Counting the Public In

POWER, CONFLICT, AND DEMOCRACY

American Politics into the Twenty-first Century
Robert Y. Shapiro, Editor

Power, Conflict, and Democracy:
American Politics into the Twenty-first Century
Robert Y. Shapiro, Editor

This series focuses on how the will of the people and the public interest are promoted, encouraged, or thwarted. It aims to question not only the direction American politics will take as it enters the twenty-first century but also the direction American politics has already taken.

The series addresses the role of interest groups and social and political movements; openness in American politics; important developments in institutions such as the executive, legislative, and judicial branches at all levels of government as well as the bureaucracies thus created; the changing behavior of politicians and political parties; the role of public opinion; and the functioning of mass media. Because problems drive politics, the series also examines important policy issues in both domestic and foreign affairs.

The series welcomes all theoretical perspectives, methodologies, and types of evidence that answer important questions about trends in American politics.

John G. Geer, *From Tea Leaves to Opinion Polls: A Theory of Democratic Leadership*

Kim Fridkin Kahn, *The Political Consequences of Being a Woman: How Stereotypes Influence the Conduct and Consequences of Political Campaigns*

Kelly D. Patterson, *Political Parties and the Maintenance of Liberal Democracy*

Dona Cooper Hamilton and Charles V. Hamilton, *The Dual Agenda: Race and Social Welfare Policies of Civil Rights Organizations*

Hanes Walton, Jr., *African-American Power and Politics: The Political Context Variable*

Amy Fried, *Muffled Echoes: Oliver North and the Politics of Public Opinion*

Russell D. Riley, *The Presidency and the Politics of Racial Inequality: Nation-Keeping from 1831 to 1965*

Robert W. Bailey, *Gay Politics, Urban Politics: Identity and Economics in the Urban Setting*

Ronald T. Libby, *ECO-WARS: Political Campaigns and Social Movements*

Counting the Public In

Presidents, Public Opinion, and Foreign Policy

Douglas C. Foyle

COLUMBIA UNIVERSITY PRESS

NEW YORK

Columbia University Press
Publishers Since 1893
New York   Chichester, West Sussex

Grateful acknowledgment is made to the Seeley G. Mudd Manuscript Library, Princeton
University Library, for permission to use the John Foster Dulles Oral History Collection, the
John Foster Dulles Papers, the Emmet Hughes Papers, and the Karl Lott Rankin Papers.

Grateful acknowledgment is made to Robert Bowie for permission to cite and/or quote from his
oral history in the John Foster Dulles Oral History Collection, Seeley G. Mudd Manuscript
Library, Princeton University Library.

Grateful acknowledgment is made to the Oral History Collection of Columbia University for
permission to cite and/or quote from James Hagerty Oral History #91, Arthur Kimball Oral
History #66, and Carl McCardle Oral History #116. Published with the permission of the Oral
History Collection of Columbia University.

Portions of Chapters 1, 2, and 3 were first published in "Public Opinion and Foreign Policy: Elite
Beliefs as a Mediating Variable," *International Studies Quarterly* 41 (March 1997): 141–169. Used
by permission of Blackwell Publishers and the International Studies Association.

Library of Congress Cataloging-in-Publication Data

Foyle, Douglas C.
    Counting the public in : presidents, public opinion, and foreign
policy / Douglas C. Foyle
       p. cm. — (Power, conflict, and democracy)
    Includes bibliographical references and index.
    ISBN 0-231-11068-5 (cl. : alk. paper). — ISBN 0-231-11069-3 (alk.
paper)
       1. United States—Foreign relations—Public opinion.
    2. Presidents—United States—Decision making.   I. Title.
II. Series.
JZ1480.F69   1999
327.73—dc21   98–45781

∞

Casebound editions of Columbia University Press books are printed on
permanent and durable acid-free paper.
Printed in the United States of America
c 10 9 8 7 6 5 4 3 2 1
p 10 9 8 7 6 5 4 3 2 1

To Laura

My interest in the connection between public opinion and foreign policy grew out of a fascination with the broader topic of the domestic determinants of international relations. In explanations of international outcomes, even though much of the international relations literature has traditionally de-emphasized factors internal to the state, my training and reading have led me to think otherwise. Sometimes a state's international position is so restricting that domestic politics has little influence, but most of the time domestic factors figure prominently in international choices. As the recent literature on the interaction between domestic factors and international relations suggests, national leaders consider more than just the international environment. Because leaders' political fortunes (regardless of whether they live in a democratic or an authoritarian nation) depend in part on the success or failure of their foreign policies, they base their decisions on the domestic context as well. Accordingly, any analysis that overlooks the domestic component of a state's policies leaves out a significant part of the causal explanation for international outcomes.

This book considers one aspect of the domestic sources of international politics: the potential linkage between public opinion and foreign policy. I argue that the influence of public opinion on foreign policy outcomes is determined by the interaction between a decision maker's beliefs about the proper role of public opinion in foreign policy formulation and the decision context in which a foreign policy choice must be made. My research suggests that some people's beliefs open them to consider public preferences when making foreign policy choices. Other officials' views make them relatively unresponsive to the public's wishes. Because the conditions under which a choice must be made can alter the type of information that leaders have about public opinion and their perception of their ability to develop public support, I maintain that an individual's beliefs about public opinion and the decision context in which a choice must be made interact to determine the influence of public opinion. I explore this argument by analyzing the beliefs of American presidents from Harry Truman through Bill Clinton. I then examine the connections between these beliefs and foreign policy decisions in case studies of the choices of presidents holding a wide range of views about public opinion. Based on this analysis, I conclude that public opinion can play an important constraining role in foreign policy choices.

This project would have been difficult to complete without the advice, assistance, and support of several persons and institutions. At the top of this list is my graduate school adviser and mentor, Ole Holsti. I attribute my expeditious and successful passage through graduate school to advice he gave to my entering graduate class on our first day. His counsel to "kill two birds with one stone" by directing every course paper to either developing a workable dissertation or a publication became the touchstone of my early graduate work. His presence from the beginning also helped channel my interests in the domestic determinants of foreign policy to fertile research grounds. He patiently read every draft I gave him of first my dissertation and then my book manuscript and provided both advice and encouragement throughout the long process leading up to publication. On a practical level, he helped in the more mundane issues of finding fellowship support, providing guidance in developing and writing a dissertation, finding a publisher for my work, and bringing it to its published form. To say the least, his guidance reflects the model of the role that a mentor should play. He will always have my profound gratitude.

My thanks also go to the other members of my dissertation committee, who provided invaluable comments and assistance on my dissertation. Although I significantly reworked the form and added a great deal of substance to the book, my original ideas were developed in my dissertation. In addition to helping shape the original research plan, John Brehm and Peter Feaver generously read rough drafts of each chapter. Their comments on the evolving dissertation were always insightful and had a profound influence on the final product. Albert Eldridge provided a great deal of assistance in forming my dissertation and developing my approach to the subject as well as commenting critically on the draft itself. Historian Alex Roland helped me select cases and form an archival research strategy and sensitized me to the need to remain attentive to the uniqueness of historical circumstances. These people's help and advice improved my work in incalculable ways.

Other scholars provided helpful comments on papers based on the larger work or in conversations on my project. Many thanks for their advice go to Badredine Arfi, Larry Baum, Bob Billings, Bill Boettcher, Ralph Carter, Rick Herrmann, Heidi Hobbs, Lynn Kuzma, Richard Ned Lebow, Timothy Lomperis, Ed Mansfield, Randall Peterson, Tom Preston, Mark Schafer, Keith Shimko, John Sullivan, Don Sylvan, Philip Tetlock, Stuart Thorson, Steve Walker, Yaacov Vertzberger, and Jim Voss. Several scholars assisted me by reading and providing valuable comments on the final draft of this book. My thanks in this regard go to Harvey Foyle, Patrick Haney, Margaret Hermann, and Philip Powlick.

Several archivists shared their knowledge and expertise of their library's holdings. At the Eisenhower Library in Abilene, Kansas, David Haight and Herb Pankratz were always helpful in suggesting potentially useful collections to check and in helping me examine the library's papers. At the Seeley G. Mudd Manuscript Library of Princeton University, Monica Ruscil and the rest of the staff were always eager to answer questions and provide guidance on their collections. At the National Archives in Washington, D.C., Kenneth Heger and John VanDereedt in the Civil Branch and Kenneth Schlesinger in the Modern Military Branch shared their knowledge of the archives' expansive collections. Their assistance greatly helped in sifting through the chaff to locate key files and documents. At the U.S. Army Military History Institute in Carlisle, Pennsylvania, Richard J. Sommers and David A. Keough made my examination of their collections productive.

I would not have been able to make the trips to these archives or written this book without financial assistance from several sources. A postdoctoral fellowship at the Mershon Center of The Ohio State University allowed me the freedom to conduct additional research and improve the manuscript. I benefited greatly from a fellowship from the National Science Foundation Grant (DIR-9113599) to the Mershon

Center Research Training Group on the Role of Cognition in Collective Political Decision Making at The Ohio State University, which provided both living expenses and research support. A Hubert H. Humphrey Fellowship from the U.S. Arms Control and Disarmament Agency provided living and tuition support to allow me to concentrate on writing. A travel grant from the Eisenhower World Affairs Institute provided financial support for one of my trips to the Eisenhower Library. Summer research grants from the political science department at Duke University also defrayed the costs of my archival work and costs associated with completing my dissertation. Thanks go to Randall Calvert, chair of the political science department at the University of Rochester, New York, for allowing me access to the university's resources during time I spent there.

At Columbia University Press, acquiring editor John Michel provided invaluable guidance and insight into the publication process. His assistant, Alexander Thorp, responded to my inquiries in rapid order. Assistant managing editor Ronald Harris shepherded my manuscript through the editorial process and smoothed the inevitable bumps along the way. Margaret B. Yamashita copyedited the book with conscientiousness and professionalism. The anonymous reviewers for the press provided valuable comments and suggestions. I have produced a better book because of their assistance.

Robert Bowie graciously granted his permission to cite his oral history comments. The Columbia University Oral History Research Office also gave me permission to quote from and cite interviews from James Hagerty Oral History 91, Arthur Kimball Oral History 66, and Carl McCardle Oral History 116. The International Studies Association and Blackwell Publishers granted their permission to use material that appeared in my article "Public Opinion and Foreign Policy: Elite Beliefs as a Mediating Variable," *International Studies Quarterly* 41 (1997):141–69. Materials from the John Foster Dulles Oral History Collection, the John Foster Dulles Papers, the Emmet Hughes Papers, and the Karl Lott Rankin Papers are used by permission of the Princeton University Libraries.

On a more personal level, I want to thank my parents, Harvey and Joanne Foyle, for providing emotional and financial support during my undergraduate and graduate careers. They never doubted my ability to persevere and complete what I started. I would not have accomplished this task without them. My parents-in-law, Philip Wurtz and Rita

Wurtz, and other family members always were interested in my work and supportive of my efforts.

Finally, my wife, Laura, remained a constant source of support throughout graduate school and in producing this book. She listened to endless one-sided conversations with good humor and patience and read countless drafts. Her editing skills and attention to detail were much appreciated. The issues on which her advice proved valuable are too numerous to count. Throughout the years of graduate work and beyond, she constantly supported me in both big and small ways, even as the pressures from her own doctoral program and work as a clinical psychologist placed demands on her. I can only hope that I gave her half the assistance and support that she gave me.

Counting the Public In

CHAPTER ONE

Linking Public Opinion and Foreign Policy

After the U.S. Marine barracks in Beirut, Lebanon, was bombed on October 23, 1983, killing 241 marines, it took the full efforts of administration officials and congressional Republicans to persuade President Ronald Reagan to redeploy American forces offshore on February 7, 1984, despite the strong public sentiment opposing the continued American involvement. But after 18 American soldiers were killed and 78 wounded in Somalia on October 3, 1993, President Bill Clinton quickly reversed his policy on October 7 in the face of a similar negative public reaction, by announcing the withdrawal of American troops by March 31, 1994. Even though public opinion moved sharply against a continued U.S. commitment in both cases after American troops died, one president chose to ignore public opposition, and another reacted quickly to it.

This variation in reaction to public opinion emerges on longer-term issues as well. After a lengthy interagency review, President Dwight D. Eisenhower in 1954 announced a new strategic doctrine emphasizing nuclear weapons, even though he harbored serious private doubts regarding the policy's efficacy. Although the public did not clamor for a dramatic revision of strategic doctrine, Eisenhower believed that radical action was necessary to sustain long-term public support. In 1983, however, Reagan announced his vision for strategic defenses against missiles without consulting with his main foreign and defense policy advisers.

The public may have been disenchanted with the existing strategic doctrine and subsequently approved of Reagan's decision, but this did not influence his policy choice. (For a discussion of the Reagan and Clinton cases, see chapters 8 and 9; the Eisenhower decision is discussed in chapter 6.) That is, one president reacted to public opinion when it approved of the status quo, and another ignored the public when pressured for a policy change. Although I will examine later the factors that accounted for these different reactions, these brief examples suggest that policymakers do not necessarily evaluate public opinion in similar ways. These instances illustrate a key point, that the prevailing public opinion does not directly translate into policy outcomes.

Instead, the differing influence of public opinion is mediated largely through a president's beliefs about the proper influence that public opinion should have on foreign policymaking. The theory presented in this book explains why presidents undertake different policy initiatives when faced with similar public sentiments and why some presidents react to public opinion in what appears to be a counterintuitive manner based on objective circumstances. Building on recent work demonstrating a conditional influence of public opinion, I develop the theory that a decision maker's reaction to public opinion is based on the interaction between the person's beliefs about the proper role of public opinion in formulating foreign policy and the prevailing decision context. My findings suggest that some individuals' beliefs make them relatively open to decisions responding to public opinion, whereas others' beliefs cause them to ignore the public's view when contemplating foreign policy choices. As the strictures of time and information change, the influence of public opinion on these persons shifts in a predictable manner. Through an examination of cases from post–World War II American presidential administrations, this book explores the plausibility of the theory's explanation of when and why decision makers become concerned with public opinion when formulating foreign policy.

This exploration is informed by earlier perspectives that provide a range of answers to the question of how, if at all, public opinion affects foreign policy. Long-standing debates in American politics and international relations point to normative tensions surrounding the role of public opinion in determining foreign policy. From American politics, two strands of democratic theory suggest alternative views of the manner in which elected officials respond to public opinion.

The *delegate view* of democratic representation contends that officials act as the public's representative by acting on their constituents' wishes. Public opinion, it is argued, should play a vital role in formulating policy, and policies should reflect public preferences on important matters, as expressed through available mechanisms (e.g., voting, polls, interest-group activity).[1] Abraham Lincoln supported this view in 1836: "While acting as [his constituents'] representative, I shall be governed by their will on all subjects on which I have the means of knowing what their will is; and on all others, I shall do what my own judgment teaches me will best advance their interests." Then in 1848, he noted, "The primary, the cardinal, the one great living principle of all democratic representative government—the principle that the representative is bound to carry out the known will of his constituents."[2] This view implies that policymakers carefully consider and even follow the dictates of public opinion when formulating policy.

The *trustee view* of democratic representation suggests that elected officials rely more on their own judgment than on the presumably uninformed opinions of their constituents. In this view, officials handle the complicated issues facing the government, and the public's involvement is limited primarily to selecting candidates at the ballot box. Because this view portrays the public as uninformed, proponents tend to regard any response to public opinion between elections as unwise and undesirable. In the *Federalist Papers* 71, Alexander Hamilton argued,

> The republican principle demands that the deliberate sense of the community should govern the conduct of those to whom they intrust the management of their affairs; but it does not require an unqualified complaisance to every sudden breeze or passion. [Instead,] when occasions present themselves in which the interests of the people are at variance with their inclinations, it is the duty of persons whom they have appointed to be guardians of those interests, to withstand the temporary delusion in order to give them time and opportunity for more cool and sedate reflection.

Edmund Burke made a similar argument:

> [A representative's] unbiased opinion, his mature judgment, his enlightened conscience, he ought not to sacrifice to you, to any man, or to any set of men living. . . . Your representative owes you, not his industry only, but his judgment; and he betrays, instead of serving you, if he sacrifices it to your opinion.[3]

According to this view, the public's role should be limited to selecting the best persons at elections and then standing back to allow them to determine the public's best interests. Although most modern analysts believe that a balance between the delegate and trustee perspectives is best for democratic governance,[4] this book argues that individuals have particular patterns of response to public opinion—only some of which reflect a balance between the delegate and trustee views—based on their beliefs about the proper role of public opinion in their decisions.

Another theoretical debate in the international relations literature concerns the disagreement between realists and Wilsonian liberals over the influence of public opinion on foreign policy. Despite believing that public opinion usually has little influence, classical realists (whose view is related to the trustee perspective), such as Hans Morgenthau and Walter Lippmann, contend that when public opinion does affect decisions, it perniciously constrains the free hand of policymakers to make wise foreign policy. Morgenthau speaks for most realists in holding that "the rational requirements of good foreign policy cannot from the outset count on the support of a public opinion whose preferences are emotional rather than rational." According to him, the public's preferences contradict the necessities of sound policy and would "sacrifice tomorrow's real benefit for today's apparent advantage."[5] Lippmann argued that the public's slow response to events and lack of relevant information threatens the well-being of any nation that relies on public opinion to guide its foreign policy:

> The unhappy truth is that the prevailing public opinion has been destructively wrong at the critical junctures. The people have imposed a veto on the judgments of informed and responsible officials. They have compelled the government, which usually knew what would have been wiser, or was necessary, or was more expedient, to be too late with too little, or too long with too much, too pacifist in peace and too bellicose in war, too neutralist or appeasing in negotiation or too intransigent.[6]

Even though Lippmann was emphasizing here the constraining influence of public opinion, most realists contend that public opinion rarely influences foreign policy choices.

Although realists concede that public opinion has sometimes caused difficulties for decision makers, these scholars conclude that elites usually either ignore the public's preferences altogether or persuade the public to support their chosen policy. Realists argue that formulating foreign policy requires complicated trade-offs, access to secret information, and sophisticated reasoning, which the public lacks. Given the emotional or moody foundations of public opinion, realists recommend that policymakers not consider public opinion as they formulate foreign policy. Instead, after deciding on a policy, officials might work to build public support for the chosen alternative. This view suggests that policymakers will likely develop policy with attention only to national security requirements while largely leaving public sentiments out of the equation. Having chosen an alternative, officials might then move to secure public support for a policy through educational efforts to change public opinion. Even though public opinion and foreign policy might eventually align with each other, the realists contend this result occurs primarily because of policymakers' efforts to alter public opinion. This realist perspective, which Ole R. Holsti labels the "Almond-Lippmann consensus," dominated thinking about public opinion and foreign policy for much of the period after World War II.[7]

Although not usually concerned with public opinion and foreign policy, neorealist views on this subject are similar to the thinking of classical realists. Neorealists such as Kenneth Waltz distinguish between theories of foreign policy choice and systemic theories of international outcomes but still echo the sentiments of classical realists regarding public opinion and foreign policy. For example, John Mearsheimer observes, "Public opinion on national security issues is notoriously fickle and responsive to elite manipulation and world events."[8] To the extent that neorealists do consider public opinion, elites are expected either to ignore or to educate the public in national security policy, in much the same manner as described by the classical realists. (Given these similarities, the term *realist* is used throughout this book with the understanding that it applies to both classical realist and neorealist expectations.)

In contrast to the realists, Wilsonian liberals (whose view is closely related to the delegate perspective) argue that public opinion should affect foreign policy formulation because of democratic norms and the public's moderating influence on possibly adventurous and overambitious elites.[9] Like other liberals, Woodrow Wilson believed the public possessed an inherent virtuous quality that supplied a valuable and steady direction to a nation's foreign policy. In his mind, public opinion provided the only prudent guide to foreign policy, because "only a free people could hold their purpose and their honor steady to a common end and prefer the interests of mankind to any narrow interest of their own." He insisted that reason, not passion or ignorance, directed the public's opinion on the weighty matters of state. Given public opinion's sound foundation and constancy of purpose, he maintained that democratic leaders should discern and implement the public's will.[10]

Wilsonian liberals believe that public opinion affects foreign policy formulation by limiting extreme elite tendencies, providing policy innovations, and leading the government to select the policy the public prefers. Since democracies ultimately require the consent of the governed, Wilsonian liberals note that public opinion can provide a brake on elite adventurism or dissuade policymakers from attempting dangerously risky actions for fear of losing public support. As a result, in decisions requiring quick action, public opinion might constrain the range of action that policymakers perceive as possible. Because it can take a great deal of time for public opinion (through letters, protests, interest group activity, etc.) to communicate its demands to government officials, Wilsonian liberals suggest that officials respond to public opinion when making decisions on issues that develop over a longer period of time. Accordingly, government officials might actually choose to implement foreign policies that the public prefers. In contrast to the realists, Wilsonian liberals think that public opinion and foreign policy eventually align because public opinion can alter the policy choices of elected officials.

The realist and Wilsonian liberal perspectives spawned a large literature examining the question of public opinion's influence on foreign policy. Despite the high degree of consistency (92 percent) between public opinion and foreign policy at the aggregate level,[11] research has provided varying explanations for this correlation between the public's view and the actions of elected officials. First, some scholars maintain that the public supports the government's actions because of the elite's manipulation of public perceptions, its educational/leadership efforts, or the public's general tendency to support the elite's foreign policy. Accordingly, public opinion plays little or no role in determining policy and responds directly to the elite's actions. Although many scholars have supported this view, Bernard Cohen provides perhaps the strongest statement of the public's limited influence. Based on his interviews with State Department officials in the 1950s and 1960s, he argued to the extent that these officials considered public opinion, they attempted to shape it, not follow it. In a poignant statement that Cohen found typical of the views held in the State Department, one official remarked, "To hell with public opinion. . . . We should lead, and not follow."[12] To varying degrees, other analysts have emphasized the ability of elites to generate support for their policies through efforts to change public opinion, to shape the conduct and reporting of polls, and/or to manipulate events.[13] This position represents the consensus realist position after

World War II which argued that most correlations between policy and opinion existed because of expressions of public support after the government had taken action.[14]

In regard to decision making, this literature suggests that public opinion receives little, if any, consideration during policy formulation. To the extent that decision makers do weigh it, elites try to shape public opinion to support their chosen policies. This view implies two separate forms of behavior: (1) Decision makers ignore public opinion (with public support automatically following policy), and (2) decision makers ignore public opinion during policy formulation but make concerted efforts to change the public's mind after settling on a policy.

A second group of scholars argue that public opinion is consistently considered in foreign policy formulation but mostly influences policy by eliminating options as unacceptable because of public opposition. These proponents contend that mass opinion may not cause policymakers to choose a specific policy but that it does set the parameters of acceptable alternatives by "ruling out" one or more policies. These researchers emphasize that public opinion broadly constrains decision makers because either they anticipate the future electoral consequences of their policy or they react to the public opinion of the moment. For example, Bruce Russett observed, "Public opinion sets broad limits of constraint, identifying a range of policies in which decision makers can choose, and in which they must choose if they are not to face rejection in the voting booths." By allowing several acceptable policies, he contended, opinion and policy "interact" in such a way that leaders both react to and manipulate public opinion.[15] In his study of American policy toward China between 1949 and 1979, Leonard Kusnitz noted that public opinion limited the range of viable policy options because officials anticipated the public's reaction and feared electoral retribution.[16] In a study methodologically similar to Cohen's and employing intensive interviews with both State Department and National Security Council staff members during the final years of the Reagan administration, Philip Powlick found that public opinion acted as a rough first cut at policy options, since officials thought that a successful policy needed to have public support or at least a lack of public disapproval.[17] Other researchers provide specific examples from case studies in which public opinion limited the policy options that decision makers considered or in which public constraint and elite leadership interacted.[18] Despite varying degrees of emphasis, these researchers agreed that public opinion does limit the range of choices available but still leaves open a number of options.

They also refrained from contending that public opinion leads to the selection of one specific policy or, rather, is merely manipulated by the elites. Instead, public opinion and policy are thought to interact in a manner that lies somewhere between these extremes.

A third line of research, mostly employing quantitative correlational methods, contends that mass public opinion can cause decision makers to choose policies the public prefers. Most notable is Benjamin Page and Robert Shapiro's extensive examination of public opinion surveys and policies which revealed a high degree of congruence (defined as consistency between opinion and policy and whether changes in policy and changes in opinion occurred at the same time) between public preferences and foreign policies. Although expressing a note of caution, the authors concluded that public opinion affected policy more often than policy altered opinion, with opinion often acting as a proximate cause of policy change.[19] Public opinion also appears to influence aggregate levels of defense spending, congressional vote decisions related to defense issues, and presidential decisions during wartime.[20] High public approval ratings seem to influence presidential decisions to employ military force more than international conditions do.[21] This research also suggests that democratic responsiveness and elite efforts at manipulation can exist at the same time. Even though democratic governments developed sophisticated polling operations in an attempt to manipulate public opinion or to increase their leverage relative to other political actors, these actions also had a "recoil effect" that caused them to become more sensitive and responsive to public preferences.[22] These proponents paint a picture of an elite that may often turn to public opinion to assess policy means and ends.

Finally, other research emphasizes a conditional view of when these three influence processes may occur. Thomas Graham's extensive study of public opinion and arms control policy found that public opinion often affected policy but that this influence depended greatly on the level of public support for a policy option.[23] He concluded that decision makers could successfully oppose public preferences if less than 59 percent of the public supported a policy option. But levels of 60 percent or more did significantly affect decision making. In addition to the level of public support, Graham pointed to the effectiveness of elite communication strategies, the stage of the policy process, and elite awareness of the dimensions of public opinion as other possible conditions affecting public influence.[24] Several other conditions also may affect the public's influence, including domestic structure,[25] close proximity of a decision to the next election,[26] the type of issue under consideration,[27] individual sensitivity to public opinion,[28] and the decision context.[29]

The Argument

We now have a better understanding of the connection between opinion and policy based on this earlier work, but we still have much to learn about this relationship, the possible linkages between public opinion and decision making, and the potential causes of variance in the public's influence.[30] This book seeks to provide partial answers to these questions by investigating two of the conditioning variables of public opinion's influence: sensitivity to public opinion (which is measured through individual beliefs) and decision context. To examine these influences, I use case studies to track possible influence patterns and to evaluate these conditional variables.

Much of the book's argument rests on the importance of beliefs in determining a policymaker's response to public opinion. Earlier research found that beliefs affect how people interpret and respond to the political environment, help guide actions in the political realm, and alter foreign policy behavior.[31] A belief contains "the information that a person has about other people, objects, and issues. The information may be factual or it may only be one person's opinion."[32] A belief system is "the set of lenses through which information concerning the physical and social environment is received."[33] These lenses "usually include principles and general ideas on the nature of the social and physical environment that constitutes the policymaker's field of action."[34]

Beliefs may shape and constrain decision making indirectly by providing a prism or filter through which the world is perceived; they may affect how decision makers evaluate policy possibilities; and they may define the kinds and levels of political support that is desirable or necessary.[35] These findings suggest important implications for potential linkage processes. If decision makers believe that public opinion has little relevance to a foreign policy's success, they may ignore it when formulating policy. However, if elites believe that foreign policies face serious difficulties because of public opposition, they may be more inclined to factor public opinion into their assessments of policy options.

A leader's personal beliefs and characteristics are more likely to affect policy choices (1) in more ambiguous and nonroutine situations,

(2) in decisions made at the top of the hierarchical ladder in which the leader is likely to participate and has final authority for the decision, and (3) when the person has available a broad range of possible actions.[36] These conditions imply that beliefs about public opinion held by presidential-level policymakers may affect decision-making behavior to a greater extent than is found at lower echelons.[37] Since decision makers' views about how public opinion has reacted to and affected policy in the past may determine how policymakers respond to public opinion in subsequent decision making, an examination of the beliefs at the presidential level may enhance our understanding of the connection between opinion and policy by linking these individual perspectives with policy choices.

This research examines individual beliefs about public opinion in two areas: (1) normative beliefs and (2) practical beliefs. *Normative beliefs* consist of an individual's judgment concerning the *desirability* of input from public opinion affecting foreign policy choices. Part of this view rests on the decision maker's assessment of the character of public opinion (i.e., whether it is emotional, stable, informed, etc.). *Practical beliefs* represent the decision maker's assessment of the *necessity* of public support of a foreign policy for it to be successful. The combination of an individual's normative and practical beliefs may affect when and how that person responds to public opinion. Although previous research implied that the least common view among policymakers is the combination of a desire for little public input and a denial of the need for public support ("guardians" in the terminology employed later), policymakers expressed a range of attitudes toward similar questions, roughly along these dimensions.[38]

Using normative and practical beliefs as the defining dimensions, four distinct belief orientations are possible (see table 1.1; the labels were chosen for their descriptive value). For clarity, these orientations are presented as theoretical ideal types. In reality, these beliefs are likely to exist along a continuum, and individuals may have specific variations. Along with a description of the orientation and suggestions of its influence on behavior, two examples are given for each. One example is taken from statements by former American secretaries of state, and the other comes from private interviews with American foreign policy officials reported in earlier research. (These examples are for illustrative purposes only. A more extensive analysis such as reported in this study would be necessary before actually determining these individuals' beliefs.)

TABLE 1.1 Beliefs Orientations

		Is public support of a foreign policy necessary?	
		Yes	No
Is it desirable for input from public opinion to affect foreign policy choices?	Yes	Delegate	Executor
	No	Pragmatist	Guardian

Delegates

Delegates believe that it is desirable for public opinion to influence policy choices and necessary to have public support for a successful foreign policy. These individuals view their position as agents for the public, having been sent to pursue certain policies or as acting as the public would want them to do on a given issue.[39] Delegates will probably use public opinion extensively to assess foreign policy means and goals, and public opinion is a prime consideration in their choice of any policy, with the policymaker attempting to implement the public will or at least not acting against the public's wishes. After making a decision, delegates are likely to try to educate the public about how the policy they selected responds to the public's preferences.

In addition to policy substance, delegates may be sensitive about the timing of their foreign policies. That is, they may postpone policy initiatives until public support develops for an action, either on its own or after educational efforts. Although individuals with different beliefs may try to persuade the public to support their policy *once they have acted,* delegates are more apt to postpone the policy until after public support has materialized. In this case, the delegates would not choose a policy based on the public's view but would be sensitive to the public's desires regarding the time at which a policy initiative was pursued. This behavior might be particularly noticeable on issues that allow a longer decision time.

James F. Byrnes, secretary of state for President Harry Truman, provides an example of a statement reflecting the delegate orientation: "We must have an institution [in charge of foreign policy] that is responsive to the will of the people and able to translate our policies into effective action." Noting the increased attention to public opinion in the State Department, he observed that "behind these efforts is the firm realization that our foreign policy must be responsive to and have the firm support of the American people." More recently, a State Department official in the East Asian and Pacific Affairs Bureau commented,

> I think any good policy from a more experienced professional almost instinctively takes public opinion into account when they [*sic*] formulate foreign policy. You really cannot have a successful policy that does not enjoy popular support, and the idea that you can pursue something and eventually persuade people to buy it. . . . Maybe you can, but I think that's an approach to policy that is fraught with peril. It's much better to know that you have solid support for policy early on.[40]

Executors

Executors are people who carry out or perform tasks for other people. Even though they are chosen by others and consider their input, executors do not necessarily require the active support of the persons for whom they perform the tasks (e.g., the executor of a will). In the context of this book, executors feel that the public's input into policy formulation is desirable but believe that its support is not necessary for a successful policy. For executors, public opinion should be one of the initial factors considered in foreign policy formulation, and it might limit the options under consideration or suggest possible alternatives. If executors do not have information on public opinion or disagree with it, they will likely rely on their own best judgment because they do not believe in the need for public opinion actively supporting each policy. Executors will probably not pay much attention to leading the public. If they do consider leading it, they will likely only think about it instrumentally, with the goal of affecting other actors, such as Congress, rather than as an end in itself.

President Lyndon Johnson's secretary of state, Dean Rusk, expressed views falling under the executor orientation:

> One flaw of government officials is that they often underestimate the capacity of ordinary citizens to make sensible judgments about public issues. Political leaders and policy officers must always remember to ask, "What would the American people think about this issue if they knew about it tomorrow morning?" This doesn't mean that the passing whims of the American people are suitable guidelines for policy. Edmund Burke once reminded the electors of Bristol that he was not in Parliament simply to represent their every whim, but to bring to bear his conscience, his abilities, and his judgment on the issues.[41]

Likewise, a deputy assistant secretary in the State Department remarked, "My own personal inclination is that, by and large, the executive is in need of a balance out there in the public, and the chances of pursuing a policy that's either unwise or short-sighted is lessened because of the role public opinion plays."[42]

Pragmatists

Pragmatists believe that even though public input affecting foreign policy choices is not desirable, public support of the chosen policy is necessary. The pragmatist's views are reminiscent of the perspective of scholar Hans Morgenthau, who believed that policymakers in a democracy must balance the rational requirements of foreign policy dictated by the national interest with the necessity of maintaining support from the public.[43] He likened this process to the diplomat performing the "highest feat of statesmanship: trimming his sails to the winds of popular passion while using them to carry the ship of state to the port of good foreign policy, on however roundabout and zigzag a course."[44] Pragmatists should attempt to lead the public to gain support for their preferred option and to use their own best judgment as the "first cut" in determining a sound foreign policy. In contrast to delegates, who seek to demonstrate how policy aligns with public preferences, pragmatists will likely approach explanatory efforts with the sole purpose of creating public support. If generating public support does not appear possible, then public opinion may limit the range of feasible options.

Consonant with the pragmatist belief system, President Bill Clinton's secretary of state, Madeleine Albright, stated that she would "talk about foreign policy, not in abstract terms, but in human terms and in bipartisan terms," ... "because in our democracy, we cannot pursue policies abroad that are not understood and supported here at home." Similarly, a former assistant secretary for public affairs in the State Department explained, "You should study the problem carefully in terms of the national interest and decide on the ideal course. Only then should you consider congressional and public opinion with an eye towards educating such opinion in the necessities of the situation."[45]

Guardians

Finally, *guardians* find public input into foreign policy choices to be undesirable and believe that the public's support is not necessary for a successful foreign policy. Once in power, guardians may see themselves as best left on their own as experts to act in the national interest.[46] The noted newspaper columnist Walter Lippmann argued, "[The people] can elect the government. They can remove it. They can approve or disapprove its performance. But they cannot administer the government. . . . A mass cannot govern."[47]

Similarly, the former diplomat George Kennan found public opinion a poor basis for policy, contending that it "can be easily led astray into areas of emotionalism and subjectivity which make it a poor and inadequate guide for national action." Kennan recommended moving against the tide of public opinion if required by the dictates of national interest: "History does not forgive us our national mistakes because they are explicable in terms of our domestic politics." To rectify this problem, he suggested developing a principle of professionalism that might shield foreign policy from domestic tides.[48]

Guardians will probably ignore public opinion in their decisions and determine foreign policy based on their own judgment with little reference to public support. In contrast to delegates, guardians may try to educate the public, to show them not how a policy aligns with public preferences but how the policy serves the national interest.

A statement by Ronald Reagan's secretary of state, George Shultz, is typical of the guardian's belief system: "My view is that democratically elected and accountable individuals have been placed in positions where they can and must make decisions to defend our national security. The risk and burden of leadership is that those decision will receive, or not receive, the support of the people on their merits." Echoing this sentiment, a desk officer in the State Department's Bureau of African Affairs reported, "I don't think anyone is terribly anxious to find out more about public opinion to use as a guide to policy. The tendency in this building is you would rather not deal with it because it's a wild card and it's an impediment to rational policymaking."[49]

This book argues that beliefs about public opinion interact with the decision context and affect the influence of public opinion on foreign policy. A *decision context* is defined by (1) the level of threat to important values or goals (high or low), (2) the length of the available decision time (short or long), and (3) the policymaker's awareness of the need for a decision on an issue (surprise or anticipation).[50] A high-threat situation exists when policymakers "recognize that achievement of their goal or objective can be impeded or entirely obstructed." A decision time is short when decision makers perceive that "in a restricted period of time the situation will be altered in some major way. After the situation is modified, a decision is either no longer possible or must be made under less favorable circumstances." Finally, surprise refers to "the absence of awareness on the part of policymakers that the situation is likely to occur."[51]

These three characteristics combine to create situational ideal types with separate expectations of decision-making behavior. Because this study focuses on presidential decision making, I looked only at cases with a high threat to important values, since presidents are likely to be involved in these decisions.[52] The two remaining decision context factors, decision time and awareness, mainly affect the amount and type of information that the decision makers possess. High threat combined with the other two factors yields four decision contexts: (1) crisis (short decision time and surprise), (2) reflexive (short decision time and anticipation), (3) innovative (extended decision time and surprise), and (4) deliberative (extended decision time and anticipation).[53]

The decision-making process should vary between these contexts in a predictable manner. Since the crisis context allows the circumvention of normal bureaucratic procedures and information may be in short supply, decision makers may react quickly based on their preconceived notions. Reflexive contexts may be characterized by limited information searches because of the time pressure, but decision makers may rely heavily on previously developed contingency plans and not consider many alternatives because of the anticipation of the issue. Innovative contexts are likely to contain an extensive search of options and information instigated by the high threat and allowed by the extended time. Since the surprise and long decision time may "shake up" entrenched patterns of behavior, policymakers have an opportunity to propose new policy approaches to old problems. Finally, deliberative contexts usually lead to an intensive search for options and information that involve many agencies and possibly cause organizational conflicts.[54]

These situational pressures should interact with belief orientations. When only a short amount of time is available to make a decision, the restricted amount of time for information searches may result in officials' having only vague ideas about public opinion. Delegates, who are most concerned with public opinion, will not have enough information to follow it. Since these people will want to consider public opinion but will lack the information, they are probably broadly constrained by their impression of public preferences. Since executors do not feel they need public support for their foreign policies to succeed and usually do not have much information about the public's view, public opinion will likely have no influence on their decisions in these contexts. If executors do learn information about public opinion, the public's influence will probably depend on the strength of their policy preferences. If executors have strong preferences, public opinion should still have no influence on their policy decision. But if they have only weak preferences, public opinion will likely limit their decision. In any case, executors will probably remain open to information about public opinion in reaching a decision. Because of their focus on public support, pragmatists are probably constrained by public opinion for fear of losing public support. The short decision time allowed for a choice is likely to prevent them from feeling confident that they can successfully persuade the public to support a policy it does not already accept. Guardians will likely ignore the public, given their lack of information about public opinion and the need for a quick decision.

When the decision time is long, policymakers have more information about public opinion. Accordingly, delegates are likely use the longer period to determine public preferences and to follow them when making their choice. If the public opposes a policy that a delegate favors, he will probably wait for the public to support the preferred policy alternative (either on its own or after education efforts) before embarking on it. Depending on the strength of their preferences, executors will likely be either constrained by public opinion (if they lack a strong view) or be unaffected by public opinion (if they have a strong preference). If an executor has strong preferences, she may attempt to persuade the public to soften its opposition. In any case, the executor should be open to information about public opinion. Pragmatists should use the extended time to gain the public's support for the policy. Guardians are likely to use this information to mitigate public opposition by leading the public to support their preferred policy.

A summary of these predictions appears in table 1.2. At this idealized level, the surprise/anticipation factor is not expected to interact with beliefs in determining an individual's reaction to public opinion. As a result, the predictions for the reflexive context are the same as those for the crisis context, and the innovative context behavior is expected to be like the deliberative context. For this reason, table 1.2 outlines predictions only for the crisis and deliberative contexts. Of course, individuals could hold beliefs that would differentiate between decisions with surprise or anticipation.

TABLE 1.2 Predictions for Orientations

Decision Contexts	Orientations			
	DELEGATE	EXECUTOR	PRAGMATIST	GUARDIAN
Crisis	Constrain	No impact/ *Constrain*	Constrain	No impact
Deliberative	Follow	Lead/ *Constrain*	Lead	Lead

Note: The behavior prediction for the executor is in roman type if the individual has strong policy preferences and is in italics if the individual has weak preferences.

Alternative Explanations

In contrast to the beliefs model, realist and Wilsonian liberal theories provide the prevailing expectations of public opinion's influence on policymaking. By offering an alternative that is contingent on the person making the decision, the beliefs model challenges the explanatory framework proposed by these theories. First, as discussed earlier, realists believe that policymakers ignore public opinion when making a decision and lead the public to support their chosen alternative when implementing the policy. Given the time pressure, informational constraints, and the severe threat inherent in a crisis, realist views imply that public opinion has little impact in this context, since policymakers give it little, if any, attention. If policymakers consider public opinion at all, they think about it only in regard to leading it when implementing their chosen policy.

Realists argue that as the decision context becomes less crisislike (moving from the crisis context to the reflexive, innovative, and deliberative contexts) and allows more opportunities for reflection, decision makers continue to discount public opinion when selecting a policy but pay more attention to leading the public when implementing it. In the reflexive context, the realist view implies that public opinion will continue to have little effect given the premium on time and high threat to security. However, since this situation was anticipated, decision makers may use this opportunity to examine the issue and formulate contingency plans, including plans to lead public opinion. In the innovative and deliberative contexts, realist theory suggests that to generate public support, decision makers may employ the considerable decision time allowed to assess and instigate an effort to educate the public about the policy. Realists feel that public opinion may also restrict these longer-term decisions in a pernicious manner as the public becomes mobilized either to support or oppose specific policy options. This constraining role might be expected to be more apparent in the deliberative context than in the innovative context because the extended time and anticipation in a deliberative situation allow many groups both inside and outside the government to attempt to influence the handling of a specific problem.

As discussed earlier, regardless of the situation, Wilsonian liberals describe an extensive linkage between public opinion and foreign policy. However, this influence may vary among decision contexts because of information limitations. Crises are characterized by informational shortages and pressures for a quick decision. In these situations, Wilsonian liberals suggest that policymakers may be constrained by public opinion as they pay heed to their impressions of the broad limitations set by the public. In the reflexive context, decision makers may use their anticipation of the issue to attempt to assess public opinion, which may give decision makers a keener perception of public opinion. Even though this effort may give decision makers a clearer idea of the public's desires, the short decision time may still prevent extensive amounts of information regarding public opinion from reaching them, thereby making a constraining influence most likely. In both these contexts, public opinion may also limit extreme or risky responses by policymakers.

Given the longer time allowed for decision making in the innovative and deliberative contexts, Wilsonian liberals see decision makers searching out relevant public opinion information. Public preferences may be more clearly formed and provide a better basis for policy. In addition, decision makers may be more susceptible to pressures from outside the government. In combination, these factors can cause decision makers to follow public opinion. Table 1.3 compares the predictions based on the realist and Wilsonian liberal perspectives.

Implications

This book's exploration of the connection between public opinion and foreign policy contributes to our knowledge in three areas, each of which is revisited in the concluding chapter. First, regarding public opinion's influence on foreign policy, this research adds to our understanding of why and under what conditions public opinion affects the formulation of foreign policy. It also continues the trend of focusing on

TABLE 1.3 **Alternative Explanations**

Situation (all high threat)	Realist	Wilsonian Liberal
Crisis short time/surprise	No impact/*Lead*	Constrain
Reflexive short time/anticipation	Lead	Constrain
Innovative long time/surprise	Lead	Follow
Deliberative long time/anticipation	Lead/*Constrain*	Follow

Note: Italics indicate conditional predictions.

the conditions under which public opinion influences policy outcomes. Beliefs orientations, as argued in the rest of this book, provide a better explanation of the dynamics of public opinion's influence across a range of presidents than is provided by the realist or Wilsonian liberal perspectives alone. The beliefs model suggests that the realist and Wilsonian liberal predictions and democratic theory's delegate and trustee views can sometimes accurately describe policymaking dynamics, but it depends greatly on the individual and decision context. The beliefs and decision context variables thus offer two important determining conditions regarding whether and how public opinion influences foreign policy. As a result, the descriptive and predictive accuracy of the realist, Wilsonian liberal, and democratic theories depends greatly on processes that these other views have overlooked.

Second, this intensive case study analysis contributes to our understanding of the linkage between public opinion and foreign policy. A persistent question in the literature is, "If public opinion influences foreign policy, how does it do so?"[55] Several linkage processes have been proposed, including anticipated future opinion, perceptions of the current opinion context, and specific indicators of opinion (such as polls and newspapers). Although each of these factors may influence policy, we still do not know which ones, when, and under what conditions.

Public opinion can affect policymaking through a decision maker's anticipation of the public's future reactions.[56] Anticipations may be limited to a policymaker's view of the public's potential reaction in the very near future, such as how the public will react when a policy is announced. The anticipation may also be directed to how the public will react in the next election to the government's handling of the issue. To form these anticipations, decision makers may use their past experiences to project the public's future option preferences or reactions, especially onto policies on which no specific information about public opinion exists.[57]

This form of opinion linkage might be especially evident in issues of major foreign policy importance that policymakers believe may become factors in the next election.[58] Even though public opinion at a particular point favors one option, policymakers may sense that the public's view in the future will change. As a result, even when information about public opinion is available, decision makers may react more to their anticipation of future opinion as it is expected to be manifested in future elections than to the current public mood. These politicians may respond to their anticipation of opinion by framing policies to generate the most positive future public view or avoid a negative future public reaction. This linkage process implies that decision makers could act against current public opinion because they expect that future opinion will view the situation differently. What appears at first to be a disconnect between opinion and policy may actually represent a more nuanced understanding of opinion by policymakers. This form of linkage has been evident in crises when other information about public opinion was lacking, and earlier research found that this process operated under more normal conditions, especially when public opinion had not been formed.[59]

Images of the existing public opinion context may also affect policy, as Walter Lippmann described in regard to the importance of the "pictures" of public opinion in decision makers' heads as the basis for their reactions to it.[60] Much of public opinion's influence may be linked to the policy process through these broad, impressionistic views of the prevailing context of opinion. V. O. Key argued that the opinion context, "as it is perceived by those responsible for action, conditions many of the acts of those who must make what we may call 'opinion-related decisions.' "[61] Bernard Cohen referred to the opinion context as affecting a decision maker "by creating in the policy-maker an impression of a public attitude or attitudes, or by becoming part of the environment and cultural milieu that help to shape his own thinking, [which] may consciously affect his official behavior."[62] Some scholars have even suggested that relationship between public opinion and foreign policy relies entirely on these perceptions.[63] As with anticipated future opinion, this linkage process does not necessarily rely on direct knowledge by the policymaker of any immediate expression of public opinion. Even so, since these perceptions of opinion can affect how decision makers perceive international events and how they view and weigh their policy choices, the process may be a critical factor in the opinion and policy connection.

Decision makers may also turn to specific indicators of opinion before making a choice. We often assume that policymakers rely on polling data for all their impressions of public opinion, but other factors (such as letters, editorial opinion, and the views of close associates) may also reveal public opinion. Key defined public opinion as "those opinions held by private persons which governments find it prudent to heed." This definition, Key conceded, relies on ascertaining the attitudes of government officials to determine which opinions they value.[64] Previous work shows that State Department and National Security Council officials rely on a range of indicators and use the news media and elected representatives the most often, mass opinion (such as polls and letters) to a lesser extent, and other elites and interest-group activity the least often.[65] Since these indicators are most commonly associated with public opinion, it would come as no surprise if decision makers turned to these to determine the public's view.

My investigation of American foreign policy decision making shows that although each of the three linkage processes can be found in decision making, the strongest are the anticipation of future opinion and the perceptions of the opinion context. Contrary to what is commonly believed, the least influential linkage process is specific indicators of opinion. Although polls were available throughout each of the decisions I examined, the decision makers were more concerned with how the public would eventually come to view the issue or with their own perceptions of the opinion context. This result was found across a range of presidencies and indicates the importance of a decision maker's perceptions in assessing the linkage between public opinion and foreign policy.

Finally, my work also emphasizes the domestic sources of international relations. One view, usually identified with the neorealist perspective, is that internal factors rarely influence state decisions both in crises and under normal conditions.[66] These proponents contend that especially in crises, the increased secrecy, concentration of authority, and the premium on quick and decisive action brought on by the heightened threat dramatically reduce or eliminate the impact of domestic factors on decision making.[67] In addition, since public opinion polls reveal a marked increase in the approval of the president's actions during crises, regardless of whether a policy succeeds or fails, decision makers may be less inclined to consider public opinion under these conditions.[68] These researchers contend that the limited influence of domestic factors extends to noncrisis contexts as well.[69]

Liberal theories of international relations emphasize that domestic structure, processes, and societal influences can affect state choices as much as international circumstances and pressures, an emphasis that has contributed to a recent rethinking about the influence of domestic policy on international relations.[70] Scholars now consider domestic influences to be an important determinant of foreign policy behavior. These proponents argue that domestic considerations affect perceptions of the values at stake, the development of options and policy choices, and the timing of international action in both crises and ordinary circumstances.[71] Domestic factors are now thought to influence a range of international behavior, including crisis initiation, crisis escalation, the use of force, international bargaining, and broader strategic policy.[72] According to these proponents, analyses of international behavior cannot be limited to the international conditions, since domestic considerations do significantly affect foreign policy choices.[73] This book's findings support this perspective by suggesting that domestic factors such as public opinion can have an important influence on how decision makers perceive their choices and select among the available alternatives.

Method

To reach these conclusions, I followed a qualitative research design to assess the beliefs model's predictive value and to evaluate the power of alternative approaches to explain the pattern of public opinion's influence on foreign policy.[74] I derived my data from sources such as archival collections, public documents, and memoirs and examined them through congruence and process-tracing procedures. To provide depth, I explored the influence of public opinion on the decisions of President Dwight Eisenhower and Secretary of State John Foster Dulles across the range of decision contexts discussed earlier. To provide breadth, I considered the decision making of Presidents Jimmy Carter, Ronald Reagan, George Bush, and Bill Clinton across a more limited set of cases. (For a detailed discussion of data acquisition and analysis, see the methods appendix.)

I measured beliefs using a qualitative content analysis. My analysis of Eisenhower's and Dulles's beliefs examined public and private communications, speeches, and public writings found in archives and other public sources to formulate a coherent picture of the individual's beliefs. As a validity check after I had analyzed the primary materials, I considered the oral history recollections of individuals close to both men concerning Eisenhower's and Dulles's beliefs about public opinion. Because these individuals formed their impression of Eisenhower's and Dulles's beliefs apart from my own analysis, I could use their assessments to judge the accuracy of the qualitative content analysis.[75] For the other post–World War II presidents, I relied on statements of their beliefs made during their presidencies and in their published memoirs. (The theoretical foundation and mechanics of the qualitative content analysis are discussed in the methods appendix.)

A final note about the presentation of primary sources: Some of the sources used in this analysis are records of discussions or minutes of meetings written by note takers rather than transcripts of the meetings. For this reason, some of my quotations report an individual speaking in the third person. Except when noted, documents listed as either a memorandum of conversation or a memorandum of discussion are summaries of the conversations that took place.

Variables and Operationalization

I examined each case as a series of decisions made in four stages: (1) problem representation (which contains two observation points that are analyzed separately: agenda setting and definition of the situation), (2) option generation, (3) policy selection, and (4) policy implementation.[76] *Problem representation* refers to the manner in which decision makers define the stakes involved in a policy. Policymakers assess the interests threatened, possible opportunities, and why they must choose a policy. Agenda setting concerns the choice to consider the issue and the factors that affect this choice. When policymakers define a situation, they look at the issue in terms of the threats and opportunities it might create. Next, *option generation* refers to the identification of possible policies to address the issue and their potential consequences. *Policy selection* is the process of choosing a policy from the possible options, and *policy implementation* refers to the choices necessary to execute the selected alternative. The dependent variable is the choice made during each of these stages and allows an assessment of whether public opinion influences decision making differently across these stages, as suggested by some earlier researchers.

The first independent variable, the decision-making context, is defined according to the previously mentioned determinants of the policymaking context (threat to important values, decision time, and awareness). Four contexts were selected: crisis, reflexive, innovative, and deliberative. For the more recent presidents, I considered only the more extreme crisis and deliberative contexts.

The second independent variable is the president's normative and practical beliefs about public opinion (Dulles is included in the Eisenhower cases).

The third independent variable is the president's (and Dulles's in the Eisenhower cases) assessment of public opinion. This variable consists of the individual's views of what public opinion is on an issue and what the public wants done either at that time or in the future. The influence of this variable, relative to the fourth independent variable (other interests), on the choices made by policymakers is coded at the end of each case.

The fourth independent variable, which for the sake of simplicity is referred to as *other interests*, consists of all the interest-based (security, economic, etc.) reasons for which policymakers may make decisions, except for public opinion. For example, a decision not to intervene in a conflict because of the possible damage to the United States' strategic position would represent such an interest (whereas a decision not to intervene because of possible divisions in the public would represent a public opinion–based interest). Exactly what the other reasons may be are not important to this study except for the fact that they are not public opinion, since if decision makers see these elements compelling them to make a particular choice, the influence of public opinion will necessarily be diminished.

Finally, three other variables are used as *control variables* to ensure that the effects of the study's explanatory variables are isolated.

First, all cases contain a large national security component, since national security issues provide the most difficult test of the impact of public opinion on policy.[77] Economic policy may be a factor in these cases, but the overriding consideration in these decisions is security. Public opinion is commonly believed, especially in realist circles, to have the least influence on purely national security issues, because it is thought that concerns related to the national interest predominate in these matters. Since this study's cases all involve a high threat to important values, the influence of public opinion is most likely to comply with the realists' predictions. For this reason, the results of the study are biased toward finding support for the realist perspective and away from finding an influence of public opinion. As a result, evidence in support of public opinion's influence in these cases would provide more convincing evidence of public opinion's impact on foreign policy.[78]

The second control variable is the president's public approval rating. My cases are from periods when the president's public approval rating was high (above 50 percent). Presidents may concern themselves with approval ratings in large part because they see them as a measurement of their success and power, and so more popular presidents may have more options in regard to foreign policy because a high approval rating may reduce domestic constraints.[79] For this reason, when approval ratings are high, presidents are probably less concerned about public opinion than at other times. In a more negative opinion context, the president may become increasingly focused on taking a more "popular" action rather than a presidentially preferred (based on national security, ideology, etc.), less popular alternative (assuming that the "popular" and "preferred" options are not the same policy).[80] In addition, as support from key domestic groups wanes, presidents may become more tempted to act internationally to bolster their flagging domestic fortunes.[81] In any event, since presidents usually are less concerned with public opinion when they are popular relative to when they are not popular, this control variable biases this study's findings toward the realist model and away from finding an influence of public opinion.

The third control variable is the temporal proximity of the case to the next presidential election. As presidential elections approach, presidents may become unusually concerned about public opinion because of its relation to the election's outcome. If the next presidential election has any effect on the sensitivity of decision makers to public opinion, this effect should decrease as the distance from the next election increases. For this reason, I used a distance of at least one year before the next presidential election. As with the other control variables, this factor serves to ensure that any bias in case selection is slanted away from finding an influence of public opinion, in favor of realist propositions.

Selecting cases that focused on national security and that occurred when the president's approval rating was high and outside an election year provides a set of conditions when public opinion was less likely to be influential. Unless otherwise noted, all the cases fit these control variables. In addition, when combined with the decision context variable, these conditions create the types of situations when the beliefs variable is more likely to have a noticeable influence, especially during the crisis cases. As a result of this case selection process, if beliefs do affect public opinion's influence on foreign policy, it should be noticed under the circumstances examined in this study.

Case Selection

The case studies that I selected are based on the decision context explanatory variable and the three control variables (national security issue, approval rating, electoral proximity). To evaluate the beliefs model and the alternative explanations, I performed an analysis that contained both depth, to trace the decision-making process, and breadth across the various beliefs orientations. When I began my research, I chose the Eisenhower administration for an in-depth analysis because it was the most recent administration for which the majority of archival materials were open to the public. The extensive archival material available in both Eisenhower's and Dulles's personal and official papers allowed access to and insight into their beliefs and policymaking behavior. In addition, the existence of polling during this period provided a context sufficiently similar to that of later administrations. I then identified potential cases focusing on national security and assessed them in relation to the president's approval rating and the temporal proximity to the next presidential election. If they satisfied the qualifications of the control variables, I selected those cases that conformed to the context independent variable, with one case for each of the four contexts. If more than one case fit all these conditions, I chose the one that came closest to the "ideal." The following cases were chosen for intensive analysis: (1) crisis case: Formosa Straits crisis, September through November 1954; (2) reflexive case: possible U.S. intervention to relieve the French garrison at Dien Bien Phu, January through May 1954; (3) innovative case: U.S. reaction to Soviet launching of *Sputnik*, October 1957 through August 1958; and (4) deliberative case: development of the New Look defense strategy, December 1952 through July 1954. After selecting the Eisenhower administration and the cases, I determined the values of the independent variables concerning beliefs (both Eisenhower and Dulles were subsequently categorized as pragmatists), the assessment of public opinion, and the other interests involved in the cases.

When my analysis of the Eisenhower cases suggested the value of the beliefs model, I looked at several more cases from other administrations to determine the generalizability of the model. To evaluate the breadth of the beliefs model's application, I performed a qualitative content analysis of the beliefs of all the remaining post–World War II presidents and chose four presidents representative of the four beliefs orientations: Carter (executor), Reagan (guardian), Bush (pragmatist), and Clinton (delegate). Because the archival record for these recent cases was still unavailable at the time of this analysis, I could not explore these cases at the same level of detail as the Eisenhower ones. These additional cases were selected following the same criteria as for the Eisenhower cases. Because of the focus on the beliefs variable and the results from the Eisenhower cases showing that surprise did not have a major effect on public opinion's influence, a crisis and a deliberative case were chosen for each president. The crisis cases are (1) Carter: Soviet invasion of Afghanistan, 1979–1980; (2) Reagan: Beirut marine barracks bombing, 1983–1984; (3) Bush: Gulf War, 1990–1991; and (4) Clinton: Somalia, 1993. The deliberative cases are (1) Carter: Panama Canal treaties, 1977–1978; (2) Reagan: origins of the Strategic Defense Initiative, 1983; (3) Bush: reunification of Germany, 1989–1990; and (4) Clinton: intervention in Bosnia, 1995. In two cases (Carter Afghanistan, Reagan Lebanon), the most crisislike cases for the administration barely missed the election distance requirement. Because of the focus on the decision context variable in these follow-on cases, I relaxed the election control variable and remained sensitive to this situation in the analysis and conclusions.

Coding the Influence of Public Opinion and Beliefs

I used two coding schemes to describe the influence of public opinion and beliefs. Once I had determined the influence of the independent variables on the dependent variable, I coded the influence of the policymaker's assessments of public opinion on the decision, relative to other interests, regarding four public opinion influence categories derived from the literature (i.e., no impact, lead, constrain, and follow). In addition, for the categories indicating that public opinion does influence policy (constrain and follow), I coded the strength of this influence. The following paragraphs report the indicators used to code the assessment and strength of public opinion's influence.

First, the *no-impact category* indicates that decision makers ignore, or largely ignore, public opinion during policy deliberations (and refrain from attempts to lead public opinion). Any correlation between public opinion and policy results only because public support for policy came after the elites' decisions and not because the elites considered public opinion in their deliberations or expended much effort to generate public support. To receive this coding, public opinion was mentioned seldom or not at all during discussions. Less stringently, public opinion information might have been mentioned but was dismissed or discounted during deliberations. Although some explanation of decisions is expected after a policy decision, concerted public relations efforts to generate public support should remain absent.[82]

Second, the *lead category* describes situations in which public opinion does not affect policy choices, but decision makers do expend considerable effort to generate public support for the government's policies through attempts to lead the public.[83] Unlike the view that policymakers may completely ignore public opinion, this view implies at least some concern about public opinion. Under this coding, public opinion is considered after a decision has already been made and/or only in reference to how the policy might be explained to the public or how the public might be educated about the policy. Deliberation about public opinion focuses on activities to shape public opinion and not on considerations of whether the policy will receive public support or opposition (except to determine the level of effort to dedicate to leading the public).

Third, the *constrain category* describes public opinion as limiting the options available to decision makers while at the same time allowing a band of acceptable policies from which decision makers can choose. Certain options are ruled out, removed from consideration, or dismissed because of potential public opposition. In their decisions, actors might have preferred certain options but discarded them once potential public reaction was assessed.

Fourth, the final coding outcome is the *follow category*. To receive this coding, policies that conform to the perceived public's preferences were adopted. Evidence supporting this option is a concern by decision makers with implementing exactly or nearly exactly the policy the public wants. Government leaders, too, may show a concern with public opinion as a guide to both policy options and policy choice.

The constrain and follow categories indicate that public opinion did affect the decision. The influence of public opinion ranges from being the sole factor driving a decision to being merely one minor concern of many in shaping a policy. For this reason, the strength of public opinion's influence was coded when a constrain or follow category influence was found. A *strong* influence signifies that the decision was based mostly on public opinion. Other factors, such as security interests, did not account for the choice reached. A *moderate* influence of public opinion indicates that public opinion was one of the primary factors in a decision but that other issues were also significant to decision makers. Finally, a *mild* influence indicates that considerations other than public opinion accounted for the decision. Public opinion did affect the choice, but it mainly reinforced other factors and was only one of several factors that influenced the decision.

The influence of beliefs was coded according to a congruence procedure and process tracing (see the methods appendix for more information on these processes). Behavior was labeled *inconsistent* if it did not fit predictions based on beliefs. If behavior was congruent with predictions, it was labeled as *consistent.* If the behavior was consistent with predictions and the evidence pointed to an explicit consideration of public opinion in the manner predicted by beliefs, this influence was labeled as *causal.* Sometimes the influence of beliefs was found in more than one of these codings. If behavior fell in both the *causal* and *consistent* categories, it was labeled as *supportive.* If any part of the coding was inconsistent, the component parts are given in the order of their descriptive value.

The remainder of this book reports the findings of this research. The results of the qualitative content analysis of Eisenhower's and Dulles's public opinion beliefs and a comparison of the specific expectations of their behavior based on their beliefs orientation with realist and Wilsonian liberal predictions are presented in chapter 2. The four case studies selected from the Eisenhower administration are examined in successive chapters: chapter 3 discusses the crisis context (1954 Formosa Straits case); chapter 4 considers the reflexive context (1954 Dien Bien Phu case); chapter 5 evaluates the innovative context (1957–1958 *Sputnik* case); and chapter 6 analyzes the deliberative context (1953–1954 New Look case). Chapter 7 reports the findings of the content analysis of the other post–World War II presidents. Brief crisis and deliberative case studies from the Carter, Reagan, Bush, and Clinton presidencies are discussed in chapters 8 and 9, respectively. Finally, chapter 10 discusses the study's findings and outlines their implications for several areas of research.

CHAPTER TWO

Preserving Public Support

Eisenhower and Dulles as Pragmatists

Both President Dwight D. Eisenhower and his secretary of state, John Foster Dulles, placed primary importance on sustaining public support for their policies in both the short and long term. Although they believed in creating foreign policies based on the demands of the national security interests at stake, they also knew that any successful policy required the public's support. According to the analysis of their beliefs, Eisenhower held the normative belief that public opinion should not influence his foreign policy choices and thought its role in policy formulation should be limited to being informed about the policy the government had selected. This view complements his practical belief that public support was necessary and was best achieved through elite leadership efforts. However, if he thought he could not lead the public on a particular policy, he would, as a final resort, adjust his policies to the limits of public acceptance. Whereas Dulles was willing to take guidance on basic foreign policy objectives from the public, his normative beliefs regarding other foreign policies suggest that he thought the government should choose the best policy based on its own determination of the national interest. Like Eisenhower, Dulles saw, in his practical beliefs, public support as a necessary component of foreign policy that could best be achieved through elite leadership efforts.

These beliefs identify both Eisenhower and Dulles as pragmatists. Although the variations in their beliefs affected their behavior in certain instances, the model predicts that both would act consistently with the *lead category* unless they regarded effective leadership as impossible. In these instances, public opinion would limit their actions consistent with the *constrain category*.

This chapter examines both Eisenhower's and Dulles's beliefs. In addition to the qualitative analysis, I discuss, as a construct validity check, the oral history recollections of individuals close to both men. Finally, I compare the predictions of behavior expected from these two individuals based on their beliefs with predictions from the realist and Wilsonian liberal models.

Public Opinion Beliefs: Eisenhower

Normative Beliefs

Eisenhower did not want input from public opinion to affect his formulation of policy. For this reason, he believed that the republican form of government, outlined in the U.S. Constitution, represented the best framework for governing the nation because it shielded decision makers, to a certain extent, from the whims of public opinion. For example, a memorandum of conversation records Eisenhower as opposing a change in the electoral college because it would move the United States "closer to a democracy & less of a republic. Right now you have a truly representative body here, with more responsibility. . . . We can't let just a popular majority sweep us in one direction, because then you can't recover."[1] In the formulation of policy, he was more concerned with long-term policy success than the initial public response to a policy. He feared that policymakers would lose sight of a policy's ultimate objectives if they became overly concerned with poll ratings or temporary reactions. As he observed to a friend,

> I think it is fair to say that, in this [current political and historical] situation only a leadership that is based on honesty of purpose, calmness and inexhaustible patience in conference and persuasion, and refusal to be diverted from basic principles can, in the long run, win out. I further believe that we must never lose sight of the ultimate objectives we are trying to attain. Immediate reaction is relatively unimportant—it is particularly unimportant if it affects only my own current standing in the

popular polls. These are the principles by which I *try* to live. I regret that I so often fail.[2]

Eisenhower believed that the public's influence on policy should be mainly through the selection of qualified representatives at elections to make policy decisions without reference to public opinion. He had faith in the public's ability to make the correct choice at the ballot box. This faith was reflected in a private letter in which he wrote that he rejected the idea that the electoral decisions reached by "popular majorities" could not be trusted.[3] Outside elections, he felt comfortable circumscribing the influence of public opinion on issues about which the public might know little, such as national security matters. He argued at a July 1953 National Security Council (NSC) meeting that "members of the Administration gave the people guides as to policy every time they appeared in public. The Administration should take the public into its confidence where the public has to make decisions or form public opinion. However, we did not have to tell everything."[4] At another point, he noted, "We will get the best effect in reaching difficult decisions if our public is fully and properly informed—or that is achieved so far as it may be practicable to do" within the strictures of national security. Suggesting that public opinion was unqualified to affect foreign affairs, he continued,

> I believe that the rule to apply is, Can, with the facts, the American public actually make a decision in this particular point? Should they? And I think it is easy to see that if the subject is sufficiently professional or technical, there would be no possibility of a great electorate making a decision anyway.[5]

Instead of relying on public opinion as a basis for policy, Eisenhower felt he should first select policies without reference to their popularity and then, if possible, lead the public to support the policies he deemed appropriate. In a memorandum to top administration officials outlining the need for better public relations, he explained his philosophy:

> We have a task that is not unlike the advertising and sales activity of a great industrial organization. It is first necessary to have a good product to sell; next it is necessary to have an effective and persuasive way of informing the public of the excellence of that product.[6]

Eisenhower explained to a friend that he considered it the obligation of the president to "have the courage and the strength to stand up and tell the truth and to keep repeating the truth regardless of vilification and abuse" until the people accepted the facts that drove the decision. Because of the four-year election cycle, he felt that the president had "a longer assured opportunity to teach an unpleasant fact" and convince the public of the veracity of his arguments. "On the other hand, we have a Congress in which the members must be selected every two years, and they are sensitive indeed to even transitory resentments in their several districts."[7]

Eisenhower's preferences in dealing with the public derived from his estimation of public opinion. The public's support of government policies during World War II signified to him that the public was "grown up" and capable of assuming the responsibilities associated with American action in the international sphere.[8] Even though he felt that the public would respond positively if fully informed, he believed the complex nature of foreign affairs and the information necessary to make a proper judgment made public opinion a poor guide for choosing a policy. He remained concerned that the public might not always stand behind the correct policy and could force the government to act imprudently. During a discussion of nuclear weapons at a May 1953 NSC meeting, the memorandum of conversation reported that Eisenhower concluded the following:

> It seemed to him at least possible that some action could occur that would force the Government's hand and cause us to resort to atomic bombardment. He noted that popular pressure had forced the Government's hand in the Spanish American War. Accordingly, though Secretary [of Defense Charles] Wilson was generally correct [that the United States would never be the first to use nuclear weapons in a conflict with the Soviets], he should not be so certain in view of the temper of the American people.[9]

Although Eisenhower thought that the public reacted responsibly to news during World War II, the rapidness with which the public lost interest in foreign affairs concerned him. He commented:

> Right after the World War the great cry was for demobilization. . . . Along with it we suffered a certain distaste for anything that smacked of war and therefore almost smacked of foreign news. . . . The local story assumed its ancient and traditional importance in our lives . . . hope was strong that peace was with us, and we felt that one subject that we could now ignore—and turn back to our more accustomed paths and pur-

suits—was war, the foreign problems with which we were beset. . . . And then, one day we awoke with a great shock.[10]

He feared this tendency by the public could deprive the government of the support necessary for its conduct of foreign affairs. Eisenhower also worried that the public might not always sufficiently understand foreign affairs, since it, unlike government officials, lacked a sufficient background in military affairs to avoid confusion and misunderstandings concerning international relations.[11]

Given this ambivalence about public opinion, Eisenhower believed that government efforts to inform the public were necessary to head off potential problems. He confided to an associate that he tried to speak about foreign affairs a great deal because "Americans understand it less than anything else."[12] He felt that public opinion could be shaped to favor the administration's goals, arguing "that much of our so-called 'public opinion' is merely a reflection of some commentator's reports which, as you so well know, bear little relation to the truth. By the same token, I believe that public opinion based on such flimsy foundations can be changed rapidly."[13] Even so, he was shocked at the seeming futility of his efforts to inform the public on important matters, lamenting at one point the "almost complete lack of information the American people have on subjects we have talked about time and time again."[14]

In summary, Eisenhower had a fairly limited view of what it meant to have the public involved in the formulation of foreign policy. Although the public could cope with broad foreign policy questions, he believed that it would sometimes, if not often, fail to understand specific issues. Accordingly, the public should take an essentially passive role in policy formulation. In short, Eisenhower believed that the primary direction of influence in foreign policy formulation should be from the government to the public.

Practical Beliefs

Eisenhower thought that the influence of public opinion on his foreign policy choices should be minimal, but he did believe that the public's support of a foreign policy was necessary for it to succeed, especially concerning issues of major importance such as the broad purposes of American foreign policy and, in particular, national security policy. He commented, "I am not pleading . . . for some utopian state on which in every minor question complete unanimity of opinion and conviction will be achieved. I am talking merely about the basic purposes that our country is trying to achieve in the world."[15] Related to his notions of a free government, he felt that an informed public was necessary for its proper functioning. At a May 1956 NSC meeting, he noted that the "first task was to educate the American people and Congress. The National Security Council could be as wise as so many Solomons and yet end in complete failure if we cannot convince the public and the Congress of the wisdom of our decisions."[16] On questions involving war, Eisenhower felt that public support was a prerequisite for any successful action, especially given the Korean War experience. Reflecting this concern at an August 1954 NSC meeting, the minutes report that Eisenhower commented:

> Since the Civil War there [has] been only one war in which the United States participated which . . . evoked continuous and vociferous criticism from the American public. This was the Korean war. The President thought that a democracy such as the United States could not be led into war unless public opinion so overwhelmingly favored war that a Congressional declaration of war was merely an automatic registering of public opinion. . . . The country would have to be behind any action taken by our military forces."[17]

Public opinion could also play a critical part in diplomatic relations. Eisenhower observed that "if we can show the world that [John Foster Dulles's] words and thoughts represent the words and thoughts of the mass of Americans, his capacity for serving us all would be greatly enhanced."[18] On both diplomatic and national security policy, he saw public support as critical to its successful implementation.

In large part because of this view, Eisenhower saw his primary responsibility as leading the public. An internal memorandum records that "he felt his big job was selling the people of America the things that they have for the best of all the people."[19] To achieve this goal, he believed that "anyone who accepts a position of responsibility must, by that very fact, exert the leadership required in that position."[20] Public information programs provided the linchpin in his strategy. He was quoted as defining public relations as "nothing in the world but getting ideas put out in such a way that your purpose is actually understood by all the people that need to understand it in order to get it done efficiently and well."[21] These efforts placed a premium on information, education, and the presentation of facts to the public through congressional speeches, press conferences, and, especially, presidential speeches.[22]

While emphasizing the necessity of leading the public, Eisenhower also perceived the limited ability of any leader to sway the public. He recognized "that as far as speaking goes, any one, including himself, has only so much credit in the bank—people get tired of him."[23] In a long letter to his former speech writer Emmet Hughes, Eisenhower argued that the government's responsibility was to focus mainly on the job of government and not to become overly concerned about public relations. A popular president could alter the public's view, but usually only by deeds, rather than words, and the public would support the policy once it succeeded. "Occasionally I must go on the air and let the people have direct knowledge of the important and comprehensive programs that are in the mill."[24]

In perhaps the clearest explication of his beliefs, Eisenhower wrote to a friend about how he reached foreign policy decisions:

> More and more I find myself . . . tending to strip each problem down to its simplest possible form. Having gotten the issue well defined in my mind, I try in the next step to determine what answer would best serve the *long term* advantage and welfare of the United States and the free world. I then consider the *immediate problem* and what solution can we get that will best conform to the long term interests of the country and at the same time *can command a sufficient approval in this country so as to secure the necessary Congressional action.*[25]

Eisenhower's practical beliefs centered on the need for the support of public opinion, which could usually be achieved through concerted efforts to lead and inform the people about the administration's policy. Despite the importance of public relations in his approach, he believed that most of his attention should be on constructing suitable policies. Policy came first, followed by efforts to lead and explain the chosen alternative to the public to gain its support. But Eisenhower did not rule out adjusting his policy to conform with public opinion if he concluded he could not generate public support. In short, Eisenhower felt that by making the correct decisions, taking the proper action, and defending these choices in the public sphere, he usually could gradually persuade the public to accept the policies he deemed necessary, even if the public did not initially accept them.

Eisenhower's normative beliefs—reflecting a desire to formulate foreign policy without input from public opinion—and practical beliefs— viewing public opinion as a necessary component of a successful foreign policy—are characteristic of the pragmatist belief orientation. Like

Eisenhower's, Dulles's beliefs also identify him as a pragmatist, but Dulles differed in two important respects. In his normative beliefs, Dulles thought that public opinion should guide the nation's broad foreign policy objectives. In his practical beliefs, he assumed that with given enough time, he could lead the public to support the policy he deemed best, but without enough time, he probably could not do so. Other than these important differences, the analysis of their beliefs suggests that they largely agreed on their approach to public opinion.

Public Opinion Beliefs: Dulles

Normative Beliefs

Dulles did not want public input to affect the government's foreign policy choices regarding anything but the nation's broad and long-term foreign policies.

> The fact that the American people historically have certain objectives is not, however, in itself a foreign policy. The task of the President and the Secretary of State is to find the ways to accomplish this basic objective of the American people. It is the ways whereby our government proposes to accomplish that result that constitute a foreign policy.[26]

While in office, in an extemporaneous and off-the-record speech to interest-group representatives (the groups are not clear from the documentation), Dulles emphasized the broad nature of information he desired from the public. He commented that much of his time in the State Department was spent on "day by day problems." However, regarding "long-range problems" and the ability to "look ahead," he noted that "we [in the State Department] don't believe that we have a monopoly of out-giving; we want to get that kind of enlightenment from you. I can assure you that when your organizations make constructive suggestions to us that they get serious attention and that that is the kind of thing which we welcome."[27]

Dulles thought that the general outlines of national policy would be determined mainly at election time. In particular, he felt that presidential elections gave the public the means to determine broad foreign policy goals, observing that "national elections give the opportunity to translate the public will into action."[28] Dulles spoke positively regarding public opinion and its ability to cope with these larger issues, believing that the American people "possessed to a high degree the ability to see clearly and to think straight."[29] At the time of his appointment as special counsel to the State Department during the Truman administration, he observed, "In the past, the American people have always developed a unity of purpose which has enabled them to repel successfully the successive challenges which come inevitably to every nation."[30] At another time, he commented, "The American people have always responded, once it was made clear to them that a need was vital. Our greatest lapses have been due to the fact that those in authority have been afraid to trust the American people and have kept from them unpleasant truths."[31] At least on the large and vital issues, he felt that the public could be trusted to do the correct thing.

Dulles had less faith in public opinion on specific policies than on broad foreign policy objectives. He judged it necessary for the government to reach its own decisions in the creation of foreign policy and not be limited by concerns regarding public opinion, since he did not believe the public would always react reasonably. Dulles privately told an associate:

> I give great importance to public opinion but I can't abdicate to such opinion the leadership I feel I must exercise. My responsibility, under the President, is to choose and carry out foreign policies most likely to contribute to the security and advancement of the American people. I often have to make decisions before the state of public opinion can be ascertained, and often such decisions have to be based on circumstances so complicated that it's next to impossible for the majority of the people to understand them. In other words, you can't make foreign policy on the basis of public opinion polls.[32]

During a February 1957 NSC discussion about whether the government should give information to the public regarding the possible consequences of a nuclear attack, Dulles argued strongly that this sort of information should not be given to the American public because it would seriously limit the government's ability to formulate policy. The memorandum of the discussion records his saying:

> It was clear in [Dulles's] own mind that the Government ought never [to give this sort of information to the public]. We were here involved with a very dangerous and delicate problem which called for our best judgment. In the circumstances, we certainly could not carry out the program ... without creating a mob psychology which would compel us against our better judgment to accept a dangerously faulty disarmament program or else to undertake a vast and costly shelter program.... Sec-

retary Dulles insisted that we do not wish to incorporate this kind of information in the minds of our people.[33]

This hesitance concerning the public's opinion of specific policies resulted from several defects in public opinion that Dulles thought could harm the formulation of policy. He decided that the public was not able to identify improper leadership and could be misled by this wrongheaded guidance.[34] This problem could be aggravated by the possibility that the public could develop a "mob psychology" if it became too aroused and that many foreign policy issues were too complicated for the public to understand. The public, he felt, could become too fixated on immediate results, making it difficult to maintain a consistent foreign policy. He remarked that "one of the weaknesses perhaps of the American people is that we want things to happen very quickly, and if they don't happen very quickly we become disappointed and turn away and try something else."[35] Although Dulles's overall view of public opinion was positive, he conceded that an uninformed or misguided public could suffer from problems at either of two extremes: it could be either too committed and adamant about a policy, regardless of its value, or too focused on short-term success.

In sum, Dulles felt that public opinion should play a role in policy formulation and believed that government leaders should try to achieve the public's basic foreign policy objectives. However, on specific policies, he deemed it acceptable to pursue the correct policy despite the public's preferences.

Practical Beliefs

Dulles believed that a successful foreign policy required public support. For example, he observed early in the Eisenhower administration:

> Under our form of society, foreign policy is not a matter just for diplomats, however astute they may be. Foreign policies to be successful must be understood and supported by the people. And I have stated that it will be my purpose, as far as it is possible, to see to it that our foreign policies are simple, so that they can be understood; that they are made public, so that the people will have a chance to understand them.[36]

In a private conversation with an associate, he linked the necessity of domestic support with a foreign policy's international success:

> There's no question that we need public support for our foreign policies. We can't get too far ahead of public opinion, and we must do everything

we can to bring it along with us. Any United States foreign policy, to be effective, has to have a compelling majority of American public opinion behind it. Other nations are more inclined to listen to proposals or objections from the President and me if they know that the American people are thoroughly behind us. They are more inclined to hold back if they know the American public is divided.[37]

To gain this support, he wanted to

> make radio and television talks to the American people in an effort to bring them to feel that we really wanted them to know what was in our minds so that we could have a full exchange of thoughts and we could have the popular backing which is indispensable in our representative form of government.[38]

At the beginning of the Cold War, Dulles was particularly troubled by the possibility of disunity, especially as it affected American power:

> Power is not merely the existence of material power, whether it be in terms of weapons or goods. It includes unity of purpose, without which material things cannot be geared into an effective program. The United States still has great potential power but it is not effective power if its use is paralyzed by internal divisions, by distrusts, and by political rivalries. . . . Internal disunity always means ineffectual foreign policies.[39]

If disunity reigned, then the United States could not act decisively, thereby undercutting American leadership, whereas a united foreign policy held the possibility of enhancing American leadership.

Dulles sensed no contradiction between the necessities of policy and the requirement of public support. In fact, he saw the ever-changing machinations of power politics as both undesirable and unworkable in the United States.

> It is quite impractical for the United States to operate on a "freewheeling" basis in the field of foreign affairs. In a democracy like ours foreign policy must be understood by the people and supported by the people. We have had during these postwar years a foreign policy which has on the whole been successful, and which has had bipartisan support, whenever it was a policy that was understood and approved by our people. But the American people could never understand and put their weight behind a foreign policy which was erratic and, indeed, shifty in character. They cannot be led in devious and unpredictable paths by a govern-

ment which chooses to operate on the basis of day-to-day expediency rather than of principle.[40]

Because public support was necessary, Dulles considered it vital to prepare public opinion and lead it to support a policy before implementing it. This requirement meant the United States would often move slowly because of the necessity for a "prolonged" preparation of public opinion before acting.[41]

To achieve this support, he sought consistent public information efforts. In a private letter regarding his concern for public opinion during his pre-Eisenhower government service, Dulles explained,

> Whenever I have been at meetings either of the Council of Foreign Ministers or of the U.N. I have, on my return, always made a report to the public. . . . This has both informed the public and invited public discussion, and afforded interested individuals an opportunity to exert an intelligent influence.[42]

Even so, as discussed earlier, Dulles remained prepared to withhold information from the public if the situation warranted it, in his judgment.

Dulles's practical beliefs concerning public opinion revolved around the need for the public's support. Any sizable public disagreement on the fundamentals of foreign policy would necessarily lead to difficulties. In addition, on specific actions, he did not feel comfortable acting quickly without public support. To gain the necessary support in these situations, he felt that a certain amount of time was necessary to prepare the public to accept the government's policy, and he believed that the best way to ensure the public's support of foreign policy was to inform it simply and clearly. In sum, Dulles believed that the government should use its best judgment to formulate foreign policy, consistent with the public's basic objectives, and to inform the public about this policy to obtain its acceptance. These beliefs are consistent with the pragmatist beliefs orientation.

Validity

Oral history recollections by people who knew Eisenhower and Dulles allow a validity test of the qualitative content analysis. Examining how those close to these two decision makers believed that Eisenhower and Dulles saw public opinion, confirmed the qualitative content analysis.

White House Press Secretary James Hagerty noted that Eisenhower did not use polls to guide policy:

> Most of the time [Eisenhower] would say, in effect, "Well, that may be so but I'm going to do what I think is right." Now, if the polls agreed with what he was doing, well and good. If they didn't, it didn't make the slightest bit of difference in what he thought was best for the nation or the world on whatever he was proposing.[43]

Even though he valued public support, the oral histories demonstrate that Eisenhower felt he should decide on policy based on other factors and then generate support for the proper policy by leading the public. The president's brother, Milton Eisenhower, compared Dwight Eisenhower's views with those of other presidents:

> I worked for eight [presidents]. The effect on the vote is always so important. As a matter of fact in Washington today the reason we don't solve our problems is because everybody is voting for what will get him reelected rather than for what is right. He [President Eisenhower] was never that way. If an essential policy or decision happened to have a bad political effect, too damn bad. But he really had enough confidence in the American people that he believed that they would accept the truth and then act wisely.[44]

Arthur Larson, who served as special assistant to the president, agreed with this assessment.

> Eisenhower could be said to be a man who made his decisions on the basis of principle rather than politics. . . . I've always said that Eisenhower was completely nonpolitical in the sense that in the scale of motivations for a decision, political advantage, the effect on votes and so forth, was not only low on the list, it was absolutely non-existent. If you wanted to get thrown out of the Oval Room, all you had to say is, "Look, Mr. President, this is going to cost you votes in West Virginia." Well, you wouldn't get past "West"—you'd be out.[45]

Andrew Goodpaster, who was Eisenhower's staff secretary and close associate, echoed this assessment and described Eisenhower as feeling strongly about the need to lead public opinion to support his policies. He recalled that Eisenhower "recognized that there was a great leadership responsibility in forming and advising public opinion, particularly in difficult areas removed from their own experience, such as foreign affairs and military activity."[46]

I think that [Eisenhower] saw [the office of president] as the crucial place in government for the consideration, as he put it, of what's good for America—from the standpoint of what's good for America, insofar as the government was concerned. And then came the responsibility of trying to bring that about, working through the Congress, working directly with the people. . . . On occasion [Eisenhower] would see in addition to trying to lead public opinion, or have a role in forming public opinion, that it would be his task to create public interest in some topic that was of deep importance.[47]

The director of the Office of Defense Mobilization and a member of the National Security Council, Arthur Flemming, confirmed the notion that Eisenhower cared deeply about public support. Flemming found Eisenhower's reaction to the British, French, and Israeli seizure of the Suez Canal representative of his views concerning public opinion. He recalled that Eisenhower said:

"I don't understand why they've done it. . . . To my knowledge this is the first time that a nation resting on a democratic foundation has committed its forces without the support of its people. . . . It won't work." [Flemming added,] The support of the people was at the center of his thinking, the center of his administration whether dealing with foreign policy or dealing with domestic policy. He recognized that under a democracy you had to work to get the support of a bill. I don't mean by that that he was just sitting around waiting to see whether or not a particular policy had the support of the people but he had the feeling that if he was going to get any place with a policy in which he believed that one of the things he had to do was to work on getting the support of the people.[48]

The oral history accounts portray Eisenhower as feeling that he should not follow public opinion but instead should determine the best policy for the nation. After he decided on a policy, he believed that he should gain the necessary public support by vigorous leadership efforts. In sum, the views of those close to Eisenhower largely echo the findings of the qualitative content analysis.

Oral history accounts of Dulles's beliefs also support the qualitative content analysis. These recollections identify Dulles as interested in public opinion, but not in terms of seeking guidance for policy. Former Vice President Richard Nixon agreed that Dulles strongly felt the need to lead the public:

Dulles knew that you had to win politically in order to have your policies go through. . . . Some political leaders in the decision making process would put their finger in the air and say, what do the people want. Dulles never believed in decision-making by Gallup Poll. Dulles on the other hand, having decided what ought to be done, then wanted to check the Gallup Poll to see what was possible, and then he believed in educating the people and bringing them along to what ought to be done. He often said to me that that was the job of a statesman, never to find out what public opinion was, he said—"After all, you don't take a Gallup Poll to find out what you ought to do in Nepal. Most people don't know where Nepal is, let alone, most Congressmen and Senators. But what you do is to determine what policy should be, and then if there's a controversy and if there's a need for public understanding, you educate the public."[49]

The former assistant secretary of state for public affairs, Andrew Berding, reported that Dulles read State Department analyses of public opinion in the form of

newspaper editorials, the columns of something like thirty columnists, as I recall it, also public statements by leading figures, statements made in Congress, occasionally letters by outstanding people to the editors, resolutions passed by national organizations, and the like. A compendium of all that, and an analysis of all that, was made and submitted to him on different aspects of American foreign policy.[50]

The special assistant to the secretary of state (among other positions), William Butts Macomber, reported that Dulles used polls to determine whether public opposition was building against a policy. Macomber recalled that Dulles would pay attention to polls

if he thought that the US polls were indicating that public concern and opposition were building up against some policy or action he thought was awfully important. Then, you can be sure, he would look at those polls, and he would chart out some kind of a campaign to persuade people that what he was doing was right. So he used them as warning signs.[51]

The oral histories also confirm Dulles's recognition that the public's support of policy was necessary for a successful foreign policy. The director of the policy-planning staff of the State Department, Robert Bowie, explained,

I think, also, he felt very strongly that it was important to carry along public opinion with foreign policy and that the Secretary had a responsibility for trying to fulfill that role, too. He was deeply concerned I think, at all times, with the fear that the democratic opinion might be misled or might be too easily tempted to let down and drop its guard or to cease to support the necessary measures.[52]

Macomber echoed these sentiments and noted that Dulles was more concerned with potential opposition:

[Dulles] told me once that to have a successful policy you don't really have to mobilize over fifty per cent of the people behind you. But it will not be a successful policy if at any time over fifty per cent of the people of this country are against it. . . . So he worked very hard on explaining to the public why he was for something. He wasn't trying to get a huge majority behind him, but he always thought that no policy—no matter how good it was intrinsically—was going to work if over fifty per cent of the country was opposed to it. So he worked very hard to explain his policies in a way that would prevent a build up of opposition to the point where they would be overcome and shot down.[53]

As argued in the qualitative content analysis, the information given to the public played a critical role in Dulles's conception of how to avoid a loss of support. Assistant Secretary of State for Public Affairs Carl McCardle reports that Dulles saw one of his duties as secretary of state as "holding press conferences and keeping the people informed."[54] Special Assistant to the Secretary of State Roderic O'Connor also emphasized this point, stating, "There's no question in my mind but that [Dulles] felt that his relations with the press and keeping people informed was an extremely important part of his mission. . . . And he [gave a large number of press conferences] because he thought it was essential that people be kept informed about what he was doing."[55]

The oral histories portray Dulles as being very concerned about public support, especially potential public opposition. They support the qualitative content analysis's conclusion that even though he believed public support to be important, he did not believe in determining policy based on what would be popular. These reports also indicate that to gain public support and avoid opposition, he considered the best action to be to lead public opinion by explaining the policy.

Predictions

This qualitative content analysis suggests a range of predictions for Eisenhower's and Dulles's behavior which, taken as a whole, present a pattern of expected reactions to public opinion different from that of the realist or Wilsonian liberal models. Eisenhower's beliefs corresponded most closely to a desire to lead the public. In his decision making, he would have attempted to formulate the best policy and then tried to convince the public of the value of that approach (assuming that he thought that the public would respond to his leadership). The role of public opinion in his behavior, in general, will likely be captured by the *lead category*. However, public opinion could constrain Eisenhower if he felt that he could not generate public support for his policy. He might have then adjusted his policy to fall within the acceptable range of public opinion. This influence would be particularly pronounced if the decision concerned involvement in war, because he saw public backing as necessary before engaging in military action. In these cases, the *constrain category* will probably describe his behavior. He would not have followed public opinion because of his view that the public was often uninformed about the critical details of policy. But he would not have ignored public opinion, either, since he felt that the public's support of foreign policy was too important to be taken for granted. Therefore, the *follow and no-impact categories* will not be indicative of Eisenhower's decision-making behavior.

These expectations, combined with the decision context variable, suggest predictions of behavior in particular situations. To the extent that the crisis and reflexive cases entailed the use of force, Eisenhower would have searched for other alternatives if he perceived the public was unsupportive. Under these circumstances, the *constrain category* would best capture Eisenhower's decision making. If public support was not problematic, then the *lead category* would be expected. In the innovative and deliberative cases, the *lead category* will likely best describe Eisenhower's behavior. In any of these cases, Eisenhower would likely act consistently with the *constrain category* if he found the public's opposition to his preferred policy to be unmovable.

Dulles's general beliefs also suggest he would have acted according to the *lead category*. He believed that the government should formulate policy first and then generate public support. If he did not see public opinion as a problem, he would have attempted to discern and implement the best policy from a national security standpoint. If he perceived that the public might be divided over the government's policy, Dulles would have reacted in one of two ways. If he had adequate time to educate the public, he would have pursued vigorous leadership efforts and/or stretched out the policy's implementation to generate public support for the policy as outlined in the *lead category*. If he thought that the public might remain divided or there was not enough time to lead the public, he would have adjusted his policy recommendations to meet what the public would accept, as described by the *constrain category*. In addition, as found in his normative beliefs, Dulles expressed a willingness to consider the public's input on broad foreign policy objectives, especially as represented in electoral outcomes. In decisions involving these questions, he might have reacted to public opinion by either attempting to achieve the public's expressed goals, in accordance with the *follow category*, or at least by being limited by them, in accordance with the *constrain category*. In this sense, decisions involving broad foreign policy objectives are an exception to these predictions based on Dulles's pragmatist beliefs (since he would be acting much like a delegate). Except in this case, the *follow category* would not characterize his decision making. In addition, his concern for gaining public support of policy suggests that he would not have ignored public opinion, which rules out the *no-impact category*.

As with Eisenhower, combining the implications of the beliefs and context variables results in situational predictions. Dulles emphasized the need to have time to prepare the public adequately for the government's actions (allowing the government to lead on policy). The lack of time and need for preparation would be most pressing in a crisis context, given the short decision time and surprise. Thus the *constrain category* would likely describe Dulles's actions in a crisis context (assuming that he saw no immediate way of preparing the public for possible government action). Because of his concern with informing the public if the time allowed, Dulles would have acted consistently with the *lead category* in the reflexive, innovative, and deliberative contexts. The anticipation in the reflexive context and the long decision time in the innovative and deliberative contexts would have given him the time he believed necessary to lead public opinion. If a question arose concerning the broad objectives of American foreign policy, Dulles would have been affected by public opinion, as described in the *follow* or *constrain categories*.

Table 2.1 summarizes these predictions for both Eisenhower and Dulles, along with the decision contexts and cases examined. For comparison purposes, this chart also reports the predictions of the realists and Wilsonian liberals presented in chapter 1.

As the table indicates, in crises, the predictions based on beliefs largely agree with the Wilsonian liberal predictions. For reflexive cases, the beliefs predictions suggest that Eisenhower would have acted as the

TABLE 2.1 Prediction Comparisons

Situation (all high threat)	Case	Realist	Wilsonian Liberal	Beliefs
Crisis short time/ surprise	Formosa Straits, 1954	No Impact/ *Lead*	Constrain	DDE: Constrain/ *Lead* JFD: Constrain
Reflexive short time/ anticipation	Dien Bien Phu, 1954	Lead	Constrain	DDE: Constrain/ *Lead* JFD: Lead
Innovative long time/ surprise	Sputnik, 1957–58	Lead	Follow	DDE: Lead/ *Constrain* JFD: Lead
Deliberative long time/ anticipation	New Look, 1953–54	Lead/ *Constrain*	Follow	DDE: Lead/ *Constrain* JFD: Lead/*Follow on broad foreign policy*

Note: Italics indicate conditional predictions.

Wilsonian liberals describe and Dulles would have acted more as the realists predict. For the innovative and deliberative cases, both decision makers are predicted to act more consistently with realist views, except for Dulles on broad foreign policy questions. In the next four chapters, these contexts are considered in reference to the expectations of each of these models.

CHAPTER THREE

The Crisis Context:

Anticipating Domestic Opposition
over the Offshore Islands

Tensions in the Formosa Straits in the late summer of 1954 rose against the larger background of America's Cold War fear of Soviet-directed global communist expansion and Communist Chinese regional aggression.[1] After the Communist victory over the Nationalists on the mainland in the Chinese civil war in 1949, the defeated Nationalists, led by Chiang Kai-shek, took refuge on the island of Formosa (now more commonly referred to as Taiwan) and a series of offshore islands in close proximity to the mainland (which can be seen with the naked eye), in hopes of an eventual return. Because American decision makers saw Communist Chinese actions as directed by the Soviet Union, Communist aggression took on a broader global significance as part of the United States' grand strategy of containing Soviet expansion. With the outbreak of the Korean War in June 1950, the United States took explicit action to protect Formosa with President Harry Truman's order to the Seventh Fleet to interpose itself between Formosa and the mainland. By the time Eisenhower took office, Formosa had become an important bulwark (although not formalized through treaty) in containing communist expansion. Although the American commitment to protect the offshore islands remained intentionally ambiguous, any U.S. response to aggression against them would inevitably have had greater global consequences.

American policy toward Communist China also implied serious domestic implications, given the acrimonious debate over "who lost China" following the Communist victory in 1949. Support in Congress was strong, especially among the more conservative members of the Republican Party—Senator William Knowland (R, Calif.) in particular—for giving the Nationalists political and military assistance in their continuing effort to take back the mainland. So when the Communist Chinese took aggressive action in the late summer of 1954, more was at stake for American decision makers than several tiny islands.

On September 3, 1954, Communist Chinese forces began heavy shelling of the Nationalist-held coastal island of Quemoy, which raised the specter of a move against the whole chain of offshore islands. Given the importance of the Nationalists as an ally and the potential damage to American prestige from the loss of Quemoy or the other offshore islands, the Eisenhower administration decided that Formosa and the offshore islands, which also included the island of Matsu and the Tachen chain, needed to remain in friendly hands. But the United States also equally feared war over the islands, and even though all decision makers agreed that Formosa needed to be defended, a definite policy toward the offshore islands remained elusive. The administration considered a range of options, from publicly refusing to defend them to using nuclear weapons to protect them.

After intense deliberations, Eisenhower attempted to avoid either of these extremes by adopting a two-track policy: the dispute over the offshore islands would be submitted to the United Nations Security Council by a "neutral" third party, and in the meantime, the United States would negotiate a defense treaty with the Nationalists. In early 1955, to show its support for the administration's approach, Congress approved a resolution authorizing the president to use force to protect Formosa, the Pescadores, and "related territories of that area now in friendly hands." Despite these moves, tensions later grew in February, March, and April, with the administration seriously considering the use of nuclear weapons amid growing fears of an imminent Communist invasion of Formosa. War was averted, however, when in April 1955 Communist Chinese leader Chou En-lai offered to negotiate.[2] Although the offshore islands remained the center of intense concern through mid-1955, the case study considers the period when the Eisenhower administration initially debated and formulated a response (September, October, and November 1954—from the outbreak of the shelling to the beginning of negotiations on the mutual defense treaty).

Although the Communist threat to the offshore islands did not star-
tle decision makers (Eisenhower later recalled in his memoirs that it "did
not come as a complete surprise"), the administration was surprised by
the scale of action and the timing of the assault, since they expected only
minor skirmishes. In his August 5 report on the Far East, Dulles stressed
that "diversionary" attacks on the offshore islands were possible, but he
expected no major moves from the communists in the area, and instead
thought that the Communist Chinese would make the offshore islands
a diplomatic issue. When the mainland Chinese spoke threateningly
about Formosa during the summer, State Department analysts interpreted their statements as propaganda moves to attract international
attention. After the Communists engaged in minor artillery shelling of
the islands, military analysts described it as merely a "pinprick" of little
significance following the previous propaganda. Military observers also
dismissed an August buildup across from Quemoy as not an immediate
threat to the islands. But the larger scale of the Communist Chinese
assault in September defied these expectations, as did the timing of the
attack, since on August 18, military officials observed that no invasion of
the islands in the area was anticipated in the near future. The end of the
"invasion season," which lasted from April to mid-July, may have reinforced these conclusions.[3]

As they confronted these issues, public opinion limited the decision
makers in significant ways and at critical junctures. Although concerns
with American prestige and the reaction by U.S. allies largely determined choices during problem representation, as policymakers continued to ponder the matter, Dulles eliminated certain options because of
potential public opposition as the administration sought to find a viable
policy. When faced with the need to choose a policy, Eisenhower rejected the use of force to defend the offshore islands primarily because he
feared public opposition. His uncertainty about potential allies' reactions also reinforced his misgivings about domestic politics. However,
the administration concluded that the United States could not abandon
the islands because of the implications for American prestige and the
psychological impact of their loss on important allies. Limited by
domestic and international pressure, the administration thus settled on
an option they hoped would avoid the choice between fighting to protect the islands or abandoning them altogether. It chose instead to submit the issue to the United Nations. The administration also decided to
negotiate a defense treaty with the Nationalists to counteract any possible political and psychological damage the UN resolution might cause.

Once committed to this policy, public opinion affected the timing, but not the substance, of the administration's implementation efforts. Although the public's influence fluctuated somewhat over the course of the case, public opinion served as an important constraint on the direction of policy after the shelling.

These actions have important implications for realist and Wilsonian liberal theories and the beliefs model. As I argued in chapter 1, of all the decision contexts considered, the realist expectation that decision makers will ignore public opinion when formulating policy is most likely to be correct in crises. Decision makers may, however, attempt to influence public opinion while implementing a decision. But Wilsonian liberals expect public opinion to influence policy in crises because decision makers may be held back by their anticipations of public opinion and perceptions of the opinion context. Since realist and Wilsonian liberal theories suggest different predictions in a case in which realist explanations are expected to predominate, this case provides a good opportunity to examine the realist and Wilsonian liberal claims concerning the influence of public opinion.

The beliefs model suggests a different pattern of public opinion's influence. If Eisenhower perceived at some point that public opinion would not support a particular policy option, especially an aggressive one, and could not be persuaded to support it, he would probably be constrained by the public's view. Otherwise, if he saw public support as unproblematic, he would have attempted to lead public opinion. Dulles would have been constrained by public opinion if he perceived public opposition, since crises usually do not allow the time necessary (in his mind) to lead public opinion. If public opposition was not an issue, he would have attempted to lead the public to support his preferred policy alternative.

As indicated after the analysis, public opinion's influence is coded for the entire case as being in the *strong constrain category*. Although the realist view does receive some support during the problem representation (when officials ignored it) and implementation (when they acted mostly to lead it) stages, realist theory cannot account for the significant constraining influence of public opinion found during option generation and policy selection. Since this case is most likely to support the realist view, this result provides significant evidence against the realist perspective. Instead, the profound influence of public opinion during option generation and policy selection implies support for the Wilsonian liberal theory. The pattern of behavior also confirms the influence of the beliefs variable. Eisenhower's and Dulles's behavior was coded as a *supportive* influence, since their choices were *consistent* with expectations at every decision stage, and process tracing suggested a *causal* influence for Dulles's beliefs during option generation, policy selection, and implementation and for Eisenhower's beliefs during the critical policy selection stage.

Problem Representation: Setting the Agenda

When initially faced with the shelling, security interests dominated the decision makers' deliberations. The initial reports to Eisenhower stressed that the situation "may require basic decisions as a matter of urgency" given the threat of an impending Communist Chinese invasion and American strategic interests in the area.[4] The significance of this region put any overt threat to the offshore islands or Formosa on the administration's discussion agenda. The United States' position on the offshore islands remained decidedly vague, in large part because Eisenhower did not want to commit to defend them, nor did he want to exclude them from protection for fear of the message it would communicate to the Communists, Nationalists, and domestic sectors supportive of the Nationalists. The Communist Chinese attack caught the administration in the midst of a reevaluation of the American defense perimeter in Asia. Although they remained concerned about a Communist miscalculation of American resolve following the Indochina incident (see chapter 4) and troop withdrawals from the region based on the New Look defense strategy (see chapter 6), Dulles noted in a late August letter to the U.S. ambassador to Japan that U.S. policy in the region was still fluid and that the administration had not yet decided which of the islands to defend.[5]

Although the United States had made no public or private commitments to defend the islands, both Eisenhower and Dulles publicly recognized the importance of the offshore islands and their connection to the defense of Formosa. On August 17, Eisenhower stated that any attempt to cross the Formosa Straits to attack the main island of Formosa would have to run over the U.S. Navy, and he even observed that a possible invasion of Formosa would make a good target for atomic weapons. Although Dulles acknowledged that the military needed to make the final determination (the NSC had directed the Joint Chiefs of Staff [JCS] in mid-August to consider the viability of defending the offshore islands from a Chinese attack), he explicitly connected the offshore islands with U.S. interests on August 25 when he argued the off-shore islands might, from a military standpoint, be "so intimately connected with the defense of Formosa that the military would be justified in concluding that the defense of Formosa comprehended a defense of those islands." In this context, the shelling of the offshore islands raised the possibility of a Communist Chinese invasion in the minds of decision makers and necessitated an expeditious decision regarding the administration's position.[6]

Problem Representation: Defining the Situation

The government did not immediately agree on a definition of the problem. Given the speed with which the events occurred and the various locations of key individuals (Dulles was attending an international conference in the Philippines, and Eisenhower was at his "summer White House" in Denver), policymakers reached their own conclusions about the threat confronting the administration.

Eisenhower defined the implications of the threat to the islands as physical and psychological and thought that the security of Formosa was intimately connected with the fate of the offshore islands. In August, he stated that he "had imagined [the offshore islands] were vital outposts for the defense of Formosa."[7] He recalled later that the Communist Chinese shelling posed a threat to both the offshore islands, on the one hand, and Formosa and the Pescadores, on the other, because the Nationalists' possession of them made an amphibious invasion of Formosa more difficult. During later discussions, however, Eisenhower stressed the islands' psychological importance to the Nationalist Chinese rather than their physical value, mentioning later that the islands meant "everything" in terms of morale for the Nationalists.[8]

Since Eisenhower saw allied support for American regional policy as vital, he also worried about how American allies, particularly the British, would perceive and react to the shelling and feared that an aggressive American response might drive a wedge between the United States and its international friends.[9] At the August 18 NSC meeting, he expressed his feeling that unilateral American involvement in a large regional war would be disastrous and speculated that the United States might even lose it if allied opinion turned against the American policy. Nonetheless, he concluded that the United States "should go as far as possible to defend [the offshore islands] without inflaming world opinion against us."[10] The real possibility of war in the area only enhanced these anxieties.[11] In the end, Eisenhower formed a picture of the threat from the shelling in terms of both a physical and a psychological threat to Formosa's security, with additional implications for allied relations deriving from the possibility of war.

Dulles also fretted about the potential reaction of American allies should the United States become involved in a regional war and feared unwanted complications if it led to conflicts with important allies, Great Britain in particular, or disturbed domestic opinion in these nations. More than even Eisenhower, Dulles viewed the attack on the islands in terms of their psychological value. In addition to speculating that the islands might be "intimately connected" to Formosan defenses from a military standpoint, Dulles told Secretary of Defense Charles Wilson that the loss of the offshore islands would deal a severe psychological and political blow to the Nationalists. But he also thought the situation might contribute to American prestige if handled correctly. On August 31 during a State Department meeting, he emphasized the need for a belligerent military policy regarding the offshore islands, even though this would entail some dangers, in order to recoup the prestige lost from the Indochina situation earlier that year. Although this policy did entail some risks, Dulles maintained that the benefits in terms of American prestige were worth the danger, which in any event, he did not see as considerable. He underscored the need for a flexible policy regarding the offshore islands that would respond to "political and military considerations," because even though it was critical to keep Formosa permanently out of communist hands, the same did not hold true for the offshore islands.[12]

When the shelling occurred, Dulles dramatically outlined his perception of the situation confronting American policymakers in a telegram dated September 4 from the Philippines. He explained that the loss of Quemoy would cause "grave psychological repercussions and lead to mounting Communist action against deteriorating anti-Communist morale so that this would be [the] beginning of [a] chain of events which could gravely jeopardize [the] entire off-shore position [Formosa, Japan, New Zealand, Australia, the Ryukyu Islands, and the Philippines]." He argued that the United States should attempt to hold the islands if they were judged defensible with American assistance, even if the real estate contained no intrinsic value and such a defense necessitated attacking the Chinese mainland. Given the seriousness of the threat, he recommended immediate consultations with at least the leadership of Congress as a matter of "urgency" to ensure congressional backing.[13] In sum, Dulles's view centered on the psychological threat that would result from the loss of the islands and on the opportunity for the United States to recoup lost prestige.

Option Generation

To remedy this situation, decision makers developed a range of alternatives, from doing nothing to responding aggressively. Given his perception of the threat, Eisenhower preferred a policy of procrastination which would allow him to avoid choosing among several unattractive alternatives. Although Dulles initially favored an aggressive response, he significantly altered his policy position in response to anticipated public opinion, to support a more middle-of-the-road stance more closely approaching the direction that Eisenhower preferred. There was division in the Defense Department, however, with the JCS (led by its chair, Admiral Arthur Radford) pressing for decisive action to protect the islands and others (mainly Secretary of Defense Charles Wilson and Army Chief of Staff General Matthew Ridgway) recommending backing away completely from a commitment to defend them.

Given the dilemma that Eisenhower saw as inherent in the policy toward the islands, the option he preferred boiled down to taking a "wait and see" attitude toward action. Although he did not wish to abandon the offshore islands, he preferred to achieve his goals by keeping the American position vague and avoiding an explicit commitment. Eisenhower also remained uncertain about how to achieve this end. He firmly believed that the island of Formosa had be defended, since it entailed a clear American national security interest. In addition, he felt "certain that American public opinion overwhelmingly favors any necessary action on our part to make certain of the defeat of any such attempt" to take the island. State Department polling supported his feeling.[14]

While Eisenhower worried about the ramifications for the Nationalists' morale of allowing the offshore islands to fall into Communist hands, more bellicose action posed a problem as well. He feared a commitment to defend the islands would irretrievably engage American prestige in a possibly doomed defensive action. Furthermore, the implications of an American-backed evacuation of the Nationalist troops on Quemoy in the event of an invasion troubled him, and he noted that "my hunch is that once we get tied up in any one of these things our prestige is so completely involved."[15] Eisenhower felt strongly that the administration should not pledge to protect the offshore islands unless they could be defended, something he found a risky prospect given their proximity to the mainland. A commitment to defend the islands, he believed, also might anger important allies.[16]

Although Eisenhower believed as late as mid-August that the offshore islands themselves were "vital outposts" of Formosa's defense, he now appeared to be weighing the costs of defending them in terms of potential damage the country's prestige and allied relations. Facing the prospect of balancing a policy between abandoning and defending the islands while avoiding the irretrievable commitment of American prestige, he settled on procrastination as the only policy that could allay his concerns by avoiding a commitment, keeping several options open, and leaving the decision up to the Communist Chinese.

Unlike Eisenhower, Dulles initially supported a more forceful stance, recommending the defense of the offshore islands because of the opportunity to regain American prestige and the possible damage to the American position in the region from their loss. During the first week of the crisis, he saw the psychological value of the islands as so great that he was willing to commit to their defense even if it meant risking a larger war, attacking the Chinese mainland, and, possibly, using nuclear weapons. He thought that if the islands were not defensible, the United States should distance itself from their fate to avoid its own Dien Bien Phu (see chapter 4). He apparently held this view at least until September 9 when Undersecretary of State Bedell Smith presented Dulles's views to a NSC meeting.[17] Although his insistence on the protection of Formosa never wavered, Dulles soon shifted to a less confrontational option of submitting the issue to the United Nations for consideration, a middle option between defending and abandoning the offshore islands that became attractive mainly because of his concerns with public opinion.

While returning from his trip to Asia on September 12, Dulles composed a detailed analysis of the offshore islands situation and proposed a possible solution to the crisis.[18] The memo reveals that his views had developed considerably since his initial reaction a week earlier. Dulles observed, "Quemoy cannot be held *indefinitely* without general war with Red China in which the Communists are defeated." The administration, he reasoned, could use President Harry Truman's 1950 order to the Seventh Fleet to defend Formosa against a Communist Chinese invasion to justify the defense of the offshore islands. In a comment reflecting his evolving viewpoint, he pointed out that this move would "undoubtedly" result in a "serious attack on the Administration, and a sharply divided Congress and nation, if the Executive sought to use his authority to order U.S. forces to defend also Quemoy, Tachen etc." Dulles believed that the islands were "not demonstrably essential to the defense of Formosa, as shown by the fact that for four years they have not been included in the area the Fleet is ordered to defend." This perception sharply contrasts with his previous views when he argued the opposite regarding the importance of the islands.

If the administration attempted to gain broader authority to act regarding the offshore islands, Dulles reasoned that the Congress and public would "probably," but not necessarily, "respond to an all-out appeal to the Congress" on the basis that the United States could not be "acquiescent" to further communist gains in Asia. However, the current congressional elections would complicate attempts at leadership. A commitment to defend the islands would "alienate" world opinion and American allies (Europe, Australia, and New Zealand), especially since the situation "would probably lead to our initiating the use of atomic weapons." But even though the United States did not necessarily need to "disassociate" itself immediately from the islands if it decided not to fight to defend them, Dulles believed that the loss of the offshore islands (because of the implied commitment to defend them, given American aid to Formosa and American military personnel on Quemoy) would likely harm both American prestige and Nationalist morale.

To resolve this problem, Dulles concluded that the issue should be submitted to the United Nations Security Council by a "neutral," but interested, nation, such as New Zealand, with a call for preserving the status quo and studying the issue further. Although the United States would relinquish control of the issue to the international body, Dulles found certain advantages in this option. If the Soviet Union vetoed the resolution, the United States would gain standing in world opinion and with its allies and could claim the moral high ground. If the Soviets chose not to veto the resolution, the Soviets and Communist Chinese might split, and Communist China would become an "international outcast" if it still chose to act. He foresaw the ultimate outcome of the UN option as the permanent independence of Formosa and the Pescadores. As he recognized in the presentation of his proposal at the September 12 NSC meeting, the UN option placed the administration in a better position to lead the public to support a defense of the islands if it became necessary later.

The reasoning of this memorandum reflects an important shift in Dulles's thinking regarding this crisis. Although he initially felt strongly about the need to defend the islands, his arguments now recognized a tension between competing interests and motives and, to an extent, began to express a view of the situation similar to Eisenhower's. Instead of relying on unilateral military action to defend the islands, Dulles now suggested pursuing a multilateral diplomatic course that would reduce American control but still meet the administration's policy objectives.

What accounts for Dulles's shift in position from recommending a commitment to defend the offshore islands at great risk to one desperately seeking an alternative between withdrawing or fighting? One possibility is his initial concerns about the defensibility of the islands had not been met. However, given the information he received during the intervening period, this conclusion appears unlikely. On September 7, Dulles noted that the Defense Department was currently considering the defensibility issue and that the answer looked negative. But on a September 9 stopover in Formosa for consultations, Major General William Chase, U.S. army chief of the Military Assistance Advisory Group to Formosa, gave an "optimistic" report of the military situation and recommended that the United States announce its intention to defend the islands. The U.S. ambassador to Formosa, Karl Lott Rankin, while noting that some of the islands might not be defensible, recommended that the United States keep the Communist Chinese guessing and provide military assistance where it would be helpful. In contrast to Dulles's September 7 statement, the majority of the Joint Chiefs on September 11 concluded the offshore islands were important to the defense of Formosa and defensible with American assistance.[19] Finally, while Dulles's concern about the damage to American prestige and Nationalist morale continued, the reasoning of his September 12 memorandum did not discuss the potential defensibility of the islands.

Instead of defensive issues, Dulles's memorandum focused on a new element concerning the probable negative domestic reaction if the administration acted to defend the islands. This new concern with domestic division appeared to have caused him to shift his policy recommendation from defending the islands to pursuing the possible midrange alternative of the UN option and was derived from new information that appeared regarding public opinion between his September 4 and September 12 memoranda. During this time, State Department public opinion analyses, on which Dulles heavily relied for information on public opinion, reported that the public would be divided if the

United States took aggressive action. The September 2–8 China Telegram, a report distributed to American diplomatic posts in the Far East where Dulles was attending the signing of the Southeast Asia Treaty Organization (SEATO) treaty, observed that American newspaper editors were divided on the policy the American government should choose. The following week's report indicated an even more pronounced division among commentators. In addition, other internal State Department reports warned that significant divisions in elite opinion were growing and that the possibility existed for serious divisions in the larger public should the United States use force.[20] Dulles's presentation to the NSC on September 12 emphasized the influence of public opinion to an even greater extent. In both his memorandum and his oral presentation, he stressed the future reaction of public opinion to the administration's actions. Based on this information and the reasoning in the memorandum, the shift in Dulles's policy recommendations seems to stem from this new information regarding public opinion and suggests that it heavily influenced Dulles's thinking regarding policy options to resolve the crisis.

Unlike Dulles, the JCS and Chairman Radford developed the most hawkish position based on their view of the political, psychological, and military significance of the islands and recommended several steps necessary to defend them in a September 11 memorandum to Secretary of Defense Wilson.[21] The JCS saw the offshore islands as important, among other reasons, to the Nationalists' morale, commando raiding, and intelligence gathering. Although Quemoy was not "essential" to the defense of Formosa, since the Communists could invade the larger island without the smaller one, the JCS deemed Quemoy as "substantially related" to Formosa's defense because its possession could prevent the Communists from using the best harbor in the area from which to launch an invasion. The JCS felt the offshore islands would be defensible if the United States committed naval and air forces to the area and gave the American commander the freedom "to strike when and where necessary" to thwart an actual invasion or preparations to invade. They indicated that the use of nuclear weapons would be considered "if and when" the need arose, but "with the understanding now that if essential to victory their use would be accorded."

In contrast to the JCS majority, who were willing to risk nuclear war to prevent the Communist Chinese from taking the offshore islands, Secretary of Defense Wilson and Army Chief of Staff General Matthew Ridgway argued against an American commitment to defend the islands. Wilson believed a distinction needed to be made between the offshore islands (of little consequence) and Formosa and the Pescadores (which remained important). The basic problem arose because "it would be extremely difficult to explain, either to the people of the United States or to our allies why, after refusing to go to war with Communist China over Korea and Indochina, we were perfectly willing to fight over these small islands." Ridgway disagreed with the JCS on two major points. First, he argued that the offshore islands were not *militarily* related to the defense of Formosa, and he rejected the JCS majority's political and psychological reasoning as outside the military's purview and rightly in the hands of political authorities. Quemoy, in particular, would be of "minuscule importance" during a war because the Communists could bypass the area in an invasion of Formosa, and it offered no major objectives for counteroffensive targeting. Second, he argued that a successful defense of the islands would require a major commitment of at least a division of American ground forces, along with air and naval assets which would need to be given a free hand to attack the Chinese mainland.[22]

Policy Selection

With this range of options before them, the administration reached a policy decision on the crisis during a special NSC meeting on September 12.[23] At this session, Dulles presented, and Eisenhower approved, Dulles's recommendation for investigating the United Nations option. For the next several months, the administration focused on implementing the decision reached at this meeting.

The meeting opened with a briefing by Dulles about his trip to the Far East and meeting with Nationalist leader Chiang Kai-shek, who asked for a mutual security treaty with the United States. Special Assistant to the President Robert Cutler introduced the offshore islands issue by recalling that the policy toward Formosa and the offshore islands, established in November 1953, was to "effectively incorporate" Formosa and the Pescadores into the American defensive perimeter and to protect them from a hostile takeover even "at grave risk of general war." Concerning the offshore islands, the United States would "encourage and assist" the Nationalists to defend them "without committing U.S. forces, unless Formosa or the Pescadores are attacked." Regarding the Communist reaction, the director of the Central Intelligence Agency (CIA), Allen Dulles, stated that the new interagency intelligence estimate was that the Communists would not act if they felt the United States would respond militarily.[24] JCS Chair Radford then weighed in with the views of the hawkish JCS majority, Ridgway's dissent, and CINCPAC (Commander in Chief, Pacific) Admiral Felix Stump, who emphasized the importance of the offshore islands for the defense of Formosa.

Attention then turned to the question of whether the president possessed the constitutional authority to protect the offshore islands based on Truman's 1950 orders to the Seventh Fleet. Eisenhower and Attorney General Herbert Brownell expressed trepidation about the legal standing of such action. Wilson then added his support for continuing the current policy because of the difference he saw between the offshore islands, on the one hand, and Formosa and the Pescadores, on the other, and he noted that the choice lay between the damage to morale from losing the islands or the danger of precipitating a war with China that would be difficult to stop. While Radford pressed the military reasons for holding the islands, Brownell offered a memorandum on past congressional positions on Formosa indicating that Congress had not previously understood the offshore islands to be included in the Seventh Fleet's orders.[25]

After hearing this dispute among his advisers, Eisenhower then expressed views that roughly conformed with his previous perspective on the significance of the islands by underscoring their psychological value and lack of relevance to the actual defense of Formosa. Speaking generally about the approach to these types of issues, he warned that the United States needed to be careful in reacting to every possible communist threat, because if the communists found they could tie down the United States by "making faces," they would use this tactic throughout the world. If a large-scale war was to be the result, he preferred to confront the "head of the snake" (meaning the Soviet Union rather than China). After comments by Radford describing the level of action necessary to protect the offshore islands (including attacks on the Chinese mainland), Eisenhower insisted that such aggressive action, since it implied war, required congressional approval. To do otherwise, he maintained, "would be logical grounds for impeachment" and "he was damned if he knew" how important allies, especially Britain, would react to American involvement in such a war. Perhaps feeling pressure from the NSC for belligerent action, Eisenhower "said that the Council must get one thing clear in their heads, and that is that they are talking about war." Based on a reference to "not holding back" as had been done in Korea, Eisenhower clearly saw a decision to defend the offshore islands against a Communist Chinese assault as tantamount to a commitment to a large-scale war.[26]

At this point in the discussion, Dulles introduced his proposal for UN consideration of the crisis as a means to alleviate the dilemma facing the administration. He pointed out that both sides could find support for their arguments. American weakness could lead to further Communist probing, resulting in a fight in "less advantageous conditions," with possibly "disastrous consequences in Korea, Japan, Formosa, and the Philippines." But war with the Communist Chinese over the offshore islands at this point could undermine the American position. "Outside of [South Korean leader Syngman] Rhee and Chiang [Kai-shek], the rest of the world would condemn us, as well as a substantial part of the U.S. people. The British fear atomic war and would not consider the reasons for our action to be justified. Possibly very few Americans would agree." The United States faced a "horrible dilemma." To alleviate this condition, Dulles advised submitting the issue to the United Nations to "obtain an injunction to maintain the *status quo*." If the Soviets vetoed the resolution against the UN majority will, the administration would find a "totally different atmosphere regarding our allies and the American people." If the Soviets went along, the move could be the first step in stabilizing the region. Dulles asserted that the proposal held the possibility of avoiding the two unacceptable extremes of the "moral condemnation of the world" for choosing war or the outright loss of islands. He thought that the United States also had to consult with the Nationalists and the British and added that his information indicated that no decision on the defense of the islands was necessary in the short term, since the Chinese were acting cautiously because of the immediate Nationalist reaction and uncertainty of American action.[27]

Eisenhower "heartily endorsed" Dulles's proposal and stressed the need to find out the British reaction. He saw advantages to the UN resolution, since it might allow America to act without congressional authority, as had occurred in Korea. Dulles noted that if the United States acted in the present atmosphere, the administration would have to act without congressional authorization and would "not have anyone in the United States with us." However, the UN resolution would enable congressional authorization that otherwise would not be forthcoming. After further discussion of the UN option, Eisenhower's concern for domestic opinion became apparent. According to the minutes:

> [Eisenhower] did not believe that we could put the proposition of going to war over with the American people at this time. The West Coast might agree, but his letters from the farm areas elsewhere constantly say don't send our boys to war. It will be a big job to explain to the American people the importance of these islands to U.S. security. Moreover, if we shuck the U.N., and say we are going to be the world's policeman, we had better get ready to go to war, because we'll get it. The president said that while he was in general agreement with everything that had been said, we must enlist world support and the approval of the American people.[28]

Although Eisenhower thought he might be able to generate congressional and public support if he labeled the islands as an essential national security interest, he believed that he would have to make a "terrific case." He insisted that the group "must recognize that Quemoy is not our ship. Letters to him constantly say what do we care what happens to those yellow people out there?"[29]

Continuing the NSC discussion, Vice President Richard Nixon joined the JCS majority concerning the psychological and political importance of the islands. If the United States decided to do nothing, he recommended not announcing the decision, in order to keep the Communists guessing and to take a chance on the consequences. He argued that a significant segment of the American population still felt the UN had "kept our boys from doing what should have been done in Korea" and worried that the administration might be criticized for "becoming engaged in another war under UN auspices after the example of Korea." Dulles

> agreed that there was a very vocal segment of the United States which was against the UN, but that all the polls indicated an overwhelming majority (about 75%) who were still for the UN. He thought that his proposal would be responsive to the real wishes of the American people that we exhaust all peaceful means before taking military action.

To this, Eisenhower reiterated his belief that the administration "must be able to explain our actions to the American people." Eisenhower concluded the meeting saying that only he should comment on the substance of discussions and decided to have the secretary of state explore the possibility and desirability of the UN option.

Eisenhower's perception of divisions in the American public is supported by polling from this period. Although the public supported some form of aid to Formosa (then the current policy), it was sharply divided over the question of sending in American troops, with only a fraction of the public supporting such a move. A September 1954 State Department poll found that 53 percent of the population supported "giving the Chinese Nationalist government on Formosa all the help it needs to attack the Chinese Communists on the mainland of China," with 33 percent disapproving and 14 percent with no opinion—figures essentially unchanged since March 1952. The 53 percent supporting assistance to the Nationalist Chinese were asked what type of assistance the United States should give. Expressed as a percentage of the total sample, of which 33 percent opposed aid, the poll indicated that 20 percent supported sending troops to assist the Chinese Nationalists in this effort and 31 percent opposed troops but supported some sort of undefined aid (the remaining 2 percent of the original 53 percent gave no opinion on the use of troops).[30]

A more specific question on the defense of Formosa also revealed significant divisions in the public. A Gallup poll taken after the critical NSC meeting, during the week of September 16 through 21 and released on October 6, asked: "If Formosa is invaded by Communist China, which one of the following statements (on card) comes closest to your own view of what the United States should do?" Ten percent answered "have US planes bomb airfields and factories on the China mainland"; 31 percent indicated "have US planes and ships help keep Communist China from invading Formosa"; 28 percent responded "have US supply guns and other war materials but take no active part in fighting"; 21 percent preferred to "have the United States keep out of Formosa altogether and let them fight it out themselves"; and 10 percent gave no opinion.[31] These surveys revealed a significant division in the public over the level of American assistance to Formosa and a special concern about the use of ground troops. Even greater public opposition to an American use of force would be expected regarding the offshore islands, since even the American government questioned their strategic significance.

Public opinion strongly affected Eisenhower's choice to support Dulles's policy proposal. Even though the psychological importance of the islands provided a reason not to simply abandon them, Eisenhower was less inclined to agree with the proponents of action (such as the JCS majority) and, because the islands held little physical value, seemed hesitant to risk war and its consequences in public opinion. He clearly believed that public support for military action and congressional authorization would not be forthcoming at the time and felt that the majority of the public would oppose any unilateral action by the United States that resulted in war. While recognizing that the islands had psychological importance and that a full-fledged education campaign might create public support for American action, Eisenhower desperately wanted to avoid another Asian war, because of the risk of domestic division. The UN option seemed to resolve the conflict between the extreme choices, held the possibility of avoiding war at least in the short term, and placed the administration in a better position to obtain the required public support should more aggressive action prove necessary at a later date. Although he was interested in leading public opinion on this issue, Eisenhower recognized that his ability to do so was limited and found a less confrontational approach more consonant with his reading of public opinion. Along with lingering concerns about the United States' allies, public opinion virtually eliminated the option of war or a strong stand regarding the offshore islands at that time.

Policy Implementation

As decided at the September 12 NSC meeting, the administration's comment on the content of the discussion was both brief and ambiguous, with Eisenhower noting that it merely entailed consultations on the region and reaffirmed old decisions. In response to inquires from the press, Dulles commented that he would keep both the Communist Chinese and the press guessing about the administration's intentions.[32]

While the administration held its cards closely in public, Dulles began consulting with the British concerning the United Nations option. The British supported the American effort to pursue a middle course between abandoning the islands and precipitating a war and were particularly relieved that the administration was attempting to avoid general war and the implied use of nuclear weapons. The United States and the British agreed to approach New Zealand about introducing the UN resolution, with subsequent negotiations among the three nations lasting through mid-October. Even though Dulles spent a great deal of time in Europe addressing these issues, the subject of the negotiations was effectively kept out of the press.[33]

During these negotiations, anxiety heightened in the administration about the potential Nationalist reaction to the UN option. In a September 30 telegram to Dulles, Undersecretary of State Bedell Smith and the U.S. ambassador to the UN, Henry Cabot Lodge, asked for his views concerning the timing of the resolution's introduction. In particular, Smith and Lodge were concerned about the upcoming 1954 midterm congressional elections which might be complicated because of "unfavorable reaction once [the Nationalist Chinese] learn of [the] proposal and realize its full implications and this would be almost certain to generate considerable emotion in certain domestic political circles." Dulles's reply stressed the need to have the resolution under consideration by the Security Council before the United States faced the choice of losing the islands or intervening. Dulles noted that the military situation should dictate the timing, but he recommended that the resolution be introduced "either in November or when [a] serious attack [was] mounting, whichever comes first." While recognizing that some domestic sectors and the Nationalists might be upset by the resolution, he felt the action was defensible as the only available option to keep the offshore islands in Nationalist hands without American intervention, something that he thought the United States would not undertake, since it would entail a large-scale war that might include the use of atomic weapons.[34] Although Dulles's choice of timing made the military situation the top priority, by suggesting a delay on the resolution until after the November election, he attempted to avoid any possible division and negative electoral consequences if the administration's efforts became publicly known.

In a slight change in timing, on October 4, Dulles recommended proceeding with the Security Council resolution, regardless of the campaign and without prior consultation with congressional leaders. He reasoned that delaying action might reduce its effect and the resolution might even help in the election: "It is hard for me to believe that [news of the effort] will have any adverse effect, and indeed the effect might be favorable on net balance."[35] He believed that the resolution would be supported by the majority in Congress and the American public and that only a "handful" of the public favored war over the islands. Since he felt almost certain that the communists would reject the resolution, it would provide a good basis from which to bring the public to support the administration position.[36] Even so, Eisenhower and Dulles decided to delay notifying Congress about the resolution until right before its introduction, since bipartisan consultation would be difficult during the campaign. Instead, they decided to inform Senate Majority Leader Senator William Knowland (R, Calif.) immediately before the resolution's submission, because New Zealand would be introducing it, and they would be guilty of bad faith if they consulted with Congress beforehand. Eisenhower "could not conceive of any reason why in the conduct of foreign affairs we should not follow our own best judgments," and Nixon said it would be unnecessary and dangerous for prior consultation with Congress.[37]

It soon became apparent, however, that Nationalist opposition to the UN resolution needed to be taken more seriously. On October 5, Ambassador Lodge, alluding to the upcoming elections, warned Dulles that a confrontation with the Nationalists could be politically dangerous.[38] In addition, the U.S. ambassador to Formosa, Karl Rankin, alerted Washington to a "violently unfavorable reaction" regarding the UN resolution from Chiang, who would interpret it as "another Yalta."[39] Because of Rankin's message, the assistant secretary of state for far eastern affairs, Walter Robertson, recommended to Dulles on October 7 that the United States pursue a mutual defense treaty (which had been under consideration for some time) covering Formosa and the Pescadores, in order to bolster Nationalist morale and counteract any damage to relations that the UN resolution might create. The treaty might also serve to deter the communists from taking more aggressive action in the region. Robertson's memorandum apparently had an impact. In a discussion with Eisenhower on October 7, Dulles said that the United States should be willing to grant Chiang a defensive treaty if he went along with the resolution in the Security Council. Eisenhower agreed.[40]

During discussions with the Nationalists regarding the UN resolution, Chiang requested that the defense treaty be concluded first before the resolution was introduced, which Dulles and Eisenhower found acceptable if key members of the Congress assented. By October 18, the administration had already received favorable replies from some members of the Republican congressional leadership on the treaty, including Nationalist supporter Senator Knowland, and decided that the Democratic leadership should be consulted as soon as possible. On October 19, Lodge again warned Dulles that he feared Chiang would excite the "China lobby" because of his foul mood. Dulles noted that the administration was attempting to assuage Chiang with the mutual defense treaty, since the Nationalists wanted it so badly and observed that an announcement on the treaty might be forthcoming should consultations with the Congress go well.[41]

The upcoming election also influenced the timing of the announcement of the treaty negotiations. The influential Senate Foreign Relations Committee member, Michael Mansfield (D, Mont.) recommended holding off on the treaty until after the congressional elections because it would likely become a partisan issue, much to the detriment of a bipartisan foreign policy. The timing weighed heavily on Dulles's mind and surfaced in his discussions with Nationalist Chinese officials. In an effort to head off Nationalist efforts to cause domestic problems for the administration by playing on their desire for a treaty, Dulles stressed that should the Republicans lose the midterm elections, congressional consultations would have to begin again regarding the treaty because of the change in leadership. Because of possible conflicts with the elections, Dulles observed, even though negotiations could begin before the election, no announcement should be made regarding the treaty until afterward.[42]

After Eisenhower formally approved negotiation of the treaty at the October 28 NSC meeting, the administration announced the opening of defense treaty negotiations on November 6, two days before the congressional elections, with observers expecting it to pass the Senate. Talks continued throughout November (even though the Democrats regained control of Congress from the Republicans) and concluded with the initialing of a treaty on November 23 committing the United States to defend only Formosa and the nearby Pescadores. That same day, the Communist Chinese announcement that it would imprison captured American flyers for espionage led some, including Senator Knowland, to call for a blockade of mainland China.[43]

The public reaction to the imprisonment announcement caused considerable consternation for the administration. In discussions on the resolution's introduction with New Zealand and the United Kingdom, Dulles pressed for holding off until the public's reaction to the treaty could be ascertained. He thought it would take a few days for the public to understand the treaty and feared that people might misread the resolution as retaliation for the Communist imprisonment of the American flyers. In this context, he thought the UN resolution might only exacerbate the domestic situation rather than improve it. Although Eisenhower and he were attempting to have a calming influence, he emphasized the need to proceed carefully, since public reaction to a Communist Chinese attack on the offshore islands, in this charged political atmosphere, might force the United States into a conflict. In the aftermath of these actions, Dulles recommended delaying the resolution until the public had quieted down or hostilities appeared imminent.[44]

Dulles's arguments apparently were persuasive. The mutual defense treaty was publicly signed on December 2 and ratified by the Senate on

February 9, 1955. New Zealand introduced its resolution on January 28, 1955, after new attacks by the Communists on the offshore islands. Although the Soviets introduced their own resolution condemning American aggression, the New Zealand resolution passed the Security Council on January 31. However, Communist Chinese leader Chou En-lai's refusal to accept an invitation to discuss the matter at the Security Council effectively ended the UN's involvement.[45] Even though the administration successfully implemented its alternatives, the policies failed to relieve the pressure on the Nationalist Chinese position. After worsening in early 1955, the crisis was defused, and the shelling tapered off after a Communist Chinese offer in April for discussions on the Formosa Straits was accepted by the United States. Although the Nationalists abandoned the Tachen islands in January at the urging of the United States, they retained possession of the main offshore islands of Quemoy and Matsu.

With the adoption of a two-track policy encompassing the UN resolution and the mutual defense treaty, the administration hoped its policy would avoid war yet keep the offshore islands in Nationalist hands. The policy at the time seemed to meet all significant requirements. It avoided public opposition to a unilateral commitment of American forces to protect the offshore islands, and in the view of high-level officials, it also placed the administration in a good position to lead the public and American allies to take action at a later date if the Communist Chinese pursued additional aggressive action. It successfully assuaged the Nationalists' concerns and maintained the support of other American allies by not appearing too bellicose. It also held out the possibility of deterring further Communist aggression. In the end, the administration selected the policy that it felt successfully balanced all its near-term interests and provided the political foundation for more aggressive action at a later time if it became necessary.

Variables

Although the decision makers' assessments of public opinion played an important part in the determination of the outcome, their effect varied throughout the case. As officials formed their initial impressions of the situation, they largely ignored public opinion. However, as they began to formulate options and select policies, their assessments of public preferences became more closely connected to the policy process. Dulles's assessment of public opinion dramatically altered his policy position to support the less belligerent UN option when he found that the public would not support the more rigorous defensive option he initially recommended. In considering the policy, he stressed the difficulty, at that time, of building public support for aggressive action and emphasized the UN option's ability to give the administration the time and opportunity to lead the public to support a more assertive policy if it became necessary. Dulles remained acutely aware of the dynamics of public opinion as he attempted to implement the alternative by trying to keep the administration's negotiations out of electoral politics and favoring a defense treaty with Formosa to head off Nationalist efforts to make administration policy an electoral issue. Given his concerns with public opinion, he also worked to ensure that the timing of the resolution and treaty aligned with the public's ability to support the policies. Throughout this case, public opinion proved to be a constant concern for Dulles, especially as he formulated a response to the threat.

Like Dulles, Eisenhower remained painfully aware of the limits of public opinion, which constrained both the maximum and minimum policy he could accept when evaluating possible policies. Although public opinion did not influence his initial conceptions of the attack, it reinforced his view that the administration, at the very least, had to defend Formosa. As is clear from the NSC deliberations, Eisenhower concluded that the public would not support war over the offshore islands, which would make acquiring authorization from Congress prohibitive. When confronted with the need to make a decision and pressed by the military to adopt a rigorous defense of the offshore islands, his perception of the public's lack of stomach for war steeled his rejection of these suggestions. This concern continued as Dulles implemented the policy regarding the resolution and treaty negotiations.

The effect of the assessment of public opinion increased as the case proceeded, whereas the impact of other interests correspondingly waned. Decision makers focused on national security issues in the early going as they formed their opinions about the need for an American response. Dulles framed the problem in terms of threats to the American position in the region, since the damage to American prestige associated with the loss of the islands would have psychological implications for the United States' regional allies and the Nationalists in particular. Even though Dulles thought that the American position with its Asian allies would be bolstered by a strong response, perhaps even recouping some lost prestige, he knew the European partners were just as worried that the Americans would respond too vigorously. Dulles placed more weight on the reaction of the Asian allies early in the crisis, but once public opinion caused him to favor a more restrained alternative, his focus shifted to a balance between satisfying America's Asian and European friends when implementing the policy.

Eisenhower saw the importance of the islands as deriving mostly from their psychological significance to the Nationalists' morale, although he also attributed some military value to them. His concerns with American prestige also reinforced his desire to respond firmly to the Chinese threat. Like Dulles, as he turned to specific options to confront the threat, he balanced these interests partly against the European allies' fear of a hotheaded American response. Although Eisenhower focused a great deal on allied responses when implementing the UN option, European trepidation only partially militated against a strong American response, which was determined mostly by his concern with the domestic divisions that would erupt if he responded too vigorously to the shelling.

The influence of beliefs was apparent throughout this case, with Eisenhower's and Dulles's behavior consistent with their beliefs throughout and causally influencing their choices at critical junctures. Eisenhower was expected to formulate his views based on national security interests and then attempt to lead the public to support the chosen policy unless he perceived public opposition. During both the problem representation and the option generation stages, he reacted *consistently* with his beliefs, by focusing on national security interests rather than on public opinion. As he faced the need for a decision, these beliefs had a *causal* influence on him, by limiting the options he saw as being available. At the critical meeting to decide the policy, he almost exclusively relied on public opinion as a reason to avoid war over the offshore islands. His statements reveal that he understood that the public would not accept war, and so leading the public on the issue would be extremely difficult. Dulles's alternative provided Eisenhower with an option to rectify his competing concerns with the loss of Nationalist morale, on the one hand, and the limitations provided by public opinion, on the other. As he moved to implement the policy, his behavior remained *consistent* with his beliefs, since once he had selected the UN option, his policy implementation decisions were driven mostly by national security concerns. Eisenhower focused on his prerogatives to set foreign policy when considering a discussion of the resolution with Congress and agreed to negotiate a treaty after it was linked to Nationalist support of the UN option. When public reaction in late November threatened to undermine his policy approach, he attempted to calm the people to preserve support for his policies. By reacting consistently with his beliefs at all times and causally at the vital decision points, the effect of Eisenhower's beliefs receives a *supportive* coding.

Dulles's beliefs suggest that he would have preferred to make decisions based on the national security determinants of policy and then lead public opinion to support it. In cases such as this one, which allow only a short amount of decision time, if he perceived public opposition to his policy, he would be constrained by it, since he would be unlikely to find the extended time he thought was needed to generate public support. While forming his initial conceptions of the threat, he focused on the national security concerns, a tactic that was *consistent* with his beliefs. While he formulated his perceptions of the policy options and the administration was selecting and implementing the policy, his beliefs had a *causal* influence. Dulles decided to change his policy recommendation after information on possible divisions in the public over aggressive action became available and was reflected in both the reasoning of his memorandum and his presentation at the September 12 NSC meeting. The UN option also gave him an issue and the time he felt necessary to persuade the public to support a more belligerent policy if it were required. As the administration moved to implement the policy, he shifted to leading public opinion as the time to create support for it became available. Even though concern with negative public reaction at first made Dulles hesitant to introduce the resolution in October, he eventually chose that month because of its positive influence on leading public opinion to support administration policy (although it was later delayed because of the treaty negotiations). His decision on the treaty reflected his desire to obtain Nationalist Chinese political agreement, although he may have been partially concerned with their influence on domestic opinion. When the Chinese announcement of the imprisonment of the American flyers raised his concern about public overreaction, he pressed the British to delay the resolution until the public could be properly led to support the treaty. This combination of influences suggests a *supportive* coding of the effect on Dulles's actions of the beliefs variable.

Coding the Influence of Public Opinion

The influence of public opinion is coded for the case in the *strong constrain category*. Although other interests affected decision makers throughout the case and largely determined decisions during the problem representation (when decision makers focused on American prestige and the Nationalists' reactions) and policy implementation (when they focused on allied and congressional relations and public opinion affected the timing of when some alternatives were acted on) stages, public opinion greatly conditioned the choice of the UN option itself. During the option generation and policy selection stages, public opinion greatly limited the options that Dulles felt were available and forced him to seek an alternative policy to defending the islands because of mounting public divisions over the proper reaction to the crisis. During the policy selection stage, although concerns about the reactions of American allies remained, Eisenhower's perceptions of public opposition severely limited the range of alternatives he felt were available and largely eliminated the option of aggressive action.

The influence of public opinion in this case supports the Wilsonian liberal perspective, which suggests that public opinion would constrain decision makers. It provides only minor support for the realist view, which implies that decision makers would largely ignore public opinion except to lead it when implementing a policy. Support for the Wilsonian liberal viewpoint appeared as decision makers began to tackle the question of how to respond to the threat occasioned by the Communist Chinese shelling and, although it waned somewhat during the policy implementation stage, lasted throughout the rest of the case. The realist view is supported during the problem representation stage because decision makers across the board saw the situation primarily in terms of national security interests (allied relations, American international prestige) and during the problem implementation stage, when decision makers also tried, in part, to lead public opinion. However, realist predictions cannot account for the behavior at the other stages of decision in which the strength of public opinion's influence provides disconfirming evidence. This finding is particularly strong, since this case was selected to bias results in favor of realist views. National security interests remained in decision makers' minds when they confronted many of these decisions, but they relied more on public opinion than these other factors. Given these dynamics, the case largely disconfirms realist predictions.

Although the Wilsonian liberal model is mostly supported and the realist model is only partially supported by the case, the beliefs model fully accounts for the case's dynamics, in which officials focused on other interests at the beginning of the crisis and then shifted toward

TABLE 3.1 Influence Coding: Crisis Case

Predicted Public Influence			Actual Public Influence	Influence of Beliefs
REALIST	WILSONIAN LIBERAL	BELIEFS		
No Impact/ Lead	Constrain	DDE: Constrain/ Lead	Constrain (strong)	DDE: Supportive
		JFD: Constrain		JFD: Supportive

Note: Italics indicate conditional predictions.

public opinion as they began to develop policy options. This finding is particularly important because beliefs are expected to have the most influence in the crisis context. In this sense, the beliefs model is correct where it should be strongest while at the same time the realist model is fairly weak where it should be strongest, and the Wilsonian liberal model is fairly strong where it should be weakest (see table 3.1).

Under crisis conditions, it is often argued that public opinion does not have adequate time to influence policy decisions. However, since decision makers applied data gathered in other contexts to the decision they faced in this case and even relied on reports of current public opinion to assess future public views, time did not prohibit public opinion's influence. Perhaps the strongest link connecting public opinion and policy outcomes was formed by the decision makers' anticipations of public preferences. These anticipations were often based on either perceptions of the existing opinion context or on particular evidence of the public's view. For example, this influence was most noticeable on Dulles when he projected a "serious attack" on the administration and a divided Congress and nation if the administration took aggressive action. This view was based in large part on his reading of the State Department's internal reports of how elite opinion was reacting to the shelling. His preference for the UN alternative appears at least partially a response to his reading of polling results indicating that the public approved of the UN as a vehicle to resolve international disputes. This effect can be detected in Eisenhower as well. He formed his perception of the public's attitude toward war in the area based on letters he had received (relating to the entire Asian region). Based on these data, he understood the opinion context as opposing American involvement in an Asian war, and he also saw (undoubtedly spurred by the public's opposition to the Korean war) that the public was skeptical of claims based on national security in the region. He then used this information to anticipate that public opinion could not be easily led to support aggressive American action.

In the end, although decision makers largely formulated and implemented policy away from the public eye, public opinion still played an integral part in their deliberations, but not because a great deal of information about public preferences was available or because of a large public outcry. There was none. Instead, public opinion influenced policy because the beliefs of key decision makers predisposed them to consider public opinion an important part of the decision process. These officials used the information they had gathered in other contexts and indicators of public sentiment that they found during the crisis to formulate nuanced perceptions of future public views. This same process remains abundantly clear in their reaction to the threat to Dien Bien Phu. However, as discussed in the next chapter, because the decision context changed, officials also reacted to public opinion differently than they did in the Formosa Straits case, as would be expected from their beliefs about public opinion.

CHAPTER FOUR

The Reflexive Context

Boxed in by Public Opinion at Dien Bien Phu

During the winter and early spring of 1954, members of the Eisenhower administration reached a decision on intervening at Dien Bien Phu in Indochina. They were expecting an urgent request for assistance from the French, who were then fighting a communist insurgent group called the Viet Minh in the French colony of the Associated States of Indochina, composed of Vietnam, Laos, and Cambodia. By 1954, France had committed a large number of forces to the war and had received significant financial and material assistance from the United States. On November 20 and 21, 1953, the French sent in a sizable number of their best troops to seize and occupy the remote Dien Bien Phu fortress, which could be resupplied only by air, in an attempt to draw the Viet Minh into a decisive battle. Eisenhower recalled being "horror stricken" that they would try to defend such an isolated location:[1] "I can't think of anything crazier. No experienced soldier would ever establish a force, an immobile force, in a place, in a fortress, and then ask the enemy to come and get it." Observing that those sorts of situations always ended with the garrison's surrender, he remarked, "Just as I expected, it became a desperate position."[2]

In early January 1954, the administration considered the conditions under which it might intervene in the Indochinese conflict in general and at Dien Bien Phu in particular. During the spring and after an intense examination of the question, the administration developed a policy supporting "united action" to combat communism in Indochina. Conceived as both a temporary reaction to Dien Bien Phu and a long-term effort regarding the larger threat to Indochina, the vaguely defined policy envisioned a multilateral coalition, including the British and other regional powers, to deter Communist Chinese intervention in Indochina and to intervene itself if necessary. After the situation at Dien Bien Phu worsened in early April, the administration decided to intervene to relieve the outpost if three conditions were met: (1) the action was multilateral; (2) the French promised independence to the Associated States; and (3) Congress gave its approval. Since Congress made its approval contingent on multilateral action (with the British in particular), the administration focused on obtaining commitments from the British and French. Although these efforts failed, the administration stuck to its conditions by rejecting in April two desperate French requests for unilateral American intervention. The fortress fell in early May.

The administration's deliberations reflected a blend of attention to both domestic and international imperatives. Believing that a communist victory in Indochina would seriously damage American interests and rejecting unilateral intervention because of public opposition, Eisenhower decided that multilateral intervention provided the only viable policy alternative. Dulles, instead of seeing multilateral intervention as the best alternative allowed by public opinion, favored multilateral intervention almost from the beginning as the best policy to address American interests.

Initially, the prospect of American intervention arose because of fears that the French regional position might be seriously damaged if the battle for Dien Bien Phu were lost. As Eisenhower dealt with this prospect, public opinion limited his perceptions of the range of viable policy alternatives. He feared a repeat of the Korean War experience, in which an unpopular war undermined the Democrats' electoral fortunes (which he took advantage of as the Republican candidate in the 1952 presidential election). To do nothing meant the possible repeat of the "loss of China" debate (but this time the blame would be on his Republican administration), which would cost him politically, especially since he had run for office on a platform of liberating communist nations. Eisenhower also reacted to public opposition to unilateral intervention and action tainted by colonialism by requiring that any intervention be multilateral. National security concerns drove Dulles's thinking throughout the case. When implementing the multilateral policy, both Eisenhower and Dulles took actions to lead public opinion to support their chosen policy.[3]

As I described in chapter 1, realist and Wilsonian liberal theories lead to divergent expectations of behavior in the reflexive context. As in the crisis context, realist theories suggest that public opinion has no influence on choices, with policymakers leading the public to support the policy selected by the government. The Wilsonian liberal approach, however, states that decision makers will be constrained by public opinion.

According to the beliefs model, Eisenhower and Dulles would have reacted in different ways to public opinion. As in the crisis context, because Eisenhower believed that the support of public opinion was necessary, especially in cases of war and the commitment of American troops, his actions would be expected to be constrained in terms of war and on issues in which he perceived the public could not be led. Otherwise, he would have decided on the policy that best supported the national interest and then attempted to lead the public. But since Dulles's concern regarding public opinion centered on his belief in the need for time to generate public support, he would have supported the "best" policy based on other factors and then used the extended time allowed by anticipation to formulate a public education program to generate support.

The influence of public opinion for this case is coded in a *moderate constrain category* influence, with a lesser *lead category* influence. Although other interests had a significant effect, public opinion acted as an important factor limiting the administration's range of action. On the one hand, Eisenhower's decisions, which public opinion constrained, largely conformed to expectations of the Wilsonian liberal perspective, as does the main case finding, because he made the final decisions. On the other hand, Dulles's actions were generally what the realists expected, since he developed his view without reference to public opinion and then attempted to lead the public to support his chosen policy. The beliefs variable predicts this divergence between Eisenhower and Dulles and is largely supported by this case, since it accounts for when and why they reached their positions. The behavior of both actors was coded as *supportive* of the beliefs model because their behavior was *consistent* at all points and a *causal* influence was suggested at both the policy selection and implementation stages.

Problem Representation: Setting the Agenda

Early in its tenure, the administration recognized the importance of Indochina. Shortly after taking office, the secretary of state, John Foster

Dulles, recorded the consensus of an Oval Office meeting with Eisenhower and others that Indochina "had probably the top priority in foreign policy, being in some ways more important than Korea because the consequences of loss there could not be localized, but would spread throughout Asia and Europe."[4]

At a meeting on January 8, 1954, when the Viet Minh had surrounded Dien Bien Phu, the NSC considered Dien Bien Phu, intervention, and Indochina. Eisenhower expressed his strong opposition to using ground troops to confront the problem. As the minutes of the meeting state:

> For himself, said the President with great force, he simply could not imagine the United States putting ground forces anywhere in Southeast Asia, except possibly in Malaya, which we would have to defend as a bulwark to our off-shore island chain. . . . I can not tell you, said the President with vehemence, how bitterly opposed I am to such a course of action. This war in Indochina would absorb our troops by divisions![5]

In response to the recommendation of the JCS chair, Admiral Arthur Radford, that the United States do all in its power to prevent the loss of Dien Bien Phu even if it entailed using carrier aircraft, Eisenhower supported a quick air intervention. Despite noting his concern with keeping American troops out of Indochina, he insisted that the United States had to keep its vital interests in mind. While NSC adviser Robert Cutler and Secretary of the Treasury George Humphrey worried air intervention might draw the United States into a larger commitment, Eisenhower commented, "What you've got here is a leaky dike, and with leaky dikes it's sometimes better to put a finger in than to let the whole structure be washed away."[6] Although this meeting reached no final determination of policy, Eisenhower directed the CIA and Defense Department to report to the NSC on the feasible steps, short of actual intervention, that the United States might take to assist the French.

Problem Representation: Defining the Situation

From January 8 through mid-March 1954, the administration developed its definition of the situation as it related to two important issues: (1) the broader international and domestic political context regarding intervention in Indochina and (2) intervention at Dien Bien Phu after it was attacked on March 13.

The still-fresh memory of the Korean War, under an armistice for less than a year, remained on the decision makers' minds. Eisenhower ran for president in 1952 on the platform of ending the divisive conflict and had succeeded in achieving a cease-fire in the summer of 1953. The prospect of another wrenching experience like the Korean War would clearly have caused him to hesitate before embarking on another limited conflict.[7] In his memoirs, Assistant to the President Sherman Adams attributed Eisenhower's eventual decision to forgo intervention to his desire to avoid another Korea and believed that Eisenhower's anxiety derived from his perception of the public's reluctance to fight another Asian war.[8]

By the same token, Indochina also attained significance because of the broader political context. Holding the line against further communist expansion supplied an unchallenged assumption, given Eisenhower's 1952 presidential campaign stressing the "liberation" of communist-held nations. In addition, during the election, Eisenhower exploited the 1949 "loss of China" to the communists, which occurred on Democratic President Harry Truman's watch, which made the prospect of ceding a nation to the communist sphere uncomfortable at best.[9] In fact, Eisenhower explicitly made this linkage himself at a cabinet meeting, noting that he could not afford to have the Democrats ask, "Who lost Vietnam?"[10]

The Korean and Chinese analogies provided two contradictory legacies with which the administration needed to grapple. If it became involved in a limited war in Indochina, the government faced the prospect that a war-weary public would turn against the policy and the administration. But doing nothing and allowing the communists to take over Indochina gave the Democrats a political and electoral issue to exploit. Consequently, the administration confronted a public opinion climate hostile to both unilateral intervention to prevent Indochina's fall and any policy that would allow the communists to take over the country.

Whereas the Korean and Chinese analogies formed the domestic background for intervention, the NSC 5405 policy paper on American policy in Southeast Asia outlined the national security interests at stake. Approved by Eisenhower on January 16, NSC 5405 described the loss of Indochina as having severe repercussions for American interests around the world and recognized that a weakening of French resolve was a more serious threat to the region's security than even intervention by the Chinese.[11] Soon after the approval of NSC 5405, a furor erupted in

Washington on January 27 when Joseph and Stewart Alsop revealed in their *Washington Post* column that the administration was considering sending two hundred uniformed air force mechanics to Indochina to assist the French.[12] This leak led Senator John Stennis (D, Miss.), an influential member of the Senate Armed Services Committee, to express publicly his deep opposition to sending the mechanics and American troops to Indochina because he feared more American personnel would inevitably follow. At the February 3 press conference at which Eisenhower announced he would send the two hundred mechanics, along with additional equipment, he attempted to reduce this concern by emphasizing that the mechanics would not take part in the fighting. However, his announcement only further stimulated press and congressional apprehension, which forced Eisenhower to hold a meeting with the congressional leadership to allay their anxieties. But before the meeting could take place, another press leak on February 4 revealed the existence of the Special Committee on Southeast Asia, which was created to coordinate American efforts on Indochina and French assistance and had considered the mechanics issue. This revelation further undercut confidence in the administration's position because it implied that it was developing policy that could lead to American involvement in the war, without consulting with Congress.[13]

The administration then began a brief but intense public campaign to reduce congressional and public concerns. At his February 7 press conference, Eisenhower emphasized, "No one could be more bitterly opposed to ever getting the United States involved in a hot war in that region than I am; consequently, every move I authorize is calculated, so far as humans can do it, to make certain that that does not happen."[14] When congressional leaders observed that the opposition would quiet down if Eisenhower pledged to remove the mechanics by June 15, he made this commitment in addition to assuring them he would not rashly commit American troops to the conflict and promised to consult with Congress if the situation in Indochina changed dramatically. He further attempted to deflate public and congressional worries at his February 17 press conference when he reaffirmed that he would not take the nation into war unless it resulted from constitutional processes—meaning congressional involvement. These efforts succeeded in calming public and congressional anxiety.[15]

Eisenhower took away from this experience a renewed understanding of the public opposition to American participation in the Indochina war. In the original draft pages of his memoir *Mandate for Change*, he included a long retrospective on why he did not intervene in Indochina. In addition to other factors (such as the French and Indochinese leaders' shortcomings, the ineffectiveness of air strikes, and potential American association with colonialism), Eisenhower argued, "One measure . . . advocated by some, I felt completely unfeasible—and do to this day: commitment of large formations of U.S. ground troops." In a statement implying that he used congressional sentiment on this issue as reflecting public opinion, he attributed his concern to the public's opposition, as exemplified by Stennis's reaction to the "modest" step of sending mechanics and the negative response to Nixon's April 16 comment on intervention.[16] He could only surmise that public opposition would be even greater if he sent American ground troops into Indochina. Although the rest of this quotation indicates that Eisenhower weighed the military viability of action more heavily, it suggests that opposition from public opinion somewhat constrained his outlook toward intervention.

Polling numbers from this period reveal a constant and significant level of public opposition to the use of ground troops in Indochina and support Eisenhower's conclusion. In anticipation of later decisions, Eisenhower recruited pollster Alfred Politz to conduct a poll in the summer of 1953 to sound out public opinion on the subject.[17] The subsequent memorandum to Eisenhower indicated that if it seemed that the communists were going to invade Indochina, 47 percent of the public thought the United States should help fight; 32 percent disagreed; and 21 percent did not know. Several follow-up questions were asked of the 68 percent answering "yes" and "don't know" regarding specific policy options to fight the communists. The results found that as a percentage of the entire sample, the public opposed almost all forms of action except for increased arms supplies: (1) for "American soldiers fighting in Indo-China" 30 percent favored it, 23 percent opposed it, and 15 percent did not know; (2) if the United States supplied most of the money and men 16 percent favored action; 39 percent opposed it; and 13 percent did not know; (3) concerning unilateral U.S. involvement without UN cooperation 11 percent favored it, 42 percent opposed it, and 15 percent did not know; and (4) regarding "increasing armament supplies to Indo-China," 46 percent favored it, 9 percent opposed it, and 13 percent did not know.

These poll results reveal the American public's tentativeness regarding intervention. In the portion favoring some kind of assistance, small pluralities favored sending American soldiers, and large pluralities adopted a multilateral approach by opposing both the United States acting as the primary supplier of troops and material, as had been done in Korea, and unilateral action without the support of the international community. When the original question's 32 percent opposition is factored in, a majority of the public opposed sending American soldiers to fight, supplying most of the men and material, and acting without international cooperation.

Later polls found that the public opposed ground troops but would favor air intervention under certain conditions. A September 18, 1953, Gallup poll stated, "The United States is now sending war materials to help the French fight the Communists in Indochina. Would you approve or disapprove of sending United States soldiers to take part in the fighting there?" Only 8 percent of the public supported this move; 85 percent disapproved; and 7 percent expressed no opinion—a level of opposition that the report stated was "unusually significant." The same did not hold for the use of air power. An October 1953 poll by the State Department found that 53 percent approved and 34 percent disapproved of using the air force "if it looks like the Communists might take over all of Indochina."[18]

This potential public opposition dovetailed with Eisenhower's other concerns regarding military intervention in Indochina and made him realize that military involvement with large numbers of troops would be unwise. Even before taking office, he had doubts about the viability of a military solution to the communist threat in Indochina. In a March 17, 1951, diary entry, Eisenhower reasoned that even if the French were able to pacify all of Indochina, it would still be threatened by the "inexhaustible" communist Chinese manpower across the border. He concluded that "I am convinced no military victory is possible in that kind of theater."[19] In the continuation of the earlier quotation from the draft of his memoirs discussing the problems of potential public opposition, he linked the military viability of intervention with his ability to overcome domestic opposition:

> But [public opposition] in itself should not be overriding. Indeed had the circumstances lent themselves to a reasonable chance for a victory or a chance to avert a defeat for freedom, then I feel the task of explaining to the American public the necessity for sacrifice would have been a simple one indeed. But this was the wrong war for such action. The jungles of Indochina would have swallowed up division after division of U.S. troops.[20]

Although Eisenhower felt he could have led the public to support ground intervention if the military conditions in Indochina had favored such action, he was not willing to risk an unsuccessful intervention in Indochina given the underlying public opposition. But if the military conditions had been favorable, he might have attempted to lead the public.

In addition to these concerns, Eisenhower focused on two other considerations throughout his deliberations: (1) the domestic and international implications of American support for French colonialism and (2) the linked issue of independence for Indochina. In a March 26, 1953, meeting with French Prime Minister René Mayer, Eisenhower stressed that in order for the American government to give more financial support to the French war effort, the American public would have to be convinced both that the French were not pursuing colonialism and that Indochina would soon be granted full independence. Eisenhower also advised Mayer to emphasize the threat from communism in his statements because "unfortunately many Americans continue to think of the war in Indo-China as a French colonial operation rather than as a part of the struggle of the free world against the forces of Soviet Communism."[21]

In sum, Eisenhower saw the situation in Indochina as fraught with threats at varying levels. He believed that vital American interests were involved in Indochina and preferred to take action short of military involvement to preserve them. Although the introduction of American ground troops would lead to dire consequences both militarily and domestically, he remained open to air intervention or a quick strike to support American interests. In addition, the perception of French and American actions as supporting the independence of the Associated States rather than colonial interests was required to gain domestic support. In short, Eisenhower perceived a series of threats emanating from Indochina, ranging from American regional and global national security concerns to anxieties about domestic support for intervention.

Dulles viewed American interests in Indochina in a similar manner. At a January 5, 1954, briefing of the bipartisan congressional leadership, he observed that Indochina was "fraught with anxiety and danger" and expressed his fear that the French would quit the war if the United States cut off aid, since they had lost their desire for a successful prosecution of the war after promising negotiations on independence in the summer of 1953.[22] Later, at the January 8 NSC meeting, Dulles linked his concern regarding the danger to Indochina with the possibility of military action.

The Pentagon's notes of the meeting show Dulles arguing that the French position in Indochina was so critical as "to force the U.S. to decide now to utilize U.S. forces in the fighting in Southeast Asia."[23] Aside from the situation in Indochina, Dulles perceived potential domestic problems for the administration. In a February 24, 1954, conversation with Eisenhower, Dulles warned that based on his recent meeting with the Senate Foreign Affairs Committee, the administration should anticipate possible domestic attacks, given the lack of domestic preparedness for French setbacks in Indochina.[24] The implications, given the memory of the "who lost China" debate, must have been clear.

Dulles perceived a situation dangerous to American interests but still salvageable. He thought that Indochina needed to remain out of communist hands in order to preserve the American position in the region and felt that the current French government represented the best hope to achieve that end, since the French opposition parties would likely abandon the cause altogether.[25] Although Dulles favored intervention to prevent Indochina from becoming communist, he believed the current French government would continue to prosecute the war, barring a serious setback. Since he had already heard rumblings reminiscent of the outcry after China became communist, he thought that the "loss" of Indochina could have significant domestic ramifications.

Against this background, the Viet Minh made their first large-scale assault on Dien Bien Phu on March 13. On March 18, Eisenhower described in a letter to his friend Swede Hazlett the consequences of the battle's outcome in mainly psychological rather than military terms:

> The situation [at Dien Bien Phu] there becomes increasingly disturbing. I hope the French will have the stamina to stick it out; because a defeat in that area will inevitably have a serious psychological effect on the French. I suspect that this particular attack was launched by the Communists to gain an advantage to be used at the Geneva Conference.[26]

At the March 18 NSC meeting, Dulles, like Eisenhower, interpreted the Viet Minh attack at Dien Bien Phu as a ploy to gain a negotiating advantage at the Geneva Conference, which was scheduled to include a discussion of Indochina. He recalled his warning to French Foreign Minister Georges Bidault that "on the basis of the American experience in Korea, that if Indochina were put on the agenda for the Geneva Conference it would be the signal for violent Vietminh attacks on the French Union forces in Indochina. This was precisely what had happened."[27]

Option Generation

Possible options were evaluated during March and focused on three interrelated questions: (1) whether or not to intervene, (2) whether intervention would be unilateral or multilateral, and (3) whether to use air and naval forces alone or ground forces as well. After the Viet Minh attack, the military began to make the necessary arrangements to intervene at Dien Bien Phu. On March 19, an American carrier task force was told to prepare for action off the Indochinese coast and be ready to act on three hours' notice. On March 22, the carrier task force was ordered to prepare to attack the communist forces at Dien Bien Phu if ordered to do so.[28]

In this atmosphere, the administration began more intense discussions regarding potential intervention. On March 23, after Eisenhower approved visiting French Chief of Staff Paul Ély's requests for matériel to help Dien Bien Phu hold out, Dulles, Radford, and Ély met to discuss American policy. Ély pressed for clarification of American thinking on intervention, whereas Dulles only referred to the broad political preconditions necessary (regarding independence and American training of indigenous forces) before the United States would become involved, because once engaged, it would be difficult to extract American forces.[29]

On March 24, Radford and Dulles spoke privately regarding the French situation. Dulles noted his concern that the French were creating vacuums throughout the world and that the United States faced the critical decision of how it could fill them. Appearing somewhat apprehensive about domestic criticism, Radford replied that the French might withdraw in two to three weeks if they did not achieve victory and speculated that the administration would "look bad here to our own people. The appearances he will have to make—hearings, etc.—can be embarrassing."[30] To avoid domestic criticism, Dulles suggested, pending a clarification of the political situation, the United States might step up activities along Formosa's coast and increase direct contacts with the Associated States. He even worried, "We could lose Europe, Asia, and Africa all at once if we don't watch out."[31]

After meeting again with Ély, who probed Radford on whether and how the United States would intervene, Radford warned that the dire situation at Dien Bien Phu and the political and psychological implications in France caused him to be

gravely fearful that the measures being taken by the French will prove to be inadequate and initiated too late to prevent a progressive deterioration of the situation. The consequences can well lead to the loss of all of S.E. Asia to Communist domination. If this is to be avoided, I consider that the U.S. must be prepared to act promptly and in force possibly to a frantic and belated request by the French for U.S. intervention.[32]

While Radford conducted a series of meetings with Ély, the broader administration policy concerning Indochina continued to develop. On March 21, Eisenhower met with his top-level advisers (including John Foster Dulles, CIA Director Allen Dulles, Secretary of Defense Charles Wilson, and Postmaster General Arthur Summerfield, a top political adviser to Eisenhower). Although there is no record of this meeting, its timing, the content of the legislative leaders' meeting the next day, and the presence of Summerfield suggests that they discussed a proposal by Dulles for multilateral intervention (united action) and its political ramifications.[33] On March 22, Eisenhower, Dulles, and Radford met with a select group of Republican legislative leaders to notify them of the administration's plans. Dulles informed the leaders that the administration was considering publicly proposing united action in Indochina and wished to have their endorsement of the proposal, which the leaders gave.[34]

Eisenhower and Dulles met again on March 24. As Dulles reported, they first discussed Dulles's and Radford's conversation with Ély on the previous day. Dulles remembered that Eisenhower "agreed basically that we should not get involved in fighting in Indochina unless there were the political pre-conditions necessary for a successful outcome. He did not, however, wholly exclude the possibility of a single strike, if it were almost certain this would produce decisive results." Given the content of Dulles's memorandum concerning his March 23 conversation with Ély, the political preconditions seemingly pertained to factors internal to the Associated States, such as independence and training issues. Dulles then raised the subject of his united action speech set for March 29. In hopes of checking the drift toward appeasement of the Chinese by France and Britain, he felt that "it would be useful for me in my speech Monday night to talk about Indochina and its importance to the free world." While Eisenhower agreed, he cautioned that nothing should be said that would commit the United States to any particular action.[35]

The March 25 NSC meeting concerned several reports that recommended considering intervention.[36] Both Dulles and Wilson agreed that the interagency NSC Planning Board should consider intervention. Eisenhower supported the examination saying, "What he was asking for was the extent to which we should go in employing ground forces to save Indochina from the Communists." However, he "did not see how the United States or other free world nations could go full-out in support of the Associated States without UN approval and assistance." He added that a request from the Associated States for intervention would also be necessary. Furthermore, Eisenhower "was clear that the Congress would have to be in on any move by the United States to intervene in Indochina. It was simply academic to imagine otherwise."[37]

After a brief discussion of executive prerogatives on intervention, Eisenhower suggested that the administration begin to explore the level of support in Congress for intervention. Since he thought the UN might not support the coalition and reasoned that the administration could get the necessary two thirds support from the Senate for a treaty, Eisenhower wondered whether the United States could intervene as part of a regional group limited to nations in Southeast Asia based on an Indochinese invitation (after the negotiation of a treaty to form the multilateral coalition). Whereas Wilson proposed forgetting about Indochina and concentrating on the other nations in the region, Eisenhower "expressed great doubt as to the feasibility of such a proposal, since he believed that the collapse of Indochina would produce a chain reaction which would result in the fall of all of Southeast Asia to the Communists." By the end of the meeting, Eisenhower had come up with three conditions for American intervention: (1) an invitation from the Associated States, (2) congressional support, and (3) either UN action or a regional grouping. The Planning Board was ordered to consider the "circumstances and conditions" under which the United States would intervene either multilaterally or unilaterally to prevent the fall of Indochina.[38]

Dulles expanded on his view regarding the importance of Dien Bien Phu at the March 26 cabinet meeting. He stressed that the United States must help the French win or else the communists would "cut our defense line in half."[39] Given the danger, he was "inclined to believe [a] situation may develop requiring [the] U.S. to take some strong risks— but less than [the] risks or action would be later." The French, he believed, were interested in American assistance but only under the condition that their prestige would not be damaged. Indochina was an "extremely serious situation which may require going to Congress for more extensive action" and a multilateral political understanding.[40]

By March 26, the administration had several options on the table. Unilateral action to relieve Dien Bien Phu remained a strong possibility, and both Eisenhower and Dulles would accept a single air strike if it were decisive (although they both preferred multilateral intervention over unilateral action). Eisenhower remained wary of using ground forces under any conditions. Given the seriousness of the threat, both Eisenhower and Dulles supported discussions with Congress about possible intervention. Implicit in the discussion was the option of staying out completely if the conditions proposed by Eisenhower were not met.

Policy Selection

During the final week of March, the administration concentrated on presenting the united action proposal to Congress and the public. Dulles went over a draft of his March 29 speech with Eisenhower who, thinking it was "very fine," approved it on March 27 with only minor changes. Dulles hoped that a strong statement would stem the French drift toward accommodation with the Viet Minh and deter Chinese intervention (without committing troops) and that American intervention would not be necessary. Since the administration had made no final decision, the vague speech committed the United States to no one policy.[41]

Dulles's perception of public opinion did affect how he tried to build support, but he chose the policy of united action because he thought it best addressed national security requirements. On March 27, he discussed his perceptions of public opinion with Assistant Secretary of State for Public Affairs Carl McCardle. Dulles noted that the director of the Policy Planning Staff in the State Department, Robert Bowie, "thinks the country will not be willing to go along with a tough program" (presumably a reference to intervention) and thought the administration might have to compromise. The telephone minutes recorded, "The Sec. said if [the public] won't go along with a strong policy, it won't go along on appeasement. Neither policy is popular—we better take the one that is right. The President agreed,—though the Sec. said he is not as critical."[42]

Dulles perceived domestic problems with both intervention (the Korean War analogy) and "appeasement" that would allow Indochina to become communist (the China analogy). Despite this domestic pressure, Dulles felt that the administration needed to pursue the policy that best met the challenges of the international situation. As he outlined in his March 26 presentation to the cabinet, the national security considerations pointed to united action as the best alternative.

What Eisenhower agreed with is not clear from this quotation. It could refer to either the unpopularity of appeasement and intervention or the need to adopt the "right" policy. Later reasoning by Eisenhower, in which he felt limited by public opinion, appears to rule out his insistence on adopting the "right" policy, regardless of public opinion. Other information supports the view that Eisenhower believed both intervention and appeasement were unpopular with the public and that he and Dulles agreed on which policy was "right" (multilateral intervention)—although I concluded that they reached this judgment for different reasons. Given this information, the statement probably indicates that Eisenhower and Dulles agreed on multilateral intervention. For Eisenhower, being less "critical" probably refers to his willingness to compromise rather than pursue a strong policy of intervention.[43]

Dulles gave his televised address, entitled "The Threat of a Red Asia," on March 29. He stressed the French pledge for independence and argued that Southeast Asia's strategic position made the region vital to American security interests. Concerning American action, he recalled his recent statements, "to impress on potential aggressors" that the United States would respond to aggression at "places and by means of free world choosing" to ensure that aggression would not be rewarded and that the threat "should not be passively accepted, but should be met by united action." After the speech, he thought he had met his objectives by warning the Chinese of potential aggression, implying to the French the continued American commitment to Indochina, outlining the potential danger to the American public to build support for potential action, and issuing a call for action vague enough to commit the country to no particular policy. The nation's and Congress's response to the speech was muted but indicative of "broad support." When asked at his March 31 press conference whether united action would mean direct intervention with American troops, Eisenhower remained noncommittal, noting the great disadvantage of employing American forces around the world in response to every situation but also adding that each case needed to be evaluated on its own merits.[44]

While the effort to build support for the united action policy progressed, the administration continued consulting with congressional leaders over the ever-worsening situation at Dien Bien Phu. On March 29, in a meeting with Republican legislative leaders, Nixon reported that Eisenhower stated, "very simply, but dramatically," that "I am bringing this up at this time because at any time in the space of forty-eight hours, it might be necessary to move into the battle of Dien Bien Phu in order to keep it from going against us, and in that case I will be calling in the Democrats as well as our Republican leaders to inform them of the actions we're taking."[45]

The situation soon became more precarious during March 30–April 1 when the Viet Minh took the fortress's central defensive position. With Indochina sinking fast, the NSC again considered the question of intervention on April 1. When Radford warned that unless conditions were reversed, there would be "no way to save the situation," Eisenhower concluded, "The plight of the French certainly raised the question whether the United States ought now to consider any kind of intervention to save Dien Bien Phu." He noted his understanding that all but Radford of the JCS opposed an American air strike.[46] Eisenhower commented that although he could see a "thousand variants in the equation and very terrible risks, there was no reason for the Council to avoid considering the intervention issue." In response to a question by Dulles as to what could be done to save the fortress, Radford replied that American forces could help by the next day if the decision were made. At this point, Eisenhower adjourned the NSC to discuss the issue with a more limited group in the Oval Office.[47]

Unfortunately, no memorandum of the conversation in this meeting has been found in the State Department files or at the Eisenhower Library. However, based on the actions taken after the meeting, the evidence points to a decision to consult Congress over possible intervention to save Dien Bien Phu.[48] Following the Oval Office meeting, Dulles told Attorney General Herbert Brownell that "something fairly serious had come up after the morning NSC meeting." Presumably this statement refers to a possible congressional resolution on intervention, since Dulles noted he was "working on it with Legal Adviser [Herman] Phleger" and he hoped to have something to present to Congress.[49] He later informed Eisenhower that he had approved an April 2 meeting, in keeping with the action Eisenhower promised if the administration were contemplating intervention, with four members from both the Senate and House (two from each party), and hoped to have something to show Eisenhower the next morning.[50] After Eisenhower approved the meeting, Dulles spoke to Radford, "We need to think about the whole range of things we can do with sea and air power which might hold and so involve the Chinese Communists that they won't think of further adventures in SE Asia." Radford and Dulles agreed that they must "satisfy" Congress "that for the particular job we want to do, it can be done without sending manpower to Asia."[51]

As of April 1, Eisenhower still had not completely ruled out unilateral intervention at Dien Bien Phu. He told two newspaper editor friends that even though he would have to deny it forever, the United States might have to use carrier planes to bomb the area around Dien Bien Phu to prevent it from falling into enemy hands.[52] But his view soon changed. On April 2, Eisenhower met with Dulles, Wilson, Radford, and Cutler to consider the congressional resolution on intervening.[53] After approving Dulles's congressional resolution, Eisenhower decided "that the tactical procedure should be to develop first the thinking of congressional leaders without actually submitting in the first instance a resolution drafted by ourselves." Dulles agreed and indicated that he and Radford did differ on the resolution. Dulles viewed the resolution as a deterrent action and a measure to bolster the American position from which the United States could form a coalition including France, the Associated States, Thailand, Indonesia, the United Kingdom, the Philippines, Australia, and New Zealand. He felt that "it [was] very important from the standpoint of congressional and public opinion that adequate participation in any defensive efforts should be made by these other countries." Dulles thought that Radford, however, saw the resolution as authority for immediate use in a "strike," regardless of "any prior development of an adequate measure of allied unity." But Radford, the staunchest proponent of action, now pulled back, stating that although he had previously favored intervention to save Dien Bien Phu, "he [now] felt that the outcome there would be determined in a matter of hours, and the situation was not one which called for any US participation."[54]

At this meeting, the administration reached an important decision by resolving to pursue a congressional resolution authorizing American intervention in the hopes of deterring Chinese intervention, bolstering French morale, and authorizing the pursuit of united action. The resolution also served the additional function of assisting in the acquisition of support from regional actors. Although officials recognized that international support would rely in part on the administration's ability to obtain domestic support, Dulles in particular realized that an international coalition would make intervention more acceptable to domestic opinion. In this sense, congressional, public, and international support for united action each relied in part on the others.

On April 3, Dulles and Radford outlined to the congressional delegation the administration's case for a resolution granting authority to

Eisenhower to use sea and airpower. Senate Majority Leader Knowland expressed his immediate support, but further discussion "developed a unanimous reaction" by the members that Congress would not act until "the Secretary had obtained commitments of a political and material nature from our allies." Congressional leaders were unanimous in wanting "no more Koreas with the United States furnishing 90% of the manpower." Radford and Dulles stated that they did not contemplate the use of ground troops, but the members of Congress felt that "once the flag was committed the use of land forces would inevitably follow." The group decided that Dulles should attempt to get commitments from the British and others. If he could get their acceptance, "the consensus was that a Congressional resolution could be passed, giving the President power to commit armed forces in the area."[55]

Afterward, Dulles reported to Eisenhower that "on the whole it went pretty well,—although it raised some serious problems." Dulles indicated that Congress would "go along on some vigorous action" as long as those in the area participated (as he expected), and he concluded that he could move forward on united action. Again, Dulles returned to the need for multilateral participation in order to gain public support for united action: "The Sec. said the position of Britain is what they were thinking of. It is hard to get the American people excited if they are not [involved]."[56]

This analysis suggests that Eisenhower did seriously consider intervention and felt that he needed congressional approval but that the atmosphere in Congress did not create for him additional obstacles to intervention.[57] In a meeting with his advisers on April 4, Eisenhower set the conditions that provided the foundation for the administration's policy. Sherman Adams reported that at this meeting, "Eisenhower had agreed with Dulles and Radford on a plan to send American forces to Indo-China under certain strict conditions." The conditions were first "joint action" with British, Australian, and New Zealand troops and other regional actors (such as the Philippines and Thailand) if possible. Second, the French would continue to fight with full participation until the end. Third, "Eisenhower was also concerned that American intervention in Indo-China might be interpreted as protection of French colonialism. He added a condition that the French would need to guarantee future independence" to Indochina.[58] These conditions were directly linked to Eisenhower's perception of public opinion. Multilateral involvement ensured that the United States would not be faced with almost total reliance on American forces in a protracted war, as in Korea. In addition,

Eisenhower could defuse domestic concerns about colonialism because of the independence condition. These actions also served to address the anxieties raised by congressional leaders in the April 3 meeting.[59]

The discussion at the afternoon NSC meeting on April 6 points to many of the factors that weighed on decision makers' minds during this period.[60] At this meeting, Eisenhower opposed unilateral American intervention because of opposition from Congress and the public. But although Dulles believed that the United States should pursue united action first, he did not rule out unilateral action if the coalition option failed. Eisenhower clearly rejected unilateral action, but he maintained his support for multilateral action as a necessary move to create domestic support.

According to the minutes, Eisenhower stated:

> As far as he was concerned, said the President with great emphasis, there was no possibility whatever of U.S. unilateral intervention in Indochina, and we had best face that fact. Even if we tried such a course, we would have to take it to Congress and fight for it like dogs, with very little hope of success. At the very least, also, we would have to be invited in by the Vietnamese.

Dulles supported this assessment, indicating that based on his April 3 meeting with congressional leaders, "it would be impossible to get Congressional authorization for U.S. unilateral action in Indochina." He argued that "to secure the necessary Congressional support," three conditions would have to be met: (1) united action, including nations in the region; (2) French acceleration of the independence program; and (3) a French commitment to continue the war.[61]

Echoing his comments from April 2, Dulles saw the decision that day "as not primarily a decision to intervene with military forces in Indochina, but as an effort to build up strength in the Southeast Asia area to such a point that military intervention might prove unnecessary." Dulles thought,

> If we could build a good political foundation in and around Southeast Asia, it might not be necessary to intervene with our own armed forces. If, on the other hand, the United States failed to get results in its efforts to build up a regional grouping, it would certainly be necessary to contemplate armed intervention.[62]

Since Congress would support intervention under certain conditions, Dulles recommended concentrating on developing the regional grouping before the Geneva negotiation in order to bolster French morale and make the communists back down. But even though he made multilateral intervention the priority, he did not rule out going it alone if necessary.

Eisenhower endorsed the long-term coalitional approach and "expressed warm approval" for the creation of the organization even if Indochina were lost. He concluded, "The creation of such a political organization for defense would be better than emergency action." He later expressed the view that the "thing to do was to try to get our major allies to recognize the vital need to join in a coalition to prevent further Communist imperialism in Southeast Asia."[63] However, multilateral action remained the sine qua non of American policy, and Eisenhower stated "with great conviction that we certainly could not intervene in Indochina and become the colonial power which succeeded France. The Associated States would certainly not agree to invite our intervention unless we had other Asiatic nations with us."[64]

Eisenhower clearly was worried about the implications of a communist takeover of Indochina and saw the regional grouping as a means to secure public support and avoid unilateral intervention:

> Indochina was the first in a row of dominoes. If it fell its neighbors would shortly thereafter fall with it, and where would the process end? If he was correct, said the President, it would end with the United States directly behind the 8-ball. We are not prepared now to take action with respect to Dien Bien Phu in and by itself, but the coalition program for Southeast Asia must go forward as a matter of the greatest urgency. If we can secure this regional grouping for the defense of Indochina, the battle is two-thirds won. This grouping would give us the needed popular support of domestic opinion and of allied governments, and we might thereafter not be required to contemplate a unilateral American intervention in Indochina.[65]

Essentially deciding to pursue the previous policy, the NSC postponed a decision regarding intervention in lieu of seeking British support for a regional grouping to defend Southeast Asia and pressing the French to "accelerate" the movement for independence. The minutes indicated Eisenhower's intention to seek congressional authorization for American participation in this regional grouping if an agreement was reached. Much to his chagrin, Nixon concluded that Eisenhower had

> backed down considerably from the strong position he had taken on Indochina the latter part of the previous week. He seemed resigned to

doing nothing at all unless we could get the allies and the country to go along with whatever was suggested and he did not seem inclined to put much pressure on to get them to come along.[66]

Although Eisenhower felt something needed to be done about Southeast Asia, he rejected any unilateral action because it would not receive public support.

Eisenhower and Dulles reached essentially the same position on the multilateral approach, but public opinion affected their policy positions in different ways. Whereas Eisenhower was held back by public opinion, Dulles tried to lead it. Eisenhower believed that national security and a fear of the electoral repercussions of another "who lost China" debate made protecting Indochina from the communists necessary. For Eisenhower, public opinion and the resulting congressional sentiment precluded unilateral action. In January and in earlier pronouncements, Eisenhower had ruled out the use of ground troops in Indochina because of their military viability and political considerations. However, he had accepted some form of unilateral action throughout the winter and spring, even indicating on April 2 that the United States might have to pursue this action. But by April 6, Eisenhower clearly opposed unilateral action at the NSC meeting. His reasoning reflected a concern that public opinion would oppose unilateral action, thus making it exceedingly difficult, if not impossible, to obtain congressional authorization. His concern regarding a repeat of the Korean War was probably heightened by congressional sentiment expressed at the April 3 meeting. Even though public opinion restricted his view of unilateral intervention, he felt that public opinion would support American action if it were multilateral and clean of the taint of colonialism. But he did not want to use ground troops, given his judgment of their utility, or unilateral action, because of opposition at home. This process of elimination left multilateral intervention as the only way of preserving Indochina.

Eisenhower's openness to unilateral intervention on April 1 and his opposition to it on April 4 and 6 suggests that he received the information about public opinion that influenced this view between these two days. Congress's opposition to unilateral intervention on April 3 probably gave him the current reading of public opinion (he also had recent polling information suggesting the same thing). Since Eisenhower was already sensitive to the Korean analogy, the insistence by the congressional leaders on "no more Koreas" in which the United States acted unilaterally would have made him concerned about public opinion. Given his comments at the April 6 NSC meeting, it appears he had indeed read congressional sentiment as reflecting the public's general opinion.

Dulles also preferred multilateral action. In addition to being the easiest policy for which to generate public support for intervention, he found other reasons to recommend it. A multilateral grouping would serve three purposes that would remove the threat from Indochina: (1) strengthening the French will to continue the fight, (2) preventing further communist aggression, and (3) forcing the communists to back down at Geneva. His comments at the April 6 NSC meeting also indicated his openness to unilateral intervention if multilateral action failed (something that Eisenhower was not prepared to accept). Whereas Eisenhower saw multilateral action as the only option available to the administration, Dulles saw it as the best way to achieve American objectives, regardless of domestic constraints. Instead of being held back by public opinion, Dulles attempted to lead it, as evidenced by the March 29 speech and later efforts during the policy's implementation.

Policy Implementation

As the United States began trying to build international support for united action, the French made their first informal request for American intervention late in the day on April 4. The American ambassador to France, Douglas Dillon, cabled Washington that the French government had notified him that "immediate armed intervention of US carrier aircraft at Dien Bien Phu is now necessary to save the situation."[67] Although administration leaders quickly rejected the French proposal as inconsistent with their policy decision to pursue united action, the request set off a flurry of activity in the American government the morning of April 5. Dulles telephoned Eisenhower and informed him of Dillon's telegram. Recalling the outcome of the April 3 meeting with Congress, Dulles said that in principle, the United States had already answered the question by deciding that other nations needed to be included to ensure the United States did not act alone. Eisenhower replied that unilateral action would be "unconstitutional and indefensible" unless the administration had some way of gaining congressional support. Although Eisenhower suggested "taking a look to see if anything else can be done," he also insisted that "we cannot engage in active war" and chose to continue to seek united action.[68]

In his response to Dillon, Dulles reaffirmed the administration's conditions on intervention and reminded him that everything was being done "to prepare [the] public, [and the] Congressional and Constitutional basis for united action in Indochina."[69] After the April 6 NSC meeting, Dulles told Dillon that he could tell the French that "it can hardly be expected that this momentous decision [for intervention] could be taken without preparation when our nation is not itself directly attacked. There must be adequate public understanding and Congressional support and action and international preparation." He regretted the political delay, but congressional support depended on united action.[70] In sum, the administration's response to the French request for intervention was to implement the decision that had been made on April 4 to pursue united action. In their deliberations regarding the French telegram, Dulles and Eisenhower felt limited by Congress's conditions concerning intervention, and in his messages to Dillon, Dulles stressed the need (and the actions being taken) to prepare the public for action.

The administration continued this effort to prepare the public for multilateral intervention in the week following the April 4 decision. In speeches and press conferences, the administration underscored the importance of Indochina.[71] In addition to these efforts, the State Department started an intensive program to generate domestic support for intervention. Reporter Richard Rovere attended one of these sessions and broke the story on April 8. He reported that Dulles was

> conducting what must undoubtedly be one of the boldest campaigns of political suasion ever undertaken by an American statesman. Congressmen, political leaders of all shadings of opinion, newspapermen, and radio and television personalities have been rounded up in droves and escorted to lectures and briefings on what the State Department regards as the American stake in Indo-China.[72]

At the April 9 cabinet meeting, Eisenhower continued to reject unilateral action. He added that the domestic situation in the United States would greatly improve if the British and others agreed to participate, given the American aversion to "go it alone."[73] The next day, April 10, Dulles left on a trip to Europe to persuade America's allies to join a united action coalition. When he returned on April 15, Dulles felt that he had accomplished his purpose by getting the French and British to agree to joint action. However, the main result of the trip, a vaguely worded communiqué, committed the British only to "an examination of the possibility of establishing a collective defense . . . to assure the peace security and freedom of Southeast Asia and the Western Pacific."[74] Although Dulles claimed that the British statement reflected its agreement to undertake a collective defense, the British privately rejected joint military intervention (a key aspect of united action) and instead preferred a collective security arrangement that did *not* include Indochina.[75] For their part, the French objected to the American timetable for action and insisted that any movement toward a collective security arrangement before Geneva would be impossible because it would appear to their own people that they had decided the conference would fail.[76] Although Dulles did not appear to realize it at the time, the British had rejected the substance of united action, and the French had spurned any coalitional effort before Geneva, thereby making his vision of united action impossible to achieve.

In addition, the administration faced a domestic uproar when on April 16, Vice President Nixon stated that if the French withdrew and American troops provided the only way to save Indochina, "I believe that the executive branch of the government has to take the politically unpopular position of facing up to it and doing it [i.e., sending troops], and I personally would support such a decision."[77] The statement, perceived as an administration trial balloon on sending troops, met with both sharp and widespread opposition. Both parties in Congress reacted negatively, based on concerns that the administration had once again cut them out of foreign policy decision making. The American and world press also responded harshly.[78] Apparently scared by the interventionist talk, on April 18, the British undercut the administration's united action strategy by pulling out of an April 20 meeting at which the collective security arrangements were to be discussed.[79] Although Dulles did not appear overly concerned with Nixon's statement, this incident strongly reinforced Eisenhower's aversion to unilateral intervention because of public opposition.[80]

The public remained wary of involving American ground troops, as Eisenhower suspected, but it nonetheless supported the main lines of the administration's policy. Referring to a February Gallup Poll finding that only 11 percent of the public favored dispatching ground troops to Indochina, a State Department report on public opinion concluded that "editorial opinion, Congressional statements, and public opinion polls all point to ['an unwillingness to send troops to participate in the fighting']." The report provided summaries of previous polls from 1953 that showed approval of sending in the American air force if the communists tried to take over Indochina, but an unpublished March 1954 Gallup Poll found public opposition to action by any forces. The poll asked: "Suppose things got so bad in Indo-China it looked as if the Communists were going to beat the French and take over all of Indo-China. Which *one* of these things do you think the United States should then do?" Nine percent said to "send American soldiers and flyers to take part in the fighting there"; 33 percent preferred to "send the French more supplies than we do now—but *no* soldiers or flyers"; 45 percent wanted to "try to arrange for an armistice and a peaceful settlement by negotiation"; and 13 percent expressed no opinion. The report also noted that commentators voiced "widespread and strong" support for Dulles's united action policy and viewed his trip to Europe as a success.[81] This report largely supported the multilateral American policy and Eisenhower's perception of public opinion as extremely wary of any use of troops and concerned with the independence of the Associated States.

At a North Atlantic Treaty Organization (NATO) ministers' meeting in Europe on April 22, French Minister of Foreign Affairs Georges Bidault informed Dulles that the situation at Dien Bien Phu was "virtually hopeless" and only a "massive" air intervention by the United States could avert disaster. Bidault now favored internationalizing the war (although he had previously opposed it) and hoped that the United States would take action.[82] Dulles reported on April 23 that he felt Dien Bien Phu had become a symbol "out of all proportion to its military importance" and believed that if it fell, the French government would be taken over by "defeatists." In this climate, Dulles reported that the French commander in Indochina now felt that his only alternatives were either a massive B-29 bombing by American planes or a cease-fire which Dulles assumed would be limited to the area around Dien Bien Phu.[83] Much to Dulles's dismay, he learned over dinner that the cease-fire that the commander had in mind encompassed all of Indochina rather than merely Dien Bien Phu. British Foreign Minister Anthony Eden also informed Dulles the British were unlikely to become involved militarily for fear of igniting World War III.[84]

Although frustrated by the spiraling situation, the Eisenhower administration stuck to its original position taken in early April. On April 24, Eisenhower complained that the French wanted the United States to enter the war as "junior partners and provide materials, etc." while the French remained in charge. He could not "go along with them on that on any such notion" and expressed his exasperation at the British position. Apparently resigned to the fortress's collapse, Eisenhower asked Undersecretary of State Bedell Smith to have a draft message prepared for that eventuality.[85] Later that day, Dulles informed Bidault that American military involvement remained conditioned on prior "congressional authorization," which was not "obtainable in a matter of hours" and not "at all except in the framework of a political understanding" with other interested parties in the region.[86]

In the rapidly shifting situation, Dulles now doubted that even unilateral action would save the day. On April 25, Dulles cabled Washington of his opposition to "armed intervention by executive action." He now opposed intervention because American security was not directly threatened; it was not clear such action would "protect our long-range interests"; it was "unlikely" that air intervention would save the fortress; immediate intervention without the British might strain American relations with the United Kingdom, Australia, and New Zealand; and the United Stated had not reached a political understanding with the French.[87]

Eisenhower met with Republican congressional leaders on April 26 to discuss Dien Bien Phu. Despite the deteriorating situation, Eisenhower remained opposed to unilateral intervention, and he reiterated his belief that any American intervention would need to occur through united action so as to free it from the taint of colonialism. Even though the fortress might fall, Eisenhower indicated that the administration was still trying to form a collective grouping for intervention, but under no circumstance did he foresee introducing American ground troops. One legislator raised the potential problem that the administration would be criticized for not sufficiently emphasizing the danger in Indochina. Eisenhower agreed and noted the criticism that Truman and the Democrats had suffered after China became communist.[88] They all agreed that the administration might be attacked for "losing" Indochina. Eisenhower attempted to redirect these concerns toward America's hesitant allies. The problem was that "neither the French nor the British had risen to the occasion, and so Dien Bien Phu would be lost."[89] Perhaps in response to this concern, Eisenhower held a press conference on April 29 to underscore the administration's efforts.[90]

At the NSC meeting on April 29, Eisenhower approved explorations of a regional grouping without the British and at the same time fended off pressure from within the administration to intervene unilaterally, possibly with ground troops.[91] The director for foreign operations, Harold Stassen, spoke favorably of unilateral American intervention and stated his belief that Congress and the public would support direct intervention if Eisenhower explained the action as necessary for American interests. Eisenhower seriously questioned this assessment. Arguing that he could not lead public opinion on this issue, the minutes recorded that "the President expressed considerable doubt as to whether Governor Stassen's diagnosis of the attitude of the Congress and people in this contingency was correct." Eisenhower also suggested that unilateral intervention would be viewed as merely replacing "French colonialism with American colonialism." He feared that the Chinese and possibly the Soviet Union would respond if the United States intervened unilaterally and observed that collective action was the only policy consistent with the broader American national security policy. He thought that unilateral action would amount to an attempt to "police the entire world" and would cause a significant loss of support in the free world, since the United States would be "accused of imperialistic ambitions." Eisenhower observed that "if the United States were to permit its ground forces to be drawn into a conflict in a great variety of places throughout the world, the end result would be gravely to weaken the defensive position of the United States."[92]

To avoid this option, Undersecretary Smith suggested a multilateral air strike that would both meet the coalition conditions imposed by Congress and provide the necessary assistance to keep the French in the war. Nixon pointed out that even though the air strikes would not influence the military situation, it could have a positive effect on the world's perceptions of American resolve. Expressing an opinion he had long held, Eisenhower said he would agree to put the multilateral air intervention proposal before Congress if the French would stay and fight. Although he supported multilateral action, he

> wanted to end the meeting with one word of warning. If we wanted to win over the Congress and the people of the United States to an understanding of their stake in Southeast Asia, let us not talk of intervention with United States ground forces. People were frightened, and were opposed to this idea.[93]

Similarly, Nixon reported, "the President himself said that he could not visualize a ground troop operation in Indochina that would be supported by the people of the United States and which would not in the long run put our defense too far out of balance."[94] Smith reported to Dulles in Europe that Eisenhower "feels sure that neither Congressional nor public opinion would accept a last minute partnership with the French" without a multilateral coalition joined "by [the] most exposed and interested nations."[95] In the face of pressure from his advisers for more aggressive action, Eisenhower held to his position of supporting multilateral action but rejected ground troops and unilateral action of any kind.

On May 5, the administration resigned itself to the fall of Dien Bien Phu. At a White House meeting attended by Eisenhower, Dulles, and Cutler, the top decision makers reflected on their choices and accepted the loss of the fortress. Perhaps to blunt possible domestic criticism, Eisenhower suggested that Dulles give "a chronology of the U.S. actions to Congress in his bipartisan briefing to show that throughout we had adhered to the principle of collective security." He reaffirmed his rejection of an overt unilateral American intervention because it would raise "a colonial stigma on the U.S., and because it would exhaust the U.S. eventually." Dulles and Eisenhower agreed that the "conditions did not justify the U.S. entry into Indochina as a belligerent at this time" and decided to proceed with efforts to organize a regional grouping and find out where the United States and British might be able to agree.[96] Later that day, Dulles briefed a bipartisan congressional group, partly to head off possible criticism of the administration after the inevitable fall of Dien Bien Phu and to explain the administration's efforts toward united action.[97]

The French troops at Dien Bien Phu surrendered on May 7. After failing to create a multilateral coalition, Dulles publicly announced on June 8 that the administration would not be asking for congressional authorization for intervention. On June 12, the French government fell on a vote concerning Indochina and a government led by Pierre Mendès-France—who was committed to a negotiated settlement and against asking for American intervention—replaced it on June 17. On July 22, negotiators in Geneva reached a cease-fire agreement, called the Geneva Accords of 1954, which required a temporary partition of Vietnam at the seventeenth parallel followed by national elections in 1956. Neither the United States nor the Vietnamese government signed the accords. The Southeast Asia Treaty Organization (SEATO), negotiated in September 1954, created the collective grouping that American decision makers had sought throughout the crisis, made up of Australia, Britain, France, New Zealand, Pakistan, the Philippines, Thailand, and the United States. These nations agreed to "meet common danger" and recognized that threats to Laos, Cambodia, and southern Vietnam would "endanger" the signatories' security.[98]

With the fall of both Dien Bien Phu and the French government, serious consideration of American intervention in Indochina during

1954 ended. Although it appeared late in the process that Congress might assent to unilateral American intervention, the administration could not build the multilateral coalition that Eisenhower felt was necessary for public approval, nor would the French grant the assurances he wanted. Eisenhower refused to relent to internal pressure from his advisers to send American troops into the region unilaterally. Throughout the process, the American public remained opposed to any commitment of American ground troops and unilateral intervention—views that weighed on Eisenhower's mind. In the end, despite his concern about American interests in the region and pressure from within the administration to intervene, Eisenhower concluded that the necessary conditions for a successful intervention had not been met.

Variables

Assessments of public opinion influenced these decision makers' policy stances, especially Eisenhower's. The effect of another war on the American public, which Eisenhower believed would oppose intervention, concerned him greatly, especially if ground troops were employed. In the broader political context, he thought he needed to avoid both another Korea (limited war) and another China (loss of a country to the communists) and also perceived that the colonialism and independence issues could affect public support. The positions that Eisenhower eventually adopted were consistent with his perceptions of public opinion regarding independence, colonialism, and ground troops. In fact, the conditions for American involvement that he established were selected in part to reduce public opposition. He reasoned that public concerns about colonialism could be assuaged by an invitation from the Associated States before intervention. Eisenhower felt that the public opposed unilateral action and he ruled it out for this reason, but he favored multilateral intervention, as did the public. As the administration moved toward united action, Eisenhower's concern with public opinion emerged during his discussions with Republican congressional leaders regarding the potential criticism that Democrats might level against them if Indochina fell. To alleviate these fears, he moved to frame the issue for the public by emphasizing both the importance of American interests in Indochina and the administration's efforts to protect them.

Dulles's focus on public opinion emerged during the selection of the policy responding to the threat to Dien Bien Phu. Dulles perceived public opposition to caving in to the communists and also to taking more aggressive action. Given this view, he recommended pursuing the "right" policy (which he determined was the united action policy). Since he believed that the participation of other nations would generate domestic support, the policy was at once the best one, in his view, from a national security perspective and designed to create the greatest public support. As the administration moved toward implementation, he concentrated on leading the public, as suggested in many of his communications and the far-reaching State Department briefing program to persuade opinion leaders to support intervention.

Other interests had a significant influence on policymakers, especially Dulles, and helped determine the placement of intervention on the agenda. Because the administration perceived Indochina as a bulwark against further communist expansion in the region, American national security interests in the region and around the globe might be seriously threatened if it fell. In addition, should the French lose the battle for Dien Bien Phu, the political and psychological ramifications might lead to a new French government, which might seriously jeopardize France's commitment to the Indochina war. As Dulles presented it at the March 26 NSC meeting, united action, regardless of the domestic imperatives, best served American interests in the region. His reluctance to support unilateral action of any kind was related to his belief that the policy had a slim chance of working.

Other interests affected Eisenhower. Fearing that the political and psychological consequences of losing Dien Bien Phu could seriously threaten French stamina, he favored an examination of limited intervention, implying with his finger-in-the-dike metaphor that limited early action might alleviate the need for more dramatic action later. But even though Eisenhower saw Indochina as vital to national security, he viewed a larger-scale ground intervention negatively because of his misgivings about the viability of such action. This left unilateral and multilateral air or naval action as possible alternatives. Eisenhower also insisted on united action and independence for the Associated States in part because of his fear that world opinion might see unilateral American action as merely replacing French colonialism with American colonialism.

Both Dulles and Eisenhower acted according to their beliefs throughout the decision process, and these beliefs had a causal influence at the critical junctures, thereby yielding a *supportive* influence coding of beliefs. Although they both reached the same policy conclusion, their beliefs caused them to do so for different reasons, and they were prepared to support different policies if conditions changed.

According to his beliefs, Eisenhower would have been constrained by public opinion if opposition to a policy, especially war, were immovable. Otherwise, he would have attempted to lead the public to support the policy he deemed best for national security. In addition to the national security interests at stake, he felt he needed to take action on Indochina because of the potential public reaction if another country fell to communism. Process tracing reveals that public opinion limited his range of action by causing him to reject unilateral intervention and reinforcing his aversion to using ground troops. The conditions that Eisenhower imposed on American intervention stemmed from his concern with having domestic support. Given the public's aversion to the Korean War and colonialism, he found it necessary to impose the multilateral and independence conditions on intervention. Once he chose to support multilateral intervention, he moved to drum up support for his selected alternative. This behavior is *consistent* with expectations based on beliefs in setting the agenda, defining the situation, and generating options and suggests a *causal* influence on policy selection and implementation.

For Dulles, beliefs predictions suggest that if he saw public opinion as a problem, he would have formulated an education program if he had had enough time. Dulles regarded multilateral intervention as the best approach from a national security standpoint and attempted to lead the public to support it. Although he did not think it necessary, he supported unilateral intervention. He anticipated potential domestic criticism from either letting Indochina become communist or taking overly aggressive action, but these issues did not limit his view of the situation. Instead, he used the anticipation of these views to construct a public information program to create support for multilateral intervention which he thought would prevent Indochina's fall. As the administration moved to implement the policy, Dulles continued to attempt to lead public opinion and actively worked to achieve this goal through briefings at the State Department. His behavior is *consistent* with his beliefs during the agenda setting, the definition of the situation, and the option generation stages, and they had a *causal* influence during policy selection and implementation.

Coding the Influence of Public Opinion

When considered as a whole, the effect of public opinion falls into a *moderate constrain category* influence, with a smaller influence as within the *lead category*. In addition to damaging the U.S. strategic position, Eisenhower feared a possibly divisive and politically damaging domestic debate about "who lost Indochina" if the communists won the war. When formulating a policy to confront this problem, public opinion and Eisenhower's own trepidation based on his military experience together ruled out ground intervention. Worried about the domestic reaction to "another" Korean War, public opinion also played a stronger role in eliminating a unilateral American action and pressured Eisenhower to insist on guarantees of independence. He supported the united action proposal because it fit American interests in Indochina and the region and it alleviated his concerns regarding colonialism and the independence of the Associated States. In regard to the strength of influence, public opinion was one of the primary determinants of policy, along with concerns about the viability of intervention. Public opinion set a range of acceptable and unacceptable policy options, but other interests also had an important influence on policy choices. For this reason, public opinion acted as a *moderate* constraint on decision making. Dulles's perceptions and actions throughout the case fall into the lead category, as do some of Eisenhower's actions at the implementation stage when he attempted to build support for united action. This behavior warrants a lesser coding of the *lead category*.

As in the crisis context, public opinion affected policy outcomes through the more perceptual linkages, with the strongest connection resulting from perceptions of the opinion context. This linkage influenced decision makers on a number of issues, perhaps most clearly through Eisenhower's use of the Korean and Chinese analogies in the formation of his attitudes. Anticipated reactions affected how decision makers defined the conditions for intervention, with both Dulles and Eisenhower feeling that the public would be receptive to intervention if it were multilateral and Eisenhower attending to the colonialism and independence issues because of the potential reaction by the public. In addition, based on his reading of the opinion context, Dulles anticipated that the public would not support either the policy of appeasement or intervention in Indochina.

Specific measures of opinion entered decision making through congressional opinion, press reactions to the administration's actions (the technicians and Nixon's April 16 speech), and polling information. Whereas decision makers relied on the more vague measures of public opinion to formulate their views, the heightened attention given to the issue allowed more expressions of public opinion to enter the process.

Decision makers in the offshore islands crisis context were able to formulate policy largely outside the public view, but the Dien Bien Phu issue, which continued to be front-page news because of its inherent drama, activated congressional, press, and public attention that allowed these more specific expressions of public sentiment to become relevant. Even so, the overall linkage process did not change dramatically from the crisis case.

This case provides mixed support for both the Wilsonian liberal and the realist viewpoints (see table 4.1). Support for the Wilsonian liberal perspective comes primarily through the actions of Eisenhower, who throughout responded to the perceived constraints of public opinion. Because his actions had a strong influence on the overall coding of public opinion, the Wilsonian liberal view more accurately describes the generation of options and policy choice. The realist perspective—according to which decision makers should lead public opinion to support the policy that they select for national security reasons—is supported most by Dulles's actions. Throughout, Dulles based his decisions on his perception of the nation's security interests and then attempted to lead the public to support them. More broadly, agenda setting and policy implementation align more closely with this view.

This divergence between Eisenhower and Dulles results largely because of the differing influence of their beliefs on their behavior. Because of his concerns with staying in the range acceptable to public opinion, Eisenhower remained limited by public opinion's view of the situation, much as he had during the crisis case. Dulles, however, now found—given the administration's anticipation of the issue—the time necessary to formulate and lead the public to support the policy he

---

TABLE 4.1 Influence Coding: Reflexive Case

Predicted Public Influence			Actual Public Influence	Influence of Beliefs
REALIST	WILSONIAN LIBERAL	BELIEFS		
Lead	Constrain	DDE: Constrain/*Lead*	Constrain (moderate)/ with lesser	DDE: Supportive
		JFD: Lead	Lead	JFD: Supportive

Note: Italics indicate conditional predictions.

deemed best. Thus, even though Eisenhower and Dulles agreed on the same policy, they reached that point in two very different manners. These results imply that beliefs can be a vital variable in explaining and predicting how public opinion influences policymaking. But chapter 5's discussion of the administration's response to the Soviet Union's launch of *Sputnik* points to the possible limits of the influence of beliefs when confronted with strong situational pressures.

CHAPTER FIVE

The Innovative Context

Standing Firm, Pushing Forward, and Giving Way After *Sputnik*

On October 4, 1957, the Soviet Union launched a 184-pound satellite called *Sputnik* into outer space, causing a global sensation. Although the American government quickly concluded that the satellite provided no immediate threat, it did, in combination with other Soviet technological advancements, pose a potential long-term threat to U.S. national security. Accordingly, the administration quickly decided that it needed to organize its scientific effort better and encourage more students to study the sciences. Sensing the new public concern could allow him to overcome entrenched opposition, Eisenhower began a campaign to reorganize the Defense Department. After a second larger Russian satellite was launched in early November, the administration moved to raise defense spending and to launch its own satellite to mollify the public's apprehension. In the end, the administration adopted a series of policies based on both national security and public opinion, including a public information program, a backup and higher-priority satellite program, the creation of a science adviser position in the White House, reorganization of the defense establishment, an education bill, an increase in defense spending and acceleration of the missile program, a plan for space exploration, and a civilian space agency.[1]

Because the Soviets combined their ballistic missile and satellite programs (the United States had separate programs), *Sputnik* implied a significant booster capability for Soviet warheads. Even though the Soviets still had problems with guidance and reentry, the booster thrust (of *Sputnik II* in particular) in combination with a Soviet high-yield thermonuclear weapons test the previous summer and a series of recent missile tests suggested that they did possess the range and throw weight capability necessary for a successful intercontinental ballistic missile (ICBM).[2] This capability came as a distinct surprise not only to the media, Congress, and public but to the administration as well. According to the notes of the NSC meeting the day afterward, Deputy Secretary of Defense Donald Quarles reported that the Soviets "possess a competence in long-range rocketry and in auxiliary fields which is even more advanced than the competence with which we had credited them."[3] In his memoirs, Eisenhower recalled that the "size of the thrust required to propel a satellite of this weight came as a distinct surprise to us."[4] Given its Cold War propaganda value, the booster and satellite contained serious implications for American international prestige. In addition to providing the first practical threat to the continental United States in some time, the short amount of time it would take for a Soviet ICBM to reach the United States greatly reduced the American bomber force's response time and could open it to a potentially disarming first strike. The government had expected a Soviet satellite at some point (although the public did not), but it did not anticipate the specific timing of the launch.[5]

In response to this achievement, the administration initially pursued a public relations strategy to calm the public's apparent concern. After the second *Sputnik*, the administration began to see unrestrained public hysteria over the satellite as a challenge to its policy goals. They thus attempted to keep what they saw as the public's overreaction from altering security policies by developing several policies to confront the threat and allay public concern, including a public information program, defense reorganization, and an education bill. The administration continued to push these policies, but when it became clear that the public could not be calmed with these efforts alone, it adopted several additional policies (increased defense spending, missile acceleration, and a space program).

Realist and Wilsonian liberal theories generate different expectations of policy behavior for this context. As discussed in chapter 1, according to realist theory, decision makers use their best judgment to fashion a policy to meet the national security threat. Because of the surprise, realist theory also suggests that public opinion might become (irrationally) aroused by the shock of the revealed threat and may limit viable policy options. Expectations based on Wilsonian liberal theory indicate that the long decision time allows policymakers an opportunity to measure public opinion and the public an opportunity to influence policy decisions. Given these conditions, officials respond by trying to carry out the public's policy preferences.

The beliefs model offers similar behavioral predictions for Eisenhower and Dulles. As with previous cases, Eisenhower would have made the decision that best reflected his perception of national security and then tried to gain public support for the option. If he perceived public opposition to be unchangeable, it should have constrained his choices. Dulles should have attempted to persuade the public to support the policy he perceived as best for national security, since the long decision time would have allowed him the time he thought necessary to generate public support.

The *Sputnik* case provides mixed evidence for these views of decision making. The realist perspective finds support throughout, since decision makers chose certain policies to meet national security needs and then attempted to lead the public. However, decisions on defense spending, missiles, and space policy during the policy selection and implementation stages support the Wilsonian liberal view. For this reason, the influence of public opinion for the entire case is coded as a combination of the *lead* and *follow (moderate) categories*, with the lead category as the primary overall influence.

The beliefs variable also received mixed support. For several policies, Eisenhower acted according to his beliefs at both a *consistent* and a *causal* level of influence. But he relented to public pressure on defense spending, missile acceleration, and space policy, which is *inconsistent* with beliefs predictions. Even so, the presence of his public opinion beliefs remained apparent (even as he acted against them) as shown in his irritation in having to respond to public opinion. Dulles reacted to national security concerns and attempted to lead the public because of his beliefs, which implies a *causal* influence.

Problem Representation: Setting the Agenda

Before *Sputnik*, the administration recognized the link between American international prestige and satellites but regarded the missile program as paramount, which thereby limited the satellite effort. The administration decided on May 16, 1955, to launch a satellite during the

International Geophysical Year (IGY, between July 1957 and December 1958) based on the recognition of the "considerable prestige and psychological benefits" from being first, but the small ($20 million at the start and $110 million per year by May 1957) satellite program was not to interfere with the ongoing ballistic missile program.[6] At a later NSC meeting, both Eisenhower and Dulles emphasized the need to develop an ICBM capability as soon as possible because of the impact of a Soviet ICBM on America's international prestige and domestic public opinion. According to the meeting's notes, Dulles warned that the administration needed to consider "how to minimize the consequences of a Russian achievement of these weapons prior to the United States" because "it was going to be very difficult to persuade public opinion on this score" given the inevitable Soviet propaganda efforts. Eisenhower stressed that he was "absolutely determined not to tolerate any fooling with this thing. We [have] simply got to achieve such missiles as promptly as possible, if only because of the enormous psychological and political significance of ballistic missiles." Although the notes reveal that he was thinking primarily about the international reaction, Eisenhower punctuated his comments with references to the many telegrams and letters he received from the public calling for the quick development of an American ballistic missile.[7]

After the October 4, 1957, launch, press comment largely mirrored the administration's fears that the satellite would enhance Soviet prestige and provide significant propaganda leverage. Press reports linked the satellite achievement to the Soviets' ICBM capacity (with the implied threat to the American mainland), and some called for a reexamination of American defense policies and missile programs. Sensing an opportunity, Democratic leaders took the administration to task for allowing American continental defenses to waste away through spending cuts and issued calls for unrestrained efforts to catch up.[8]

The administration's initial response focused on the scientific aspects of the Soviet achievement and downplayed the military implications. Because Eisenhower remained at his Gettysburg retreat over the weekend, Press Secretary James C. Hagerty issued the administration's first response on Saturday, October 5. He emphasized that the administration was not surprised, did not think of the satellite program as a race, and suggested that the administration was following *Sputnik* because "of great scientific interest." Other administration statements to minimize the Soviet achievement were less polished and even increased public concern by appearing to misunderstand the satellite's significance.

Secretary of Defense Charles Wilson called *Sputnik* "a nice scientific trick," and Assistant to the President Sherman Adams dismissed exaggerated efforts to catch up by asserting that the United States would not take part in "an outer space basketball game." On Monday October 7, Eisenhower returned from Gettysburg to a chaotic White House. Despite a calm outward appearance, the fact that he hit golf balls (an activity he used to relieve stress) for a considerable period of time in the evening reflected his worries about *Sputnik*.[9] Later Adams recalled that "although Eisenhower maintained an official air of serenity, he was privately as concerned as everybody else in the country by the jump ahead that the Russians had made in scientific enterprise."[10] Eisenhower recollected, "There was no point in trying to minimize the accomplishment or the warning it gave that we must take added efforts to ensure maximum progress in missile and other scientific programs."[11]

Problem Representation: Defining the Situation

Eisenhower later recalled that *Sputnik* created two problems: "The first, a short term one, was to find ways of affording perspective to our people and so relieve the current wave of near-hysteria; the second, to take all feasible measures to accelerate missile and satellite programs."[12] This retrospective is consistent with the administration's actions during the first months after *Sputnik,* which centered on the satellite's public relations and propaganda implications. The administration believed that to resolve this problem, it needed only to reassure the public (by accelerating the Project *Vanguard* satellite program and making comforting statements) rather than change the broader national security program. Soon after the launch, in a move to attempt to head off congressional action, Eisenhower instructed his advisers to communicate that the government had formulated a solid approach to satellites and planned no immediate changes.[13] Privately, Eisenhower cautioned his cabinet about the long-term threat implied by *Sputnik.* The notes record his saying that he expected Congress to request new legislation and that *Sputnik* created "increased tensions with which we would have to learn to live for a long time."[14] In a week, administration discussions moved to consider the possible long-term threats to national security revealed by *Sputnik* concerning education and defense reorganization.

The initial efforts to assess the threat were made at an October 8 meeting that began with a presentation of a Pentagon memorandum on *Sputnik.*[15] The report noted two Cold War implications: "(1) the impact on public imagination of the first successful invasion and conquest of outer space, and (2) the inferences, if any, that can be drawn about the status of [the Soviet] development of military rocketry." The paper recommended no change in satellite or missile programs, concluded that the lack of an American satellite had no military significance, and proposed a public statement to this effect. It further advised that no effort be made to push up the planned December 1 launch date of an "experimental part-size" American satellite, since this would only increase the chance of failure.

According to a memorandum of conversation, after the presentation of the Pentagon memorandum, Eisenhower asked whether an army *Redstone* missile could have placed an American satellite into orbit earlier.[16] Upon hearing that it could have, Eisenhower immediately seized on the political implications and noted that the Democratic Congress would press the administration about failing to use the *Redstone*. At odds with statements from 1955, Eisenhower asserted that the "timing was never given too much importance in our own program" as long as it protected military secrets and succeeded during the IGY. Sensing the possible benefits from overhead satellite reconnaissance in terms of estimating Soviet military capabilities, Eisenhower told the group to think five years ahead and referred to the reconnaissance satellite program. He rejected a "sudden shift" in the satellite program because it would "belie the attitude we have had all along."

In fact, Hagerty and Dulles had agreed in the morning of October 8 that Eisenhower needed to have a press conference to put *Sputnik* "in proper perspective."[17] Eisenhower actively prepared for the press conference and outlined several pieces of information he wanted: the history of ballistic missile programs, the status of the missile and satellite programs when Eisenhower came into office in 1953, a chronology of costs, and an explanation for cost increases.[18] Undoubtedly, several of these items were directed at documenting the previous Truman administration's and Democratic Congresses' lack of interest in and funding for missiles. Continuing his public relations focus, Eisenhower went over his press conference statement and said he wanted "to allay histeria [*sic*] and alarm" and "bring out that the Russian action is simply proof of a thrust mechanism of a certain power accuracy and reliability."[19]

At his last meeting with Secretary of Defense Wilson on October 8 (Neil McElroy was scheduled to replace him the next day), Eisenhower and Wilson seemed unaware of the pressures for increased spending that *Sputnik* would generate. Since Congress had actually cut the administration's fiscal year (FY) 58 defense budget request the previous summer, Wilson predicted that Congress would again cut his request.[20] This political assessment, though correct just five days before, failed to consider the rising sentiment in Congress and the press for increased spending. Wilson assumed that *Sputnik* would bring more attention to the missile program and recommended removing overtime restrictions because of political perceptions. Although the restrictions' cost and influence were minor, Wilson felt that some members of Congress would contend the limitations slowed the missile program. Eisenhower agreed and suggested a backup to the *Vanguard* system in case it failed or was significantly slowed. At this meeting, neither Wilson nor Eisenhower saw a large policy influence from *Sputnik*, so both concentrated on alleviating potential near-term public relations problems rather than substantive policy responses.

Dulles, too, focused on the public relations aspects of the satellite, writing in an unused draft statement for Eisenhower that the satellite was "an event of considerable technical and scientific importance" but that its significance "should not be exaggerated."[21] He attributed the launch to the high priority the Soviets had given the project, the German scientists that the Soviets had captured at the end of World War II, and the rigid nature of Soviet society.

Eisenhower continued to concentrate on public relations on October 9. At a meeting with the newly sworn in secretary of defense, McElroy, and other top Defense officials, Eisenhower instructed them on the "attitude that the group should maintain in the present satellite situation." He recalled the intentional separation of the military and scientific components and warned them that they gave "exactly the wrong impression" by making "the matter look like a 'race'" when they claimed other missiles could have put a satellite into orbit earlier.[22]

At his pre-press conference briefing that same day, Eisenhower asserted that *Sputnik* did not necessitate "revamping foreign policy" and had no implications concerning the arms race.[23] At his press conference (rebroadcast on television), the press was hostile to Eisenhower's attempts to downplay the incident and the perception of threat.[24] The public statement he released emphasized the scientific nature of the American satellite program, the separation of the military missile program and scientific satellite program (hence, satellite progress had nothing to do with military security), and the absence of a satellite race.[25] Attempting to project a sense of calm, he insisted that "so far as the satellite is concerned, that does not raise my apprehensions, not one iota." He expressed confidence in American security, since the American ICBM and intermediate-range ballistic missile (IRBM) programs were moving ahead without delay and could counter any Soviet ICBM achievements. Because the American satellite program had never received the same level of priority as the missile program, he found no reason to grow "hysterical" about it. He rejected the notion that missiles made bombers obsolete and stressed that his administration had provided maximum funding for missiles. He reminded his audience that science, not political considerations or interservice rivalry, had determined the decisions regarding the satellite program. Perhaps as an afterthought, he committed the administration to a December satellite launch.

This effort failed, however, to quiet press criticism of the administration's program. By adopting a subdued attitude toward the satellite and continually referring to advice from experts, Eisenhower appeared unmoved by *Sputnik's* implications, which served only to heighten rather than reduce anxiety.[26]

Despite the common assumption in the administration, the press, and the world that the American public suffered from "hysteria," the available information does not support this view. Unlike the dire assessments in the press and Congress, public opinion remained largely restrained in *Sputnik's* immediate aftermath and accepted the administration's explanations, as shown in two Gallup polls, one taken before *Sputnik* and the other in the days immediately afterward (see table 5.1).[27]

Indeed, the public appeared more concerned about school integration, because of Little Rock, Arkansas, as evidenced by the dramatic rise in the surveys' ranking of integration and race relations. In fact, the importance of relations with Russia even dropped somewhat. Even though some respondents now listed *Sputnik*, missiles, and defense preparedness as the most important problems, combining these responses with general Russian relations (yielding 39 percent) creates an increase of only 5 percent over the previous month. These results hardly represent a "hysterical" reaction to *Sputnik*. Public opinion researcher Samuel Lubell, who was conducting interviews immediately before and after *Sputnik*, reported similar findings. From his anecdotal evidence he concluded that most of the public's responses followed the administration's position rather than the press's criticism.[28]

When asked in an October 25 poll why the Russians were the first to launch a satellite, Americans gave several reasons: 22 percent said the Russians worked harder and longer on the program; 14 percent indicat-

TABLE 5.1 Poll: "What do you think is the most important problem facing this country today?"

September 15, 1957 (Interview dates, August 27–September 4, 1957)		November 6, 1957 (Interview Dates, October 10–15, 1957)	
Keeping out of war, relations with Russia	34%	Integration, race problems	29%
High cost of living, threat of inflation	22%	Keeping the peace, foreign policy, dealing with Russia	26%
Integration problems	10%	Economic, money problems	12%
Don't know any	13%	Defense, preparedness	7%
Nuclear tests, atomic control, juvenile deliquency, foreign aid, need of religion, farm problems, labor unions, labor corruption, and others were each less than 10%		Sputnik, missiles	6%
		Other social problems	4%
		Farm problems	2%
		Miscellaneous	5%
		None, can't say	9%

ed they had better scientists (notably the German scientists); 7 percent blamed a poorly organized American program (because of interservice rivalry); and 7 percent thought the Russians gave more money to the program. The first and fourth reasons reflected the administration's explanations.[29] Although Americans did worry about *Sputnik* (as did the administration), opinion in the first weeks after *Sputnik* was more restrained than hysterical, whereas the press and elite commentary is more indicative of a "media riot."[30]

In the face of mounting press and congressional criticism and calls from within the administration for a more dramatic response, Eisenhower remained determined to maintain the established programs and public relations approach. At the October 10 NSC meeting, anticipating press and congressional questions of NSC members, Eisenhower instructed them that "he could imagine nothing more important than . . . [standing] firmly by the existing earth satellite program . . . In short, we should answer inquiries by stating we have a plan—a good plan—and that we are going to stick to it." When one adviser suggested a program for human space flight or a trip to the moon, Eisenhower, perhaps sensing the costs of such public relations endeavors, countered, "We must, above all, still seek a military posture that the Russians will respect."[31]

Although the administration had always denied that interservice rivalry was a problem, Eisenhower felt that a question at a press conference on possible delays in the missile program caused by interservice rivalries "showed the widespread belief in our country that we are competing among ourselves rather than with the Russians." Even though Eisenhower had accepted slight delays in the missile program in the summer of 1957 to save money, he now announced that "nothing should be allowed to stand in the way of getting [a successful IRBM tested]." The meeting's minutes report that Eisenhower reverted to his 1955 position, reminding the NSC of "the great political and psychological advantage of the first achievement of an IRBM and an ICBM. He noted that from the inception of the ballistic missiles program, the Council had agreed that these political and psychological considerations were perhaps even more important than the strictly military considerations."[32] As a result, Eisenhower approved the continuation of both the *Jupiter* and *Thor* IRBM programs until one had a successful test flight, thereby making a choice possible.

Perhaps based on the October 9 press conference and his reading of the newspapers, Eisenhower's perception of public pressure for policy alternations changed. At the October 11 cabinet meeting, he now expected Congress to press for increased defense spending beyond the $38 billion target for FY59, but he still believed that the administration should hold the line, resist new legislation, and "try to keep [the American] fiscal house in order despite increased tensions with which we would have to learn to live for a long time." He believed the administration would have to "ride the black horse this year" and thought the best approach would be to propose a low figure for defense even if it had to be raised later.[33] He warned McElroy that some in his department would try to force a choice between "security and a sound budget." Eisenhower stated that he believed both were necessary and the administration needed to find the proper balance. Vice President Richard Nixon warned, and Eisenhower concurred, that "the satellite development could change the temper of the country rapidly." On October 14, Eisenhower observed that Congress would appropriate $41 billion (rather than his preferred $38 billion figure) for defense in FY59, barring "some striking military development in the coming months." Given the probable decline in revenues from the growing recession and a possible budget deficit, he feared that a rise in the debt limit "might induce a popular reaction. . . . Members of Congress will face a troublesome dilemma in meeting economy pressures from one side and demagogic temptations for more defense spending on the other."[34] In essence, he saw both spending imbalances and a pared-down budget as potentially unpopular.

Eisenhower's perception of the *Sputnik* threat crystallized during an October 15 meeting with scientists from the Office of Defense Management Science Advisory Committee (SAC). He expressed his exasperation about public opinion, saying, "I can't understand why the American people have got so worked up over this thing."[35] He said he had been reflecting on the government's scientific activities and wondered whether American science was being "outdistanced."[36] I. I. Rabi, the head of SAC, expressed concern at the Soviets' tremendous progress in science and warned that they could rapidly pass the United States unless corrective actions were taken. Believing that the Soviets inspired their public's interest in science, Edwin H. Land, who invented the Polaroid Land camera, wondered whether there was "not some way in which the President could inspire the country" to value science. Eisenhower thought he could try to create a nationwide respect and enthusiasm for science through speeches and reasoned that "now is a good time to try such a thing. People are alarmed and thinking about science, and perhaps this alarm could be turned to a constructive result." However, he believed that scientific research could not be allowed to undermine the priority of ICBM and IRBM testing because of their psychological necessity. Eisenhower concluded from this meeting that Soviet scientific progress could dangerously outpace American science, threatening the nation's security if the administration took no action. He also now realized that public unease over *Sputnik* would not go away with the administration's limited public relations effort.[37]

Dulles continued to downplay the significance of *Sputnik* and to reject hasty policy changes. At his press conference on October 16, he attributed the Soviets' success to their continuous efforts since World War II, their capture of German rocket scientists, and their single-minded focus on one objective. He reiterated his belief in the superiority of American power, especially bombers, which, he argued, would be important for years to come. He also observed that *Sputnik* might serve a useful purpose by awakening the public and Congress, which had cut defense and foreign aid spending in the summer of 1957, from complacency on missiles.[38] Privately, he admitted to Eisenhower a possibly "discouraging future for the free world unless current trends can be reversed."[39] He viewed the shock caused by *Sputnik* to "free world opinion" as an "indispensable first step" in reversing the decline and reasoned that the shock could have the same influence on "galvanizing" the world to confront the Soviet threat as Pearl Harbor had had on the American public. Dulles clearly hoped that *Sputnik* would create greater support for American global policy both at home and abroad.

Option Generation

The administration developed several options between mid-October and early November, ranging from continued public relations efforts and relatively minor organizational changes (satellite work, a science adviser position) to major policy initiatives (defense reorganization, an education bill, increased defense spending, and adjustments in the missile program). Eisenhower continued to resist the perceived pressure from public opinion to increase defense spending and expand the space exploration program and considered policy options that might direct attention to less costly areas (such as education).

Almost from the first news of *Sputnik*, Eisenhower saw an opportunity to pursue his long-desired goal of reorganizing the Defense Department. He had advocated reforms since the end of World War II (testifying before Congress in favor of them in 1945, 1947, and 1951) and had attempted to mount a significant but ultimately unsatisfactory reorganization effort in 1953.[40] Nelson Rockefeller, chair of the President's Advisory Committee on Government Organization (PACGO), had suggested reorganization even before *Sputnik*. Although Eisenhower preferred to wait until about six weeks after McElroy took office (mid-November), he sensed that *Sputnik* provided an opportunity to progress rapidly on this front.[41] Eisenhower hoped that reorganization would, without sacrificing quality, achieve greater efficiency and savings while keeping expenditures at the same level. The real obstacle continued to be convincing Congress.[42] Recognizing that *Sputnik* might mitigate this problem, he commented that "in the present climate a giant step toward unification could be made. This might permit the secretary of defense to close out numerous installations, cut down overhead, etc."[43]

The October 15 SAC discussions resulted in three additional policy directions. First, Eisenhower pushed forward consideration of a new position of science adviser to the president. Second, on October 22, he announced a series of speeches on defense and education to raise public awareness, as suggested by the scientists. Third, he attempted to channel public and political pressures away from more costly programs such as space exploration and defense spending and into less expensive improvements in education and defense organization to benefit national security.[44]

The SAC recommendations dovetailed with previous administration plans for education. By October 2, before *Sputnik*, the Department of Health, Education and Welfare (HEW; now the Department of Health and Human Services) had nearly finished drawing up a list of alternatives (which eventually were presented to Eisenhower after *Sputnik*) to the administration's school construction bill which Congress had earlier rejected.[45] After *Sputnik*, Eisenhower saw the SAC proposal for science education as a focused educational effort that would provide a cheaper alternative to the rejected school construction bill while at the same time fulfilling a national security need.[46] The SAC convinced him to act in two ways to rectify the paucity of scientists: (1) create public awareness of the problem and (2) provide federal assistance for the sciences.[47] Eisenhower emphasized these two factors as he began his attempt to divert the public's attention away from defense spending and toward education at his October 30 press conference, saying that "[the scientist's] chief concern is not the relative position of ourselves today in scientific advancement with any other nation, but where we are going to be in ten years."[48]

Eisenhower also continued to pay a great deal of attention to American missile programs and potential IRBM deployments in Europe. After the pivotal October 15 SAC meeting, Eisenhower maintained these programs at the highest defense priority (over that of the satellite program).[49] At the same time, he ordered overtime restrictions on missile work to be removed, as Wilson had suggested on October 8.[50]

Dulles, too, remained concerned about the missile program in response to the United States' relations with its allies. He convinced Eisenhower on October 31 that they should use the forthcoming December NATO meeting to complete an IRBM deployment agreement with Britain and convince other countries to accept them.[51] Given the shock of *Sputnik* and the perception of threat, Dulles wanted an announcement—particularly one by Eisenhower at the NATO conference—concerning the acceleration of IRBM deployments because it might bolster flagging European morale.[52]

Although Eisenhower placed less priority on the satellite program than on the missile program, he understood the need for an American satellite as soon as possible, for public relations and political reasons.[53] Based on the satellite's importance, McElroy suggested to Eisenhower that they use a modified army *Redstone* rocket (called the *Jupiter-C*) as a backup to the navy's *Vanguard* rocket to "make sure we fire a satellite at an early date." Although irritated that the Defense Department had earlier rejected a similar suggestion, Eisenhower approved the backup.[54] Eisenhower realized that the satellite program had taken on great political and prestige significance and believed that much of the pressure for action would be relieved after a successful satellite launch.

Finally, pressure increased for more defense spending in response to *Sputnik* even as Eisenhower continued to oppose it. His philosophical approach to defense spending and the Cold War, based on restraint and preparations for a long-term conflict, remained unchanged after *Sputnik*. Eisenhower wrote to one acquaintance that a program to defeat the Soviets "must be designed for indefinite use and endurance. Hasty and extraordinary effort under the impetus of sudden fear" or complacency because "of the lack, over a period, of overt aggressive action" would not provide adequate security. Given *Sputnik*, he anticipated that the next Congress would support large appropriations for defense. The problem he saw with this view was that the nation faced "not a temporary emergency, such as a war, but a long term responsibility." He believed that the challenge was to renew public support and understanding for this long-term effort, which rested on predictable levels of defense spending.[55].

Eisenhower continued his public explanation at his October 30 press conference, acknowledging that some increases in defense spending beyond the $38 billion figure might be necessary, but he attributed this rise to an increase in inflation rather than an enhanced national security need.[56] Accordingly, he tried to deflect concern about national security into an effort to increase education spending. Dulles agreed with this approach and suggested leading the public to support this view. He wrote to Eisenhower that he feared *Sputnik* would "lead Congress to be liberal with military appropriations, perhaps even with the military aspects of mutual security, but will offset this by cutting down on the economic aid."[57]

By the end of October, the administration was considering a range of options: defense reorganization, an education bill, a new science adviser, additional funding for space R&D, a satellite program, adjustments in the IRBM program, and increased defense spending. Eisenhower opposed options that might greatly increase government spending (defense spending, space research), added an alternative when he saw an opportunity to pursue his own policy objectives (defense reorganization), reacted to perceived threats to the national interest (education bill, missile deployment, science adviser), and moved to decrease public pressure on the administration (satellite programs).

Policy Selection

The administration chose several alternatives to respond to *Sputnik*. To calm the public, Eisenhower adopted the special assistant proposal, gave speeches, and pushed to put a satellite into orbit. Although he resisted increasing defense spending, Eisenhower eventually accepted moderate increases and approved an accelerated IRBM program because of the perceived pressure of public opinion. The administration also moved to develop policy on defense reorganization and an education bill designed to address scientific shortcomings and national security needs. The administration eventually relented to congressional pressure in early 1958 and drew up a plan for a new civilian space agency and space exploration.

In the week after the October 15 SAC meeting, the administration prepared a formal proposal for improving the White House's coordination of science through a special assistant to the president for science and technology. The SAC would be transferred from the Defense Department to the White House and be reconstituted as the President's Scientific Advisory Committee (PSAC).[58] Eisenhower decided to announce the new appointment of James Killian, the president of MIT, at the first speech of his series.[59]

But before Eisenhower could give his first speech to reassure the nation, the Soviets announced another startling achievement: orbiting a satellite, called *Sputnik II*, which weighed 1,121 pounds and carried the first living organism (a dog) into space. The missile's thrust capacity was estimated at 500,000 pounds, which was clearly enough to propel an ICBM from the Soviet Union to the United States. The press reacted with heightened alarm and pressed for greater attention and financial commitments from the administration.[60] Although privately, Dulles acknowledged the importance of "the weight of this thing" to Eisenhower, publicly he downplayed the launch, as did the rest of the administration, by saying that it revealed nothing new about Soviet ICBM capabilities.[61]

In response to *Sputnik II*, Eisenhower decided on November 4 to move up the first of his "chins-up" speeches to November 7, which he would deliver from the Oval Office (instead of waiting until a planned November 13 speech from Oklahoma City), and would address national security rather than science (which he left for the Oklahoma speech).[62] While acknowledging public "complacency would be worse," Eisenhower believed that he could "allay some of the fears" the public felt through his speeches.[63] He hoped to create a "spiral of confidence and optimism" that could sustain public support of the long-term program to combat the Soviet threat.[64]

Eisenhower personally shaped his November 7 speech around a focus on national security because there were "so many parts of the defense problem that have *really* to be put before the American people." He emphasized that "money alone will not solve this problem" and intended to end with a statement of his "complete conviction that the American people can meet every one of these problems and these threats if we turn our minds to it."[65] His confidence in his persuasive abilities made it easier for him not to reveal information gathered from the secret U-2 spy plane program that regularly overflew the Soviet Union and gave him an accurate picture of Soviet missile activities. The U-2 information indicated that the Soviets were only a few months ahead of the United States in its ICBM research and that they had not taken steps toward deploying the missiles.[66] Although revealing this information and capability might have ended the criticism of the administration's handling of national security and removed the pressure for increased defense spending, Eisenhower did not want to jeopardize the source of this valuable information.[67] He wrote to one friend that regarding relative Soviet and American military capabilities, "You can understand that there are many things that I don't dare to allude to publicly, yet some of them would do much to allay the fears of our people."[68]

In the evening of November 7, Eisenhower gave his first speech from the Oval Office to a radio and television audience. After describing the United States' defensive capabilities, he identified four areas needing improvement to prevent the country from falling behind: (1) scientific education, (2) greater public and private research, (3) the sharing of scientific information with American allies, and (4) better government organization and effort concerning science, technology, and missiles. Leaving the first two subjects for the later speech, he announced Killian's appointment to ensure that interservice rivalries did not harm R&D, as well as other actions to streamline the missile programs. He rejected calls to increase spending and acknowledged that "certainly, we need to feel a high sense of urgency. But this does not mean that we should mount our charger and try to ride off in all directions at once."[69] By emphasizing these alternatives, he attempted to direct public attention to those areas he believed required government action to confront the *Sputnik* threat: science education and defense reorganization to reduce interservice rivalry. The press, however, did not view his proposals in the same light, with comments ranging from "biting criticism to lukewarm praise."[70]

Eisenhower gave his second speech on November 13 from Oklahoma City, also to a radio and television audience. He outlined a series of actions to preserve America's retaliation capability, including accelerated bomber dispersal, improvements in bomber response time, increased warning capabilities, and active missile defenses. He added that because his science experts regarded science education as even more important than defense programs, he was suggesting several actions to improve the quality of science teaching and the attractiveness of scientific careers.[71] The press reacted favorably to this second speech, which continued Eisenhower's effort to direct the public's concern about *Sputnik* to less expensive areas such as education reforms.[72] He believed that his messages had reassured the public and hoped that additional speeches would further convince the public that his administration was addressing the nation's defense needs.[73] However, these speeches were never given, because Eisenhower suffered a mild stroke on November 25, effectively scuttling the information campaign.[74] Although he soon recovered from the stroke, polls reveal an increasingly apprehensive public after *Sputnik II*. A November 24 Gallup Poll (taken during the week of November 7–12) asked whether the public was "satisfied with the present defense policies of the United States—or do you think there is a need to take a new look at our defense policies?" Only 26 percent reported being satisfied with the current policies, and 53 percent wanted a new examination (21 percent gave no opinion).[75]

On November 25, the day on which Eisenhower suffered his stroke, Senate Majority Leader Lyndon Johnson (D, Tex.) opened several months of hearings before the Defense Preparedness Subcommittee of the Senate Armed Services Committee. Witnesses described the urgency with which the United States needed to address its shortcomings in science and technology, defense organization, and defense spending. Even though the hearings made Eisenhower's case for defense reorganization easier to make, the extensive criticism also undermined Eisenhower's prestige in an area in which his competence had not been previously challenged.[76]

Whatever Eisenhower hoped to gain from the *Vanguard* launch disappeared when the missile exploded on the launch platform on December 6. Subsequent editorials extensively criticized the administration, chastising the American failure as "Kaputnik" and "Flopnik."[77] Dulles complained to Nixon that he had seldom been this despondent and surmised that the United States was well behind the Soviets.[78] After the *Vanguard* failure, the administration pinned its hopes on the *Jupiter-C* missile launch, scheduled for late January. Senator William Knowland (R, Calif.) explicitly linked the satellite program to efforts to restrain defense spending when he reported that unless the administration had a successful satellite launch soon, congressional demands for increased defense spending would go "hog-wild."[79] Fearing such an eventuality, Eisenhower raised the *Vanguard* and *Jupiter-C* satellite programs to the highest level of priority in the Defense Department (equal to that of the missile programs), even though the Defense Department recommended maintaining the satellites at the lower priority level.[80] But these efforts paid off on January 31 when the army's *Jupiter-C* orbited the first American satellite, named *Explorer*, and relieved some of the pressure on the administration.

Eisenhower had hoped that a successful satellite launch would reduce pressure for more defense spending, but he was forced to fight a progressively more difficult battle to restrain it. In early November, the Security Resources Panel, formed by Eisenhower in early 1957 to examine the viability of a national shelter program for nuclear defense, delivered its analysis, commonly known as the Gaither report. During its deliberations, the panel had expanded its purview to recommend changes in active measures to protect civilians and enhance the nuclear retaliatory force. The plan's costs were staggering. It called for $44 billion in increased defense spending over a five-year period, nearly $9 billion a year on average—almost a 25 percent increase over Eisenhower's preferred $38 billion defense budget.[81]

The panel members met with Eisenhower on November 4 and warned him that a surprise bomber attack could destroy the American strategic bomber force on the ground and predicted that by 1959, the Soviets would have enough operational ICBMs to threaten the American bomber force and population. Eisenhower remained unconvinced and disputed the vulnerability of the American deterrent. Even when it was argued to Eisenhower that the American bomber force's slow response time (when not on alert) would enable a Soviet bomber strike to disarm it, both Eisenhower and Dulles calmly dismissed the possibility of such an attack.[82] Instead of focusing on the military aspects, Eisenhower recalled the October 15 recommendations of his scientists:

> We are not behind now, but we must make great exertions in order not to fall behind. This means we must educate our people for the scientific and technological needs, and must also educate our people so they will support what is required. The difficult thing is that, in our democracies, we can apparently only do this with crisis, and we do not think government by crisis is the right process. The crux is, therefore, how to keep up interest and support without hysteria. . . . Americans will carry a challenging load for a couple of years, but it is very hard to obtain the commitments to indefinite burdens.[83]

Although Eisenhower agreed with some recommendations (such as the dispersal of bombers), he reiterated his support for the $38 billion defense ceiling, recognizing that "an increase above $38 billion is inevitable," especially because of inflation.

At the November 7 panel presentation to the NSC, Eisenhower stated his support for neither a "panicked" nor a "complacent" attitude and instead asked for a comprehensive survey of what "could and should be done." He reasoned that "in this context, perhaps the advent of *Sputnik* had been helpful" but cautioned that "we certainly did not wish to appear frightened and he had received information today indicating that fear had pervaded the population of the United States. The President believed that we could correct this situation." Eisenhower observed he could not just accept the report without regard for its impact on the public, since "we have before us a big job of molding public opinion as well as of avoiding extremes. We must get the American public to understand that we are confronting a tough problem but one that we can lick."[84] In fact, Eisenhower began the series of speeches that evening to correct this fear and direct public attention to the problem of education. Dulles worried that the report, because of its attention solely to the military problem, had failed to consider the other aspects of security.[85]

Although Eisenhower accepted some of the report's minor recommendations such as improvements in bomber dispersal and reaction time, he essentially rejected the Gaither report's call for dramatically increased defense spending. He decided that the level of spending required to implement the report's proposals would undermine the economy, necessitate economic controls, and harm individual freedoms by an eventual resort to a garrison state. He later, however, did accept some relatively minor enhancements, but he held the line against vastly increased defense spending in circumstances in which he could have easily relented.[86]

Eisenhower met on November 11 with McElroy and Quarles to discuss the FY59 defense budget. McElroy recommended a series of spending increases above the $38 billion base to improve the strategic forces and reaction time. Eisenhower accepted his recommendations, noting the $38 billion ceiling was not "sacrosanct." Combined with other cuts, he thought the defense budget could be kept between $39 billion and $39.5 billion.[87]

The Pentagon presented the FY59 Defense Department budget to the NSC on November 14. When Eisenhower realized that the Defense figures assumed it would continue working on two ICBMs (the *Titan* and *Atlas*) and two IRBMs (the *Jupiter* and *Thor*), he protested, opposing the production of large numbers of these missiles until they were proved effective through testing—an insistence he soon abandoned because of public opinion. Despite Eisenhower's complaints about the requested defense increases, he eventually accepted the budget, reasoning that one unbalanced budget would not create a problem. Eisenhower's willingness to accept increases in defense spending may have been influenced by a new intelligence estimate that the Soviets might have ten operational ICBMs by 1959, one hundred by 1960, and five hundred by 1961, with U.S. plans, calling for only twenty-four ICBMs in 1960 and sixty-five in 1961.[88]

A November 22 meeting on the FY59 defense budget concerned the issue of an additional $573 million to place an increased number of *Jupiter* and *Thor* IRBMs into production and to complete them at an earlier date.[89] With McElroy and Killian in attendance, Eisenhower opened the discussion saying that he "wanted to approach these [defense budget] proposals not on the basis of 'can we do it in response to public outcry,' but 'should we do it.' The matter is not one of justification, but rather of need." Although Eisenhower agreed to produce both missiles, he returned to his point that "we should not spend money simply because of public pressure, but should do what is based on real need."[90]

At a NSC meeting on November 22, the Defense Department presented its revised defense figures.[91] McElroy supported a decision to deploy one squadron of IRBMs by the end of 1958 to bolster the allies' morale. Dulles noted, however, that it was unlikely the Europeans could deploy missiles before the end of 1959 (the date he recommended). Although he did not mention it then, Dulles later told Eisenhower that he feared public and congressional fixation on spending on missile programs would undercut financial support for other necessary national security programs such as foreign military and economic aid.[92] Perhaps sensing that domestic pressure, despite the technological shortcomings, necessitated the acceleration of IRBMs, Eisenhower hinted that he would eventually relent to public opinion, saying "that when the Council had first become involved directly in the ballistic missiles programs he had expressed the opinion that the effect of ballistic missiles would be more important in the psychological area than in the area of military weapons."

A meeting of top administration officials discussed the acceleration of IRBMs on November 26 when Eisenhower was recovering from his stroke. In McElroy's view, "the chief reason for taking the action is psychological—to stiffen the confidence and allay the concern particularly of our own people. Militarily, the acceleration is not needed." When McElroy suggested that he announce the production of IRBMs the following day at the Senate preparedness hearings, Eisenhower's liaison with Congress, Wilton Persons, agreed, observing, "There is great pressure from the Congress to do this or something like it." Dulles resisted this line of action, maintaining that American bomber forces would be a strong enough deterrent during 1959 and 1960 even if the Soviets acquired nuclear missiles that could threaten Europe. He argued that the pressure for the missiles came not from the Europeans "but rather our own people, who feel exposed to attack for the first time." However, McElroy found public concern as reason enough for acceleration, as "this would tend to calm our people down." Dulles tried again to dissuade the group, suggesting that he "could get along much better in the foreign policy field with a full military aid program and a lower missile program than vice versa."[93] Despite Dulles's protests, because Eisenhower had approved the decisions, McElroy announced the decision to place the *Jupiter* and *Thor* into production the next day during his testimony at the Senate preparedness hearings.[94] A recovered Eisenhower led the American delegation to the NATO conference in mid-December, where his personal involvement in the proceedings and the IRBM commitment helped restore European confidence in the administration.[95]

Even though he rejected an excessive reaction to what he perceived as public panic, Eisenhower realized that public opinion had influenced his defense spending decisions. At a December 5 meeting with McElroy to approve the $1.26 billion in additional FY58 spending and a $39 billion FY59 defense budget, the notes record that

> the President said what he is really giving a lot of thought to is what is the figure that will create confidence. He thought that a feeling of greater confidence in the security sphere might go over into economic confidence as well, and thus help the economic picture. The President said that he thought that about two-thirds of the supplementary funds are more to stabilize public opinion than to meet [the] real need for acceleration, and Mr. McElroy agreed.[96]

Not only had Eisenhower increased defense spending, but he had approved the simultaneous production of both the *Thor* and the *Jupiter*, which he had long opposed. He also increased the number of planned IRBMs by the end of 1960 from 60 to 120 (by adding 60 *Jupiter* missiles to the planned deployment of 60 *Thor* missiles).[97] Eisenhower grudgingly took into account public opinion and even rationalized that the spending might help the faltering economy. Despite his reaction to public opinion, he believed that he had been restrained in light of the pressures for even greater spending, such as suggested by the Gaither report. Given the choice, Eisenhower accepted a relatively small increase in defense spending, which he believed was not militarily warranted, to reassure the public and head off possible greater increases which he felt would more seriously threaten the nation's economic health, his presidency, and possibly political freedoms.[98]

Although Eisenhower did react to public opinion on defense spending, he used the context of public opinion after *Sputnik* to press for reorganization of the Defense Department. That is, Eisenhower saw public opinion as a resource that he could use to press his case, pointing out that "the present feeling in the country supports some such change."[99] Eisenhower held a dinner with the JCS and secretaries of the military departments on November 4 to sound out the military on reorganization and to push their thinking in his direction, with public opinion as a prod.[100] He discussed his support for reorganization and admonished them to rise above interservice rivalries and "take the stance of soldier-statesmen." When Defense Department officials balked, Eisenhower insisted that he "wanted the American people to have a complete faith in the services" and that "the American public has lost a large measure of confidence in the services" because of interservice rivalries. According to the notes of the meeting, "The United States is disturbed over the security situation. He [Eisenhower] does not want to be complacent about it, or hysterical. But he thinks that our people now believe the services are more interested in the struggle with each other than against an outside foe."

Eisenhower also worked to build public support for reorganization, personally writing the portion of his State of the Union message on it.[101] He saw the speech as critical to forming public opinion on the subject and told Republican legislative leaders that although several instances of interservice rivalry had been revealed, he believed that "what is important is what [the] public thinks about it—so I devote several pages [of the State of the Union address] to what we intend to do."[102]

As Eisenhower pushed forward on reorganization, he also made certain that the administration was focusing on the education proposals. At a November 6 meeting on the education bill, Eisenhower stated that even though Congress would not pass a school construction bill, he felt that "it was necessary to get something new and in the present public mood."[103] At the November 15 cabinet meeting, HEW Secretary Marion Folsom presented a broad outline of the education bill, which included improvements in graduate schools, scholarships, and fellowships for college and graduate school students; aptitude testing of high school students; improvements in equipment for and the teaching of math and science in high schools; and improvements in teaching foreign languages.[104] Eisenhower later stated his belief "that anything you could hook on the defense situation would get by. He said 'I can't understand the United States being quite as panicky as they really are.'" Although he was not wholeheartedly enthusiastic about the proposal, it did meet his concerns about the education of future scientists. When the National Defense Education Act of 1958 was announced in late December, the most common reaction to the expanded four-year $884 million program was that it was too small.[105]

Unlike the education program, Eisenhower resisted efforts to commit large amounts of money to space research, since he feared it would be wasted on spurious research projects such as sending a rocket to the moon.[106] As a result, the administration did not seriously consider a new civilian-based government organization for space research until pressure from Congress forced the issue in January and February 1958.[107] The issue of whether the space agency should be in the Defense Department or be separate arose at the February 4 Republican legislative leaders' meeting.[108] After hearing Killian's outline of possible future exploration projects, the notes record Eisenhower as stating that he was "firmly of the opinion that a rule of reason had to be applied to these Space projects—that we couldn't pour unlimited funds into these costly projects where there was nothing of early value to the Nation's security."

Although Senator Knowland strongly favored being first with a lunar probe because of the psychological impact, Eisenhower did not "want to just rush an all-out effort on each one of these possible glamor [*sic*] performances without a full appreciation of their great cost." As this discussion reveals, the costs of the potential program and a focus on the defensive implications largely affected Eisenhower's views on space research and organizational options.

A month later on March 5, Killian presented the PSAC proposal for NASA to Eisenhower, saying that the limited nature of military space activity made necessary a civilian agency to handle the civil aspects and that the military would control defense-related space research.[109] Eisenhower relented. He reasoned that military aspects concerned the "application of knowledge," whereas most areas of basic "discovery" research, except ballistic missiles, were scientific rather than military in nature. Although not mentioned in the notes of the meeting, Killian's memorandum stressed civil interest in space exploration, along with "public and foreign relations considerations" as reasons for adopting separate civilian and military programs for space research.[110] The minimum estimated costs for the space exploration program were $275 million for the first year, reaching $650 million a year by 1965, as compared with some congressional proposals to spend upward of $1 billion in the next year.[111]

Policy Implementation

The administration worked throughout 1958 to secure the passage of its chosen policies in four areas. First, the administration gathered support for its defense budget and considered the Gaither report's recommendation for faster development of ICBMs. In response to congressional pressure, the administration chose to augment FY59 defense spending to purchase additional missiles. Second, the administration started a largely successful public information program to promote its defense reorganization plan. The third and fourth policies concerned the education program and NASA bill. Once the administration presented its proposals, most of the activity involved congressional wrangling over their exact form.

The political context at the end of 1957 and early 1958 provided more bad news for the administration. On December 20, a *Washington Post* article gave a mostly accurate version of the highly classified Gaither report, much to the administration's dismay.[112] The report's view of imminent danger and calls for increased spending and negative year-end press assessments of Eisenhower and the American global position further unsettled the public.[113]

Public opinion, however, remained fairly sanguine about the American position. A February 2 poll on the most important problem rated keeping the peace (30 percent) and economic problems (18 percent) highest. *Sputnik*/space problems (11 percent) and national defense (9 percent) were mentioned by one out of five respondents. Eisenhower had raised the importance of education (6 percent), and integration remained a concern for a much smaller percentage (4 percent) than in the November poll. A March 23 Gallup poll on the most important problem again pointed to factors other than *Sputnik*, with the following distribution: economic conditions (40 percent), keeping the peace (17 percent), *Sputnik*/space problems (7 percent), integration (4 percent), and defense (3 percent).[114] *Life* magazine asked the public to evaluate the administration's handling of defense, and 18 percent judged it as very good; 53 percent as fairly good; and 19 percent as poor (10 percent held no opinion). The most important problems were seen as catching up with the Russians in defense, producing more scientists, and taxes.[115]

At the January 3 cabinet meeting, both Eisenhower and Dulles observed that a Soviet ICBM capacity did not change near-term American security.[116] Eisenhower reasoned that Soviet ICBMs did not neutralize American bomber power, and Dulles added that the key was having "sufficient military power to deter aggression" rather than superiority. Since missiles constituted a change in the means of delivery (requiring greater attention to warning) but not in destructive capacity, Dulles thought the American deterrent remained robust.

As the administration began to discuss the Gaither report's recommendation to increase the planned ICBM force, Republican congressional leaders pressed the administration to calm the public. Noting the "defeatism" in the newspapers, the leaders urged Eisenhower to use his State of the Union address to make "a strong personal-type statement to inspire the trust and confidence of the American people." Eisenhower compared the situation with the gloom following Pearl Harbor and recalled how a speech he made in 1942 seemed "a very effective antidote."[117]

Eisenhower designed his State of the Union address, delivered on January 9, to provide the confidence-boosting statement about American defenses that the Republican leaders desired.[118] In the speech, he briefly reviewed the country's defense strengths and the administration's action to confront the Soviet threat and outlined several areas that required action, including defense reorganization, an accelerated defense effort, education, research, and a balanced budget.[119] Press and congressional reactions greeted the speech positively.[120] A week later, Dulles added his own comment, noting that *Sputnik* had "jolted the American people" and created "a wave of mortification, anger and fresh determination" that had led to "a more serious appraisal of the struggle" with the Soviets and "an increasing willingness to make the kind of efforts and sacrifices needed to win that struggle."[121]

Even as the administration attempted to reduce the pressure for increased defense spending, the demands for action continued. Eisenhower complained about the shifting sentiment in Congress on military spending, saying that whereas six months ago, "the Congress was a group of economizers and cut the budget," it now wanted to increase defense spending, even though the world threat remained the same. He concluded that the reason for this behavior was "the heat that comes on the Congress from the States."[122] In other words, Eisenhower saw Congress as worried about public opinion back home rather than national security.

Although the administration did feel the pressure for increased defense spending, the problem of projected Soviet missile developments continued. When Eisenhower learned that American solid-propellant ICBMs would not be ready until 1965/66, the administration had to face the question of how many of the quickly obsolete, liquid-fueled ICBMs (*Atlas* and *Titan*) to produce, given the projected Soviet capabilities. On March 10, he decided to wait to deploy solid-fueled ICBMs until mid-1965, when they would be perfected. In the meantime, the *Atlas* ICBM would be used until it could be replaced with the *Titan II* (which used an improved liquid fuel, allowing it to be stored in hardened silos). By using the *Titan II* as a transitional weapon, Eisenhower resisted the air force's pressure to accelerate the development of solid-fuel ICBMs (and accept the greater associated costs) and effectively provided for the shift from liquid- to solid-fueled missiles.[123]

Eisenhower remained concerned about public opinion and continued to attempt to control its influence, for two reasons. First, he feared that high defense spending would hurt the economy. On March 20, he commented to his brother Milton Eisenhower that he would "try to show [in a planned speech] what the enormous expenditures for defense are doing to our economy." Defense spending needed to be restrained "to keep this thing in the size a free economy can carry indefinitely."[124]

He also told Republican legislative leaders on March 25 that he was trying to "exert some reasonable control" and to reject calls based on "hysteria and demagoguery" for increased defense spending.[125] Second,
because he believed that high levels of defense spending could be maintained only in a crisis atmosphere such as that created by *Sputnik*, he
thought that the public would soon oppose higher defense spending,
thus creating a feast-or-famine cycle in defense spending he wished to
avoid. Eisenhower told Dulles he worried about

> the costs of relative security with the attendant possibilities of, either:
> (1). Seeing the American people get so tired of these huge expenditures
> as to cause them to refuse to support necessary appropriations and thus
> expose us to unacceptable risks. (2). Imposing on our people such politi-
> cal and economic controls as would imply a dangerous degree of regi-
> mentation. . . . I personally believe that one of the main objectives of our
> own efforts should be to encourage our entire people to see, with clear
> eyes, the changing character of our difficulties, and to convince them
> that we must be vigilant, energetic, imaginative and incapable of surren-
> der through fatigue or lack of courage. . . . A part of [the job of achieving
> reliable settlements with the Soviets] is educating and informing our
> own people—so that they will support every burden we must carry.[126]

Eisenhower continued to fight an increasingly difficult holding
action on defense spending. In the spring, the military departments
asked for a $10 billion augmentation to the FY59 program (a figure that
Eisenhower said indicated a lack of responsibility). The Defense
Department later pared down the request to an additional $1.6 bil-
lion.[127] Eisenhower claimed a "moral victory" after McElroy shaved an
additional $200 million off the augmentations, returning it to $1.6 billion after it had been increased again to $1.8 billion.[128]

At the April 24 NSC meeting, the administration returned to the
question of producing ICBMs and IRBMs.[129] Despite the military's
request, Eisenhower refused to increase beyond 130 the number of
ICBMs planned by the end of FY64. The military also requested an
increase to 180 in the number of liquid-fueled IRBMs from the December estimate of 120 missiles in 1960. Although the decision astonished
those in the room, Eisenhower approved the increase to 180 IRBMs but
noted that it "did not constitute the austerity program" he preferred.
The reasoning for this decision remains unclear, but Robert Divine
believed that Eisenhower chose to spend more than he wanted to
"hedge his bets" against a potential missile gap and go slow on the more

important solid-fueled missiles while averting the huge increases suggested by the Gaither report and the Democrats.[130]

Believing that too much defense spending could harm the nation's economy, Eisenhower continued to complain about congressional pressure, accusing Congress of planning to "kill every Russian three times."[131] But he eventually relented to this pressure on the condition that the new funds came in the form of new obligational authority rather than expenditures (which had to be spent in a particular year)—making it possible to spend the money only if necessary.[132] With this compromise, Eisenhower grudgingly approved Congress's $39.6 billion budget for FY59 appropriations ($815 million more than the administration request but $1 billion less than the Democrats wanted).[133] As he had previously, Eisenhower approved a relatively small amount more than he preferred (because of congressional pressure based on public opinion) in order to avoid spending a great deal more than he thought wise.

To complement this effort, Eisenhower hoped that his defense reorganization plan would reduce defense spending by eliminating waste and duplication. He had learned two things from the Truman administration's 1947 reform effort. First, Eisenhower felt Truman made a mistake by first deciding on the plan and then allowing public discussion. Instead, he thought that public discussion should come first or Truman should have at least pressed his case once having made the decision. Second, since Pentagon opposition could effectively scuttle any change, he saw agreement by the Defense Department as necessary for lasting reform.[134] Eisenhower had already felt "political heat" from newspaper reports for not moving fast enough and so urged McElroy to speed his advisory committee's consideration of policy specifics.[135]

Eisenhower influenced the Pentagon deliberations by ensuring that his PACGO representative attended all consultant meetings.[136] In fact, the PACGO continued to develop proposals for reorganization and to have them approved by Eisenhower. His representative then presented these proposals to the Pentagon committee, thus making sure that the president had previously approved many of the proposals eventually adopted.[137]

Given his strong feelings, Eisenhower said he was prepared "to lead, persuade, cajole and of course to some degree compel" the necessary action and at one point inserted himself into the process when he attended a Pentagon committee meeting, at the suggestion of an aide, to shift the balance away from the military.[138] At this meeting, Eisenhower pressed the military to act, pointing out that they could not "laugh off the present criticism," since "public opinion . . . is a strong force and must be respected."[139] Following these discussions, Eisenhower approved the Defense Department plan on March 27.[140]

To gain public support for his proposals, Eisenhower recognized the need to undertake an education campaign.[141] Accordingly, he gave a series of speeches to several different groups in which he stressed how much money defense reorganization would save.[142] In tandem with this effort, Eisenhower wrote to top business executives to enlist their support and encourage them to pressure Congress to support his reorganization plan.[143] As reports from Congress indicated, this letter-writing campaign prooured Congreoo to be more accepting of the administration's proposals, and after some congressional wrangling, Eisenhower eventually got most of what he wanted in the measure he signed on August 6.[144]

Eisenhower took a similar approach on the education bill. When Secretary Folsom reported that they had not encountered serious opposition, Eisenhower assumed that it "certainly was a good political move to put all [the] new [administration education proposals] into this security effort."[145] Eisenhower presented his four-year, $1 billion education program on January 27. The Congress eventually passed the bill in August, and Eisenhower signed it on September 2.

As with the education program, implementation of the NASA bill centered on congressional negotiations, and the administration tried to cool public and congressional expectations by outlining a moderate program.[146] In discussions with Congress, Eisenhower rejected early lunar probes to achieve a psychological advantage because of the costs, his desire to avoid a space race with the Russians, and his fear that concentrating on this might cause the United States to fall behind in other areas.[147] However, Eisenhower relented on March 24 to public pressure for a plan to reach the moon before the Soviets did when he approved the requests for space research funding.[148] As part of his attempt to limit expenditures, on March 26, he released the administration's plan for space exploration, entitled "Introduction to Outer Space," and asked the press to publish the paper (which it did) to ensure wide dissemination.[149] By emphasizing instrumented projects with no early goals, the administration hoped that the paper would relieve the public pressure for quick, costly achievements and for competition with the Soviets.[150] Despite a great deal of attention early on, Eisenhower's signing of the NASA bill on July 29 seemed to go unnoticed by much of the public.[151]

Variables

Assessments of the state of public opinion figured prominently in the administration's deliberations after *Sputnik*. Although Eisenhower feared that public opinion might persuade Congress to try to increase defense spending, he thought relatively little explanation could allay public concern and so sought at the October 9 press conference to convince the public that *Sputnik* required little corrective action. Although polling data and anecdotal reports suggest that public opinion remained fairly restrained, press and elite opinion remained inconsolable regarding *Sputnik's* possibly dire consequences. Given these reports, Eisenhower remained perplexed by what he perceived as the public's continuing concern with *Sputnik*, despite the country's defensive position and his assurances. In the face of this pressure, he attempted to channel public apprehension into directions that would be responsive to his security-oriented concerns and that might be difficult to achieve under other circumstances (reorganization, education) rather than into areas that he viewed as costly and unproductive (defense spending, space exploration).

To do this, Eisenhower embarked on a public information campaign to calm what he saw as continuing and irrational public hysteria about defense. Believing in his ability to lead the public (based on his public opinion beliefs), he thought he could combat the rising tide of skepticism with a series of speeches. The administration's satellite policy went hand in hand with this effort because he thought an orbiting satellite would reduce public concern and pressure for action. But as public anxiety built after *Sputnik II* and the December *Vanguard* failure, the need for an American satellite increased, forcing him to approve a backup satellite program and increase its defense priority. Fearing the Gaither report would panic the public into approving what he saw as needless defense spending, Eisenhower continued to try to generate public support for a steady defense program for the "long haul" rather than massive increases in response to Soviet achievements.

Soon after the Oklahoma speech, however, it became clear to Eisenhower that his efforts would not quiet the storm, and so he adjusted his policy. He increased defense spending, authorized the production of technologically questionable IRBMs, and approved the production of two types of IRBMs simultaneously—all of which he had previously opposed. Still, he resisted the greatly enlarged program recommended by the Gaither report because he feared that once the crisis had abated, public support would wane, causing a "feast-and-famine" cycle he greatly wanted to avoid.

This public pressure also affected the administration's position on space exploration research. Although Eisenhower initially wanted to leave such research in the Pentagon, at the prompting of his advisers, he soon relented to congressional (and possibly public opinion) pressure for a civilian agency but used this proposal to deflect attention from other, more costly alternatives.

Although the information on Dulles is not as extensive, he appeared to focus mostly on public relations, seeing the heightened public concern as an opportunity to galvanize American and world opinion behind the government's policy to combat the Soviet Union. Accordingly, he lectured the public on the need to react correctly to the threat and reasoned that *Sputnik* had performed a positive function by awakening the nation to the possible danger.

Other interests also played a prominent role in policy deliberations. The importance of missile and satellite programs for American national security, international prestige, and the size of the Soviet booster forced the administration to respond to *Sputnik*. But Eisenhower did not see a need for changes in the satellite program, defense spending, funding for R&D, or foreign policy. As a long-time proponent of the reorganization of the Defense Department to improve national security, he now found an opportunity to put his preferences into operation in the new public opinion climate. The information from the scientists on October 15 also confirmed in his mind the need for limited federal action to improve U.S. science and science education. Dulles, too, focused on national security concerns. Although he saw no need to alter the present defense program, he believed that *Sputnik* had created an atmosphere of domestic and world opinion more conducive to pursuing the policies he felt were necessary to win the Cold War.

At the same time, Eisenhower and Dulles feared that overreacting would harm national security. Eisenhower chose to create the position of special assistant for science and technology because of the SAC's recommendations in mid-October. He also rejected the Gaither report's recommendations because he felt the level of increased spending was unnecessary, given the threat, and would undermine the American economy and political freedoms. Dulles rejected the report's single-minded focus on the Cold War's military components to the exclusion of other factors (i.e., economic, political, and relations with allies) and feared the program would hurt the administration's foreign policy program. On IRBM programs, although he eventually relented, Eisenhower opposed procuring missiles before they were fully tested, so as to avoid waste, and preferred keeping the spending for missiles at the previously established pace because he thought bombers were a sufficient deterrent. Dulles rejected domestic public opinion as a reason for accelerating the missile program and concentrated instead on the allies' reactions (pointing to practical problems with the missiles' deployment) and the need to spend the money elsewhere (such as on mutual security programs).

Beliefs predictions suggested that Eisenhower would have attempted to lead the public to support the policy that best enhanced national security, but public opinion might have constrained his view in the face of unyielding opposition. Initially, national security drove his decisions across several issues, such as the speech program, defense spending, and defense reorganization, with references to public opinion in these discussions as predicted from beliefs. His statements reveal that he saw his efforts directed at either calming public opinion through public relations or persuading the public to support his policy preferences. He attempted to use the satellite effort to relieve pressure for policy adjustments and tried to generate support for defense reorganization and the education program. However, as the public's anxiety continued and his broader leadership efforts failed to help, he responded to public opinion by (1) approving the production of IRBMs, although he opposed it; (2) authorizing defense spending increases when he thought it unnecessary; (3) supporting a civilian space agency when he thought the Pentagon alone should control space research; and (4) accelerating the satellite program. Although upset about adopting these policies in reaction to public opinion, he saw them as necessary in the political context.

Although Eisenhower's behavior did not follow predictions, the influence of his public opinion beliefs still is evident. He reluctantly reacted to public opinion on both defense spending and the space agency and saw his actions in both these cases as the best possible alternatives. The defense increases he authorized were small relative to other options, especially compared with the Gaither report's recommendations. The space program he approved also cost much less than some congressional proposals. So even though Eisenhower responded to public opinion, he reacted in what he saw as the most minimal manner possible consistent with maintaining public confidence—an action congruent with his belief in the necessity of public support. Eisenhower's discernible reluctance suggests that although he found public opinion an irresistible force on these issues, his beliefs still affected his actions. In sum, he did not act happily against his normative beliefs about how foreign policy should be formulated. Even though this case does not completely support the beliefs predictions of his behavior, the evidence does show that Eisenhower's public opinion beliefs influenced his perceptions of policy.

Dulles's beliefs indicate that he would attempt to lead public opinion. Indeed, at first, Dulles focused on national security, worked to calm the public with reassuring statements, and saw an opportunity to build broader support for foreign policy. Later, he recommended to Eisenhower that he appeal to the public to avoid increased defense spending at the expense of other, less popular national security programs. He also pressed for deploying missiles in Europe because of the allies' reactions, voicing his strong opinions on national security in regard to defense spending, the Gaither report, and missile acceleration. In these cases, Dulles explicitly discussed public opinion and his fear that public attitudes might undermine the policies he believed best for national security. To remedy this potential problem, he suggested a public information program.

Although the influence of beliefs remained apparent throughout all decision stages, the beliefs model receives mixed support. Despite the fewer data for Dulles, his behaviors were consistent with the prediction that he would attempt to lead public opinion. Throughout these decisions, he discussed public opinion in line with his beliefs, which points to its *causal* influence.

For many decisions, Eisenhower's actions also were consistent with the prediction that he would try to influence public opinion. His initial policy responses were determined by his perception of the national interest, and he tried to mollify the public's concern. Since he thought about public opinion in reference to his powers of persuasion, these initial views suggest a *causal* influence of public opinion. During the policy selection and implementation stages, Eisenhower took a series of actions that yield a mixed coding. Although he continued to lead the public on some aspects of policymaking (with both a *consistent* and a *causal* influence), he did relent to public pressures on defense and space policy, which was *inconsistent* with beliefs predictions.

Coding the Influence of Public Opinion

Public opinion's influence in the *Sputnik* case study receives a mixed coding overall. This case is coded in the *lead category*, with a lesser *follow (moderate) category* coding. Decision makers tried to lead public opinion throughout the case. The administration's initial efforts were directed at developing the correct policy response to the threat (special adviser, education improvements, defense reorganization), generating support for those options, and calming the public with an education campaign. These persistent attempts suggest that the primary influence of public opinion is in the *lead category*. The *follow category* describes decision making in two policy areas: defense policy and space policy. Eisenhower eventually relented to the counsel of his advisers, who recommended he increase defense spending, accelerate IRBM programs, and create a civilian space agency, largely because of perceived public pressure. He also took action to speed the satellite program in late 1957 because of public opinion. The follow category influence is strong for defense spending during policy selection, moderate for satellite policy during policy selection, and moderate and mild for space policy during policy selection and implementation, a mixture that results in a ranking at the *moderate* level.

Realist views that decision makers should attempt to lead public opinion to support the policies they see as best for national security are supported by this case (see table 5.2). Eisenhower's decisions reflected this behavioral pattern, since he based his positions on his assessment of the national interest and tried to generate support for those policies on a range of issues. Although he reacted in the most minimal way he felt possible under the circumstances, his choices of defense and space policies do not support the realist perspective. On the other hand, Dulles's actions were consistent with realist predictions throughout the case.

TABLE 5.2 Influence Coding: Innovative Case

Predicted Public Influence			Actual Public Influence	Influence of Beliefs
REALIST	WILSONIAN LIBERAL	BELIEFS		
Lead	Follow	DDE: Lead / *Constrain*	Lead/with lesser Follow	DDE: Supportive/ Inconsistent
		JFD: Lead	(moderate)	JFD: Causal

Note: Italics indicate conditional predictions.

This case also supports the Wilsonian liberal view that decision makers are responsive to the public's concerns and choose policies the public prefers. Although Eisenhower initially resisted his advisers' recommendations to increase defense spending and bolster the space program because of public opinion, he eventually gave in to the public's demand. Given the magnitude of the perceived public concern (which historian John Lewis Gaddis suggests was surpassed only by Pearl Harbor and Korea in terms of surprising revealed threat), the fact that Eisenhower gave way only after considerable pressure confirms the strength of his desire to formulate policy based on national interests.[152]

Given the level of attention to public opinion and the range of information about it, linkage processes can be found in a number of avenues. Anticipated opinion affected projections of public support for several policies (education bill, defense reorganization, defense spending). Perception of the opinion context was perhaps the strongest component of public opinion, with decision makers developing strong views about the state of public opinion ("hysterical" and "panicked"). Specific indicators of opinion also appeared in decision making, with references to newspaper articles and congressional viewpoints seen as representative of public opinion.

Despite all the information and examination of public opinion, perhaps the most striking aspect of decision makers' perceptions of the opinion context is the disjuncture between these perceptions and the polling data, especially immediately after the launch of *Sputnik*. Although newspapers were filled with comments bordering on the "hysterical," the polling data suggest that the public remained fairly subdued. The people largely accepted the administration's explanation and ranked other concerns higher, but the media and elites became obsessed with *Sputnik*, and newspapers portrayed an agitated public. This media sentiment, disconnected from the public's view, filtered into the decision-making process by creating the impression of a much greater public opinion problem than actually existed, at least right after *Sputnik*.

As a result, the decision makers' perceptions did not accurately reflect the public's views, as the people became concerned about national security only after the relentless onslaught of media attention. It is not that objective indicators of public sentiment were not available—they were. But in this instance, the government's reaction to public opinion stemmed from its reading of elite sentiments, which were assumed to reflect the public mood.

Only Eisenhower's resolve, shaped in part by his public opinion beliefs, in the face of constant political pressure, prevented a more costly and potentially damaging response to *Sputnik*. Eisenhower's shortcoming lay not in his policy response to *Sputnik*—which adequately addressed the nation's security concerns—but in his failure, over time, to quell the mounting media and subsequent public apprehension regarding national security. His failure to do so stems directly from his confidence in his own ability to lead public opinion to support his view of the foreign policy problem—a view attributable to his public opinion beliefs. In the end, his ineffective leadership effort on this general front forced him to compromise on several issues in response to a more developed public concern. Unlike the case of *Sputnik*, in which Eisenhower's perception of public opinion pushed him to adjust his policies, the next case, regarding the New Look defense policy, reveals that Eisenhower's perceptions of the steps necessary to get public support for a new strategic policy eventually caused him to adopt a major new strategic policy that he had initially opposed, in order to justify his efforts to reshape defense spending.

CHAPTER SIX

The Deliberative Context

Leadership and Limitations in the
Formulation of the New Look

The "New Look" national strategy adopted in late 1953 constituted an important shift in the U.S. definition of its national security goals and means.[1] Unlike the previous Truman strategy NSC-68, which gave higher priority to military security, the new approach deemed both economic and military security as equally important national interests. By emphasizing airpower and nuclear weapons, the New Look justified significant personnel reductions in the navy and particularly the army. In the long term, the strategy envisioned ground troops being slowly relocated from overseas bases to a central mobile and flexible reserve in the continental United States. Policymakers believed that these moves would achieve significant fiscal savings in the defense budget and contribute to the administration's efforts to adjust defense programs for the "long haul," a concept signifying the belief that the conflict with the Soviet Union would last a number of years. Previous planning under NSC-68 embodied the notion of a "critical year" in which open hostilities with the Soviet Union were thought most likely. The military used the critical year as a planning date to build up capabilities to counter the threat in that year. The shift in planning from a "year" of danger to an "age" of danger thus created potential savings, since defense expenditures could be stretched out over a longer period.

The New Look had its origin in Eisenhower's 1952 presidential campaign, which centered on four issues: Korea, communism, corruption, and lower federal government spending. After his election but before he took office, Eisenhower and his advisers began considering what he called the "great equation"—providing national security at an affordable cost. Although he remained largely noncommittal on the specific policies to reach this goal, he believed that reductions in Defense Department "waste" could largely achieve his objectives. Eisenhower's initial efforts to wring cuts from the FY54 budget ignited opposition from both Democrats, who complained about massive cuts, and Republicans, who pressed for more reductions. After meeting this stiff resistance in early 1953, he concluded that a more extensive reevaluation of the military was necessary to achieve his fiscal goal. Thus, he launched a broad study of national security, or "basic national security policy," as the administration referred to it, by the NSC and instigated a military strategy review by the JCS. Eisenhower then used these reviews to generate policy ideas and build an internal consensus on policy goals and means.

The NSC effort, designated "Project Solarium" (for the White House sun room where the meeting that originated the study was held), considered several alternative paths in the summer of 1953, ranging from then current containment policy to a rollback of communism. Eisenhower also appointed a new Joint Chiefs of Staff to reconsider American defense plans during the summer of 1953. The administration completed the new national strategy, NSC 162/2, in October, which incorporated the JCS's recommendations (identifying American overextension as the principal problem and calling for the redeployment of American forces from overseas). The new strategy identified the capacity for massive retaliation with nuclear weapons as the primary deterrent to war. Following the adoption of NSC 162/2, the JCS developed a new military strategy based on this new national strategy. This new military strategy provided significant fiscal savings, reduced personnel, and relied on airpower and nuclear weapons to offset these cuts. In January 1954, the administration presented the new military strategy and its FY55 budget to the nation (which partially implemented NSC 162/2), and Congress passed it largely intact in June. Eisenhower thus believed that he had adopted an approach to national security that provided both significant savings and a sustainable defense posture over the long term.[2]

My analysis found that public opinion had no influence on Eisenhower's determination to reduce defense spending, which he thought was necessary because of his economic philosophy. As Eisenhower pondered how he would cope with the issue, public opinion limited the options he considered and persuaded him to formulate a new strategy in order to justify the spending reductions. To persuade the public to support the new strategy, Eisenhower decided that he must head off internal government opposition to his defense reductions and so initiated the strategic reviews to build this consensus. Although policymakers considered public opinion while they developed policy options, their attention centered mainly on whether and how to lead the public to support the policies the government would eventually adopt. Because Eisenhower believed that he needed an internal consensus on the new strategy to gain public support, he accepted the policy outcome of the strategic review (reliance on nuclear weapons), even though he had significant misgivings about it. By influencing Eisenhower's choice of the process by which he would develop the new strategy, public opinion placed a broad constraint on the eventual national strategy chosen. After reaching a decision, the administration was able to persuade the public to support the new strategy and budget.

Realist and Wilsonian liberal views portray public opinion's influence in this context differently. Given the long decision time and anticipation, the realists suggest that decision makers would have used this opportunity to lead the public. But they concede that public opinion might have limited decision makers in a pernicious manner, since the extended decision time might have allowed the public to mobilize and influence policy. For this reason, the primary prediction of the realist view is for decision makers to act consistently with the *lead category*. A secondary influence of the *constrain category* is also implied.

Wilsonian liberals predict that given the extended decision time, public opinion would become an important influence on policy. Since this added time was adequate for public opinion about policy options to develop, be ascertained by the government, and influence policy, these proponents would expect public opinion to affect policy as described in the *follow category*.

Beliefs predictions suggest slightly different behavior for Eisenhower and Dulles. Eisenhower would have attempted to lead public opinion, since the extended decision time would have given him confidence in his ability to formulate an effective leadership program to build public support. Because of his belief in the necessity of public support, he still might have been constrained by public opinion if he perceived the public's opposition as immovable. Dulles would have acted consistently with the lead category, since the long decision time would have provided him the time he thought necessary to obtain public support. The one exception to this prediction would have been if the decision involved broad foreign policy goals, particularly as featured in the previous election. In this case, if Dulles perceived that the 1952 election revealed the public's preferences regarding these broad foreign policy objectives, he would have been constrained by public opinion or followed it.

During this case, public opinion affected decision making mostly according to the *lead category,* with a lesser influence from the *moderate constrain category.* For the most part, the realist perspective is accurate, since when decision makers considered public opinion, they did so with an eye toward leading the public to support the policy that they thought best. Although the need for a new strategy to persuade the public to accept the spending cuts restricted the decision makers, realists' expectations account for this form of limitation. However, realists' predictions are incorrect regarding the process by which this influence occurs. Although they expect that a mobilized public might constrain decision makers, the public stayed fairly subdued throughout the policy's formulation. Instead, decision makers were reined in by their anticipation of the public's reaction rather than a mobilized public. Except for Dulles's choices when forming his view of the issue, the Wilsonian liberal perspective is not supported, since decision makers did not follow public opinion. Although at times the decision makers adopted policies that were consistent with public opinion, process tracing reveals that they preferred these policies for other reasons.

The beliefs variable is supported in this decision context, and the influence of Eisenhower's beliefs is coded as a *supportive* influence. He expressed a desire to lead public opinion throughout the decision making and acted almost entirely consistently with this view. Because of concerns related to the necessity of public support, he was limited by public opinion in his choice of pursuing the strategic review and in accepting the policy that he had previously opposed that the strategic review produced. Dulles also acted consistently with his beliefs throughout this case, and their effect is coded as a *supportive* influence. In addition to favoring leadership of public opinion, his beliefs had a causal influence on his behavior when he suggested a broad review of American strategic policy because of the previous election results.

Problem Representation: Setting the Agenda

The impetus for reconsidering the nation's defense strategy originated with Eisenhower. Long before he entered office, he had become an advocate of reformulating American defense strategy and reconsidering its assumptions, because he feared the high defense spending and budgetary imbalances fostered by the Truman administration would harm economic security and the American position over the long term. For example, on December 11, 1952, while still president of Columbia University, Eisenhower stressed that defense policy must be sustainable over the long term as well as being capable of coping with crisis circumstances.[3] Writing in his diary on January 22, 1952, he saw large national deficits as a significant threat to the nation's economic welfare because they stifled initiative and caused high inflation. The expense of defense preparations, he reasoned, must be weighed against the long term internal cost of excessively high military budgets and deficits. Recalling America's history of neglecting the military in peacetime and then rapidly expanding it when confronted with a crisis, he felt that a more balanced policy was necessary to smooth out these precipitous surges and declines. In his view, the nation was on the "horns of a dilemma" consisting of "the danger of internal deterioration through the annual expenditure of unconscionable sums on a program of indefinite duration," on the one side, and the outside threat from the Soviet Union, on the other. To achieve a balance between these perils, Eisenhower wanted to cut the military budget to a level sustainable over the long term while maintaining the necessary military strength.[4]

Eisenhower committed himself to this view during the 1952 presidential campaign. At a September 12, 1952, meeting with Senator Robert Taft (R, Ohio), the leader of the conservative right wing of the Republican Party, Eisenhower agreed to cut the FY54 and FY55 budgets, especially defense spending, and provide tax cuts.[5] His September 25, 1952, campaign speech on defense policy reflected this meeting: "We must achieve both security and solvency. . . .[national security spending] is where the largest savings can be made. And these savings must be made without reduction of defensive power." He hoped to make these reductions through better management and planning.[6]

After winning the election, when returning from a campaign-promised trip to Korea on December 9–11 aboard the cruiser USS *Helena*, Eisenhower met with his close advisers to debate the "great equation." Their discussions led to the conclusion that the administration needed to end the Korean War honorably and to formulate a defense concept consonant with the long-haul conception.[7] Foreshadowing his future policy stance, Dulles stressed the importance of the "will and capability of reprisal at times, places and means of our choosing."[8]

Following the *Helena* discussions, Eisenhower wanted to build support for his policy both in Washington and in the public. He outlined his goals in a December 29 memorandum that he used as a basis for discussion with Senate leaders. He reiterated that the first objective must be to balance the budget, after which further reductions could be offset by tax decreases. Regarding defense, he recalled his campaign pledge to appoint a civilian group to study the workings of the Defense Department to achieve savings involving: "national purposes, problems and objectives—a field that can be termed *strategic*, in the broadest sense of that word."[9] In his February 2, 1953, State of the Union address, Eisenhower outlined his objective to "achieve adequate military strength in the limits of endurable strain on our economy" and insisted that "to amass military power without regard to our economic capacity would be to defend ourselves against one kind of disaster by inviting another."[10] Echoing his discussion with the senators a month before, he wanted to achieve the balance mainly by integrating programs and eliminating waste and duplication.

The administration soon realized, however, that the desired defense cuts would not be forthcoming without a major revision in strategy. At the February 24, 1953, NSC meeting, Secretary of Defense Charles Wilson reported that very little could be "squeezed" out of the Truman defense budget unless the administration was willing to consider either a new national strategy or a slower achievement of its objectives.[11] At the NSC meeting the next day, Eisenhower announced that he had decided to appoint "a committee of distinguished Americans . . . to participate in [the administration's] review of basic national security policies." As he envisioned at the end of December when he discussed the creation of such a group with Senate leaders, the cost of defense programs would constitute the central focus of the committee's deliberations.[12]

On another front, at the March 4 NSC meeting, Director of the Budget Joseph Dodge presented the proposed fiscal limits on the budgets of government departments, including the Defense Department. He reported that Truman's $44 billion estimate for FY55 military expenditures needed trimming by $9.4 billion to $34.6 billion.[13] The Defense

Department was directed to submit estimates of program revisions to meet these fiscal requirements and their effect on national security policies and objectives.

Problem Representation: Defining the Situation

Early in the FY54 budget process, Eisenhower still believed that he could make most of the defense cuts by reducing waste. He commented in regard to defense savings at a March 6 cabinet meeting, "I simply KNOW there are savings to be made. One thing I know too well is [the military's] luxurious use of personnel and facilities—plenty can be cut there."[14] The perceived difficulty in reaching these goals soon increased, however.

In their March 19 report to Wilson, the Joint Chiefs of Staff (chaired by Army General Omar Bradley) described the grim consequences if the administration implemented the FY54 and FY55 cuts outlined in the March 4 NSC meeting. Any reductions in the previous Truman budget projections would "increase the security risk to the United States beyond the dictates of national prudence." The limits suggested at the March 4 meeting "would so increase the risk to the United States as to pose a grave threat to the survival of our allies and the security of this nation."[15]

The Joint Chiefs presented this report at the March 25 NSC meeting. After their presentation, Eisenhower revealed his exasperation with their views by impatiently commenting that maybe a study was needed to determine whether national bankruptcy or national destruction would occur first. Although some of the meeting's participants suggested possible tax increases to fund the military, Eisenhower rejected this viewpoint out of hand. Probably with conservative congressional Republicans in mind, Eisenhower felt that the administration would face a terrific problem with Congress if he asked for tax increases instead of reductions. He expressed some irritation with the American public's view of taxes, noting that people were "yelling about the burden of their taxes." He felt it "extraordinarily difficult to get Americans to see clearly the relationship between a balanced budget and decreased taxes, on the one hand, and the threat to national security, on the other." Even though he wanted defense cuts, he clearly felt pressure from the JCS's dire assessment to maintain the current level of defense spending. As it stood, the administration remained, in Eisenhower's words, on the "horns of a dilemma" between making cuts the JCS would inevitably oppose or keeping spending at a level the nation could sustain only at the cost of continued deficits or tax increases.[16]

On March 31, Eisenhower attempted to gain some leverage when the civilian consultants presented their report on national security policy. They decided that defense expenditures could be reduced without threatening American security and that both continued budget deficits and/or increased taxes would harm the economy. To resolve this problem, they suggested reconsidering defense policy and military costs.[17]

Although Eisenhower agreed with this assessment, he felt that balancing the budget in one fell swoop was not feasible, since the government could not "suddenly cut off our developing policies and programs for national security." Instead, he wanted to show the public that the administration was moving in the direction of a balanced budget and that any failure to reach this goal could be blamed on previous Truman policies. Dismissing the suggestion to remove some American troops from Europe to save money, Eisenhower and Dulles believed that they could not pull a single division out of Europe at that time because the troops were an important physical and psychological deterrent to Soviet aggression. However, Eisenhower looked favorably on Wilson's suggestion that by adopting a "floating D-day" (instead of a specific date for readiness), expenditures could be cut significantly over time.[18]

On April 29, Eisenhower approved a new statement on basic national security policy, NSC 149/2, which placed greater emphasis on the need for gradually balancing the budget and abandoned the use of a crisis year for defense planning. Although the final budget would still run deficits in both expenditures and new obligational authority, the level of the projected shortfalls was cut significantly from the Truman estimates.[19]

The administration presented this budget and defense program to the Republican legislative leadership on April 30.[20] Based on NSC 149/2, Eisenhower underscored the dual threat to national security internally from economic and budgetary pressures and externally from the Soviet Union. In response to the presentation, Senator Robert Taft expressed his agitation at what he perceived as the lack of progress on the budgetary front. Claiming that in the public's mind, the Eisenhower revisions were no different from the Truman budget it replaced, he claimed that the result of the administration's proposed program would be large deficits or new taxes, either of which would doom future Republican electoral prospects in Congress in 1954 and in the presidential election in 1956. To resolve this problem, Taft recommended a complete resurvey of national security policy to enable more cuts in the FY55 budget.

Eisenhower became quite upset by Taft's attacks on the proposed budget reductions. After months of "sweat and study," Eisenhower defended the revisions, saying that though he felt it important to reverse the upward trend in expenditures, his proposed budget would not be "ruinous to Republican prospects in 1954."[21] He felt he could not endanger national security by approving an inadequate program and proclaimed, "No one should let budget-cutting principle override national security." They might eventually get national security expenditures to the area of $35 billion where Taft wanted them, but Eisenhower insisted that if the administration were "suddenly [to] abandon" the defense program, "we would scare our people to death."[22]

In the next few weeks, the situation crystallized for Eisenhower and his administration. At a May 1 cabinet meeting, Secretary of the Treasury George Humphrey estimated that in order to achieve the tax reductions they wanted, the administration must first end the Korean conflict and then develop a completely new military posture.[23] In addition to pressure from the Republicans for more cuts, the administration also became concerned about possible Democratic assertions that the proposed cuts would endanger national security.[24]

As pressure on both sides mounted, members of the administration considered reevaluating the national strategy. On May 2, Secretary of State John Foster Dulles invited CIA Director Allen Dulles, Undersecretary of State Bedell Smith, speech writer C. D. Jackson, and Special Assistant to the President for National Security Affairs Robert Cutler to his house to discuss his views concerning "a thorough overhaul of the prior Administration's basic national security policy." John Foster Dulles suggested, "Shouldn't we tackle a policy statement to fulfill our campaign ideas? I conceive three possible alternatives to choose from or to combine in part some way or another. To begin is the important thing." The group viewed Dulles's ideas favorably, with Cutler advising that they approach Eisenhower with the concept and Smith recommending a staff review of Dulles's options.[25]

On May 8, 1953, Eisenhower met with the May 2 group in the White House solarium. Dulles outlined the challenges facing the United States in very drastic terms. He argued that time was working against the United States and that the Soviets presented "the most terrible and fundamental" threat to the West since the invasion of Islam in the tenth century. He warned that the present defensive policy would lead to disaster because it would eventually result in the piecemeal destruction of the free world, economic bankruptcy, and the loss of the support of the Congress and American people. To avoid such a disaster, he advocated the development of a new approach to national security. The administration, he contended, should institute a study to consider the advantages and disadvantages of three possible alternatives: (1) publicly drawing a global line and notifying the Soviets that if one country on the American side fell to communism (from external aggression or internal uprising), it would mean war between the United States and the Soviet Union; (2) drawing a regional line and notifying the Soviets that if one nation fell, the United States would "take measures of our own choosing"; and (3) winning back areas already controlled by the communists. Although American allies might "shudder" at the alternatives, Dulles believed that "people look to the new Administration to appraise the alternatives and see if there is not some different way."[26] Eisenhower supported the three-task-force concept, noting that it was important to convince "ourselves and our friends" and the congressional leaders of the "rightness of the course adopted." He agreed with Humphrey's position that the present policy was "sapping our strength" and "leading to disaster" and that something had to be done "or the American people will turn against us."[27]

Eisenhower remained torn. He "desperately" wanted to win the 1954 congressional elections.[28] Although they disagreed on the timing, Taft's comments at the April 30 meeting had reinforced Eisenhower's desire for budget reductions and tax cuts. The policy to reach this goal remained elusive, however. Increasing taxes to reduce the budget deficit was philosophically and politically untenable for Eisenhower. On the contrary, he strongly wished to lower taxes and had promised to do so but would not until the United States was "reasonably secure" against the Soviet threat.[29] He found his initial attempt at reductions while maintaining security in March hindered by strident JCS opposition. As Dulles and he noted at the March 31 NSC meeting, large reductions in aid to the European allies or the removal of troops from overseas were seen as unacceptable, given the psychological damage and political ramifications that such a move might cause. As indicated at the April 30 meeting, he ruled out an abrupt shift in military strategy or the defense budget because of the potential public reaction to such a dramatic move. To add to these difficulties, the Democrats continued to criticize Wilson for the limited (in light of the reductions under consideration) defense cuts in the FY54 budget. These factors contributed to what Eisenhower called the "near impossibility of major reductions in the budget in the face of the psychology of the country which insists on maintaining the great obligations contracted in bygone times of peace, and also approves of huge defense expenditures."[30]

Eisenhower also thought the public could be persuaded to support the administration's position on the timing of balancing the budget and tax cuts. Unlike Taft, he felt the public would respond to the argument that national security should take precedence over balanced budgets (which could be achieved progressively over a number of years).[31] Even though Taft felt that immediate tax reductions were necessary to win the 1954 elections, Eisenhower believed the public could be persuaded to support the Republicans in the 1954 election if tax cuts were made at least in the FY55 budget.[32] He noted in his June 1 diary entry:

> I believe that the American public wants security ahead of tax reduction and that while we can save prodigious sums in the Defense Department without materially hurting our security, we cannot safely, this year, knock out enough to warrant an immediate tax reduction. . . . But I do believe that we can make sufficient reductions this year to show the American people that we are doing a sensible and sane and efficient job, and win an election next year on the record of economy, efficiency, and effective security. With consistent attention to these matters, I believe that we can cut government expenditures far enough to justify real tax reductions for the fiscal year '55.[33]

Poll results from earlier in the year support Eisenhower's analysis of the public's view. The public favored balancing the budget first. A March 1953 Gallup poll asked: "Some members of Congress argue that federal income taxes should be cut 10 percent beginning this July 1. Others argue that income taxes should not be cut until the budget is balanced. With which side do you agree?" Sixty-nine percent said balance the budget first, 25 percent supported cutting taxes first, and 6 percent had no opinion. The June and August 1953 polls found the same sentiment. The public may have wanted a balanced budget and tax cuts, but it also favored the current size of the military. A September 1953 poll asked: "Do you think too much of the taxes you pay is being spent for defense—or is too little being spent for defense?" Forty-five percent said the spending was about right, 20 percent saw it as too much, and 22 percent viewed it as too little.[34]

Option Generation

The administration developed its policy options between May and October 1953 through a two-track process. The May 8 solarium room meeting led to the creation of three task forces considering American national strategy, under the code name Project Solarium, which eventually resulted in the New Look's integrated national strategy statement NSC 162/2. The Defense Department and Joint Chiefs used this paper to guide both their December New Look military strategy, JCS 2101/113, and the FY55 budget. The second track instructed the newly appointed JCS to reconsider American military strategy during the summer of 1953, whose results were eventually integrated into NSC 162/2.

At the May 8 solarium room discussion, Eisenhower directed the three task forces to examine the alternatives of containment, deterrence, and rollback and to present their conclusions in terms of the "goal, risk, cost in money and men and world relations."[35] The instructions defined alternative A as the status quo policy of containment originally adopted by the Truman administration and accepted by Eisenhower in NSC 149/2.[36] Alternative A focused on maintaining "over a sustained period armed forces to provide for the security of the United States and to assist in the defense of vital areas of the free world," without risking general war. Alternative B, the deterrence option, would draw a line in the world around the Soviet bloc "beyond which the U.S. will not permit Soviet or satellite military forces to advance without general war." Finally, the rollback position, alternative C, would, at the risk of general war, "increase efforts to disturb and weaken the Soviet bloc and . . . create the maximum disruption and popular resistance throughout the Soviet bloc" to force the Soviets to concentrate on defending their possessions rather than further expansion.[37]

After more than a month of study, the three task forces presented their final reports at an expanded, full-day NSC meeting on July 16. At the end of the presentations, Eisenhower gave his analysis: "If you demand of a free people over a long period of time more than they want to give, you can obtain what you want only by using more and more controls; and the more you do this, the more you lose the individual liberty which you are trying to save and become a garrison state." He warned that the central problem was how to meet the threat posed by the Soviet Union without at the same time bankrupting the nation or sacrificing the system of government. On the domestic side, he commented, "If we are to obtain more money in taxes, there must be a vigorous campaign to educate our people—and to educate the people of our allies."[38]

On July 30, the NSC considered the task forces' reports and a memorandum on a new basic national security policy by Cutler based on his effort to provide a unified policy statement.[39] Noting that he was essentially creating task force D to combine the other task force reports, Eisenhower instructed the interagency NSC Planning Board to draft a new basic national security policy based on Cutler's memorandum and the July 30 discussion. The final modified memorandum and instructions for the Planning Board incorporated ideas from each task force, although it rejected the goals of task force C's liberation concept.[40] It directed the Planning Board members to formulate a policy based on the creation of, at the lowest possible cost, a strong retaliatory offensive capability, a continental defense capability, and a sufficient mobilization base. This Planning Board's report became NSC 162, which the NSC discussed on October 7.

In conjunction with Project Solarium and spurred by the Republican congressional leadership's suggestions in late April, Eisenhower decided on May 7 to appoint a new JCS to examine the country's military strategy and structure.[41] Political considerations—particularly the criticism he was receiving at the time from the Democrats for making too many defense cuts—drove his decision to have the new JCS perform a policy review that would both allay criticism that the cuts in the FY54 budget were jeopardizing security and lay the groundwork for cutting the FY55 budget.[42] This study, Eisenhower hoped, would assure the Congress and public that any defense cuts would be made on the basis of national security rather than fiscal austerity.

The Joint Chiefs submitted their assessment of military policy to Secretary of Defense Wilson on August 8. They warned that the United States had overcommitted itself to areas of peripheral importance and had dangerously overstretched its forces. To rectify this situation, the chiefs recommended placing first priority on "the essential military protection of our Continental U.S. vitals and the capability for delivering swift and powerful retaliatory blows." In addition, the United States should begin to withdraw its forces from peripheral overseas positions (including Europe) into a mobile reserve (in the United States), coupled with a statement indicating a "clear positive policy with respect to the use of nuclear weapons."[43]

The NSC discussed the JCS's report during its August 27 meeting (Eisenhower did not attend). When the JCS Chair Admiral Arthur

Radford indicated that the report foresaw a review of the American relationship with NATO, Dulles noted that such a troop withdrawal would mean the United States would have to place greater reliance on airpower and nuclear weapons. Although domestic opinion would be "delighted" by the proposal, Dulles warned of a "grave disaster" if not enough time were allowed to "prepare" foreign opinion on the subject. He feared that the allies would not be capable of increasing their defense budgets to compensate for a complete American withdrawal. Given their apprehension about a return to Fortress America, the United States needed to avoid a position that would either undermine free-world cohesion or completely shift the defense burden onto itself. In deference to Dulles's worries, the NSC decided to recommend to Eisenhower that the secretary of state consider the foreign policy implications of adopting that course of action.[44]

On September 2, Cutler briefed Eisenhower on the meeting, and he approved the NSC's recommendation, adding, "This concept is a crystallized and clarified statement of this administration's understanding of our national security objectives since World War II." Cutler also reported that Eisenhower "reiterated several times that the concept was not new; must and could not properly be thought of or mentioned as new." He told Cutler that "from the beginning," the stationing of American troops abroad was seen as a "temporary expedient" and he assumed that allied forces "would be able to hold vital areas with indigenous troops until American help could arrive." Eisenhower's favorable reaction to the redeployment concept at the core of the JCS report indicated a shift in his thinking from earlier in the year when he rejected redeployment because of concern over the allies' reaction.[45]

While the Solarium and JCS projects proceeded, other developments revealed the evolution of the administration's thinking on national strategy, defense strategy, and the FY55 budget. Pressure continued on Eisenhower to reduce taxes. In response to a friend who suggested that the Republicans *should* lose the Congress if they did not cut taxes, Eisenhower replied that he knew this sentiment was shared by "millions of Republicans." But he felt compelled to eliminate the deficit first by cutting spending, or the nation would face the economically debilitating prospect of continued high deficits and inflation. Although the public continually pressed him in letters for tax reductions, regardless of the deficit, Eisenhower said he would still balance the budget first: "So I spend my life trying to cut expenditures, balance the budget, and then get at the *popular* business of lowering taxes."[46]

In a September 6 memorandum to Eisenhower, Dulles again underscored his view of the current strategic problem faced by the United States and his apprehension over the possible troop pullback. Dulles argued objectively that American self-interests would best be supported by placing more emphasis on nuclear weapons, continental defense, the redeployment of troops back to the United States, and budgetary and monetary stability. Nonetheless, "the NATO concept is losing its grip" because the growing Soviet nuclear force was undercutting American nuclear superiority. This raised the prospect that the United States' vulnerability to nuclear attack might prevent it from aiding Europe or cause Europe to decide to stay out of a conflict between the United States and Soviet Union. Given this situation, Dulles felt that the August 8 JCS policy that stressed these components would be seen in Europe as the final proof of the United States' return to isolation and would destroy the alliance. Because the United States would then have to rely on itself completely for defense, the end result would be less security at a higher cost. Instead, Dulles outlined a program for a reduction of tensions with the Soviet Union, a mutual withdrawal of forces from Europe, and the creation of a strategic reserve in the continental United States that would enable a fiscally sustainable force level. This end would be accomplished through a series of nuclear and conventional arms control agreements, the opening of East-West trade, an understanding on Soviet satellites (politically free but friendly to the Soviet Union), and the Soviets' renunciation of their goal of world revolution.[47]

In his September 8 response, Eisenhower noted his general agreement with Dulles's points, especially those regarding efforts to reduce world tensions and a possible mutual troop withdrawal from Europe. In addition, he did not think it wise to place more reliance on nuclear weapons and stated that any troop withdrawal from Europe that implied a change in "*basic* intent" would "cause real turmoil abroad." Eisenhower felt that "programs for informing the American public, as well as other populations, are indispensable if we are to do anything except to drift aimlessly, probably to our own eventual destruction." He believed that even though the public wanted tax reductions, they did not understand the security implications of such a move. Consequently, "if we are to attempt [a] real revision in policies—some of which may temporarily, or even for a very extended time, involve us in vastly increased expenditures, we must begin now to educate our people in the fundamentals of these problems." Even the adoption of a well-thought-out defense program that was approved unanimously by "the President, the Cabinet, and the bipartisan leaders of the Congress would not, in themselves, be sufficient to assure the accomplishment of the resulting objectives. *We must have the enlightened support of Americans* and the informed understanding of our friends in the world." Eisenhower concluded that the government must first decide on its program, and then "a carefully thought out program of speeches, national and international conferences, articles and legislation would be in order."[48]

Eisenhower's negative reaction to the idea of further reliance on nuclear weapons was not new. He had long harbored suspicions about the viability of relying to a greater extent on the threat of massive retaliation with nuclear weapons to prevent Soviet aggression, and he had communicated these doubts to Dulles even before becoming president. After reading an advance copy of Dulles's 1952 article "A Policy of Boldness" in which he proposed a policy of massive retaliation, Eisenhower expressed his feeling that although he found the cost savings attractive, the policy would fail to confront all sources of Soviet aggression.[49] In a letter later that year, Eisenhower emphasized though the policy might be able to meet the Soviet military threat, other political, economic, and spiritual efforts were necessary to confront the Soviet political threat.[50]

Once in office, Eisenhower's doubts continued. On March 6, 1953, he observed that a policy emphasizing nuclear weapons as the decisive factor in world politics "ignores completely the facts of world politics, the whole matter of allied nations. . . .This whole idea that the bomb is a cheap way to do things is wrong."[51] At his April 30 meeting with the legislative leaders, he rejected Taft's call for greater reliance on airpower and insisted that relying on the "threat of reprisal by bombing" would not provide security. He felt that the United States needed to maintain strength in all areas or it would face "the danger of Russia taking [American allies] over gradually without having to fight."[52] Eisenhower repeated this view in public at his May 14 press conference: "For example, one extremist believes that merely in the fear of retaliation is safety. I doubt that many believe in that extreme view."[53] Although he was tempted by the cost savings of massive retaliation, he found the merits of the policy lacking.

The core problem confronting the United States remained. At the September 24 NSC meeting, Eisenhower described the central "paradox" of American policy as defending a way of life as well as saving money and protecting people. Eisenhower spoke of the need "to devise methods of meeting the Soviet threat" that "avoid transformation into a garrison state." Given the long-term threat, he preferred a minimum military establishment with a rapid mobilization base. Despite his thinking that he could get the American people to support whatever program he deemed necessary to meet the threat, he "did not want the American people to do what the Administration deemed necessary over so long a period of time that it ended in the destruction of the American way of life."[54]

The discussion of defense expenditures continued at the October 1 NSC meeting.[55] In reference to the defense program, the director of mutual security, Harold Stassen, declared that the administration should formulate its policy without regard to the opinions in Congress and move only afterward to secure its cooperation and support. Eisenhower emphasized his agreement with Stassen's analysis, saying, "You are giving my speech." Instead of increasing taxes, Eisenhower hoped that a redeployment of divisions from overseas could save a substantial amount of money. Radford contended that the only way to justify redeploying overseas forces was to claim that either the Soviet threat had diminished or, as he preferred, that the preponderance of nuclear weapons allowed a reduction in conventional forces. Wilson added that the United States could reduce its ground forces in Europe to token levels by relying more on the air force and navy, since a few divisions in Europe would not make a practical difference in the defense of Europe.

Policy Selection

After some investigation, the administration rejected Dulles's proposal. Early plans for a speech on the international control of nuclear weapons, eventually presented as the "atoms for peace" proposal in December 1953, included Dulles's mutual withdrawal concept.[56] Because of American reliance on European forward bases for nuclear retaliation, it became apparent that the United States could not abandon its position in Europe by agreeing to a mutual withdrawal without first reaching an agreement on nuclear weapons.[57] For this reason, the administration abandoned the broader mutual withdrawal proposal and removed it from the final version of the speech.[58]

The NSC considered the NSC 162 policy paper at the October 7 NSC meeting.[59] Three central issues arose in this discussion: (1) the priority of national security versus the economy and balanced budgets, (2) the redeployment issue, and (3) nuclear weapons. The meeting's participants were divided in large part between those who believed the military threat posed by the Soviet Union necessitated placing military spending above economic concerns (Dulles, Radford, and Wilson) and those who wanted equal emphasis on economic considerations (Dodge and Humphrey). Eisenhower adopted a position between these two groups.

The discussion began with a consideration of the Soviet threat, national security, and the economy. Eisenhower expressed his concern with any position that would impose extreme economic controls in the name of security and felt that the economic threat needed recognition. He "readily agreed that you could get the American people steamed up to do whatever you told them was necessary for a certain length of time. If, however, this process was to go on indefinitely, it would be necessary to resort to compulsory controls." Dulles believed, however, that balanced budgets were not critical and that security should not be sacrificed for the sake of the budget. Eisenhower and Humphrey both explained that no one was arguing that the budget should take precedence over security, merely that the economic damage from large deficits needed to be considered. Wilson countered that it would be a "terrible day" if the administration ever told the American people that the government was putting budgets ahead of security. Eisenhower reiterated his position on public opinion: "You could get the American people to make these sacrifices voluntarily for a year or for two or for three years but no eloquence would sell this proposition to the American people for the indefinite future." Despite opposition by Dulles and Wilson, Eisenhower decided to include a statement indicating the need to meet the Soviet threat without harming the economy and recognizing the importance of a strong economy over the long run for a satisfactory defense.

Although this decision established the dual threat to the economy and security, the NSC still needed to address the balanced-budget issue. In the draft paper, one side, representing all the drafting members except the Treasury and Budget representatives, emphasized meeting security needs, argued that tax levels could be increased to offset any revenue shortfalls caused by higher security costs, and concluded that the public could be persuaded to support the plan if the government explained its necessity. On the other side, the Treasury and Budget representatives stressed balancing the budget by cutting expenditures without increasing taxes (barring fundamental changes in the world situation). After discussion, the NSC agreed on a position splitting the difference between the two groups. Thus the final paper set a balanced budget as a goal but not a necessity. Although security needs would eventually predominate in any decision, the administration stressed the necessity of a sound economy.

The redeployment issue arose in this same discussion. Dulles pointed to the delicate political nature of redeployment in terms of the allies' reaction. If not embedded in a larger operation, "the redeployment could bring about the complete collapse of our coalition in Europe." Eisenhower preferred a clear statement on redeployment but agreed that news of the policy's consideration should not become public until "our Allies had also been brought to realize that such a redeployment was really good military policy," since the Europeans expected the Americans to remain indefinitely, so any abrupt withdrawal of the troops from Europe would "completely destroy" the allies' morale. Although Eisenhower was sympathetic to redeployment at some point, he approved a less vigorous statement on the issue that concentrated on American overextension, the damage a major withdrawal would cause to the Western alliance, and the need to convince America's allies that the United States' strength rested on a centrally based mobile reserve and a commitment to strike back against an aggressor.

Finally, Radford pressed Eisenhower for a positive statement regarding the use of nuclear weapons. Eisenhower expressed concern regarding the allies' reaction to any such statement at that time. While granting the point, Wilson insisted that the military needed to know "whether or not to plan for the use of these weapons. Do we intend to use weapons on which we are spending such great sums, or do we not?" Eisenhower stated that he would make any final decision and would use them if dictated by security interests but allowed that the JCS could plan to use nuclear weapons in a general war, though not in minor conflicts.

The implications of these decisions on the prospects for balancing the budget while maintaining security remained unrealized by key decision makers. The conflict between these three decisions and a balanced budget did not become clear until October 13 when the JCS presented their budget based on NSC 149/2. Eisenhower and the NSC then discovered that by rejecting immediate redeployment and avoiding further reliance on nuclear weapons, their attempts to reduce the budget deficit had fallen short of the mark.

The October 13 meeting revolved around an October 2 JCS plan based on NSC 149/2 which, instead of calling for reductions in the armed forces, actually included a slight increase.[60] Wilson presented the $43 billion Defense Department program (only a $2.5 billion cut from the Truman FY55 program) which troubled Dodge and Humphrey, who expected significant military cuts. The program contained no major reductions in combat forces because the JCS determined that they could not justify them because there were no changes in the threat from the Soviet Union, basic national security policy, or policy on the use of nuclear weapons.[61] To achieve cuts, Wilson suggested that the National Security Council needed to change American commitments, clarify the use of nuclear weapons, and/or initiate changes in overseas deployments before the JCS could reasonably make further recommendations.

Eisenhower reemphasized to Radford the need for cuts in personnel, especially in support forces, on the basis of "a respectable as opposed to a perfect posture of defense" and was particularly disturbed by the JCS proposal to increase the armed services to 3.5 million personnel when he expected a reduction to 3 million. Dulles pressed Radford over whether the JCS's force level reflected the possible use of nuclear weapons, which Radford said it did not. Wilson, Humphrey, and Radford stressed their support for greater reliance on nuclear weapons to achieve Eisenhower's desired cuts. Humphrey added the critical importance of the FY55 budget for preserving the "public confidence" in the economy and the president. If it appeared that Eisenhower was conducting business in the same way as the previous administration had done, Humphrey predicted that "the American economy will go to hell and the Republican Party will lose the next election." To this, Eisenhower commented,

> If he could be convinced that we need all this money he was prepared to fight for it everywhere and with all the energy he could summon up, although he said he did not want to scare the people to death and did want our military posture to be calculated on a long-term basis.

Despite refusing to allow the JCS to plan to use nuclear weapons, Eisenhower recognized that the redeployment of troops from Europe was not possible in FY55 because the costs of returning them would outweigh any savings and would hurt European morale. Eisenhower thus hoped to achieve the needed cuts by reducing support forces and instructed the JCS to begin deliberations on the matter.

The NSC completed the new basic national security strategy (NSC 162/2) during a discussion of a revised version of the paper (NSC 162/1) on October 29.[62] The most controversial aspect of discussion centered on a new statement calling for the creation of "a strong military posture, with emphasis on the capability of inflicting massive retaliatory damage by offensive striking power."[63] Although the JCS recommended that the national strategy "include the capability" of massive retaliation as one component of the overall program rather than as the strategy's focal point, this proposed change made nuclear retaliation the central component of the national strategy rather than just one part of a broader approach.[64] Eisenhower supported the new wording and felt the "with emphasis" phrase communicated the administration's intention of not equally building all types of military strength. After further discussion, Eisenhower accepted the "with emphasis" phrase, since the administration intended to "keep the minimum respectable posture of defense while emphasizing this particular offensive capability." The paper also changed the status of nuclear weapons "as available for use as other munitions" and rejected any major withdrawal of troops from Europe. As Radford had recommended at the previous NSC meeting, the national strategy placed greater reliance on nuclear weapons at both the strategic and tactical levels to justify budget cuts.

Eisenhower was already thinking about obtaining public support for the defense budget. He found it difficult "to get expenditures down without the country getting the impression that the Administration was throwing the country to the wolves."[65] In a letter to his brother, he again referred to his intention to have the administration reach its own decisions and then lead the public to support its action. He planned "to use 1953 largely as a period of study and formulation of programs." The "Administration Bible," as he called FY55 budget, would be brought to Congress in early 1954, and

> once we have taken our stand on that program . . . then, of course, all of us, with me in the lead, will constantly pound the drums for the necessary legislation. I suspect that all kinds of conferences, arguments, speeches and other forms of persuasive action will have to be taken, both clandestinely and publicly, to implement the program.[66]

The administration found its solution to the problem of "how to provide necessary security and still reduce the Defense budget for '55" in an Oval Office conference of Dulles, Wilson, Humphrey, and Eisenhower on November 11. At this meeting, Dulles proposed that the United States begin to withdraw ground troops from Korea, which would allow the administration to show its confidence in air and naval power and allow a substantial reduction in the active strength of the army. Dulles's argument was persuasive. Eisenhower noted, "It was agreed that the dependence that we are placing on new weapons would justify completely some reduction in conventional forces—that is, both ground troops and certain parts of the Navy." Eisenhower also decided that defense savings would come through reductions in personnel by decreasing the number of divisions in Korea and cutting overhead and support personnel in Europe.[67] By allowing a minor redeployment of troops and cuts in the aggregate force levels, the reliance on nuclear weapons gave the administration the solution it needed to simultaneously preserve security and cut defense spending in an attempt to balance the budget. Even though Eisenhower initially rejected the military's request for greater authority to plan to use nuclear weapons, his views shifted after the JCS budget presented on October 13 provided a slight increase in defense spending. On reflection, Radford's suggestion to rely on nuclear weapons to achieve defense cuts struck a chord with Eisenhower. Because he needed to justify any cuts in defense spending, Eisenhower soon gave in to the greater reliance on nuclear weapons, even though he had serious doubts about the policy's strategic validity.

On December 2, Eisenhower pressured Wilson to force the JCS to pare down the number of armed forces to 3.1 million, even if he had to "nag and worry" them. To achieve the required savings, Eisenhower stressed that the numbers needed to be brought down by "*the beginning of [the] fiscal year!*" He found it "ridiculous" that the 3.5 million Korean wartime personnel figure could not be cut, especially because the Korean armistice had been signed in the summer of 1953.[68] This prodding apparently succeeded, since the JCS eventually cut back the number of forces requested in its budget. At the December 16 NSC meeting, the JCS presented their revised military strategy, JCS 2101/113, to implement the NSC 162/2 national strategy.[69] The new military strategy emphasized the withdrawal and regrouping of some overseas forces into a central strategic reserve in the United States, a reduction in the size of the military, a reorientation toward nuclear weapons to take advantage of American technological superiority and offset a Soviet manpower advantage, and a reliance on massive retaliation.[70] The envisioned cuts in military personnel were significant. A force of 3.55 million personnel on June 30, 1953, would be decreased to approximately 3.04 million by the end of FY55 and to 2.8 million by June 30, 1957.[71]

As the administration's plans became clear, government officials gradually began to reveal to the public the results of the interagency process. On October 28, Eisenhower announced that the government planned no cuts in combat forces, and he observed that nuclear weapons would be bound to affect the "composition of your military forces," thus intimating that the air force would probably grow.[72] Wilson expanded on this sub-

ject on November 10, indicating that the new plan might end the bal-
anced-forces concept (placing equal reliance of each branch) but that a
greater reliance on airpower might allow greater strength at less cost.[73]
He later explained that the cuts in defense spending to reduce the budget
deficit would not harm security and cited the formulation of plans to
simultaneously increase security while decreasing expenses and personnel.[74] At the same time, Admiral Radford gave two speeches outlining
and defending the defense strategy, on December 2 at the American
Ordnance Association and December 14 at the National Press Club.[75]

Policy Implementation

In 1954 the administration expended considerable effort on creating
public support for its program. These activities centered on convincing
the public and Congress, through a series of public speeches, congressional hearings, and private conferences, of the value of the national
strategy, defense strategy, and budget. In large part, these efforts reflected those that Eisenhower earlier recommended be undertaken to
implement the program.

After the programs were announced, the Democrats challenged the
New Look budget on January 2, saying that the cuts in the army and
navy risked national security and played into Russian hands.[76] The
administration moved to counter these attacks at a January 5 bipartisan
leadership meeting at which Wilson presented the defense budget. He
justified the budget with reference to the JCS study and their unanimous recommendation of the budget force levels, and he accented the
evolutionary rather than revolutionary content of the strategy. When
pressed by the Democrats on a possible loss of military strength from
the program, Eisenhower replied that national defense would actually be
stronger in June 1954 than that planned by the previous administration.[77]

Eisenhower continued these themes in his January 7 State of the
Union address in which he stressed the influence of nuclear weapons on
military planning and monetary savings. He argued, "The usefulness of
these new weapons creates new relationships between men and materials. These new relationships permit economies in the use of men as we
build forces suited to our situation in the world today."[78] The logical
result, he reasoned, was the emphasis on airpower in both the navy and
the air force. He justified the defense cuts with reference to the JCS
study, stating that the defense program "is based on a new military program unanimously recommended by the Joint Chiefs of Staff and

approved by me following consideration by the National Security Council."[79]

To assess the success of his leadership efforts, Eisenhower in February asked Roy Howard, president of the Scripps-Howard newspapers, to conduct a survey of editors from around the nation for him.[80] Eisenhower wanted these editors to provide an objective assessment of the views of the people in their geographic regions on a list of issues important to him, including the public's feeling about the administration's efforts to emphasize airpower as a defense strategy.[81] Howard told Eisenhower that the editors found the people held nearly universal support for the policy and were willing to trust Eisenhower's judgment on the matter.[82]

Apparently emboldened by these reports of the strategy's popularity, at one point Eisenhower told Press Secretary James Hagerty if asked about the New Look at a press conference, he would give them a "lecture on fundamentals."[83] The opportunity for the "lecture" came later the same day at his press conference. In response to a question about whether the massive retaliation policy was really "new," Eisenhower stressed the continuity of the New Look with past policies, pointing out that it was "new" only because it was attempting to incorporate a new type of weapon into the defense strategy. He instructed, "To call it revolutionary or to act like it is something that just suddenly dropped down on us like a cloud out of the heaven, is just not true, just not true."[84] In a television and radio address on April 6, Eisenhower also stressed the nuclear retaliatory capacity as the main American deterrent toward war.[85] In all, his actions represented a concerted effort to gain the public's confidence in both the strategy he had adopted and the budget that began to implement it.

Other officials in the administration also attempted to create support for the defense program. Perhaps the most controversial and most remembered speech was Dulles's January 12 address, which outlined the "massive retaliation" strategy (although the exact phrase never appeared in the speech itself).[86] To keep defense at an affordable cost, he argued, the United States needed a long-term policy that relied on allied forces for defense around the world and a deterrent component maintained by the United States. The way to achieve this deterrent was "for the free community to be willing and able to respond vigorously at places and with means of its own choosing." As a result, the administration was "able to get more security for less cost."

Asked about the speech at his press conference the next day, Eisenhower refused to elaborate on Dulles's comments except to say that given the speed of war in the nuclear age, "about your only defense is the knowledge that there is a strong retaliatory power."[87] Dulles recognized that his speech had stirred up quite a "public and congressional controversy," which led to his decision to transform it into an article for the April issue of *Foreign Affairs*.[88] At the press conference to release the article, Dulles attempted to clarify that the *capacity* for retaliation provided the key deterrent, rather than *instantaneous* retaliation, and that the policy did not force a choice between doing everything or doing nothing (a criticism that continued to dog this approach).

On February 11, Vice President Richard Nixon argued that the new reliance on massive retaliatory power would better protect national security than would stationing troops all over the globe.[89] Admiral Radford gave an extended interview to *U.S. News & World Report*, in which he maintained that although the new strategy changed the relative emphasis on airpower and nuclear weapons, it did not alter the need for all branches of the military.[90]

Congress did not intensely investigate the New Look's basic premises and strategic approach, and the administration maintained a unified front during the program's presentation, except for a dissent from Army Chief of Staff Matthew Ridgway during congressional hearings.[91] The Democrats mounted a minor challenge to the New Look in Congress during the floor debate over the budget and in speeches elsewhere, but Congress eventually passed the FY55 defense budget, and Eisenhower signed it into law on June 30, 1954, with the administration's requests to implement the New Look remaining mostly intact.[92] Eisenhower had requested $29.9 billion in new obligational authority, resulting in $37.6 billion in expenditures for the military, and the Congress approved $28.8 billion in new obligational authority for FY55, resulting in $35.5 billion in expenditures.[93] This budget created a $3.0 billion deficit in FY55. Later years under the New Look program were more successful. FY56 supplied a $4.0 billion surplus, whereas FY57 had a $3.2 billion surplus.[94]

In the end, Eisenhower achieved his goal for FY55 by adopting a budget that established the defense spending levels that most government officials agreed provided for national security. In selecting a national and defense strategy relying on nuclear weapons, Eisenhower adopted the one policy purporting to offer both security and economy that was acceptable to the government. Since these qualities made the new strategy a useful tool to justify the cuts to the public, Eisenhower selected the policy for this reason rather than the policy's merits, since he had long opposed a heavy reliance on nuclear weapons.

Variables

The decision makers assessed public opinion throughout the policy's formulation. Because Eisenhower felt pressure to win in the 1954 election, the public's reaction to his budgetary policies remained a constant concern. He sensed that the public preferred a few, possibly contradictory results: tax cuts, a balanced budget, and an adequate national security. Even so, he recognized that the public would accept spending cuts that moved toward, but did not achieve, a balanced budget in FY54 and that tax cuts in FY55 would be enough to satisfy the public in time for the 1954 elections. Regarding strategy, Eisenhower believed that it could not be radically changed in a short period of time because it would upset the public. But he also knew that if strategy were not changed, the public would eventually turn against his administration.

Eisenhower continually repeated his belief that the public could be led to support whatever position the administration adopted. He also insisted that the administration needed public support to implement any strategic change and felt the need to educate the public on any selected policy. This concern for leading the public and maintaining public support was integrated into the Solarium study instructions, and he initiated the new JCS study in part to enhance his ability to lead the public to support whatever policy the administration selected. He believed that the security review that resulted in NSC 162/2 and the new military strategy provided a vital factor in justifying the cuts to the public and creating confidence in the government's decision.

Dulles's assessment of public opinion also affected him. He wanted the administration to examine national strategy in order to "fulfill campaign ideas," meaning that he believed that administration leaders would be held accountable for their campaign promises in the next election. If the administration did not make this assessment, he felt it would lose public support as the world situation turned against the United States. Dulles also reacted to his perception of the public's confusion about his speech by authorizing an article to clarify his positions.

Other interests, notably Eisenhower's concern with the nation's long-term economic and military vitality, primarily influenced the decision to make a balanced budget and defense reductions his priorities. The central problem, as he saw it, revolved around responding to the Soviet threat while preventing national bankruptcy, preserving the American political and economic system, avoiding a resort to a garrison state, and balancing the budget to prevent inflation. He appeared ready to support any policy that would encompass these competing interests. At a broad level, Eisenhower's policy preferences were based on his economic philosophy to eliminate budget deficits because of potential inflation. But he would not sacrifice national security in order to achieve a balanced budget and rejected immediate tax reductions in FY54 for this reason. He also rejected tax increases for philosophical reasons and the resulting congressional opposition to such action. Potential Democratic opposition to such spending cuts also worried him.

Dulles viewed the JCS report suspiciously, largely because he feared the allies' reaction to it. Accordingly, he proposed two solutions to overextension that avoided redeployment. First, he suggested a major settlement with the Soviets to reduce tension. Second, the United States could shift its strategy to rely on nuclear weapons to justify personnel cuts.

Beliefs predictions suggest that Eisenhower would have attempted to lead public opinion unless he perceived the public's opposition to be unchangeable, in which case it might have limited his decisions. Consistent with these beliefs, his approach was constrained by public opinion on two issues: (1) the need for a new national strategy to maintain long-term public support and (2) the process by which it needed to be created (the public would not support his defense cuts unless they were part of a well-formed approach to national security developed after due consideration). When the process based on these limitations produced a policy that he had long opposed, he nonetheless approved it because of his concern for public support. Despite this restriction, he thought he could lead public opinion to support the policy the administration chose. After selecting a policy, his leadership approach stressed those factors that he thought were most likely to create public support, such as his experience and knowledge, the NSC and JCS studies as the justification for the policy, and security as the basis for the policy selection rather than economy.

Dulles was predicted to lead public opinion. On broad foreign policy questions, he was predicted either to follow or be held back by public opinion, especially if it were expressed during an election. Process tracing reveals that he recommended consideration of a new basic national security policy (a broad foreign policy question) because of campaign promises and the need for public support in the future (which would be difficult to maintain if the current policy were continued). Also consistent with his beliefs, he felt the specifics of the new strategy should be developed, using the government's best judgment, to meet the Soviet threat. Dulles had long favored the massive retaliation option he put forward, and his behavior reflected the combination of following and leading public opinion expected from him on these issues. In addition, he recommended withdrawing U.S. troops from Korea to demonstrate to the public and allies the administration's confidence in the new strategic posture. Dulles also acted consistently with predictions that he would lead public opinion, as evidenced in his speech and the *Foreign Affairs* article.

In all, this analysis suggests a *supportive* coding for the influence of beliefs for both decision makers. Eisenhower acted *consistently* with his beliefs when setting the agenda and reacted to them *causally* while defining the situation, generating options, selecting a policy, and implementing it. Dulles's behavior was *consistent* with beliefs during agenda setting, option generation, policy selection, and implementation and had a *causal* influence only during the definition of the situation.

Coding the Influence of Public Opinion

Public opinion played an important part in the formation of the New Look. Eisenhower recognized that the administration faced a problem with public opinion over the long term if the nation's defense posture was not adjusted. Public opinion acted to limit how Eisenhower attempted to achieve his goal of reducing defense expenditures. The need to explain the policy to the public made it necessary for an interagency review and an administration consensus on strategy so that the country did not feel that national security was being compromised. To obtain this consensus, Eisenhower chose the solution that met the views of various government actors (reliance on massive retaliation and nuclear weapons), although he doubted the intrinsic merits of this alternative. As a result, the need for public confidence in defense decisions set into action a policy process that resulted in Eisenhower's adopting a policy about which he had deep strategic doubts. Even though public opinion did not limit policy selection specifically to the nuclear option (no evidence directly ties public opinion to the choice to rely on nuclear weapons), it did condition the decision-making process in such a way as to limit the policy outcome.

Even so, Eisenhower and others in the administration felt that they could persuade the public to support the selected policy. Most of the administration's efforts regarding public opinion were, in fact, directed at leading it. Overall, then, the coding of the entire case falls under the *lead category* because the policymakers' main concern with public opinion while making their decisions was convincing the public of the value of their selected alternative. The *constrain category* did have a *moderate* influence on the decisions by setting the broad policy context.

Realist predictions suggest that decision makers lead public opinion in this context and that they may be constrained in their choices by a mobilized public opinion (see table 6.1). This case mostly supports this view, with Eisenhower and other decision makers feeling that they could lead and taking actions to persuade the public to support their policies. The limiting influence of public opinion also was anticipated by the realists. Public opinion narrowed the decision makers' range of action because of campaign promises and, primarily, the requirements that public support placed on the formulation of a new strategic policy (need for a study, any change in strategy must occur slowly).

But this influence did not occur through the means that the realists predicted. Rather, the realists argue that public opinion may become mobilized and restrict the ability of decision makers to make policy. In this case, decision makers effectively explained the new policy to the public in such a way so as to prevent the mobilization of public opinion that might have damaged security policy. However, decision makers were limited by their anticipation of how the public might become mobilized and so took action to prevent this mobilization. Their fears of the possible public reaction, rather than the actual public reaction itself, provided the most significant constraint on decision makers. As a result,

TABLE 6.1 Influence Coding: Deliberative Case

Predicted Public Influence			Actual Public Influence	Influence of Beliefs
REALIST	WILSONIAN LIBERAL	BELIEFS		
Lead/ *Constrain*	Follow	DDE: Lead/ *Constrain*	Lead/with lesser Constrain (moderate)	DDE: Supportive
		JFD: Lead/ *Follow on broad foreign policy*		JFD: Supportive

Note: Italics indicate conditional predictions.

public opinion affected policy in the manner that the realists argued it would, although not by the process they predicted.

The Wilsonian liberal perspective suggesting that decision makers follow public opinion finds little support from this case study. Only Dulles at the definition of the situation stage turned to public opinion as a guide to action, and he was motivated in part by other concerns. This failure of predictions is striking, given that previous research on this subject showed that public opinion would have the strongest influence in this context.

Policymakers' views about public opinion derived mostly from their anticipation of the public's views. The anticipation of public opinion affected Eisenhower's conclusion that (1) the public would respond negatively to any dramatic changes in strategic policy; (2) public support would be lost if the government did not alter its strategic policy; (3) tax reductions in FY55 would be enough to help in the 1954 elections; and (4) he could win public support on his budget position by framing his actions to the public as placing national security above fiscal issues. Dulles also relied on his anticipation of opinion, since he predicted that the administration needed to work on fulfilling their campaign ideas or they would face difficulties in the next election. In addition, he believed that public opposition would soon develop if the government did not alter its national strategy. Specific measures of opinion entered the decision process when Dulles saw the election results in 1952 as a mandate to rework the national strategy and Eisenhower conducted an informal survey of newspaper editors on opinion.

As with the Formosa Straits and Indochina cases, the anticipation of opinion, especially in regard to upcoming elections, played an important part in policy deliberations. This attention to future public views, rather than readings of the public's prevailing viewpoint, reflects its potentially critical role in officials' decisions. This component is especially important given the next chapter's conclusion that several of the post–World War II presidents were likely to be responsive to public opinion.

CHAPTER SEVEN

Presidential Beliefs Orientations Since World War II

Earlier chapters demonstrated the applicability of the beliefs model to two decision makers across a range of cases. An examination of more presidents can show the broader applicability of the beliefs model. Even though this analysis does not have the same depth, an examination of the beliefs of presidents from Harry Truman through Bill Clinton reveals that though these individuals display a range of beliefs from all four orientations (see chapter 1), each view is not equally represented. Of the postwar presidents, five (including Eisenhower) are coded as pragmatists, three as guardians, and one each as an executor and a delegate. This finding suggests that a potentially broad range of reactions to public opinion might be observed in the decisions reached by the postwar presidents.

Harry S. Truman: Guardian

President Harry Truman's views regarding the place of public opinion in foreign policy decision making identify him as a *guardian*. In his normative beliefs, he thought that public input should not affect his foreign policy decisions. He decided that rather than looking to the near-term popularity of a position as a standard, he would make the "right" decision based on his evaluation of the best policy to serve American national interests and let history judge his actions. In one 1949 press conference, he insisted:

> I have no more confidence in polls than I had before the [1948] elec-
> tion. . . . I never did have any confidence in polls, and I haven't got any
> confidence now. I make my decision on whether it's right or wrong
> from my point of view, after I have all the information and all the facts I
> can get to go on. Polls have no effect on me whatever.[1]

This negative view of public influence appears to derive from Truman's
conception of the role of a leader. In his memoirs, he asserted:

> A man who is influenced by the polls or is afraid to make decisions
> which may make him unpopular is not a man to represent the welfare of
> the country. . . . I have always believed that the vast majority of people
> want to do what is right and that if the President is right and can get
> through to the people he can always persuade them.

This statement illuminates Truman's disdain for those influenced by
public opinion and his belief that if he made the "right" choice, the public would support him. He viewed the goal of doing what the public
wanted or gaining its support as diametrically opposed to what he
should be trying to accomplish. For example, he stated, "I have never
felt that popularity and glamour are fundamentals on which the Chief
Executive of the government should operate. A President has to know
where he is going and why, and he must believe in what he is doing."[2]

In his practical beliefs, Truman rejected the need for public support
of his policies and concluded that what he saw as temporary public sentiments were irrelevant to achieving the long-term objectives of the
nation. For example, he believed that leaders should go their own way
regardless of public opinion:

> I wonder how far Moses would have gone if he had taken a poll in
> Egypt? What would Jesus Christ have preached if He had taken a poll
> in the land of Israel? Where would the Reformation have gone if Mar-
> tin Luther had taken a poll? It isn't polls or public opinion alone of the
> moment that counts. It is right and wrong, and leadership—men with
> fortitude, honesty and a belief in the right that make epochs in the his-
> tory of the world.[3]

This reliance on the long-term judgment of history rather than
short-term public support was buoyed by his belief that even though his
(correct) policies might not be accepted at the time, the public would
eventually adopt his perspective. "Throughout history, those who have
tried hardest to do the right thing have often been persecuted, misrep-

resented, or even assassinated, but eventually what they stood for has come to the top and been adopted by the people." To a certain extent, he considered that unpopularity even was a job requirement, given the need to confront tough issues and make difficult choices. "A President cannot always be popular. If a President is easily influenced and interested in keeping in line with the press and the polls, he is a complete washout."[4]

Given his opposition to public input and his rejection of the need for public support, Truman would likely have relied on his perception of the national security interests at stake to make decisions. He would not have shifted his policy in accordance with potential public support or opposition. After reaching a decision, however, he might have attempted to lead the public, especially in long decision-time cases, an effort that would have emphasized the national interests at stake.

John F. Kennedy: Pragmatist

In contrast to Truman, President John Kennedy possessed the public opinion beliefs of a *pragmatist*. In his normative beliefs, he stressed the need to base his decisions on the national interest and then to cultivate the public's support. He told his pollster, Lou Harris, "You must come down on the merits of the issue, regardless of public opinion."[5] In a 1960 speech to the National Press Club, Kennedy stated that a president should do more than register the public view, that he instead has a responsibility to inspire the public in the correct direction.

> It is not enough merely to represent prevailing sentiment—to follow McKinley's practice, as described by Joe Cannon, of "keeping his ear so close to the ground he got it full of grasshoppers." We will need in the sixties a President who is willing and able to summon his national constituency to its finest hour—to alert the people to our dangers and our opportunities—to demand of them the sacrifices that will be necessary. FDR's words in his first inaugural still ring true: "In every dark hour of our national life, a leadership of frankness and vigor has met with that understanding and support of the people themselves which is essential to victory."[6]

Not only does this statement affirm Kennedy's belief in the necessity of making difficult decisions and leading the public, but by mentioning Roosevelt's statement, he was implying that public support was a necessary component of a successful policy.

Ironically, Kennedy compared his belief in the proper role of public opinion in formulating foreign policy with what he saw as the Eisenhower administration's timidity in the face of public opposition. In a 1960 speech to the California Democratic Clubs Convention, he contrasted successful foreign policy presidents who led the public and took the actions that, though unpopular, were correct with failed foreign policy presidents who "yielded to public pressure instead of educating it." He argued, "In 1960 we must elect a President who will lead the people—who will risk, if he must, his popularity for his responsibility."[7] These passages suggest both a normative belief rejecting the desirability of public input into foreign policy decision making and an emphasis on executive leadership.

In his practical beliefs, Kennedy recognized the necessity of obtaining public support for his foreign policies. In a letter to the editor of *Newsday*, he stated, "Each time we make any move or commitment in foreign affairs, I am in the need of support of the American people."[8] Despite stressing the need to lead the public to win this support, he did not completely reject the possibility of adjusting his policy in the face of persistent and strong public sentiment. In a continuation of the earlier quotation from Louis Harris, Kennedy emphasized that although a president should make decisions without regard to public opinion, he still needed to keep an eye on public support. "But if you find yourself outside those jaws of consent of the governed, then you'd better *look around fast*. You can educate the public to extend those jaws. But if you're outside them too often, then you can get voted out of office."[9]

Because Kennedy found public input into foreign policy decisions to be undesirable but believed that the public's support was necessary, Kennedy would likely have reached foreign policy decisions based on the national security interests at stake and then attempted to lead the public to support his chosen policy. If he perceived that the public would strongly oppose a policy option and that he could not persuade them to support it, then public opinion would have constrained him. This effect would have been particularly pronounced if he saw the issue as one that the public could use to vote against him or his party in the next election.

Lyndon Johnson: Guardian

As a *guardian*, President Lyndon Johnson held the normative belief that foreign policy decisions should be based on the "right" policy, with no regard to how the policy might stand up in the polls or the public's opinion. At a 1967 news conference, he reflected on popular input,

> Well, they [the polls] are never as good as you would like to have them.... We just must do what we think is best for the country, regardless of how it stands up in the polls. You never know, when you make a decision, what the end results are going to be.... You do what you think is right.

Johnson emphasized that the popularity of a policy should not be the determinant of his choice because he saw public opinion as somewhat fickle and unpredictable. At a late 1967 press conference, he recalled Truman's decision to enter the Korean War, which began as a popular choice but soon became unpopular:

> Now, those things [shifts in popularity] have happened in all of our crises—economic, domestic, and international. A President learns to expect them and learns to live with them. The important thing for every man who occupies this place is to search as best he can to get the right answer; to try to find out what is right; and then do it without regard to polls and without regard to criticism.[10]

Johnson took a relaxed view of the public's opinion on policy issues, remarking that the public would have an opportunity to express their feelings at election time. At a 1966 press conference, Johnson acknowledged, "I think we all read them [the polls] and are affected by them" and stated that he would "like to have as much approval as we can get." But "we have to make our own judgments and do what we think is right. Then we trust the judgment of the people at election time."[11]

In his practical beliefs, despite Johnson's view of public opposition to his policies as a detriment, he still believed that his policies could succeed without public support. When asked at a 1966 press conference whether he worried about public support, Johnson responded,

> No. We always would like to see what we do and what we say approved by our associates and by our constituency—but that is not always the case. When it is not, we regret it and take due notice of it and engage in proper introspection. But the polls vary from week to week, and month to month. Those are things that we do not ignore, but they are not one of my burdens.

Instead of relying on public support, Johnson saw his role as gathering the necessary information and making the judgment on his own. In his memoirs, he emphasized that when making a decision, a president must search out the best information available. He can seek the counsel of men whose wisdom and experience and judgment he values. But in the end the President must decide, and he must do so on the basis of his judgment of what is the best— for his nation and for the world.

When these judgments, which he felt were the right ones, led to public disapproval but he felt the decisions he reached were the right ones, Johnson was willing to take "it on the head."[12]

Because Johnson—much like Truman—rejected public input and the necessity of public support, he would likely have made his decisions without regard to public opinion, in accordance with his assessment of the correct policy for national security interests. Especially when he had a long decision time, he would have led the public to support his chosen policy but would not have changed his mind to suit public support or opposition.

These views suggest that Johnson would best be categorized as a guardian, although some information about his practical beliefs is somewhat contradictory. In his memoirs, Johnson made a statement that would clearly place him in the pragmatist camp. In defining the need for consensus on his policies, he explained his decision process as, "first, deciding what needed to be done regardless of the political implications and, second, convincing a majority of the Congress and the American people of the necessity for doing those things."[13] If this statement were representative of his practical beliefs, then his beliefs would appear much closer to those of Eisenhower and Kennedy. But even though this coding is less certain than for the other presidents considered, Johnson's other comments appear more like those of a guardian.[14] Given his other beliefs about the decision-making process itself, the difference in behavior based on changes in his pragmatist beliefs would likely have been manifested in a policy constraint by public opinion if he determined he could not win over the public.

Richard Nixon: Pragmatist

Like Eisenhower and Kennedy, President Richard Nixon's public opinion beliefs identify him as a *pragmatist*. In his normative beliefs, Nixon firmly believed that public opinion should not influence his foreign policy choices. For example, he rhetorically asked a radio audience several weeks before the 1972 presidential election that even though the government may respect the public's views, "Does this mean that a President should read all the public opinion polls before he acts, and then follow the opinion of the majority down the line? Of course not." At about the same time, he privately recorded the same view in his diary: "I don't give one damn what the polls say insofar as affecting my decisions. I only care about them because they may affect my ability to lead, since politicians do pay attention to them."[15]

Nixon thought of polls as a way of understanding the public's views and which ones needed changing, but he did not think he should use them to formulate his position on an issue. He expounded on this view in his book on leadership:

> If the successful leader has to know when to compromise, he also has to know when to go his own way. Too many politicians today ride toward destiny "at full Gallup." The candidate who slavishly follows the polls may get elected, but he will not be a great leader or even a good one. Polls can be useful in identifying those areas where particular persuasion is needed. But if he sets his course by them, he abdicates his role as a leader. The task of the leader is not to follow the polls but to make the polls follow him.[16]

Nixon's strong normative view complemented his practical ideas about the necessity of public support, which he thought should result from changing public opinion rather than changing his policy positions. He underscored the critical role of a leader, "A leader must be willing to take unpopular stands when they are necessary. . . . And when he does find it necessary to take an unpopular stand, he has an obligation to explain it to the people, solicit their support, and win their approval." In fact, in his reelection campaign in 1972, Nixon pledged to take the necessary steps in foreign policy, regardless of domestic support: "In the years to come, if I am returned to office, I shall not hesitate to take the action I think necessary to protect and defend this nation's best interests, whether or not those actions meet with wide popular approval."[17]

Whereas Nixon valued making the correct foreign policy choice without regard to public input or initial support, he did think that he would ultimately require the public's support of foreign policy in order for it to succeed. To obtain this support, however, policymakers needed to exert leadership through public education efforts, rather than in responding to public opposition by shifting their policy position. During an early 1969 press conference, Nixon described his decision-making obligations along similar dimensions: "It is the responsibility of a President to examine all of the options that we have, and then if he finds that the course he has to take is one that is not popular, he has to explain it to the American people and gain their support."[18] This calculus applied to wartime efforts as well:

> There are times when the Congress and the people may not recognize our vital interests in Third World conflicts. Leaders should lead and not just follow uninformed public opinion. It is their responsibility to educate the people and the Congress about where our vital interests are and then gain support for whatever military actions may be necessary to protect them. Leaders who do only what opinion polls indicate uninformed voters will support are not true leaders, and if America follows them, it will cease to be a great nation.[19]

Nixon also recognized the limitations on his ability to lead. "A leader can be out in front, ahead of public opinion, but not too far ahead. While trying to bring the public around, he often has to conceal a part of his hand, because to reveal it too soon could cost him the game."[20]

Since Nixon rejected the desirability of public input but thought its support was necessary, he would have made the decision that he regarded as being in the national interest and then taken action to persuade the public to support it. At the same time, since he thought that getting too far ahead of public opinion might cause the policy to fail, if he sensed he was pulling away from the public, he would either have worked secretly on the policy until he generated the public's support or slowed his action on the issue in order to give him time to construct the necessary base of support. In this sense, public opinion might have acted as a temporary brake on his foreign policy.

Nixon's ideas about how to win public support differ from the two other pragmatists, Eisenhower and Kennedy. In contrast, they appeared ready to adjust their policies in accordance with public opinion, if required, whereas Nixon emphasized changing public opinion to create support for his policies. Although Nixon still believed in the necessity of public support, he probably would have been less responsive to it in his decisions than either Eisenhower or Kennedy would have been. A pattern of belief similar to Nixon's is found in the remaining pragmatists, Ford and Bush. Although all these pragmatists share the same beliefs regarding public opinion, their ideas about how to achieve the needed public support varied. As indicated in the predictions for their behavior, these differences were likely to be manifested in how they reacted to potential public opposition.

Gerald Ford: Pragmatist

President Gerald Ford's beliefs suggest that he was most likely a *pragmatist*. His normative beliefs imply a desire to make decisions based on the national interest, regardless of public opinion. In an interview in early 1976, Ford stated,

> As we move ahead, we are going to try and predicate our foreign policy on the best interests of all the people in this country, as well as our allies and our adversaries, rather than to respond to a highly articulate, a very tightly organized pressure group of any kind. We cannot let America's policies be predicated on a limited part of our population or our society.

He recognized that this position might make him unpopular. In a different interview in early 1976, he commented that presidents should not focus on their popularity but instead should concentrate on the national interest. "A President has to make some decisions that are not always popular, as long as he thinks they are right. And I can assure you that I will do what is right and, hopefully, have the backing of the American people." In a similar vein, a former administration official recalled, "If I heard it once I heard it a hundred times in confidential conversations with the President: 'I [Ford] don't care what the polls say, it's the right thing to do,' or 'Whatever the election outcome, I think this is best for the country.'"[21]

In his practical beliefs, Ford considered public support to be an important component of foreign policy, but he also believed that he did not require public support at the moment of decision. Like Nixon, he emphasized leading public opinion, which he thought he could do fairly easily, rather than responding to it. When asked in early 1976 whether it was possible for him "to make decisions in the name of national security if those decisions do not reflect the popular will of the people," Ford replied,

> It does make it somewhat difficult . . . but I think it is the responsibility of a President to fully inform the American people and convince them that what we are seeking to do in foreign policy is in our best interests. And if a President carries out that responsibility, then he can and will have the support of the American people.[22]

This position seems to accept public opposition to his foreign policies with the belief that the public could eventually be persuaded to support his chosen policy.

Since Ford rejected public input as a basis for a decision, his foreign policy decisions would likely have been based on his perception of the national interest while ignoring the dictates of public opinion. After reaching a decision, Ford would have explained the decision to the public in an attempt to build public support because he thought such support was necessary. Unlike pragmatists such as Eisenhower and Kennedy, he would not have altered his policy in response to public opposition. Instead, he would have continued focusing on leading the public to generate support.

Jimmy Carter: Executor

As an *executor*, President Jimmy Carter believed that it was desirable for public opinion to influence foreign policy. In his normative beliefs, Carter thought that the public's involvement in open decision making would benefit foreign policy by preventing mistakes that might occur in a foreign policy formed in secret. In a mid-1977 interview, Carter argued for public input into foreign policy:

> But I think the openness of it [foreign policy negotiations] and the involvement of the public in the debates and discussions will prevent our making some of the mistakes that were so devastating to our country in the past. . . . I think it possibly avoids the risk of a serious mistake when a decision is made in secret without the sound judgment and the experience and the common sense of the American people and the Congress being involved in making those crucial decisions.[23]

Carter saw the process of gathering information and making a decision as a two-way street in which he would gain a greater understanding of what the public thought and could share his views with the public. But even though Carter wanted this input, he still believed that he should make his own decisions about foreign policy. In mid-1977, comparing his view with that of previous administrations, Carter stated:

> And on many of the controversial issues that in the past have been decided in a very secret way between the Secretary of State and the President, for instance, are now discussed openly with the American people. I feel that's a good move. It exposes our doubts and uncertainties and controversies on occasion, but after that debate goes back and forth in the Congress and throughout the Nation, among American people, we monitor that opinion very closely. And I think that by the time I

make a decision—which may or may not always agree with what the people are thinking at home—I have a much surer sense of what our country ought to do.[24]

In his practical beliefs, Carter felt that public support was not necessary and that he could and should make the right decision even if it cost him public support. When asked in an early 1980 interview whether unfavorable polls affected him, he replied, "No. I have never lost any sleep at all, even over matters much more important than public opinion polls. I've just done the best I could, made decisions whether they were popular or not."[25] He also expressed a commitment to address issues regardless of their popularity. In a late 1979 radio interview, Carter reflected that "I hope I never fail, as long as I'm in this office, to address a necessary and difficult question just to avoid criticisms or a lower rating in the poll." As a basis for this view, he commented,

> I didn't come here looking for glory or looking for everyone to approve what I did; I came here to do a job for our country. And if it results in either temporary or permanent criticisms or lower opinion among the American people, if I think I'm right and doing what is best for this country, I'm going to do it.[26]

Interestingly, he believed that the American public approved of his approach to decision making. He told an interviewer in mid-1978,

> I can't run the White House and make my decisions as President based on what's more popular. I have to make decisions sometimes when I know that either way that I go will be unpopular. But I think in the long run that's the kind of President the American people want.[27]

In his behavior, Carter would likely have considered public opinion in policy deliberations because he favored public input. Because he did not think that public support was necessary, he would not have felt bound by public opinion and would have led it only to affect another actor such as Congress. After factoring it in, he would have made his decision based on his conception of the national interest, even if his choice happened to be unpopular. Unlike the guardians, who thought they should rely solely on their perceptions of American national interests, Carter was willing to use public opinion as one measure of the "right" policy. If he determined that public opinion provided valuable insight, information, or the correct view of a situation, Carter might have been constrained by it. In this sense, public opinion would have provided a first cut in decision making to find out where the public stood and where he might be incorrect in his formulation of the problem, but the final basis for a decision would likely have rested on Carter's own assessment of the correct policy after taking public opinion into account.

Ronald Reagan: Guardian

President Ronald Reagan's beliefs fall into the *guardian* orientation. In his normative beliefs, Reagan expressed, several times during his career in remarkably similar fashion, his desire not to allow the potential political ramifications of his decisions affect his policy choices. In his memoirs, Reagan recalled the instructions he gave to his advisers in Sacramento when he was governor of California and in Washington when he was president:

> One of the first things I told the members of my cabinet was that when I had a decision to make, I wanted to hear all sides of the issue, but there was one thing I didn't want to hear: the *political ramifications* of my choices. The minute you begin saying, "This is good or bad politically," I said, "you start compromising principle. The only consideration I want to hear is whether it is good or bad for the people." I made the same statement at our first cabinet meeting in Washington.[28]

Again, in 1985, Reagan gave the same view with an added element:

> I told them [his staff when he became governor] that the one thing I did not want to hear was the political ramifications of any issue. I wanted only to hear debate on what was good or bad for the people, because the minute you start thinking about votes and political things, it's a bit like seeing a player's card—you can't take out of your mind that you know where that card is no matter how honest you want to be.[29]

In this last quotation, Reagan emphasized that not only did he not want to consider the potential popular support for a policy but that he also wanted to avoid contact with those considerations altogether because he felt it would contaminate his decision process. The reason that he rejected considering the political ramifications was his view that often only the president would have all the relevant information necessary for a decision.[30]

In his practical beliefs, Reagan did not think that a foreign policy required public support for it to be successful. For example, at one point,

Reagan commented that "on matters of national security, the real issue is not whether it's the popular thing, but whether it's the right thing."[31] He believed that he needed to act to protect the nation's security interests even in the face of domestic opposition especially when he needed to act quickly. However, based on Vietnam, he did express one caveat to this broader beliefs framework in reference to the long-term uses of force: "We all felt that the Vietnam War had turned into such a tragedy because military action had been undertaken without sufficient assurances that the American people were behind it."[32] If an issue concerned a protracted war, therefore, he would probably have viewed public support as necessary.

Because Reagan opposed including input from public opinion and thought that the public's support was not usually necessary, he would likely have based his decisions on his perception of the national interest and would not have included public opinion in this process. Like Truman and Johnson, especially on long-term decisions, he might have attempted to persuade the public to support his view by explaining the national security reasons for his decision. The one exception would have been a decision regarding an extended war. If public support appeared problematic, he would likely have been constrained by it.

George Bush: Pragmatist

President George Bush held public opinion beliefs most consistent with those of a *pragmatist*. In his normative beliefs, Bush thought he should not pay attention to public opinion because polls often vacillated and/or the public did not have the information necessary to make a decision. For example at a 1990 news conference, Bush commented:

> I don't believe in polls . . . . That's not the way I try to call the shots on the policy. You just raised a question about China. If I had my finger in the wind, I might have done that one differently. I might have done differently about going to Cartagena if I put my finger in the wind in terms of polls, but that's not the way I run this administration.[33]

In this quotation, Bush is emphasizing his refusal to make foreign policy decisions based on polling and his distrust in polls because of their transitory nature. He did concede in a mid-1991 interview on Air Force One that though he did not ignore polls, he did not think them very important. "From time to time I look at them [the polls], but I don't live by them or make decisions by them."[34]

Bush saw his job as making decisions based on the national interest, to which polls and public opinion would be a poor guide. In a late 1989 news conference, Bush described the responsibility he felt to reach the correct decision:

> I have an obligation as President to conduct the foreign policy of this country the way I see fit, reporting under the law to the United States Congress . . . . The whole opening to China never would have happened if Kissinger hadn't undertaken that mission. It would have fallen apart . . . . But I have mine [a job], and that is to conduct the foreign policy of this country the way I think best. If the American people don't like it, I expect they'll get somebody else to take my job, but I'm going to keep doing it.[35]

In these statements, Bush is conveying a view similar to that of a guardian, of being selected by the public to make foreign policy decisions as needed. He saw himself as responsible to the public at election time only, when the public would have an opportunity to evaluate his conduct. Bush did not see himself as needing to respond to the public on specific foreign policy decisions and, in between elections, did not feel beholden to public opinion.

In his practical beliefs, though, Bush considered public support necessary for the ultimate success of a foreign policy. However, unlike some other pragmatists who thought they either had to lead to develop public support or stay in the confines of what the public would allow, Bush believed that the public would almost automatically support his foreign policy if it were the "right" one. He told a 1990 press conference that it bothered him that the public supported his foreign policy more than his domestic policy because "perhaps it has to do with the fact that in one, I think the Vandenberg theory applies. People really basically want to support the President on foreign affairs, and partisanship does, in a sense, stop at the water's edge."[36] He took it for granted that public support would follow after merely informing the public of his decisions.[37]

Since he opposed public input, Bush would likely have chosen the foreign policy he saw as required by the national interest without regard to public opinion. Because he believed public support to be necessary, he would have regarded it as an essential component of any policy, but he also would usually have assumed that if he made the "correct" decision, the public would follow his lead. For this reason, under normal foreign policy conditions, Bush would not have been concerned about public opinion or felt burdened to pursue an extensive leadership effort to generate support. If he believed that public support was questionable, then he would have explained his policy to the public to generate support. Even so, he would not have expended much effort. If for some reason he decided that the public would not respond to his explanation, he might be constrained by it because of his belief in the need for public support of his policies. In short, under most circumstances, his dominant mode of reaction to public opinion would be to disregard it because of his assumption that public support was automatic. But when public support was doubtful, he would have coped by either leading public opinion or being constrained by it. Interestingly, although he held pragmatist beliefs, the peculiarities of his beliefs made him less likely to react to public opinion than the typical pragmatist and less likely to lead it than even some guardians.

Bill Clinton: Delegate

Bill Clinton's public opinion beliefs are consistent with those in the *delegate* orientation. In his normative beliefs, Clinton views public opinion as desirable in the decision-making process. In fact, in late 1994, he stressed to one audience the importance of both public input and his communication with the public.

> If I had to say what I needed to do to improve as a leader, it would be to find ways to be able to share with the American people what I know to be the facts here, what we're doing, and to give them some sense that I'm listening to them and they have some input, but that I'm moving the country in the right direction.[38]

Clinton believes that the public communicates its will and sets policy at election time, and he sees his obligation as acting on his campaign promises in regard to foreign policy. He told one reporter in the summer of 1993 that the voters "gave me a contract, and I'm going to fulfill it to the best of my ability, and then they can make their judgments."[39] This connection with elections does not occur just retrospectively but also in looking to the next election. Clinton told radio reporters in the fall of 1993, "I have a contract that runs for a specific limit—amount of time. I'm going to do the very best I can during that time, and then when the time is up the American people can make their own judgments."[40] In this sense, Clinton does not derive his policies from public opinion but tries to act according to the promises he made at the previous election and also to adjust a policy's timing and shape to the anticipated public reaction in the next election.[41]

By providing him with a contract to fulfill his stated campaign objectives and an opportunity for the public to judge his decisions, elections play an important part in Clinton's view of his relationship with the public, which he sees as making the correct decision for the long run and explaining the policy to the public at the next election when he will be held accountable. He focuses not so much on the near-term popularity of a policy but more on a policy's long-term (defined as the next election) political viability. In an appearance on CNN's *Larry King Live*, Clinton explained:

> What I have to do is to do the job the people gave me. And I really believe, in the world we're living in, with so much change going on and people being bombarded from all sides with so much information, people like me who are in office should not worry so much about being popular. We ought to do what we think is right for the long run and then hope—believe the election can be our friend. Because only when the elections start do people really begin to focus on it.[42]

Even though he does not face election again, Clinton, in his second term, appears to be applying his concern about public opinion to the Democrats' prospects in the next elections, since he sees these elections as judgments on his policies. Although many reports show that much of Clinton's attention has shifted to ensuring that Vice President Albert Gore succeeds him,[43] in public, Clinton has been less committed to Gore over other Democrats. For example, in December 1997, in response to a question about his support for Gore, he remarked,

> What I would say among all the Democrats is that there's plenty of time for presidential politics . . . and that the most important thing is that we show the people we can make progress on the problems of the country and on the promise of the country. As for the Vice President [Gore], himself, he needs no defense from me. I have simply said . . . He's had the most full partnership with the President of any Vice President in history and he has performed superbly.[44]

Although Clinton's endorsement of Gore was strong, he directed his comments to his performance's effect on the chances of whoever is the next Democratic nominee.

In order to anticipate the public's views, Clinton relies on polls to learn the public's perspective on an issue and sees governing as an interactive process between his preferences and public opinion. Clinton described this interaction to a reporter:

> I can tell you categorically that I do not use polls to decide what position to take. . . . I have used polling information to try to make sure I understand where the American people are, what they know and what they don't know, what information they have, and to determine what arguments might best support a position that I believe is the right position for the country.[45]

In his practical beliefs, Clinton thinks that public support remains necessary for the success of a foreign policy. As with public input, however, public support is measured over the long term at the next election, suggesting that immediate public support for a foreign policy initiative is not necessarily critical except to the extent that it indicates future public opinion about the issue. At the base level, Clinton sees public support as necessary because it gives him a freer hand in foreign policy. At one point in 1994, Clinton underscored the need for an effective communications program to develop public support for his foreign policy so that it "will give me the flexibility I need."[46] Speaking at a September 1994 press conference, Clinton emphasized the critical elements of his formulation of foreign policy: the choice of the correct policy, its possible unpopularity in the short term, and the need of public support in the long term.

> In terms of popular approval, the American people—probably wisely—are almost always against any kind of military action when they first hear about it, unless our people have been directly attacked. . . . The job of the President is to try to do what is right, particularly in matters affecting our long-term security interests. And unfortunately not all of the decisions that are right can be popular. So I don't believe that the president, that I or any other president, could conduct foreign policy by a public opinion poll, and I would hope the American people would not wish me to. . . . Any sustained endeavor involving our military forces requires the support of the people over the long run.[47]

Clinton thus does not try to make policy in response to public opinion, but he recognizes the need to select a policy that is eventually acceptable to the public. Reflecting on foreign policymaking in a democracy after Prime Minister Shimon Peres's electoral defeat in Israel, Clinton said, "You can't push people faster than they are ready to go. . . . It's the price of making foreign policy in a world increasingly composed of democracies. You can't get too far out ahead of the people, or they bring you up short."[48] Part of this process concerns educating the public about foreign policy. Reflecting on his first year in office, Clinton said he had learned

> that explaining to the American people what our interests, our values, and our policies are requires a more systematic and regular explaining. In a time when the overall framework is not clear and when people are bombarded with information, I think a President has to do that with greater frequency and to try to make a continuing effort not only to shape a new world but to find ways to explain that world to the American people.[49]

In the governing process, Clinton sees information about public opinion as a critical element in determining policy. He believes that he should behave as the public's agent, which he defines as acting as the public would want him to if it had the information he does. The important implication of this view is that he may act against the public opinion of the moment if he determines that the public eventually will wish that he had acted differently. As a result, he thinks he should evaluate the potential long-term public support of a decision in reference to its expected electoral effects, as opposed to the short-term public support of a policy as evidenced in public opinion polls. By knowing where the public stands on an issue, he can then determine how and when to move toward the policy he prefers, always keeping in mind how the policy may affect future electoral prospects. If a policy is going to hurt his future electoral prospects, he will likely avoid the issue or choose a different policy. As a result, his policy choices will usually result from an interaction between his anticipation of public opinion on an issue and what he thinks is the correct direction to move on policy.

Clinton also views communication as an important part of governing and likely sees its purpose as telling the public how his policy represents what the public wants or how his policy addresses what the public will prefer in the long term. He sees this action primarily as educating and explaining his policy to the American public rather than moving, pushing, or leading the public to support a policy that it otherwise would not.

The implications of this beliefs analysis for Clinton's second term when he will not face election again could be manifested in several ways. First, he may direct his concern with public opinion to the Democrats at the next congressional and presidential elections.[50] Second, he may focus on implementing his campaign promises from the previous election. Either of these directions would be in keeping with his beliefs as a delegate. Finally, he may make his decisions more for the long-term judgment of history rather than any near-term political calculation. To the extent that these judgments will be based on criteria other than fulfilling the public will, he may be less responsive to *public* opinion and more responsive to *historical* opinion. Although this behavior would be in keeping with Clinton's focus on the long-term popularity of his policies, his shift from public opinion would be an interesting one. Given the beliefs model, I expect him to rely more on public opinion and the electoral prospects of his party and vice president than on the judgment of history.

This survey of beliefs orientations of the post–World War II presidents reveals that these men held a wide range of views about the place of public opinion in foreign policy decision making (see table 7.1). Five of these presidents are coded as pragmatists, which is not entirely surprising, since most presidents enter office with confidence in their own abilities and feel the need to reach their own decisions, especially in the foreign policy arena. Presidents should feel somewhat driven to achieve and maintain public support for their policies, at least because public opposition can make some foreign policies practically impossible, especially if manifested in congressional opposition.

The other three beliefs orientations are represented to a lesser extent. Three of the presidents are coded as guardians. Interestingly, two of

TABLE 7.1 **Beliefs Orientations of Recent Presidents**

		Is public support of a foreign policy necessary?	
		Yes	No
Is it desirable for input from public opinion to affect foreign policy choices?	Yes	Delegate *Clinton*	Executor *Carter*
	No	Pragmatist *Eisenhower, Kennedy, Nixon, Ford, Bush*	Guardian *Truman, Johnson, Reagan*

them were known for their tenacity in support of their views and either an almost belligerent acceptance of decision responsibility (Truman: "the buck stops here") or a strong ideological approach to decision making (Reagan). The delegate (Clinton) and executor (Carter) orientations were not widely represented, with only one president of each type.

The relative lack of presidents who favor input from the public on foreign policy is striking, especially given the norms of democratic theory. Across the board, presidents were more likely to admit that they should reach their own conclusions about policies. Many of the presidents seemed to share the view that the public also does not have the information necessary to take a knowledgeable position or does not completely understand the complexities of foreign policy. Even Clinton, the lone delegate, appeared to acknowledge this view. This sentiment is reflective of the literature on public opinion and foreign policy that, at least up until the early 1980s, portrayed public opinion on foreign policy as emotional and unstructured. Since that time, a large body of research has suggested that the public holds both rational and structured views on foreign policy.[51] It will be interesting to see whether these findings in political science eventually become a commonly accepted fact in the policymaking community, as the previous negative perspective did.

The necessity of securing public support for foreign policies was shared by all but a few of the presidents. One commonly held notion is that after Vietnam, decision makers are now much more sensitive to public support when making foreign policy decisions than they were before it. Surprisingly, there has been little difference between the beliefs of the pre- and post-Vietnam presidents about the necessity of public support. With Ford as the first post–Vietnam War president, two of five presidents before the end of American military involvement in Vietnam and two of five afterward rejected the necessity of public support for foreign policy.

Interestingly, across all orientations, presidents recognized that they should or needed to do the "right" thing, but they differed in how they defined the "right" policy. Both Clinton and Carter believed that public opinion should be factored into their evaluation of policy. Clinton saw the "right" policy as partially defined by what the public would eventually view, in the long term, as the correct policy, and Carter was willing to consider input from the public on what they thought the correct policy was.

The pragmatists felt that policy should be based on their perception of the right policy to meet the national interest, but this determination was tempered by their need for public support. Even the pragmatists differed on how to react when the public opposed a policy that might serve the national interest. Under certain conditions, some decision makers (Eisenhower, Kennedy) seemed ready to change their policy positions in light of public opinion if support appeared doubtful. These presidents recognized strong limitations on a leader's ability to change public opinion. But other pragmatists (Nixon, Ford, Bush) almost exclusively emphasized a leader's ability to change public opinion to gain its support if a problem appeared. They were much more optimistic about the president's ability to mold public opinion to support administration policies, even in the face of strong potential opposition.

Finally, the guardians (Truman, Johnson, Reagan) were determined to do what was "right," regardless of public support. Truman seemed to believe that greatness was defined by sticking to his guns in the face of public opposition and counting on future generations to appreciate his policy choices. Johnson obviously preferred public support to opposition, but he still thought that he needed to implement the policy required by the national interest, despite public opposition. In a similar vein, Reagan favored pursuing policy only in response to the national interest. The guardians seemed to embrace the necessity of sometimes being out of step with public opinion on critical issues affecting the national interest.

These differences among orientations also affected how the presidents conceived of leading the public. Many presidents thought they should "lead" or "educate" the public, but what they meant by that varied according to their orientation. The delegate (Clinton) saw public education as a means of communicating to the public how his policies matched the public's long-term policy preferences. The executor (Carter) thought only about gaining public input and not about leading the public to support his policies. If he did try to lead the public, he would have done so only because it was necessary in order to affect another actor (such as Congress), rather than as an end in itself. The guardians (Truman, Johnson, Reagan) thought about leading as merely stating why a policy was necessary because of the national interest and not whether their explanations necessarily enhanced the public's support of a policy. In contrast to the guardians and delegates, when the pragmatists (Eisenhower, Kennedy, Nixon, Ford, Bush) spoke of leadership, they meant explaining the policy in terms that would create public support. In addition to affecting how public opinion was seen by the presidents, the next two chapters discuss how these differing orientations altered the formulation of foreign policy.

CHAPTER EIGHT

Crises and Recent Presidents

To provide examples from all four orientations about the influence of public opinion, in this chapter I examine a crisis case from each of the Carter, Reagan, Bush, and Clinton presidencies. The realist view says that these presidents would largely ignore public opinion; the Wilsonian liberal perspective implies that leaders would be constrained by it; and the beliefs model suggests that each president discussed in this chapter would deal with and react to public opinion in a different manner. In each case, each reacted as expected based on his beliefs. After a brief review of the expectations outlined in chapter 7, I consider a significant episode for each presidency: (1) Carter's reaction to the Soviet invasion of Afghanistan, (2) Reagan's response to the bombing of the marine barracks in Beirut, (3) Bush's decisions regarding Iraq's invasion of Kuwait, and (4) Clinton's moves after significant American casualties in Somalia.

Executor: Carter and the Soviet Invasion of Afghanistan, 1979–1980

As I argued in chapter 7, Carter favored the public's input but did not think its support was necessary. Because of these beliefs, Carter would have considered public opinion but responded to it conditionally.

If he determined that public opinion had the "right" view or if he had only weak preferences on an issue, he would likely have been constrained by it (constrain category). However, if he could not ascertain the public's opinion, disagreed with it because he thought it was wrong, or had a strong view on an issue, he would likely have relied on his own judgment in reaching a decision (no-impact category).

The Soviet Union invaded Afghanistan in late December 1979 after watching the Soviet-backed regime's control over its internal situation deteriorate for several months.[1] What began as a limited intervention with airborne troops during December 24–26 expanded into a large-scale Soviet incursion on December 27. The invasion occurred in an increasingly negative domestic and international environment for the Carter administration. Iranian students had overrun the American embassy in Tehran in November 1979 and continued to hold Americans hostage in the compound. In addition to perceptions of an increasingly hostile and interventionist Soviet Union, the administration faced domestic problems with a sour economy and a challenge by Senator Edward Kennedy (D, Mass.) for the 1980 Democratic presidential nomination.

Problem Representation

Carter sensed a broad threat from the Soviet action. His view was somewhat shaped by his feeling that the invasion signaled a new direction in Soviet policy because he (incorrectly) surmised that it was the first time the Soviets had employed troops to expand their sphere of influence since they invaded Czechoslovakia in 1948. In addition to his conclusions about the Soviets' intentions, Carter believed that the takeover gave them a greater capability to threaten the region and the Persian Gulf oil fields. In all, Carter indicated in his diary that the invasion was "the most serious international development that has occurred since I have been President."[2]

As he recalled in his memoir, Carter's initial reaction was to send "the sharpest message of my Presidency" over the hot line to Soviet leader Leonid Brezhnev, calling the Soviet action "a clear threat to the peace" that "could mark a fundamental and long-lasting turning point in our relations."[3] Brezhnev's response two days later, in which he defended the invasion as having been invited by the Afghans to combat armed aggression, reinforced Carter's initial assessment and deepened his emotional reaction. Carter found the Soviet message insulting because in his eyes, the Soviet claims were "obviously false," which led him to become emotionally agitated and angry, since he felt personally betrayed by Brezhnev. In a widely reported comment, Carter intimated that the invasion "has made a more dramatic change in my own opinion of what the Soviets' ultimate goals are than anything they've done in the previous time I've been in office."[4]

Although no evidence suggests that Carter was reacting to domestic concerns, internal factors may in fact have reinforced his strategic conclusions. Despite arguing that Carter truly reacted to what he saw as the strategic implications of the Soviet invasion, several secondary sources contend that the general domestic climate limited his range of responses. These proponents point out that the administration's dreary domestic situation and the general perception of Carter as weak on communism made a tepid reaction difficult if not impossible. These analysts conclude that domestic factors reinforced Carter's own personal predispositions rather than altering his behavior.[5]

Option Generation

In response to the Soviet invasion, the State Department and the NSC staff prepared an extensive list of possible sanctions to impose on the Soviet Union. The administration's discussions about policy responses focused on (1) directly imposing sanctions on the Soviet Union and (2) strengthening American defenses both globally and regionally. Carter eventually adopted nearly all the proposed actions.[6]

Policy Selection and Implementation

Even though Carter saw many of his possible choices as potentially damaging to him politically, he later reflected that he was "determined to make [the Soviets] pay for their unwarranted aggression without yielding to political pressures here at home."[7] When the idea of a grain embargo on American sales to the Soviets was initially raised on December 30, Vice President Walter Mondale opposed it because, he argued, it would have a negative influence on the forthcoming Iowa presidential primary. Carter deferred his decision on the issue.[8] When the administration returned to it on January 4, Mondale pointed out, "We need to be strong and firm, but that doesn't mean you have to commit political suicide!"[9] However, Carter appears to have been persuaded by several factors, other than public opinion, in deciding to impose a grain embargo. An analysis of the effects of possible sanctions found that a grain embargo would be the only one that would seriously harm the Soviet economy.[10] In addition, Carter wondered, "How I am going to lead the West and persuade our allies to impose sanctions against the Russians if we aren't willing to make some sacrifices ourselves?" He recognized that he risked electoral retribution from the farmers, especially since he had promised in the 1976 presidential election not to embargo grain except in a national emergency, but he decided, "This is an emergency and I'm going to have to impose the embargo, and we'll just have to make the best of it."[11] As a result of this and other decisions, Mondale became increasingly concerned with Carter's placing national security interests above political and electoral ramifications.[12]

A possible boycott of the summer 1980 Moscow Olympic Games was bandied about as another response that Carter thought could be damaging domestically. He wrote in his diary on January 2, 1980, that a boycott would "cause me the most trouble [domestically], and also would be the most severe blow to the Soviet Union." In his view, removing a potential public relations bonanza for the Soviets would be an extremely effective punishment of their actions.[13] The impact of this move on the Soviets appears to have been the principal reason for his decision to favor the boycott. Carter raised the possibility of a boycott on January 4 in his public address announcing the grain embargo and other sanctions and eventually made the final decision on January 18. Although he does not mention it in his memoir, some analysts have reported that domestic pressure turned in favor of a boycott after the January 4 announcement, which may have partially precipitated the need for the January 18 decision.[14] Given that Carter thought he would suffer negative domestic consequences because of the boycott, it seems unlikely, however, that he would have taken the action to gain public support.

Carter also reluctantly asked that the Senate shelve consideration of the SALT II treaty indefinitely. Although he believed that the treaty remained in the national interest and hoped to pursue ratification at a later point, his decision reflected his recognition that the Senate would not vote to approve the treaty in the aftermath of the invasion.[15] In this case, his judgment suggested that postponement of the treaty's consideration might have a better chance of achieving his policy objectives than would pressure on the Senate.

The threat to the Persian Gulf of the Soviets' action led Carter to adopt several measures to bolster American defenses. Perhaps the most controversial was restarting the peacetime registration for the draft, which he viewed as necessary to bolster American defense mobilization capabilities. In his memoirs, he wrote that he faced "a near-rebellion" from Mondale and adviser Stuart Eizenstat because they argued that the policy, which they characterized as an overreaction, would harm his reelection campaign. Despite their objections, Carter decided to proceed with the draft registration.[16] In addition, given Carter's perception of the regional threat engendered by the Soviet action, National Security Adviser Zbigniew Brzezinski gained Carter's support for a new policy toward the Persian Gulf region. Carter announced what came to be known as the Carter Doctrine in his State of the Union address, pledging that "an attempt by any outside force to gain control of the Persian Gulf regions will be regarded as an assault on the vital interests of the United States, and such an assault will be repelled by any means necessary, including military force."[17] By issuing such a strong statement, the administration hoped to deter the Soviets from further expansion in the region.

Summary

Carter's responses are consistent with those predicted by his beliefs. Although the general context of public opinion may have reinforced Carter's belief in the need for a strong reaction, national security interests seem to have been the main driving force for his choices. During the policy selection stage, Carter considered public opinion in weighing his response to the Soviet invasion. Although he initially deferred the grain embargo decision because of public opinion, his eventual choices across a range of policies—including the grain embargo, Olympic boycott, and draft registration—were based on national security concerns, despite the anticipated public opposition and negative electoral consequences. In these instances, he viewed public opinion as a legitimate factor in decision making, but since his better judgment suggested otherwise, he chose to act against what he anticipated would be the public's reaction. On SALT II, Carter deferred to a domestic factor, Senate opinion, over his judgment of the national interest, but public opinion appears not to have directly affected this choice (although it may have affected the Senate's opinion). The other major national security action, the Carter Doctrine, was predicated on Carter's perception of the extent of the Soviet threat after the invasion, and public opinion did not affect his consideration of this issue.

Consistent with his normative public opinion beliefs, Carter considered the public's input and did not attempt to keep public opinion out of his decision. In addition, since he believed that public support of a policy was not necessary for it to succeed, public opinion was not the final arbiter in his choices. At several points, when he thought the public's opinion was not correct and that the nation's security interests required a potentially unpopular policy, Carter relied on his own judgment rather than the dictates of public opinion. Thus, a *causal* influence of his beliefs is suggested at the problem representation, policy selection, and implementation stages as well as for the entire case (public opinion was not considered during option generation). The overall influence of public opinion on policy is coded in the *no-impact category*.

Guardian: Reagan and the Bombing of the Marine Barracks, 1983–1984

In most cases, since Reagan rejected public input and thought that public support was unnecessary, he would have based his decisions on national security considerations and not have been affected by public opinion (no-impact category). Nonetheless, if he considered a more protracted use of force and sensed opposition, he would have been constrained by public opinion (constrain category). On October 23, 1983, a truck bomb exploded at the marine headquarters building in Beirut, claiming 241 lives.[18] In September 1982, the marines had been sent to Beirut as part of a multilateral peacekeeping force to help the Lebanese government restore its authority. After intense negotiations, the United States pinned its hopes for rebuilding Lebanon on a May 17, 1983, agreement between Lebanon and Israel, which ended the state of war between the two nations and called for the withdrawal of Israeli troops from Lebanon. But when the casualties continued into mid-1983, Congress voted in late September to authorize the marines to remain in Lebanon for an additional eighteen months. Even so, Reagan detected a public restlessness about Lebanon, noting in his diary that according to the latest polls "on foreign policy—Lebanon—I'm way down. The people just don't know why we're there." Indeed, Gallup polls in late August and early September found that 53 percent of the public preferred withdrawing the marines and a mere 36 percent "approved of the Marine presence in Lebanon."[19]

Problem Representation

Before the bombing, Reagan believed that action by the United States could help solve Lebanon's problems. Both Reagan and Secretary of State George Shultz thought American actions in Lebanon to be critical for a successful resolution of the Lebanese situation, to prevent the Syrian and Soviet dominance of Lebanon, and to demonstrate American credibility.[20] After the bombing, Reagan's personal response was one of profound grief, which he later described as the "saddest day of my presidency, perhaps the saddest day of my life." However, his sadness soon turned to anger and a determination not to back down in the face of the terrorist attack.[21]

Option Generation

Whereas the bombing seemed to strengthen Reagan's resolve, angry reactions by both Congress and the public wilted the determination of his White House advisers, who became committed to withdrawing the marines.[22] Democrats in Congress openly criticized the administration, and Republicans privately expressed their concern. More disturbing to Reagan's advisers, James Baker and Michael Deaver in particular, were the results found by Reagan's private pollster Richard Wirthlin indicating a dramatic decline in Reagan's approval rating because of the bombing. But even while Reagan's staff wavered in their support, Reagan remained unaffected in the face of domestic opposition and continued to see the American commitment to Lebanon as a vital interest.[23] He later recalled that after the bombing,

> not surprisingly, there was new pressure in Congress to leave that country. Although I did my best to explain to the American people why our troops were there, I knew many still didn't understand it. I believed in—and still believe in—the policy and decisions that originally sent in the marines to Lebanon.[24]

Reagan's main explanation for the continued American presence in Lebanon came in his October 27 speech to the nation. He conveyed a strong anti-Communist message and linked the Beirut bombing and the recently completed American invasion of Grenada as part of the American policy to combat Soviet expansionism and compared the idea of withdrawing the marines with a surrender to terrorism.[25] Public opinion polling after the speech indicated that it had significantly increased public support for the Lebanon policy and lowered it for withdrawal.[26]

Reagan and Shultz remained adamant in their determination to hold the line, but other administration officials were just as determined to get the marines out of Lebanon. Secretary of Defense Casper Weinberger and the Joint Chiefs of Staff had long opposed the U.S. intervention, and they found willing allies in the White House and Congress who now saw the specter of Vietnam looming over Lebanon. Fearing that the intervention would seriously damage Reagan's electoral prospects in 1984, White House Chief of Staff James Baker and Senate Majority Leader Howard Baker (R, Tenn.) determined to do all in their power to extricate the marines from Lebanon, despite their fear that Reagan would not reverse himself once he had made a commitment. Unlike Reagan, who saw the October 27 speech as explaining the continued American deployment, they viewed the speech as buying the time necessary to remove the marines after a reasonable period.[27] These concerns were shared by others in the White House. A NSC staffer later recalled:

> The domestic side of the White House, James Baker, [Edwin] Meese, [Michael] Deaver, and the Vice President [George Bush], thought that the strategic interest of the U.S. was that Ronald Reagan be elected for a second term, and that if the price to be paid was humiliation in Lebanon, so be it; it would be forgotten by the summer. It was a judgment which was absolutely correct and it was supported by the JCS and Weinberger, and it was bitterly opposed by the Secretary of State.[28]

Soon after the bombing and with the exception of Shultz and the recently appointed national security adviser, Robert McFarlane, all of Reagan's major advisers turned against the Lebanon intervention and favored an expeditious withdrawal.

Policy Selection and Implementation

Even though the situation in Lebanon was worsening, Reagan remained determined to keep the marines in place. He later recalled that Lebanon, with its ineffective central government, an army incapable of restoring order, and the marines in a dreadfully exposed position, was more complex than he had initially thought. Given the loss of life in Beirut and the seemingly insurmountable problems, he conceded that the American deployment required a "second look." But with the situation deteriorating, Reagan refused to pull the marines out because it "would say to the terrorists of the world that all it took to change American foreign policy was to murder some Americans" and might even cede the region to the Soviet Union.[29]

Weinberger and other White House officials made Reagan fully aware of the growing disenchantment of both Congress and the public with the marine deployment. But those people involved in the policy discussions remember that Reagan rejected the advice of those who recommended withdrawing the troops because of concerns regarding the

1984 election. Instead, he refused to alter his policy in the face of public opposition because of the necessity of the marines' presence to support American credibility and combat Soviet influence.[30] He acknowledged the public's concern at a December 20, 1983, press conference, saying, "I can understand the public opinion [opposing the marine deployment], because they're hearing great attacks from a number of sources on our presence [in Lebanon]." Aware of this sentiment, he noted,

> There have been some suggestions made with regard to bringing [the marines] home that some of my considerations might be based on the fact that in an election year—and politics are coming up—I will tell you this: No decision regarding the lives and the safety of our servicemen will ever be made by me for a political reason.[31]

Despite Reagan's statements, support in the administration for withdrawing the marines continued to build. In January, McFarlane turned against the intervention in the face of growing public opposition, leaving Shultz the only major official beside Reagan still committed to the deployment and unaffected by the rising congressional and public opposition. But Shultz, too, had started to harbor his own doubts. He told one NSC meeting, "If I ever say send in the Marines again, somebody shoot me."[32] At the January 9 meeting, Vice President George Bush firmly supported getting out of Lebanon, which led Shultz to conclude that Bush was "panicked." After surmising that Bush's view portended an eventual withdrawal of American forces, Shultz worked to develop an alternative other than complete withdrawal and eventually settled on a plan, which Reagan supported, to replace the majority of the marines with a mobile antiterrorist force.[33]

But Reagan was not ready to give up on the mission. At a White House meeting on February 1, a virtually silent Reagan listened as Weinberger urged him to withdraw the troops, given the impossibility of implementing the terms of the May 17 agreement between Lebanon and Israel, since nearly all the Israelis had left Lebanon. Reagan remained unswayed. On February 2, he told an interviewer that "if we get out, it also means the end of Lebanon." In reference to a comment by House Speaker Tip O'Neill (D, Mass.) that the Lebanon policy had failed and the House would probably vote to withdraw the marines, Reagan commented, "Well, I'm going to respond that he may be ready to surrender, but I'm not. As long as there is a chance for peace, the mission remains the same." During his February 4 radio speech, Reagan stressed that the difficulties in Lebanon were "no reason to turn our backs and to cut and run. If we do, we'll be sending one signal to terrorists everywhere. They can gain by waging war against innocent people."[34]

The situation in Lebanon rapidly deteriorated soon after Reagan made this statement. On February 5, the central government collapsed, and on February 6, the Lebanese army ceased to function as a cohesive unit, leaving the marines in Lebanon surrounded on all sides by hostile forces and without their original purpose, to support the central Lebanese government and army. With Reagan out of town on speaking engagements, James Baker, who was traveling with Reagan, conferred with Bush in Washington and agreed that the time had arrived for the United States to withdraw completely from Lebanon. At a meeting in Washington on February 7, without Reagan in attendance, all of Reagan's top advisers, including Bush, Weinberger, and McFarlane, agreed that the marines should be withdrawn, with Undersecretary Lawrence Eagleburger, standing in for Shultz, who was out of town, the only dissenter. Bush then spoke to Reagan in a short telephone conversation and reported that all his advisers except Shultz favored a "redeployment" (a phrase used at Weinberger's suggestion) and added that the United States would still aid the Lebanese government with air support and naval fire. Despite his earlier opposition, Reagan quickly agreed.[35] The assurances of naval and air action and the characterization of the withdrawal as a redeployment reassured him that he had stuck to his goal and not "cut and run."[36] By February 26, all U.S. troops had been removed to ships offshore.

Reagan's quick assent to a withdrawal that he had so strongly opposed only days earlier was based on his conclusion that the marines' mission in Lebanon could no longer be achieved, rather than on the domestic concerns that consumed many of his closest advisers. Reagan wrote in his memoirs that when he decided to pull out the troops, it had become clear that the Lebanese army could not or would not end the civil war, making it likely to continue for some time. Given that the marines' mission could not be achieved and that "no one wanted to commit our troops to a full-scale war in the Middle East," he rejected continuing to run the risk of more casualties for a probably unachievable goal.[37] Immediately after the withdrawal decision, unnamed administration officials supported this reasoning.[38] Reports from the administration stressed that Reagan had not responded to polling on this issue and that he had "rebuffed" his advisers when they broached the subject of the political costs of the marine deployment.[39]

Summary

Throughout the Lebanon bombing case, Reagan acted consistently with predictions based on his beliefs that he would rely on the national security requirements for a decision. He focused almost exclusively on what he perceived to be the nation's security interests and largely ignored public opinion, even though many of his key advisers pressed him to act according to these considerations. Although Reagan was aware of the public's opposition and did make some minor efforts to explain his policy, he explicitly, in both public and private statements, rejected public opinion as a basis for his decision. Even in the face of almost unanimous opposition to his policy by the members of his administration, Reagan consistently held to the policy he deemed best until he was convinced that it was no longer viable. Consistent with his view that public support was needed for a protracted use of force, public opinion may have partially reinforced his opposition to expanding American involvement into a wider military effort. Reagan's behavior was *consistent* with his beliefs during the problem representation stage, and a *causal* effect is evident in the option generation, policy selection, and implementation stages. This behavior suggests a *supportive* coding for the influence of beliefs. The influence of public opinion is coded in the *no-impact category* and perhaps a *minor constrain category*, but only in regard to involvement in a wider war.

Pragmatist: Bush and the Persian Gulf War, 1990–1991

The analysis of George Bush's public opinion beliefs in chapter 7 showed he would have focused on the nation's security requirements in making a choice and not emphasized leading the public or generating support for a policy (no-impact category). If he perceived public opposition to his policy, he would have attempted to lead the public to rectify this problem to gain the needed public support (lead category). As a last resort, if he concluded he could not change public opposition, he would have been constrained by it (constrain category).

Iraq's August 2, 1990, invasion of its small neighbor Kuwait came as a surprise to American decision makers. Even though American intelligence detected the massing of Iraqi troops on the border in advance of the invasion, most American analysts and international actors (including the leaders of Egypt, Jordan, and Saudi Arabia) concluded that Iraqi leader Saddam Hussein was using the threat of invasion as leverage in his ongoing dispute with the Kuwaitis over oil prices. If Hussein did act, most American analysts thought he would, at most, take control of a Kuwaiti oil field and two small islands at the mouth of the Tigris River. After invading all of Kuwait, Iraq controlled 20 percent of the world's oil reserves and held a nearly unobstructed path to Saudi Arabia's oil fields, whose possession would give it control of 40 percent of the world's oil reserves.

Problem Representation

From the beginning, Bush perceived a significant threat to American national security from Iraq's invasion of Kuwait. He later remembered, "I had decided in my own mind in the first hours that the Iraqi aggression could not be tolerated."[40] At the time, Bush had been reading Martin Gilbert's *The Second World War* and noted Winston Churchill's conclusion that the war could have been prevented if the Allies had reacted forcefully to Adolf Hitler when he remilitarized the Rhineland in 1936. Accordingly, Bush was determined to respond to Hussein's aggression before he could reap further rewards from his action or attack other neighbors, and Bush also worried that other potential aggressors might follow Hussein's example.[41] Bush recalled that

> the overriding reason for this [need to respond to Iraq's aggression] was the fact that bold and naked aggression could not be permitted to stand. I worried that Saddam's intentions went far beyond taking over Kuwait. With an attack on Saudi Arabia, he would have gained control over a tremendous amount of the world's oil supply. . . . If he was permitted to get away with that, heaven knows where the world would have gone and what forces would have been unleashed.[42]

Other officials close to Bush confirmed his determination in the hours soon after the invasion to act strongly to counter Iraq's aggression.[43]

Option Generation

The NSC met early in the morning of August 2 (the invasion had occurred in the evening of August 1, Washington time). In a public statement before the meeting, Bush observed, "We're not discussing intervention," and in response to a question of whether he intended to send troops to the area, said, "I'm not contemplating such action." However, he intended to "have this invasion be reversed and have them get out of Kuwait." National Security Adviser Brent Scowcroft immediately concluded that Bush did not intend to suggest that intervention had been rejected as an option. Bush later confirmed that his statement had "inadvertently led to some confusion about my intent. I did not intend to rule out the use of force. At that juncture I did not wish explicitly to rule it in."[44]

The meeting itself consisted of a rambling discussion and led to no definite conclusions, but it did establish Bush's commitment to reversing the invasion. When Treasury Secretary Nicholas Brady began to talk about adapting Iraq's invasion, Bush cut him off, saying, "Let's be clear about one thing: we are not here to talk about adapting. We are not going to plan how to live with this."[45] He launched into a detailed assessment of Iraq's control of 20 percent of the world oil reserves, pointing out that Saddam Hussein might use his power to manipulate world oil prices and threaten the United States and its allies. He feared that higher oil prices would spur inflation and further damage the anemic American economy and perhaps drive it into recession. To respond, Bush endorsed a coalition effort to work through the United Nations to impose an economic embargo on Iraq. After hearing two military options (one entailed retaliatory air strikes and the other the commitment of 200,000 troops to defend Saudi Arabia), Bush approved preparations for the defensive option but made no definite commitments.[46]

On August 3, Bush met again with the NSC to discuss American policy responses. Scowcroft began by emphasizing the threat to the world and the U.S. economy posed by Iraq's action and strongly endorsed the use of force to confront it. After hearing comments by the assembled advisers endorsing military action, Bush stressed the need for economic sanctions and that "whatever we do, we've got to have the international community behind us."[47] Bush endorsed his advisers' sentiments in favor of a military response but observed that the real question was whether the Saudis would accept American assistance. He then asked for a presentation of the military options the next day at Camp David.[48]

Policy Selection

The NSC reconvened at Camp David on August 4 to discuss policy options. After hearing a presentation of the military options indicating that it would take several months for a significant defensive force to arrive in Saudi Arabia and even longer to muster an effective offensive force to remove the Iraqi forces from Kuwait, the meeting's participants returned to the question of what to do. Some advisers wondered whether the public would continue to support the policy if the American force suffered significant casualties or the commitment dragged on. But instead of focusing on the domestic component, Bush turned to a comparison between Iraq's action and the weak reaction of the Allies in the 1930s to Germany's provocations. He insisted they needed to persuade the Saudis to forgo "the appeasement option."[49] After talking with the Saudi leadership, Bush agreed to send a team to brief them on the specifics of the possible American commitment.

At this point, Bush had settled on a two-pronged policy to confront Iraq's aggression. He was determined, if the Saudis agreed, to commit American ground forces to Saudi Arabia to deter further Iraqi aggression. To persuade Saddam Hussein to withdraw, he decided to pursue a diplomatic effort to isolate Iraq and institute economic sanctions.[50]

Throughout these deliberations, Bush focused on the national security implications of the Iraqi action. When these decisions were made, public opinion had not been polled on this question, and editorial opinion had been supportive of the administration's diplomatic and economic efforts but without calling for a more aggressive response.[51] Although some of Bush's advisers, anticipating possible public opposition, raised public opinion as one reason to move cautiously regarding a military deployment, Bush remained determined to confront the aggression if he thought national security requirements dictated it, regardless of the cost in terms of public opinion. Secretary of State James Baker reported a conversation he had with Bush in the Oval Office in August. Baker recalled telling Bush,

> "I know you're aware of the fact that this has all the ingredients that brought down three of the last five Presidents: a hostage crisis, body bags, and a full-fledged economic recession caused by forty-dollar oil." The President understood it full well. "I know that, Jimmy, I know that," he said. "But we're doing what's right; we're doing what is clearly in the national interest of the United States. Whatever happens, so be it."[52]

In late August, Bush took some solace in the public's support of his Gulf policy, as reflected in public opinion polls, which he attributed to a "post-Vietnam 'maturity.' " Probably related to his concerns about domestic support, Bush worried through most of August and September that Iraq might attack the arriving American forces, with either conventional or chemical weapons, before sufficient numbers could be deployed, leading to a significant number of American deaths.[53] Despite these fears, Bush continued with the actions he saw as necessary for the nation's security.

On his return from Camp David on August 5, Bush publicly stated his private decision to reverse Iraq's invasion saying, "This will not stand. This will not stand! This aggression against Kuwait."[54] After the war, Bush explained that he saw the statement as a reflection of the internal policy deliberations and a signal of his views to the public: "I came to the conclusion that some public comment was needed to make clear my determination that the United States must do whatever might be necessary to reverse the Iraqi aggression."[55] After a presentation by American officials, the Saudis approved the defensive deployment of American troops on August 6, which President Bush authorized immediately.

Implementation

During September and October, Bush gradually moved toward increasing the number of troops to provide an offensive option. His growing impatience with economic sanctions to force the Iraqis to withdraw stemmed from his concern that the international coalition and domestic support would not continue long enough to allow the sanctions to work. Because of the harsh weather conditions in the Gulf region and the onset of Ramadan, the Muslim month of fasting, any ground war would have to take place before mid-March 1991 or be postponed for another year. Furthermore, waiting for sanctions to work would mean pushing any offensive action into 1992—a presidential election year. As one Bush adviser put it, by postponing military action until 1992, "we could have the economy in the toilet and the body bags coming home. If you're George Bush, you don't like that scenario."[56] On September 24, Bush expressed his trepidation about the staying power of international and domestic support for sanctions, "I really don't think we have time for sanctions to work."[57]

In this context, the administration saw the increased number of troops as a logical extension of their policy to drive Iraq out of Kuwait. On October 31, when Bush approved an increased deployment of around 200,000 troops to supply the offensive option, he did not see the action as tantamount to a decision for war and instead hoped that just the threat of offensive action would be enough to persuade Saddam Hussein to withdraw from Kuwait.[58]

The announcement of the troop increase led to an outpouring of congressional and public concern, at which the administration realized its failure to build public support. Beginning in October, the administration became concerned with polling results that indicated a drop in public approval of the president in general (caused in part by a domestic squabble with Congress over the federal budget) and of his Gulf policy in particular. In searching for an appropriate explanation for American policy, Bush pollster Robert Teeter discovered that though the public was not responsive to justifications based on economics (e.g., jobs, oil, recession) or principle (e.g., responding to aggression, the Hitler analogy), the public did react positively to an explanation based on the threat of Iraq's nuclear capability. Bush agreed with Teeter's view that the administration lead the public, but he refused to act on it because he felt that his competence to handle the situation, given his previous experience, was enough to gain public understanding.[59] His implicit dismissal of Teeter's call to appeal to the public was symptomatic of Bush's inattention to building public support. In fact, when public support was eroding in November, Bush consulted public relations experts to ask them what he was doing wrong. When they told him that "he had to get out every day and explain why he was there," Bush replied that "he had made his case over and over."[60] His perception notwithstanding, the common view of his leadership efforts suggest that he did little to explain either the administration's policy or the necessity of using force.[61]

Even though he feared going to war without congressional or public support, Bush decided that he would base his choice to use force on national security alone. When the UN Security Council on November 29 approved the use of all necessary means to push Iraq out of Kuwait after January 15, Bush gave in to his advisers' suggestion that he speak to the nation to explain his policy and calm the public's fears about war. On November 30, while stressing his determination to drive Iraq out after the January 15 deadline, Bush announced that he would meet with the Iraqi foreign minister, Tariq Aziz, and send Baker to Iraq to meet with Saddam Hussein "to go the extra mile for peace." The action was viewed by Bush and his top advisers as necessary to demonstrate to Congress and the public that they had exhausted all diplomatic options before resorting to war.[62]

Because Bush thought Lyndon Johnson had made a mistake by forgoing formal congressional approval of the war in Vietnam, he wished to avoid the same error, though he was equally convinced that he did not need congressional acquiescence to act.[63] In regard to the congressional debate on relying on sanctions or the offensive option, Bush was adamant: "I'll prevail . . . or I'll be impeached."[64] Bush confirmed this view later: "I believe I would have [gone ahead if the Congress had voted against war]. I know I would have. . . . But it was far better to get congressional approval. It gave it a certain legitimacy—the president's committing forces to battle—that it wouldn't have without it. I expect that impeachment papers would have been filed immediately if we'd gone into battle without sanction by the Congress."[65]

Over his Christmas vacation, Bush became even more sure that war was the correct action, based on reports of Iraqi atrocities in Kuwait.[66] Even so, he remained concerned about possible American casualties, remarking, "I don't think that support would last if it were a long, drawn-out conflagration. I think support would erode, as it did in the Vietnam conflict."[67] Bush was clearly aware of the domestic implications of a failure in the Gulf. On November 30, he had told an assembled group of bipartisan congressional members, "I know whose backside's at stake and rightfully so. It will not be a long, drawn-out mess."[68] Despite his concerns about congressional and public support, Bush was determined to go to war because he thought it was the best policy for American national security interests. He commented on January 2.

> For me, it boils down to a very moral case of good versus evil, black versus white. If I have to go, it's not going to matter to me if there isn't one congressman who supports this, or what happens to public opinion. If it's right, it's gotta be done.[69]

Bush faced none of these consequences. After asking for a congressional resolution of support on January 8, Congress voted to approve the use of force on January 12. Air attacks on Iraqi positions in Iraq and Kuwait commenced on January 16, and the ground attack began on February 23. After quick success on the ground in driving Iraqi forces out of Kuwait, Bush suspended the ground war on February 28 after only one hundred hours. Although the public was divided over the use of force before the war, Bush's public approval rating reached record levels immediately after the conflict, with 89 percent approving his performance. The figure remained at the 70 percent level until the end of August 1991.[70]

Summary

Bush's decisions were consistent with his beliefs that the public's input had no place in foreign policy and that the public's support was necessary (which he assumed would be almost automatic). Although he believed he would significantly damage his standing in public opinion if U.S. troops suffered significant casualties in the early going, he based his initial decisions in August on his perception of the nation's security requirements and largely assumed that public support would follow.

When he did run into trouble with public opinion, he appealed to the public, but only in a halfhearted manner after he had already determined the direction of his policy.

Public opinion did influence Bush's decision on the timing of the shift to the offensive option. Given the legacy of Vietnam, he feared that the public could not be led to support a long-term commitment and that waiting for sanctions would force a potentially divisive war into an election year. In combination with his concern that the international coalition also would not last this long, public opinion partially constrained his decision on the timing of the action, but not on policy goals or means.

Bush's behavior was *consistent* with his beliefs in problem representation and option generation. A *causal* influence can be seen in his policy selection and implementation, a pattern displaying a *supportive* influence of his beliefs on behavior. The influence of public opinion on policy development is principally in the *no-impact category*, with less influence of the *lead category* during implementation and a *moderate constrain category* influence on the timing of the shift to an offensive option.

Delegate: Clinton and U.S. Casualties in Somalia, October 1993

The analysis of Clinton's beliefs in chapter 7 suggests that he welcomes the public's input and thinks its support is necessary. This analysis also indicates that his response to public opinion relies primarily on his expectation of how the public will evaluate his polices in the future. Given his focus during crises on the public's input and support, public opinion should constrain his decisions when he anticipates that a policy might cause him political difficulties (constrain category).

The large-scale American involvement in Somalia began in December 1992 when President George Bush—reacting to pictures of starvation and the inability of humanitarian aid agencies and the UN to deliver needed supplies during an ongoing civil war—sent troops to protect the humanitarian relief effort. In 1993, during the first summer of the Clinton administration, the UN mission shifted from the provision of relief to nation building. When UN peacekeepers were killed, the UN authorized a search for the leader responsible for the attack, Mohamed Farah Aidid. Although it later distanced itself from this decision, the Clinton administration supported the UN's expanded role and sent specialized Ranger and Delta forces to Somalia to hunt for Aidid. After Aidid's forces shot down an American helicopter on September 25, Congress passed a nonbinding resolution requesting that Clinton secure its approval by November 15 for continuing the deployment. Then on October 3, the administration and nation were shocked when eighteen Americans were killed and seventy-eight were wounded during an attempt to capture Aidid. Television images of Somalis dragging the body of an American soldier through the streets and of a shaken American prisoner heightened domestic outrage. In the aftermath of this attack, the Clinton administration faced the decision of what, if anything, needed to be done to respond to the changing situation in Somalia.

Problem Representation

Throughout 1993, Clinton's attention to foreign affairs had been minimal because he viewed the 1992 election as an indication of the public's desire for the president to turn instead to domestic concerns. Clinton explained that "my premise was that the American people were hungry for a president who showed that he knew that something had to be done here to address our problems at home and that had been long neglected" and that this had resulted in his "conscious focus" on domestic issues. This approach not only led to his lack of involvement in many of the Somalia decisions before October 1993 but also caused him to avoid taking action to build a public consensus for his Somalia policy.[71]

In the weeks before the October 3 attack, instigated in part by a conversation with former President Jimmy Carter, Clinton had changed the administration's policy to emphasize political negotiations over military action, because the administration had decided that forceful action was not a basis on which the Somali political situation could be stabilized. In addition, the increasingly impatient Congress, bolstered by constituents' concern, pressed Clinton to clarify, by October 15, the American mission and objectives and called for a November 15 vote on authorizing the Somalia operation. Clinton knew that the administration needed to get the Somalia situation under control, for reasons related to both Somalia and its implications for other multilateral peacekeeping efforts. He feared that congressional and public opposition to the U.S. intervention in Somalia would hinder the possibility of deploying thousands of American troops in Bosnia after a settlement there. Fearing that a dramatic public reversal of policy would undercut the UN and multilateral peacekeeping—the foundation of the administration's approach to the post–Cold War world—Clinton did not suspend the hunt for Aidid, even though it contradicted the new politically focused approach.[72]

After the October 3 killings, the public and congressional reaction reached a peak. Before October 3, 46 percent of the public disapproved and 43 percent approved of "the presence of U.S. troops in Somalia," but following the deaths, 69 percent thought the U.S. troops should be pulled out and 43 percent thought they should be removed right away. The public's approval of Clinton's handling of the situation dropped from 51 percent in June to 41 percent in September before falling to an average of 31 percent in October.[73] The public's apprehension registered in Congress as well. Spurred by the pictures of a dead American dragged through the street and the emotional public reaction, Congress erupted with calls to withdraw the American forces immediately.[74]

The Somali attack and the subsequent domestic criticism took Clinton by surprise. He pressed his advisers, asking, "How could this happen?" and complained that he had not received "a realistic assessment" of the situation in Somalia and that "no one told me about the downside." Perhaps because of his concern with the long-term ramifications in public opinion of his handling of the issue, when Clinton asked political adviser David Gergen how Reagan avoided potential damage from the bombing of the marine barracks in Beirut, Gergen told him, "Because two days later we were in Grenada, and everyone knew that Ronald Reagan would bomb the hell out of somewhere."[75] The congressional reaction in particular, which one administration official described as a "near panic," astonished Clinton, who was upset with both the situation in Somalia and the lack of consensus among his advisers over how to proceed. Given the congressional reaction, the administration focused on heading off any precipitous moves and creating some breathing space in which they could evaluate their options and formulate a policy.[76]

Option Generation

Clinton met with his top advisers on the evening of October 5 to talk over the policy options. National Security Adviser Anthony Lake presented four alternatives. First, the administration could dramatically increase the military presence and work to pacify the attacking militias, but this would entail heavy fighting. Second, they could raise the number of American troops and keep pressuring Aidid militarily while trying to negotiate a settlement. Third, they could abandon the military option and seek an honorable withdrawal. Finally, they could focus on a negotiated settlement while extending the deadline for an American withdrawal but not make much of a military effort. An immediate pullout was not an option because the military needed until March 31 to shift its logistics operations to other groups and to remove its supplies and personnel.[77]

Clinton found none of the options to his liking. The group agreed that the first option, increasing military forces, was too costly, and anyway, congressional opposition made this action impossible. No one favored the face-saving exit of the third option, which was also complicated by a Somali-held American prisoner. Even though the fourth option of a negotiated settlement without military costs was favored by most members, Clinton preferred a combination of this option with the second option, which placed more emphasis on military force. He did want to help Somalia's recovery, but he now thought that this objective had to be achieved faster and with an exit strategy that he could present to Congress.[78]

A meeting that afternoon heightened congressional concerns about the administration's policy. Afraid that Congress might vote for an immediate pullout, Secretary of Defense Les Aspin and Secretary of State Warren Christopher met with more than two hundred members of Congress to reassure skittish legislators. Whereas Aspin and Christopher went in to the meeting seeking Congress's views on Somalia, the legislators expected a briefing on how the administration was planning to respond to the Somalia crisis. The result, in the words of one legislator, was "an unmitigated disaster." Instead of calming Congress's fears, the meeting only increased their anxiety and led to more calls for an immediate pullout.[79]

Congressional reactions to the deaths in Somalia were fueled in large part by pressure from the public. Throughout the U.S. intervention in Somalia, Congress paid close attention to the polls, and congressional support for intervention dropped along with public support. Their demands for an expedited pullout resulted in large part from thousands of phone calls after the October 3 attack from constituents who pressed for an immediate withdrawal.[80] The congressional stampede to leave Somalia was temporarily stemmed by senior senators from both parties who brokered a Senate agreement on October 6 to delay any vote until the following week, so as to give Clinton time to formulate a policy response and present it to Congress and the public.[81]

Policy Selection

Clinton met again with his top advisers on October 6. His political advisers, including pollster Stan Greenberg and consultants James

Carville and Mandy Grunwald, all argued for a pullout date sometime before December 31. They contended that the United States should cut its loses and depart as quickly as possible. The "home-by-Christmas" option was favored because, as one person pointed out, "The worst thing that could happen would be we set a deadline and Congress immediately moves it forward." Secretary of State Christopher argued for no deadline or an early one if required by political reasons. One official recounted, "Their argument was, really, if you can't do it by Christmas, you can't do it by March and Congress won't accept March."[82]

The military, however, argued for either no deadline or an extended one because it feared that a quick pullout would cause Somalia to return to anarchy, and the military needed a longer period to finish its political and military missions. In addition, the military insisted that it needed additional military forces to protect the troops already in Somalia until they were pulled out.[83]

After hearing these arguments, Clinton split the difference between the political and military requirements, although his decision more closely reflected the argument by the military. He approved the military's request for more troops, which more than doubled the existing number. In addition, he rejected an early withdrawal deadline because it was unacceptable to the military. Instead, he chose a March 31 deadline, the earliest date the military said was possible, because of political considerations. In addition, he abandoned the search for Aidid, ordered a stop to military action except in self-defense, and sent a former ambassador to Somalia, Robert Oakley, to negotiate a settlement.[84]

This choice balanced the political and national security pressures on Clinton. In essence, he decided to pull out of Somalia as fast as the military thought possible and announced a politically motivated deadline to stave off congressional insistence on an immediate pullout. The deadline, he hoped, would communicate to Congress and the public that the United States was not involved in an open-ended commitment. Even so, he remained prepared to move the date forward if Congress wanted an earlier deadline. In the meantime, he bolstered American forces and focused their mission on avoiding additional casualties until they could be withdrawn. Presaging Clinton's announcement the following day, a senior official noted,

> The message the president will deliver tomorrow is that it is not whether the U.S. is going to leave Somalia. It is how and when the U.S. will leave, and whether we will leave in a fashion that allows for a

reasonable chance that we can leave behind a U.N. force that can do a job or leave in a way that will virtually guarantee a return to chaos there.[85]

Implementation

Clinton met on October 7 with senior congressional leaders to explain his plan. They complained either that the March 31 deadline was not soon enough or could undermine U.S. policy by announcing the end of the American involvement. In any event, the legislators warned that Clinton needed to explain why the troops needed to remain. Despite later comments suggesting that Clinton might delay his speech on Somalia, the administration decided that Clinton had to deliver an address to the nation that evening or he would appear indecisive.[86] Although Clinton had initially been reluctant to give an evening Oval Office address for fear of drawing too much attention to the issue, his advisers convinced him that the venue would signify decisive presidential leadership on foreign policy.[87]

In addition to announcing the new policy, Clinton emphasized in his speech that "our mission from this day forward . . . is to increase our strength, do our job, bring our soldiers out and bring them home." The speech and new policy appeared to achieve Clinton's goal of mollifying congressional critics. By integrating into his speech much of the advice he had received from Congress in the previous few days and providing a clear statement of the mission and pullout date, he appeared to gain some breathing room with Congress to allow his new policy to work. Before the speech, the November 15 congressional vote on the mission seemed most likely to call for an immediate withdrawal. After the president's address, however, congressional sentiment seemed to accept the administration's plans.[88] However, the polls indicated that public opinion remained unchanged after his speech, with 52 percent disapproving of Clinton's handling of the situation.[89] In response, the administration tried to limit any public relations damage from the continual reminders of the deaths by withholding pictures of Clinton visiting the wounded and his avoiding public memorials for the troops killed. The administration also attempted to shift blame for the raid to the UN, although internal reports indicated the United States was in control of American troop actions.[90]

After visiting with constituents over the long Columbus Day weekend and noting that polls continued to show public opposition, several lawmakers, led by Senator Robert C. Byrd (D, W.Va.), who favored cutting off funding for the Somalia mission as early as January 1, pressed for a quick vote on a halt to its funding.[91] The administration's efforts to head off this movement was assisted by senior congressional members of both parties, who brokered a compromise agreement with Senator Byrd that turned Clinton's October 7 policy into law and ended funding for the mission after March 31 except for a small security force for American civilians. The last of the American forces were removed from Somalia on March 25, 1994.[92]

Summary

Clinton's behavior in this crisis was consistent with his beliefs favoring public input and support, since public opinion partially determined the issues he saw as important and partially shaped his policy decisions. Before the fall of 1993, Clinton largely ignored Somalia because of his reading of public sentiments as expressed in the 1992 election. After the October 3 raid, congressional pressure, which the administration saw as a reaction to public opinion, played a key part in determining the administration's policy. In formulating options in response to the failed raid, Clinton decided, on the advice of the military, that he could not pull out the troops immediately because it would cause chaos and further starvation in Somalia. But he also felt the pressure from Congress and the public to do something to end what appeared to be an open-ended American commitment and believed that public opposition over the issue could harm other policy initiatives.

Clinton also knew that the military deemed March 31 as the first date it could extricate itself from Somalia in an orderly fashion. Given this state of affairs, he ordered the troop increase the military wanted to protect its existing forces, adopted their earliest date for withdrawal, and publicly announced the withdrawal date to mollify congressional and public sentiment. After making the decision, he attempted to downplay the issue (unsuccessfully) and build support for the March 31 withdrawal date (successfully with Congress, unsuccessfully with public opinion) as an alternative to what he saw as a disastrous immediate withdrawal. Although several factors affected Clinton's decision to withdraw the troops, public opinion provided one constraining factor on his policy deliberations and decision to pull out the troops. Clinton's beliefs had a *causal* influence on his behavior at all stages, and the influence of public opinion in this case is coded in a *moderate constrain category* influence.

Each of these presidents reacted in accordance with his public opinion beliefs when confronting the crises examined in this chapter. This consistency with predictions across several of the beliefs orientations shows strong support for the beliefs model and accounts for the varying reactions among the presidents examined (see table 8.1). Perhaps the comparison between Carter and Reagan is most interesting because even though public opinion had nearly the same influence on their behavior, they viewed public opinion quite differently as they made their decisions. Carter wanted to know about public preferences and allowed an open discussion of them as he made his choices. While he considered the public's preferences, he ultimately decided that he needed to act against the public's view because of national security. On the other hand, Reagan largely dismissed public opinion as a factor in his policy and wanted to have only that advice regarding the American national interests at stake in Lebanon. Although neither of these actors reacted to public opinion in his final decision, they both treated the public's view differently according to their beliefs.

Both the realist and Wilsonian liberal perspectives find support in the behaviors of certain presidents, but neither can account for the behavior of all the presidents examined in this chapter. The realist model best explains Reagan's inattention to public opinion and his focus on the national interest, as well as Bush's behavior. Although the realist

TABLE 8.1 Crisis Cases and Recent Presidents

	Predicted Public Influence Based on Beliefs	Actual Public Influence	Influence of Beliefs
Carter: Executor, Afghanistan	No impact *or* Constrain	No impact	Causal
Reagan: Guardian, Lebanon	No Impact/ *Constrain*	No Impact/ with lesser Constrain (minor)	Supportive
Bush: Pragmatist, Persian Gulf	No impact/ *Lead/Constrain*	No impact/ with lesser Lead and Constrain (moderate)	Supportive
Clinton: Delegate, Somalia	Constrain	Constrain (moderate)	Causal

Note: Italics indicate conditional predictions.

view may descriptively anticipate Carter's choice, it cannot encompass the decision process that produced that outcome. The Wilsonian liberal perspective is best supported by Clinton's behavior. It partially anticipates the process by which Carter reached his decision, but not the outcome of his deliberations. In the cases, these two models find mixed support in the presidents' choices. As discussed, the beliefs model provides a much more effective account of when and why presidents turned their attention toward or away from public opinion.

Decision makers also approached leading and educating the public consistently with their beliefs. Reagan (guardian) merely referred to the national interests involved in the Lebanon situation to explain his policy. Clinton (delegate) explained the policy as being responsive to public opinion on the issue. Bush (pragmatist) focused on saying whatever would build support for the policy and weighed several alternatives before settling on the nuclear proliferation argument. Even so, he made only a limited effort to get his message out. Carter (executor) did not expend much energy building support for his policy, even though he expected public opposition. Several of these decision makers thought of their actions as "explaining" their policies to the public, but the way they approached these actions differed according to their beliefs.

An interesting parallel appeared for two of the presidents. Both Carter's and Reagan's advisers reacted more strongly to public opinion than did either president. In Carter's case, Mondale was especially concerned about the potential electoral effects of some of the responses under consideration. Although Carter encouraged Mondale to express his concerns, he reacted much less strongly to public opinion than did his vice president. Reagan's main advisers also were very concerned about the electoral implications of a continued troop deployment in Lebanon, but they generally did not mention these issues to Reagan and instead used arguments related to the national interest to persuade him to respond to their position. This pattern has two implications. First, it means that even though advisers pay attention to the type of information the president wants, they still form their own opinions based on the factors they feel are important. Second, it means that the focus on the president's decisions does not provide a full account of public opinion's role in the decision process. To the extent that Reagan's advisers were swayed by public opinion and used the arguments based on the national interest only as a ploy to convince Reagan, the coding of public opinion's influence may understate its role in the decision process.

The examination of recent presidents does provide one point of comparison implying that the beliefs orientation also affects presidential advisers and that it may explain why some advisers pay attention to public opinion, even though the president is not interested in it. Bush, as vice president during the Reagan years, acted as an adviser to Reagan on policy and reacted to public opinion in line with his beliefs. Since Bush saw public support as necessary, when he thought that the public would not support the United States' intervention in Lebanon and could not be swayed, he adjusted his policy recommendation. In much the same way that Bush later approached the Gulf War, after the bombing in Beirut, he pointed to the public's intolerance of long and costly conflicts as a reason to pull the marines out of Lebanon. Although he told other administration officials his reasons for his view, he appears to have presented a national interest perspective to Reagan. This evidence is not conclusive proof that the beliefs model can show how Reagan's advisers formed their views, but it does demonstrate that they may have formulated their views consistent with their own preferences and then presented their views to Reagan in a manner to which the president would be receptive.

As this discussion suggests, the interaction between presidents and their advisers as it affects public opinion requires more attention. Such an examination should determine the extent to which presidents and their advisers hold consonant or disconsonant views regarding public opinion and the effect of this pattern on decision making and the influence of public opinion. Although an analysis of this type is beyond the scope of this book, it does suggest a potentially useful avenue of research.

Across these cases, when public opinion did have an influence, it appeared to occur through the more perceptually based factors. Polling data (in the Reagan, Bush, and Clinton cases) and congressional reactions (in the Clinton case) formed the basis for some of these assessments, but the decision makers tended to use this information mostly to assess how the public would react to these issues. Although the polls also play an important part of the policy process in the longer-term cases examined in chapter 9, these presidents continued to pay more attention to these perceptually based influences of public opinion.

CHAPTER NINE

Deliberative Cases and Recent Presidents

Deliberative cases should provide more opportunities for public opinion to become integrated into the decision process than crisis cases do, either because the public might more easily assert itself or because its opinion might be more easily discernible by presidents. As discussed in chapter 1, even though realists expect presidents to lead the public, they also believe that an overly emotional public can perniciously constrain elite choices. Wilsonian liberals expect decision makers to follow public opinion. The beliefs model says that presidents react in a range of ways according to their views. In this chapter, I show that decision makers behave more in accordance with the beliefs model than with either the realist or the Wilsonian liberal model. The cases considered are (1) Jimmy Carter's decision to negotiate the Panama Canal treaties; (2) Ronald Reagan's origination of the Strategic Defense Initiative (SDI); (3) George Bush's handling of German reunification; and (4) Bill Clinton's decisions on intervening in Bosnia.

Executor: Carter and the Panama Canal Treaties, 1977–1978

Given Carter's positive view toward public input and rejection of the necessity of public support, he would have considered public opinion but might have acted against it if certain conditions prevailed. If he thought he had a better view of a problem than the public did, he would likely have made his decision based on other factors. Because of the long decision time, if a policy required congressional approval, he might have attempted to lead public opinion to his side to affect Congress (lead category). However, in his decision making and behavior, the target of these actions would have been Congress, and he would not have thought about generating the "necessary" public support. In this sense, he would have been treating public support instrumentally rather than as an end in itself. If he had only a weak preference on policy or thought the public had a better view, public opinion would probably have limited his actions (constrain category).

The 1903 Hay-Bunau-Varilla treaty gave the United States the right to build and operate the Panama Canal, and from its inception, it was a source of Panamanian resentment, feelings that only grew stronger with the passage of time. As a result of these rising tensions, President Lyndon Johnson began negotiations in 1964 to replace the 1903 treaty. Discussions continued throughout the Nixon administration and into the Ford administration when, finally in 1974 the United States and Panama agreed to the Kissinger-Tack principles, named for Secretary of State Henry Kissinger and Panamanian Foreign Minister Juan Tack, as a basis for an agreement. These principles foreshadowed the eventual agreement signed in 1977 and called for replacing the indefinite length of the 1903 treaty with a set end date, return of the canal to Panama, and an end to American jurisdiction. American public opposition became apparent during the 1976 election when the conservative Republican presidential primary candidate, Ronald Reagan, challenged President Gerald Ford regarding the issue, thereby stalling the negotiations until after the 1976 election. Carter, the Democratic presidential candidate, also announced, "I would not be in favor of relinquishing actual control of the Panama Canal or its use to any other nation, including Panama."[1] When Carter took office, the status of the canal thus remained a contentious domestic issue in the United States and a source of rising discontent in Panama.[2]

Problem Representation

Carter's position during the campaign had more to do with the pressures of a presidential campaign and a lack of familiarity with the issue than a firmly felt position. Sol Linowitz, Carter's negotiator for the treaties, reported that his campaign foreign policy adviser and eventual secretary of state, Cyrus Vance, assured him in October 1976 that despite the campaign rhetoric, Carter intended to move ahead with

negotiations and would "certainly want to do the right thing in connection with the Panama Canal situation." Linowitz himself rejected any
shift in Carter's fundamental perspective on Panama: "Frankly, I don't
think he had studied [the issue] in depth at the time he made his statement.[3] Soon after being elected president in 1976, Carter recognized in
discussions with his foreign policy advisers that the United States needed to sign a new treaty with Panama quickly that would relinquish its
total control over the canal and recognize Panamanian sovereignty.[4]

Option Generation

As Carter saw the situation, several factors indicated a need for
expeditious action on the treaty, even in the face of "a terrible political
fight in Congress" and public opposition. In his memoirs, he stressed
the need to correct the injustice of the original treaty which had been
presented to the Panamanian leadership as a fait accompli in 1903 and
had continued to plague American-Panamanian relations. Given the
volatility of the issue in Panamanian politics, the canal itself was coming
under increasing threat of attack or sabotage, and Carter feared that
radical groups opposed to American interests would use the issue to
undermine the stability of the Panamanian government and economy.
At a broader level, he saw the colonial overtones inherent in Panamanian–United States relations as undermining the American position with
other Latin American countries.[5]

Policy Selection

The decision to move ahead on the treaty negotiations came shortly
before the administration took office in January 1977. At an early January meeting of Carter's foreign policy advisers, the administration
decided to accept the Kissinger-Tack principles as the basis for an
agreement and to raise the priority of the negotiations. The National
Security Council adviser, Zbigniew Brzezinski, reported their conclusion was "if the new Administration did not move rapidly on the Panama issue, capitalizing on the new President's mandate, the problem
would become unmanageable and sour our relations with Latin America."[6] Vance indicated that Carter made this decision with full knowledge of the "deep emotions" and "political and foreign policy risks" that
were implied by the difficult ratification debate that any treaty was sure
to face in the Senate.[7]

In addition, the administration saw ratification of the treaty as an
important element in establishing the tone of the new government's

foreign policy. According to this view, a canal treaty would highlight the administration's new approach to foreign policy by resolving a thorny problem through an equitable agreement with a lesser power. A quick success would also establish a momentum the administration hoped would transfer to other issues. They anticipated it would undermine the president's conservative opponents by exposing them as extremists and thus ease the achievement of subsequent foreign policy objectives such as the ratification of the SALT II treaty with the Soviet Union and the normalization of relations with China. As a practical matter, some administration officials also saw the Panama treaty as an organizational "dry run" for these other issues, which they viewed as more contentious domestically.[8]

Carter decided that the foreign policy advantages outweighed potential difficulties with Congress and the public. In his memoirs, he notes,

> Despite the opposition of Congress and the public, I decided to plow ahead, believing that if the facts could be presented clearly, my advisers and I could complete action while my political popularity was still high and before we had to face the additional complication of the congressional election campaigns of 1978.[9]

Although Carter recognized that the public opposed his action, his main concern was with congressional opposition, especially in light of the need for a Senate vote on the treaty itself.

Potential difficulties with Congress also provided the main impetus for a major negotiating innovation. Linowitz thought the treaty's ratification rested on Panama's acceptance of an indefinite U.S. right to defend the canal's neutrality, an assessment that Carter shared.[10] To address this problem, the United States negotiated two treaties. One was called the neutrality treaty and concerned the permanent right of the United States to defend the canal. The other, called the Panama Canal treaty, transferred the canal to Panama. Negotiating and ratifying the neutrality treaty first, Vance believed, "would give us a clear answer to those who claimed that turning the canal over to Panama would threaten U.S. security," and both Carter and he "saw the political importance of this suggestion."[11]

Implementation

The administration faced a tough fight in the Senate to win the sixty-seven votes needed for the treaty's ratification, especially since thirty-eight senators had voted in the fall of 1975 for a Senate resolution opposing any treaty with Panama. Despite this congressional opposition and public disapproval, as reflected in public opinion polls, Carter determined to make a full press case for the treaties and to put his prestige on the line in the battle.[12] He initially hoped for a quick ratification of the treaties after they were signed on September 7, 1977, but he refused to begin the ratification campaign before the negotiations ended, which allowed the antitreaty forces to mobilize public opposition. As a result, the Senate majority leader, Robert Byrd (D, W.Va.), predicted "total disaster" if the administration pursued their quick ratification plan. Carter had originally intended to rely only on direct appeals to uncommitted senators, but this situation persuaded him to delay ratification and to adopt a more extensive public relations effort, although the main focus remained on the Senate.[13]

From the outset, Carter was determined to follow a ratification strategy that focused on changing the votes of individual senators rather than on changing public opinion. The administration concentrated their public relations effort on gaining the support of important political leaders in the states of key undecided senators, in the hopes of obtaining proratification votes. As Carter recalled,

> During the fall of 1977, I spent a lot of my time planning carefully how to get Senate votes. The task force set up for this purpose developed a somewhat limited objective: not to build up an absolute majority of support among all citizens, but to convince an acceptable number of key political leaders in each important state to give their senators some "running room."

The administration hoped that they could generate enough support for the treaties to convince concerned senators that they did not have to fear for their political lives if they voted for the treaties.[14]

The administration's public relations effort reflected these concerns. Political aide Hamilton Jordan produced a ratification strategy designed to produce at least a divided public (as opposed to the then prevailing public view that overwhelmingly opposed the treaties) and an approving one if possible. In addition to the national public opinion, they targeted public opinion in the fifteen states with uncommitted senators. But this effort paled in comparison with the other aspects of the strategy. Instead of focusing on building mass-based grassroots support (which the administration ceded to conservative, antitreaty groups), the most extensive effort went into courting a carefully selected set of local and national opinion leaders. By all accounts, this elite-focused effort was massive, with direct appeals to hundreds of opinion leaders who were flown into Washington for briefings with high-level officials, including the president. Administration officials also embarked on a public speaking campaign in support of the treaties. Intense lobbying of senators and a final televised appeal for support from the president capped this effort. Even though the administration undertook many different activities, their constant focus was on generating elite support to relieve pressure on potentially shaky Senate supporters.[15]

The premise of this strategy was that once information about the treaty became available, it would change the attitudes of opinion leaders and the public toward the treaty.[16] Although aided in the effort to generate Senate support by the perception of a late shift in public opinion, public opinion remained essentially unchanged.[17] Even so, after a seven-month ratification campaign and concessions to obtain the support of several senators, the administration achieved narrow victories in the Senate, with the neutrality treaty passing in March by a vote of sixty-eight to thirty-two and the Panama Canal treaty passing in April by the same count.[18]

Summary

Carter's reactions to public opinion were consistent with the conditional predictions based on his public opinion beliefs. When he had not thought through the issue, he deferred to the public's view and opposed the treaty. But when he devoted more attention to it, despite the public's opposition, he decided that now his view of the matter was correct and decided to act on it. Only when told that congressional support would not be forthcoming unless he relieved the pressure on uncommitted senators did he move to a public relations program. However, instead of concentrating on generating public support as an end in itself, Carter viewed public opinion instrumentally. He did not think public support was needed nor did he attempt to find it but instead tried to reduce the opposition so as to give Senate supporters room to maneuver and vote in favor of the treaties. As the evidence indicates, Carter directed his ratification efforts toward elites and senators in order to affect Senate votes without necessarily winning public support. His actions thus suggest a *supportive* influence of his beliefs, with his behavior *consistent* with his beliefs at the time of the problem representation and a *causal* influence at the other stages. The influence of public opinion on policy falls into a *lead category* influence.

Guardian: Reagan and the Origins of the Strategic Defense Initiative, 1983

Reagan did not wish to consider the public's input and did not think its support was necessary. Thus, he would have made decisions based mostly on other interests rather than public opinion. Reagan might have used the extra time available to lead the people during the implementation stage to persuade them to support his decision after he had made it based on other factors (lead category). When Reagan asked on March 23, 1983, "Wouldn't it be better to save lives than to avenge them?" and recommended that "we embark on a program to counter the awesome Soviet missile threat with measures that are defensive," he took the nation and most of his administration by surprise.[19] By proposing a defensive system, Reagan was challenging the foundations of the prevailing strategic thinking known as Mutual Assured Destruction (MAD), which held that as long as both the United States and the Soviet Union had a massive nuclear retaliation capability, neither side would launch a nuclear attack. Large-scale strategic defenses, the kind envisioned by Reagan, would dramatically undercut this "balance of terror" and were anathema to scores of arms control and strategic experts who thought that such defenses could be destabilizing if they undermined the effectiveness of one side's retaliatory force.

Reagan proposed the new research program, which he thought could render nuclear weapons "impotent and obsolete," during a time of increased tension between the Soviet Union and United States. As both sides continued their massive defense buildup, this friction worsened when Reagan labeled the Soviet Union an "evil empire" a month before his Strategic Defense Initiative (SDI) speech. At this same time, U.S. Catholic bishops questioned the moral foundations of MAD, and a popular freeze movement took shape to protest the continued American nuclear buildup. In Europe, the deployment of American cruise and Pershing II missiles led to huge public demonstrations.

Problem Representation

Reagan claimed—uncharacteristically, in biographer Lou Cannon's view—sole credit for the idea for the program, asserting that "SDI was my idea"—a conclusion supported by other sources as well.[20] Reagan's proposal for strategic defenses originated a long time before his 1983 speech. In 1979, as a presidential candidate, Reagan visited the North American Aerospace Defense Command headquarters in Colorado, from which the United States could track any incoming strategic nuclear attack, and was startled to find out that the nation had no defense against a missile attack. According to Martin Anderson, who accompanied him on the flight back to California, "It was obvious that Reagan was deeply concerned about what he had learned. . . . He slowly shook his head and said, 'We have spent all that money and have all that equipment, and there is nothing we can do to prevent a nuclear missile from hitting us.'"[21]

Reagan abhorred nuclear weapons in general and the MAD policy in particular, which he described to Cannon in 1989: "It's like you and me sitting here in a discussion where we were each pointing a loaded gun at each other and if you say anything wrong or I say anything wrong, we're going to pull the trigger. And I just thought this was ridiculous." He fundamentally disagreed with one principle of the MAD policy, embodied in the 1972 Anti-Ballistic Missile treaty (ABM), which prohibited strategic defenses. He compared this logic with the ban on chemical weapons: "We all got together in 1925 and banned the use of poison gas. But we all kept our gas masks." He dreamed that a technological breakthrough in strategic defenses would rescue the nation from relying on a strategic policy that he deemed fundamentally unsound and hoped it might advance his vision of a nuclear-free world.[22] By the time he became president in 1981, he was fully convinced of the need to move forward on strategic defenses. What remained was the opportunity to realize his vision.

Option Generation

Toward the end of 1981, a small group in the White House and a select group of outside advisers considered a renewed effort to develop a missile defense program. The group presented their findings to Reagan on January 8, 1982. After a meeting that Anderson points to as a "critical turning point," Reagan concluded that the strategic defense option would be workable.[23] However, the momentum for strategic defenses soon abated amid other pressing issues. Though firmly committed to strategic defense, Reagan lacked the scientific knowledge and military backing to inaugurate a new program in 1982. Instead, much of the administration's energy on defenses centered on building congressional support for funding the MX intercontinental ballistic missile. The House rejection of the "dense pack" MX-basing mode (in which the missiles would be placed in many silos located close together) on December 8, 1982, provided a new impetus to several proponents of strategic defense. Upset about what he perceived as the Pentagon's bungling of the MX issue, the deputy NSC adviser, Robert McFarlane, moved to provide the spark for the March 1983 speech.[24]

Unlike Reagan, McFarlane preferred to use research on strategic defenses as a bargaining chip in negotiations with the Soviets to push them for significant cuts in their missile forces. After the MX defeat cast doubt on the prospects for future American land-based strategic systems, the chief of naval operations, Admiral James Watkins, expressed his dismay over MAD and support for missile defenses to offset the Soviet land-based missile advantage to Admiral John Poindexter, who was the military assistant to the national security adviser, William Clark. Poindexter related these views to McFarlane, who saw an opportunity to push ahead on strategic defenses, and a meeting with the JCS on the subject was arranged. Reagan met with the JCS in December 1982 and asked them: "What if we began to move away from our total reliance on offense to deter a nuclear attack and moved toward a relatively greater reliance on defense?"[25] After the meeting, much to his surprise, Watkins found the other JCS members receptive to strategic defenses. Unlike Reagan, however, the JCS viewed strategic defenses as a system that would complement the present U.S. strategy rather than replace it and believed it provided a useful "middle ground" between threatening a preemptive American strike and accepting a Soviet first strike.[26]

The defeat of the MX basing mode also drove home to Reagan the difficulty of the American strategic position. His science adviser, George Keyworth, later remembered that Reagan saw "the problem . . . [as] a serious military problem: erosion in stability."[27] Like his military advisers, he thought the Soviets would continue to build their land-based forces while the United States would face continued controversy over any land-based system. The December 1982 House vote made Reagan realize that any American effort to match the Soviets in land-based missiles would encounter stumbling blocks.[28]

Policy Selection

The JCS met again with Reagan on February 11, 1983, to discuss the American strategic position. As part of the discussion, the JCS recommended reexamining strategic defense possibilities. In a phrase that Reagan later used in his March speech, Watkins asked, "Would it not be better if we could develop a system that would protect, rather than avenge, our people?" To which, Reagan replied, "Exactly."[29] Despite later controversy over the priority the JCS gave it, they all agreed that strategic defenses merited a deeper examination. Reagan seized on their recommendation: "Let's go back and look at this and get ready to push it hard."[30] Because at the meeting the JCS discussed strategic defenses only generally, they left untouched several critical issues such as the extent of the defense (e.g., All nuclear weapons? Just missiles? Military targets only? Cities?), its effect on the ABM treaty, the cost, the reactions of allies, and potential congressional views. Given these uncertainties, the JCS left the meeting thinking that the proposal would be considered further at the highest levels before a new policy was launched.[31]

However, Clark, McFarlane, and the NSC staff moved ahead rapidly and secretly on the new policy, even incorporating it into a forthcoming speech. Whereas the JCS saw strategic defenses as a means to support and improve the current strategy, Reagan had moved beyond this view and pushed for a vision in which all nuclear weapons would be rendered ineffective. When the JCS eventually found out about the planned announcement, they were shocked, and the JCS chair, General John Vessey, recommended that the speech not be given. Indeed, both Secretary of State George Shultz and Secretary of Defense Casper Weinberger were deliberately cut out of the preparations for the speech because Clark feared they would oppose the announcement.[32]

Implementation

Reagan agreed with the quick and secretive approach. He was enamored with the idea of dramatically announcing his new vision and was determined to do so despite possible concerns about administration, congressional, or allied support. Poindexter later explained, "We didn't tell anyone else what we were doing.... The chiefs didn't know. Defense didn't know. State didn't know. After we developed the insert, we talked to the president about it. And he agreed; that's what he wanted to do."[33] In fact, Reagan rejected McFarlane's suggestion that the administration seek congressional and allied support before the speech because he wanted to surprise everyone.[34] According to McFarlane, Reagan favored making the announcement as soon as possible, since "he was so swept away by his ability to stand up and announce a program that would defend Americans from nuclear war [that] he couldn't wait."[35] Reagan later stated that after the JCS "returned to me their collective judgment that development of a shield against nuclear missiles might be feasible, I decided to make public my dream and move ahead with the Strategic Defense Initiative by laying down a challenge to our scientists to solve the formidable technological problems it posed."[36]

Reagan also saw the value of making a big public relations splash with his speech. McFarlane recalled that

> Reagan's view of the political payoff was sufficient rationale as far as he was concerned. . . . By that I mean, providing the American people with an appealing answer to their fears—the intrinsic value of being able to tell Americans, "For the first time in the nuclear age, I'm doing something to save your lives. I'm telling you that we can get rid of nuclear weapons."[37]

Reagan sensed that the public would support his views and thought he could lead the people to actively support his proposed policy. Although this potential support did not affect either the choice of policy or its timing, it did reinforce his preference to move quickly on announcing it.

Following Reagan's speech and after receiving the recommendations of several advisory panels, the "Strategic Defense Initiative" was established on January 6, 1984, by presidential directive. Lieutenant General James Abrahamson was named to direct the new SDI Office in April 1984, and by 1985, SDI had become the Defense Department's largest research and development program. The program also immediately became the center of controversy in both Congress and elite circles, especially among advocates of traditional deterrence. In the face of this opposition, Reagan and Abrahamson made a concerted public relations effort to generate support for SDI. According to most public opinion polls between 1983 and 1985, the public agreed with Reagan's policy, with between one-half and three-fourths supporting the idea of strategic defenses, depending on the exact wording of the question.[38] In the end, this leadership effort and the consistent public support led Congress to grant 90 percent of the funds that Reagan requested for SDI.[39]

Summary

Throughout this case, Reagan acted consistently with his beliefs—which opposed the public's input and thought its support was unnecessary. He had long been a proponent of strategic defenses, which he saw as both morally superior to MAD and practically appealing to him because of his profound dislike of nuclear weapons. Upon hearing advice that the program was technically feasible and finding support among the JCS, Reagan saw the opportunity to pursue his vision of a nuclear-free world. As with the Lebanon case, even though Reagan's advisers appeared somewhat responsive to public opinion in their choice to support strategic defenses, Reagan's own views and choices were unaffected by public opinion. When he did consider public opinion, he did so only to generate support for the policy he preferred. Reagan's behavior was *consistent* with his beliefs in problem representation, option generation, and policy selection, and a *causal* influence was found at implementation. These codings suggest a *supportive* influence of beliefs. The connection between public opinion and policy occurred as defined under the *lead category*.

Pragmatist: Bush and German Reunification, 1989–1990

Bush's beliefs rejected public input and saw public support as a necessary but largely automatic component of a successful foreign policy. These views suggest he would have based his decisions on other interests and led the public to build support only if he perceived opposition (no-impact and lead categories).

At the end of World War II, the Allied nations of France, Britain, the United States, and the Soviet Union each occupied one of four sectors of Germany and also Berlin. France, Britain, and the United States later combined their sectors into the Federal Republic of Germany (FRG), which joined the Western NATO alliance, and the Soviet Union created the German Democratic Republic (GDR), which joined the Warsaw Pact. Each of the Allied nations retained legal rights resulting from the peace settlement at the end of World War II regarding the final disposition of the German state. Throughout the Cold War, the division of Germany remained a focal point of tension between the two alliances, with both the United States and Soviet Union maintaining significant numbers of troops on the territory of their German ally. During this period, American policy favored German reunification through peaceful means, but on the assumption that it would be best to occur later rather than sooner. However, most European nations and the Soviet Union feared a resurgent and aggressive united Germany and preferred that it remain divided.

Problem Representation

As the Cold War thawed in the late 1980s as a result of Soviet leader Mikail Gorbachev's less aggressive foreign policies, Bush, upon entering office in early 1989, saw an opportunity to achieve dramatic American objectives in Europe and exhorted his advisers to "dream big dreams." While they tried to convert Gorbachev's change in demeanor into substantive policy outcomes, they still thought German unification would take place over a number of years following political and economic reforms in the GDR.[40] Since Bush thought that the presidents who had encountered difficulties in the Soviet-American relationship had done so because they had moved too quickly, he determined to err on the side of caution. For this reason, in early 1989, Bush approved a wide-ranging review of American objectives and policy toward the Soviet Union in the hopes that the review would both provide policy guidance and insulate him from pressure from public opinion and events to act as he pondered the direction of American policy. However, the review achieved neither of these goals, as Bush found its conclusions too cautious, and domestic criticism of administration inaction in response to Soviet pronouncements mounted.[41]

The administration informally began thinking about German reunification in the spring of 1989. The issue received some attention during the policy review, but given German disinterest and the hostility of other Europeans, the State Department's review recommended not pushing the issue. In a March 1989 memorandum to Bush, however, the NSC recommended a much stronger position in favor of unification: "Today the top priority for American foreign policy in Europe should be the fate of the Federal Republic of Germany." The memo advised using the spread of democratic values as the basis for European unity within a "commonwealth of free nations" and as an alternative vision to Gorbachev's "common European home" (which assumed that the political and economic systems in Eastern Europe would remain fundamentally unchanged).[42]

Throughout the spring, the administration endured both criticism from domestic media and politicians as well as international complaints from West Europeans about a lack of ideas and action. Even though the attacks stung, Bush remained determined to move cautiously, given the stakes involved. In late spring, he complained that he was "sick and tired of getting beat up day after day for having no vision and letting Gorbachev run the show. This is not just public relations we're involved in. There's real danger in jumping ahead. Can't people *see* that?" He believed that the real opportunities afforded by Gorbachev's policies would remain, regardless of the pace of the American reaction. But if these chances evaporated, then "we'll end up realizing we were lucky—and smart—that we didn't move faster."[43] As part of the administration's response to this criticism, however, they decided to use a series of speeches in May and June to announce policy concepts to confront the evolving European situation.[44]

Option Generation

German reunification became one part of this policy process. On May 17, Bush met with Secretary of State James Baker, who stressed that the reunification issue provided one opportunity to "get ahead of the curve and exceed expectations." He advised, "There's no doubt the topic is coming back. The real question is whether Gorbachev will grab it first." Baker reported that Bush's "instinct was to emphasize the issue, building on Ronald Reagan's eloquent call" in 1987 for Gorbachev to "tear down this wall!" in reference to the Berlin Wall, which divided the city's Western and Soviet sectors. After this discussion, Bush decided to emphasize the issue on his European trip at the end of May.[45]

Moving forward on reunification squared with Bush's views. He saw himself as "less of a Europeanist, not dominated by history" and viewed Germany as a fully reformed, democratic nation, and "at some point you should let a guy up." He publicly expressed this viewpoint in May when he told an interviewer he would "love to see" unification.[46] On September 18, he commented optimistically,

> I think there has been a dramatic change in post–World War II Germany. And so, I don't fear it. . . . There is in some quarters a feeling—well, a reunified Germany would be detrimental to the peace of Europe, of Western Europe, some way; and I don't accept that at all, simply don't.[47]

The situation in Eastern Europe became more volatile during the summer as thousands of GDR citizens traveled to Hungary in hopes of crossing the border into Austria to escape communism. In August, to relieve the refugee crisis, Hungary announced that it would open its border with Austria. When the GDR cut off travel to Hungary, the flow then shifted to Czechoslovakia. Although the GDR eventually resolved this refugee problem by allowing those who made it to Czechoslovakia to emigrate and then closing the Czechoslovak border, the refugee crisis and the cutoff of travel only fueled domestic discontent.

By October 20, a three-pronged American policy emphasized a cautious approach to control developments in the GDR and still saw the possibilities for eventual unification as remote. First, the administration would encourage an evolutionary process of change in the GDR toward a more democratic and free market structure. Second, the administration would publicly begin to outline the conditions for eventual reunification, which included that unification would be voluntary and the united Germany would have an anchor in the West. Third, the United States would work with the FRG to prevent the total collapse of the GDR regime, for fear of uncontrollable instability.[48]

In an interview on October 24, Bush underscored his support for a slow and orderly reunification and gave a nod to the concerns of America's allies. He also expressed exasperation with domestic pressure to react more dramatically to the changes in Eastern Europe: "These changes we're seeing in Eastern Europe are absolutely extraordinary, but I'm not going to be stampeded into overreacting to any of this." He observed, "Democrats on Capital Hill have been calling me 'timid.' I have other, better words, like 'caution,' 'diplomatic,' 'prudent.' "[49] The pressure to react only grew stronger in the following weeks, but Bush remained steadfast in his determination to move slowly.

Perhaps the most dramatic of these events erupted onto international headlines and television screens when the GDR opened the Berlin Wall on the night of November 9, 1989. After this astounding development, Bush decided to react publicly in a way that Baker later described as "diplomatically, almost clinically—and try as best we could not to be overly emotional" in order to prevent the Soviets from feeling that in Bush's words, "we were sticking our thumb in their eye."[50] In a press conference the next day, Bush appeared subdued, which struck many observers as odd given the achievement of a major long-term American policy goal. His restrained reaction reinforced the perception of Bush as lacking "vision," and journalists and legislators alike were highly critical of his handling of the opening of the wall. These attacks frustrated Bush, who thought that the situation required a more circumspect approach and privately insisted, "I won't beat on my chest and dance on the wall."[51]

Policy Selection

Bush recognized he could have used the opening of the Berlin Wall for short-term political advantage, but he nonetheless pursued the policy he thought best for long-term American interests, regardless of the political benefits. His fears centered on two distasteful consequences that he thought might result from an overreaction. First, Bush presumed that Gorbachev was under pressure from the Soviet military and conservatives to reverse the changes in Eastern Germany and worried that a less restrained response could force Gorbachev to backtrack on the progress in Eastern Europe. Bush also believed that American exuberance could undermine Gorbachev's position in the Soviet Union, which might end possible future reforms. Second, afraid of a repeat of 1956 in Hungary during which American statements encouraged an uprising that the Soviets brutally put down, he was worried that such statements might incite other East European revolts that might force the Soviets into hostile action. He therefore opted to move carefully in the hope that reform would continue, instead of taking action that might cause a reversal in policy. To achieve this goal as smoothly as possible, the administration concluded that unity would occur regardless of American action, and so they decided to pursue a policy favoring German self-determination that moved no faster than the FRG did and was presented in a subdued manner so as not to threaten the Soviets.[52]

The American policy was met with opposition from France, Britain, other American allies, the Soviet Union, and domestic editorial opinion. Nevertheless, Bush refused to relent. In order to reassure the British and the French and to introduce American influence into the process, Baker advocated principles for unification that emphasized the need for German self-determination in NATO and the European Community, gradualism, and the inviolability of existing borders. For the remainder of 1989, the administration hoped their policy of gradualism would succeed in easing toward German unification as the basis for a stable Europe.[53]

By late 1989, polling data on the public's view of German reunification and Bush's policy toward it indicated approval of both. Polls in November and December 1989 and January 1990 all showed wide public support for German reunification. For example, a November 21 poll indicated that 64 percent of the public "would like to see Germany reunified," with only 10 percent opposed.[54] In early December, Bush's pollster Robert Teeter noted that even though Bush had been criticized as being too timid, "the public doesn't buy that criticism."[55] Despite previous concern about public opposition to his slow action, these polling results gave Bush no reason to question his gradual approach.

Events soon forced another adjustment in Bush's policy after the GDR moved elections up to mid-March from July after being pressured by the continuing flow of its citizens to the FRG. The prounification forces were expected to win the March GDR elections, making it clear that unification would now come rather quickly.[56] With the GDR collapsing before his eyes, Bush decided to abandon his policy of gradualism and move as fast as possible to achieve unification in order to avoid instability. Believing that a united Germany would remember who had supported unification, Bush wanted to stay at the forefront of the process.[57]

Implementation

Although Bush now favored moving quickly on reunification, the problem was how to do so. The Soviets favored a Four Powers conference to resolve the issue, and the British and French viewed this option somewhat favorably. The Germans preferred a solution in which the two German states would separately work out unification. The administration rejected the Soviet option as incompatible with German self-determination and the FRG's commitment to NATO and feared that the German option would lead to a policy disaster. Instead, the administration settled on another position called "Two-Plus-Four," which combined the other parties' preferred solutions. Under this process, the Germans would agree on the internal aspects of unification, and the Four Powers would be involved in its external arrangements. Although the Germans would decide most of the outlines of unification, the administration hoped the Four-Powers aspect would give the Soviets sufficient involvement to provide domestic cover for Gorbachev against attacks by his political opponents. By the end of January, the Bush administration policy had evolved into favoring fast reunification through the Two-Plus-Four process, with the goal of a united Germany in NATO.[58]

After detailed and arduous negotiations, the Soviets finally accepted the American conditions for German reunification. The Four Powers and Germans expressed their joint support for the Two-Plus-Four negotiation track on February 13. At a summit meeting in Washington with Bush on May 31, Gorbachev agreed that the Germans could decide whether they wanted to join NATO, and on July 14, Gorbachev accepted that a united Germany would become a member of NATO. With this, the final stumbling block to unification had been surmounted.[59] On September 12, 1990, the Four Powers officially surrendered their legal rights to determine Germany's fate and accepted German reunification.

Throughout this process, Bush pursued a quiet, elite-focused approach to the issue. Even though the general public's support for his policy direction allowed him to adopt this stance, it opened him to criticism for lacking vision and acting as a bystander to the unfolding events. While Bush eschewed the role of public persuader to build support for his effort, the German reunification treaty was approved by the Senate, ninety-eight to zero.[60]

Summary

Bush's behavior was consistent with predictions based on his beliefs that he would make his decision based only on national security factors and lead the public only if the support that he took for granted was not forthcoming. He approached each of his choices from the standpoint of American national security interests and focused almost exclusively on the elite's negotiations and the implications of his actions on current and future Soviet behavior. As events created domestic pressure for more dramatic action, Bush still insisted on moving slowly, without excessive emotion, because he thought this approach best served American interests. Even though his policy had broad public support, if he had found public opposition to his policy direction, he probably would have made minor efforts to create public support without changing his policy. While keeping an eye on public support, he directed most of his deliberations to other interests, used diplomacy to achieve his goals, did little to lead the people, but assumed they would support him if he made the correct decisions. Bush's beliefs influenced his behavior at the *causal* level at all stages and for the entire case, and public opinion influenced his decisions as in the *no-impact category*.

Delegate: Clinton and the Intervention in Bosnia, June–December 1995

Clinton favored the public's input and saw its support as necessary. If he anticipates opposition to a policy direction, then he will likely pull back and either avoid the policy if possible or select the alternative that will cause the fewest problems with the public (constrain category). If the public favors a particular policy direction, Clinton is likely to tailor his policy accordingly (follow category).

Fighting over the status of Bosnia in the former Yugoslavia began in 1992 as the Bosnian Serbs, consisting of 31 percent of the prewar Bosnian population, decided to unite with Serbia. The Bosnian Muslims, who made up 44 percent of the population, feared domination by a Serbian majority in the reconstituted nation (minus Croatia and Slovenia, which had declared their independence in 1991) and so sought to establish a united and independent Bosnia that included the Bosnian Serbs. In 1991, the UN imposed an arms embargo on all territories of the former Yugoslavia. Then in April and May 1993, in response to the Bosnian Serbs' military advances, the UN declared the Bosnian cities of Sarajevo, Tuzla, Zepa, Gorazde, Bhihac, and Srebrenca to be "safe areas," presumably free from attack.[61] In December 1994, in order to bolster the staying power of American allies—who were supplying UN peacekeeping troops on the ground in Bosnia—Clinton expanded his previous pledge of twenty thousand American troops to implement a peace treaty to include the evacuation of UN peacekeepers if it became necessary. In May 1995 after the failure of another cease-fire and further attacks on UN safe areas, NATO air forces bombed Serbian positions. In response, the Bosnian Serbs took several hundred UN peacekeepers hostage and chained them to potential targets. Although the peacekeepers were eventually released, the action provided the impetus for a rethinking of American policy in the summer of 1995.[62]

Domestic opinion at that time was mixed regarding American involvement in Bosnia. Polling results in June indicated the public would support American troops under certain circumstances. For example, 61 percent supported sending American troops to protect UN peacekeepers, and 78 percent supported rescuing them with American forces. However, public opinion was less supportive of more sustained aggressive action. Whereas 40 percent supported using American troops to take part in NATO efforts to punish Serbian aggression, only 37 percent supported the use of troops to enforce a cease-fire. Although 67 percent of the public supported sending troops if no Americans were killed, the number dropped to 31 percent if the question included that 100 Americans might be killed.[63]

Problem Representation

NATO's inability to respond effectively to the May Serb hostage taking began to move Clinton to search for alternative policy options. One official reported, "He saw that this was having real costs for us." The adviser reported that Clinton complained, "I want for us to be more on top of this thing, more shaping of it. If we were going to be blamed for the failures, it should at least be for concrete decisions that we had taken."[64]

At an Oval Office meeting on June 14, Clinton expressed his frustration with the continuing problem of Bosnia, which now threatened the NATO alliance, given the appearance of weakness after the Bosnian Serbs took the UN peacekeepers hostage: "We need to get the policy straight . . . or we're just going to be kicking the can down the road again. Right now we've got a situation, we've got no clear mission, no one's in control of events." As later events proved, in Clinton's mind, putting off the decision would eventually cause it to become entangled with the 1996 presidential election. Referring to efforts by Republicans in Congress, led by the future 1996 Republican presidential candidate Senator Robert Dole (R, Kans.), to lift the arms embargo against the Bosnian Muslims, Vice President Albert Gore observed that continued inaction by the United States was "driving us into a brick wall with Congress."[65]

That night Clinton discovered in a conversation with his top advisers that he did not have the flexibility he thought he did. In a discussion with Secretary of State Warren Christopher, UN Ambassador Madeleine Albright, and Assistant Secretary of State Richard Holbrooke, Clinton learned that his previous commitments had locked him into sending troops to Bosnia. Beforehand, Clinton thought he still could refuse to carry out a previously agreed-to (in December 1994) NATO plan to insert twenty thousand Americans to cover the withdrawal of UN peacekeepers from Bosnia. However, his advisers informed him otherwise. After Clinton raised the subject, Holbrooke told him, "I'm afraid that we may not have as much flexibility and options left." Clinton responded, "What do you mean? . . . I'll decide that [whether to use American troops to cover the UN withdrawal] when the time comes." Holbrooke replied, "It's been decided." When Clinton turned to Christopher to confirm Holbrooke's assertion, Christopher indicated, "That's right. . . . This is serious stuff." Clinton knew the insertion of American forces to protect the removal of the UN peacekeepers would likely be done under hostile conditions and would surely mean casualties. But reversing his commitment could cause NATO's dissolution.[66] And if Clinton did nothing, he risked his worst-case scenario: the involvement of American troops in combat as the 1996 presidential election campaign began.

Option Generation

Given the steep costs of inaction, Clinton decided in June that he needed to act to avoid the potential foreign policy debacle. Whereas he had previously allowed the Europeans to lead on the Bosnia policy, he concluded that only firm U.S. action could regain control of the situation. Several factors led him to realize that he needed to shift American policy. As the war dragged on, he began to worry that Western ineffectiveness in dealing with the issue was beginning to reflect poorly on his administration, and he watched the events of the spring and early summer with an increasing sense of foreboding. According to an official,

"We were moving from debacle to disaster in the fall or winter. . . . Desperation has a way of concentrating the mind." With the election campaign to start early the next year, Clinton knew he had to act. As a senior official put it, "The president wanted this dealt with. It was not acceptable to go into another winter as a hostage to fortune."[67]

In addition, the new French president, Jacques Chirac, was pressuring Clinton to deal more strongly with the Serbs. Thus even though the administration believed that Chirac's policy recommendations were unwise, it did provide an additional reason to act. Clinton knew what he needed to avoid [a UN pullout, humanitarian atrocities, an endless war, and congressional action to lift the arms embargo], he did not know what he should do. A senior official recalled, "We sat and watched [the situation in Bosnia] drift slowly away and the debacle of the hostage-taking . . . and Clinton got this sort of 'never-again' attitude and said to his guys, 'I need some options. I need a better way.'"[68]

One option Clinton clearly rejected because of public opinion was a permanent commitment of American troops to Bosnia. Because of public opposition to American involvement in any fighting in Bosnia, he decided that U.S. troops could play only a limited role in any potential deployment. Accordingly, the administration continued to favor the use of air strikes to respond to Serbian attacks rather than to resort to threats of ground forces.[69]

In response to Clinton's request, National Security Adviser Anthony Lake developed an approach he called the "Endgame Strategy." Lake cautioned Clinton about the risks of both failure (damage to their reputation) and success (committing American troops to enforce either the peace or a UN pullout). Clinton worried about the risks associated with a Balkan troop deployment, likened it to the beginning of Vietnam, and wondered whether the public or Congress would support such a risk. Despite the risks, he viewed the status quo as unacceptable and approved examining Lake's approach. After working on the project, Lake proposed to Clinton that he act as a messenger and communicate to the American allies that the president had reached a final decision on the United States' Bosnia policy and was prepared to implement it unilaterally. The policy promised carrots and sticks to both sides in the conflict. Lake proposed extensively bombing the Bosnian Serbs if they did not negotiate, but lifting Western economic sanctions against Serbia if it recognized Bosnia, Croatia, and Macedonia. In addition, the United States would lift the arms embargo against the Muslims if they cooperated but would withdraw from the region if they did not negotiate.[70]

The situation worsened on July 12 when Srebrenca, a safe haven, fell to the Serbs. Since NATO and the United States had promised to protect the safe havens, the Serb action seriously threatened American and NATO credibility.[71] When the Serbs killed thousands of Muslims and forced many more to flee, a senior official remarked, "We were failing, the West was failing and the Bosnian Serbs were on the march." Clinton saw the shortcomings of the Western policy and surmised the feeble response was harming American prestige. He became increasingly frustrated by his lack of options and the worsening situation.[72]

On July 14, while putting on the White House green, Clinton became even more agitated as he foresaw in the near future the likely withdrawal of UN forces and the attendant commitment of American troops. "The status quo is not acceptable. We've got to really dig in and think about this."[73] Perhaps in reference to the mounting congressional pressure for action, he insisted, "We have to seize control of this," and exclaimed, "I'm getting creamed!"[74] Some of his domestic advisers recommended a clean break from Bosnia and a UN pullout, but his foreign policy advisers pointed out that the extraction of the UN peacekeepers under fire was much more dangerous than enforcing a peace plan.[75] Though neither alternative was attractive, Clinton feared the UN extraction plan more because of its electoral implications. If he waited, he knew he would be forced to use troops to extract the peacekeepers, either on the eve of or during the 1996 election. The necessity of avoiding this potentially costly action thus spurred him to seek a diplomatic solution.[76]

Policy Selection

In addition to Clinton's concern about future problems, the immediate threat from the Serbs weighed on his mind. On July 17, he complained,

> I don't like where we are now. . . . This policy is doing enormous damage to the United States and to our standing in the world. We look weak. . . . And it can only get worse down the road. The only time we've ever made any progress is when we geared up NATO to pose a real threat to the Serbs. . . . Our position is unsustainable, it's killing the U.S. position of strength in the world.

On July 18 in a meeting in the Oval Office, Vice President Al Gore raised the issue of public opinion. In reference to Srebrenca, he referred to a front-page picture in the *Washington Post* of a woman refugee who had hanged herself. Gore stated, "My 21-year-old daughter asked about that picture.... What am I supposed to tell her? Why is this happening and we're not doing anything? ... My daughter is surprised the world is allowing this to happen ... I am too." Gore alluded to the future judgment of public opinion: "The cost of this is going to cascade over several decades. It goes to what kind of people we are. Acquiescence is the worst alternative." Clinton responded, "I've been thinking along similar lines.... So we all agree the status quo is untenable."[77]

On July 26, the day after the safe area of Zepa fell, the Senate passed Senator Bob Dole's resolution, which unilaterally lifted the arms embargo. On August 1, the House approved the Senate resolution lifting the arms embargo by a veto-proof margin. If the administration were not able to implement some solution to head off the embargo removal, Clinton now faced the worst case scenario of the collapse of the UN peacekeeping mission and its extraction under fire by American troops. Although he could veto the congressional legislation, he guessed that Congress might override it. Given this situation, he instructed Lake to move ahead briskly in his execution of the Endgame Strategy. Lake warned that they were "rolling the dice." Clinton answered, "I'm risking my presidency."[78]

But Clinton knew that the domestic risks of doing nothing were greater. Relying on polling conducted by his political consultant Dick Morris, Clinton believed that the public would support military action if it were directed at halting the killing of women and children and stopping the genocide. Nonetheless, even though the public would support peacekeeping, it remained steadfastly opposed to military involvement in any combat in Bosnia.[79] In addition to forcing the United States to intervene under fire, doing nothing implied that not only would Clinton lose control of the policy to the Republican Congress but that he also would hand his opponents an issue that they could use to attack him in the next year's presidential election. Admitting that congressional pressure influenced Clinton's desire to move quickly on the issue, administration officials still denied that the change in policy was designed to remove the issue from the 1996 election. But this position is belied by statements such as that by political consultant Dick Morris (who had the president's ear and was advising the president on foreign policy), who warned other officials, "You guys ought to take care of Bosnia before 1996 so it does not screw us up."[80]

In late summer, the Croatians launched a successful attack on the Bosnian Serbs that, by highlighting the Serbs' vulnerability and completing the almost total ethnic segregation of Bosnia and Croatia, provided a window of opportunity for an American policy initiative.[81] In this increasingly fluid situation, Clinton met on August 7 with his top advisers to discuss policy and approved the Endgame Strategy. Reflecting a desire to resolve the issue before the 1996 campaign, he emphasized, "We should bust our ass to get a settlement in the next few months. . . . We've got to exhaust every alternative, roll every die, take risks."[82]

In addition to the congressional resolutions and Croatian successes, the negative consequences of inaction on the 1996 election were increasingly coloring his decisions. The administration saw the Bosnia issue as a "political time bomb" that would go off during the 1996 election and become the primary determinant of the public's assessment of Clinton's foreign policy record. After concluding that he would be forced into deploying troops in Bosnia in the next year, regardless of his actions, and fearing that the UN mission would survive the winter only to ask to be relieved in the spring, in the middle of the 1996 campaign, Clinton chose to act on his own terms. As a senior official put it, "I don't think the President relishes going into the 1996 election hostage to fortune in the Balkans, with the Bosnian Serbs able to bring us deeper into a war."[83]

Implementation

On his trip to Europe, Lake persuaded the Europeans to support the new American policy, and negotiators were dispatched to the Balkans. On August 28, in a direct challenge to the negotiation efforts, the Bosnian Serbs launched a mortar shell attack on Sarajevo, killing thirty-seven civilians. With American and NATO credibility on the line, NATO then launched a massive air campaign—3,400 sorties—against the Bosnian Serbs that lasted until mid-September. On September 8, American negotiators used the leverage of the air attacks to get the Bosnian, Serbian, and Croatian foreign ministers to agree to several principles as the basis of negotiations. Negotiators achieved a cease-fire on October 5, and talks on a final settlement began on November 1, with a final agreement initialed on November 21.[84]

As the negotiations continued, the administration increasingly focused on winning the home front's approval of the peacekeeping troop deployment. Although Clinton found that the public disapproved of the planned troop deployment by 38 to 55 percent, he thought he had to follow through on his commitment and tried to convince the public of the appropriateness of his approach. Based on his White House polls, he decided that if he framed the issue in terms of peacekeeping, as opposed to combat, he could build public support.[85] Much of Clinton's effort to create support for his policy was thus aimed at framing the issue in these terms. Clinton realized he would have to explain his policy to the public, expected his arguments to be convincing, and used his polling as the basis to achieve public support. He told reporters, "If we can get a peace agreement, I'll go before the American people and explain it and make my argument and go before Congress and explain it and make my argument." He believed that if the public understood the limited risk and duration of the mission, he would gain "sufficient support" for the peace plan.[86]

Throughout the plan's implementation, Clinton kept the 1996 election in mind. In organizing the deployment, administration officials planned on a six- to eight-month mission, which would mean the troops would begin returning in the summer of 1996 and thus allow Clinton to talk about troop departures during the election. Since this was, in the words of a senior official, "abundantly preferable" to moving slowly on negotiations, the administration pressed for a quick end to them so as to complete the deployment as soon as possible. Although officials publicly denied that the upcoming election had any influence, an official did note privately that they "are certainly aware of the election, and I don't think it has escaped the president's attention."[87]

Following the initialing of the peace agreement, Clinton began an intense drive to gain public and congressional support for his policy and emphasized the necessity of American troops to provide peace and prevent further killing. Speaking on November 22, he announced, "The parties have chosen peace. America must choose peace as well" and stressed the need for American action because of the "senseless slaughter of so many innocent people that our fellow citizens had to watch night after night for four long years on their television screens."[88] In an address to the nation from the Oval Office on November 27, Clinton again returned to these themes, emphasizing the narrow objectives, clear exit strategy, and necessity of the mission for peace.[89] Although Congress remained divided, the deployment took place as planned.

After he took action, Clinton was amazed at the public support. Whereas 60 percent of the public had opposed the deployment of troops beforehand, its approval of his foreign policy climbed after he acted. Although Clinton thought this resulted from the lack of casualties, he also attributed it to the public's agreement with his policy. He surmised that the public responded favorably to his strong action, and he compared the public's support of sending troops to that of parents sending their children to a dentist. Even though the children might not want to go, they knew it was the right thing.[90]

Summary

Clinton's actions were consistent with his orientation toward public opinion, of doing what the public would want him to do if it had all the information. Throughout this case, Clinton's anticipation of the public's reaction in the next election affected his choices. At times, he adhered to public opinion, such as after the fall of Srebrenca, when he felt the public pressure to "do something." At the same time, he saw the constraints imposed by public opinion, especially on involvement in the ground war and on the conditions under which the public would approve of using troops. The Bosnia issue rose in importance in the summer largely because of Clinton's fear that he would have to send in American troops to cover a UN withdrawal during the presidential election. In addition to the domestic considerations, he also perceived a threat to NATO's and the United States' credibility and Europe's increasing reluctance to keep its forces in Bosnia. Given the choice between using troops to evacuate the UN force or using them in a peacekeeping role, he turned toward the peacekeeping mission. Fully recognizing that his solution might endanger his presidency, he saw the consequences of inaction as guaranteeing his failure. With this knowledge in mind, he opted for the risky option that might succeed in eliminating the issue from the 1996 campaign. When implementing the policy, Clinton used the information he had gathered from polling reports to frame his campaign to generate public support. Even though he perceived public opposition to his action, he thought he was acting as the public "really" wanted him to, given the situation, and he attempted to communicate this to the public.

Clinton's beliefs had a *causal* influence on his behavior here. The influence of public opinion on his policy in this case is coded as a *strong constrain category* influence, with lesser *follow* (strong) and *lead category* influences. He followed public opinion on the need to act in the summer of 1995, was constrained by the public as he developed his policy options, and led public opinion when implementing his policy to show the people how his actions conformed to their preferences.

This chapter's findings show solid support for the beliefs model of public opinion's influence (see table 9.1). The presidents reacted in a range

TABLE 9.1 Deliberative Cases and Recent Presidents

	Predicted Public Influence Based on Beliefs	Actual Public Influence	Influence of Beliefs
Carter: Executor, Panama Canal	Lead *or* Constrain	Lead	Supportive
Reagan: Guardian, SDI	Lead	Lead	Supportive
Bush: Pragmatist, German Reunification	No impact/ *Lead*	No impact	Causal
Clinton: Delegate, Bosnia	Constrain/ Follow	Constrain (strong)/ with lesser Follow (strong) and Lead	Causal

Note: Italics indicate conditional predictions.

of ways to public opinion, from largely ignoring it, as Reagan did, to being severely limited by it, as Clinton was. The realist perspective finds some support in these cases, especially in the manner in which Carter, Reagan, and Bush reacted. It does less well in accounting for Clinton's behavior. The Wilsonian liberal model does not accurately predict the choices of any of the decision makers, except for a small part of Clinton's approach to the Bosnian situation, which was driven in part by public opinion.

These cases best support the beliefs model, since it accounts not only for the influence of public opinion but also for the place of public opinion in the decision process. For example, even though Carter implemented a leadership program, he focused more on elites than the public in an effort to generate support for his favored policy alternative. Reagan largely ignored public opinion in his rush to shift American strategic policy. Bush dismissed public pressure for faster action on Gorbachev's initiatives and assumed that the public would support his measured approach to German reunification. Clinton responded strongly to how he thought the public would react in the next election. Each of these presidents reacted to the public in the manner expected, given their public opinion beliefs.

These decision makers also approached leading public opinion in accordance with their beliefs. Clinton (delegate) thought about and attempted to show the public how his policies conformed to public preferences as they were represented in his polling information. Carter (executor) tried to lead public opinion only when he needed to reduce public opposition in order to win undecided Senate votes. As a result, he directed his leadership efforts at influencing elite opinion, in the hopes that it would change votes. Bush (pragmatist) found the public largely in support of his policy direction and chose not to extensively lead it. Reagan (guardian) turned to leading the public once he had decided on his policy direction and focused on outlining how the policy served the national interest. As with the crisis cases, although each of these presidents considered leading the public and did so (with the exception of Bush), they varied in how they conceived of and pursued this task according to their public opinion beliefs.

Public opinion tended to enter the decision process mostly through anticipated reactions. Each president expected that his policies would be approved by the public, even though they all reacted differently to these anticipated reactions. As with the crisis case, polling information was used as a basis to project future public stances and to frame policies rather than as a basis for a particular decision at a particular time. This response to public opinion supports the trend in the influence of public opinion found in many of the cases examined across several presidents.

CHAPTER TEN

*Conclusions and Implications
for Theory and Practice*

Beliefs about public opinion help determine how leaders respond to public opinion when formulating foreign policy. Some individuals' views make them relatively open to considering public opinion when confronting threats to a nation's security. Other leaders' beliefs cause them to ignore public opinion when making decisions about similar issues. Some decision makers also have a more mixed perspective on public opinion, which results in behavior that lies in the middle on a continuum between responding to or ignoring public preferences. Individual beliefs about the role of public opinion in foreign policymaking interact with the prevailing decision context to determine the public's influence on policy outcomes on any given issue. As both the time to make a decision and the anticipated state of public opinion shift, the public's influence on the decisions of leaders with different beliefs orientations changes in a predictable manner. This perspective suggests that even though the public can significantly shape and alter foreign policy choices, its influence is highly dependent on the interaction between the leader's beliefs and the decision context.

This concluding chapter evaluates the findings of the analysis of a series of cases spanning several presidential administrations and their relevance to several areas of research. This examination suggests that even though the influence of public opinion can vary considerably from case to case and from president to president, it does so in a largely predictable manner based on the interaction between an individual's sensitivity to public opinion (as represented by his or her beliefs) and the conditions under which the decision is made.

First, I consider the pattern of the public's influence in reference to the expectations of the realist, Wilsonian liberal, and beliefs models. Although the realist and Wilsonian models account for some outcomes, the pattern of public influence most closely follows the outcome expected by the beliefs model.

Second, I discuss the information the presidents possessed about public opinion as they made their decisions and the type of information to which they reacted. As I indicated earlier, even though the presidents had a large amount of information about public opinion, its influence, surprisingly, was felt mostly through their anticipation of how the public would respond at some future time.

Third, I look at the influence of public opinion across the different decision stages. Unlike previous work suggesting that the public affected policy mainly in the early stages of policy development, my analysis unexpectedly found that public opinion influenced decisions much later in the process.

Fourth, I outline several caveats to the findings, including those conditions that might alter the public's influence.

Finally, I explore the implications of these findings for several areas of research, including democratic theories of policy choice, the domestic sources of international relations, the public opinion and foreign policy literature, and American security policy after the Cold War.

Findings

The Influence of Public Opinion

The public's influence varied across presidents and decision contexts, suggesting that public opinion has no single pattern of influence on policy. In the crisis cases, and the Eisenhower reflexive case, public opinion either had no impact or acted as a constraint on the range of acceptable policy alternatives. This variation in influence in itself is not surprising, since the realist and Wilsonian liberal models predicted both types of influence. What is surprising is that neither a lack of influence nor a constraint on policy consistently dominated the type of influence that public opinion had on short decision-time cases. As discussed later, the beliefs model of the public's influence best explained the pattern of variation.

As the decision time lengthened, the influence of public opinion did not necessarily become stronger. Instead, efforts to lead the public became more evident across all decision makers, although constraining and following influences still were apparent for some presidents. Presidents tended to have more information about the public's preferences in these cases, but they used this information largely to formulate information programs to persuade the public to support their policy approach. As with the short-term cases, even though the influence of public opinion complied with either the realist or Wilsonian liberal models, neither approach fully accounted for the pattern of influence.

The pattern of the public's influence can be *generally* described as either no-impact or constraint during crises and elite efforts to lead public opinion on longer-term decisions. However, this pattern is highly contingent on the beliefs of the individuals in power. Compared with the realist and Wilsonian liberal models, the pattern of the public's influence suggests that the beliefs model best explains public opinion's influence on policy and how presidents tried to educate the public about their policies. The beliefs model accurately explains the influence of public opinion under high-threat conditions regarding national security decisions, but it will not necessarily have the same explanatory strength in other conditions. How changing conditions alter the influence of beliefs on presidential decisions is discussed later. Table 10.1 provides a graphical presentation of the accuracy of the predictions generated from each of the perspectives based on the data and results in chapters 3 to 6 and 8 to 9.

Realists believe that decision makers either ignore public opinion or, if allowed a longer time to act, lead the public to support their position. As table 10.1 shows, the realist perspective accounts for a nontrivial number of the decisions, especially those in the Reagan and Bush cases. Reagan largely ignored public opinion in the face of strong public pressure to withdraw the marines from Lebanon and did not consider public opinion in formulating the Strategic Defense Initiative (SDI). Bush slightly adjusted the timing of his Gulf War policies in response to concerns about public support but mainly focused on the imperatives of national security, and he relied on the demands of diplomacy during the German reunification decisions. However, for other decision makers, the predictive power of the realist model diminished considerably. This model had a decidedly mixed predictive capability for Eisenhower, accounting for his choices in the deliberative case but performing less well when the cases included less decision time—exactly the opposite of

TABLE 10.1 Comparison of Model Predictions

President	Case	Realism	Wilsonian Liberalism	Beliefs Model	
Eisenhower	Formosa Straits	-	+	DDE	+
				JFD	+
	Dien Bien Phu	+/-	+/-	DDE	+
				JFD	+
	Sputnik	+/-	+/-	DDE	+/-
				JFD	+
	New Look	+	-	DDE	+
				JFD	+
Carter	Afghanistan	+/-	+/-	+	
	Panama Canal Treaty	+/-	-	+	
Reagan	Beirut	+	-	+	
	SDI	+	-	+	
Bush	Gulf War	+	-	+	
	German Reunification	+	-	+	
Clinton	Somalia	-	+	+	
	Bosnia	-	+/-	+	

Notes: + = Confirms the perspective's prediction of the decision process and choice.
    - = Disconfirms the perspective's prediction of the process and choice.
  +/- = Mixed evidence on the perspective's prediction of the decision process and choice.
      DDE = Dwight D. Eisenhower   JFD = John Foster Dulles
Source: Table format adapted from Thomas Risse-Kappen, *Cooperation Among Democracies* (Princeton, N.J.: Princeton University Press, 1995), p. 203.

realist expectations. Even though the realist model could anticipate Carter's policy choices, it did not accurately predict *how* Carter considered public opinion when reaching his decision. The realist model also did not account well for Clinton's decisions in either of the two cases. In sum, the realist model had decidedly mixed results across the range of cases examined in this study and could fully account for the process and influence of public opinion in only five of the twelve cases. Because I selected cases that would favor the realist view, these mixed results challenge the realist model of the public's influence.

Realism may accurately predict the influence of public opinion in several of the cases, but this model does not explain the dynamics of the policy process. Realists contend that decision makers simply lack relevant information about public opinion on many of the issues about which they need to make decisions and that the public reacts emotionally to foreign policy questions. In addition, some of the crisis literature suggests that policymakers are not able to consider public opinion because either the public has not developed policy preferences or these preferences cannot be communicated to the government with sufficient speed during crises.[1]

In contrast, a lack of information about public opinion did not hinder its integration into the decision process for any of the crises examined. Instead, decision makers tended to use their information and impressions about public opinion—even those that did not directly relate to the policy issue at hand—as the basis for their decisions *when they decided to integrate public opinion into their calculations.* In all cases, if policymakers were interested in public opinion, they tended to rely on their anticipation of how the public would eventually respond, even when the actual information about public opinion was available. When decision makers ignored public opinion—as Reagan did regarding the Lebanon decision—they did not ignore it because they lacked relevant information about the public's preferences.

Despite a few exceptions in the cases examined here, the public did not react in what could be characterized as an emotional manner to the foreign policy issues considered. Although the public might be accused of emotionally opposing the Panama Canal treaty and favoring the promise of a nuclear defense in the SDI case, its views agreed with significant segments of elite opinion. In addition, the *Sputnik* case is often considered a prime example in which the public reacted emotionally to a newly revealed threat. However, as the public opinion data presented in chapter 5 demonstrate, the public generally adopted Eisenhower's restrained view, at least initially, until the barrage of information from the media and other elites shifted its view. The evidence from the cases show that the public's attitude toward these foreign policy issues was quite restrained.[2]

The Wilsonian liberal model did not perform as well as the realist model across the range of cases (see table 10.1). Although it accurately accounted for the constraining influence of public opinion on Eisenhower's and Clinton's crisis decisions, as the time for a decision lengthened, the accuracy of its predictions dropped considerably. Other than the partially accurate predictions of Eisenhower's response to public opinion after *Sputnik* was launched, Carter's attention to public opinion in the Panama Canal case, and Clinton's following public opinion about the need to "do something" about Bosnia, the Wilsonian liberal model does not explain the decisions or processes of any of the long-term decisions, especially Eisenhower's development of the New Look, Reagan's development of SDI, and Bush's handling of German reunification. This pattern of influence indicates that the Wilsonian liberal model fully explains public opinion's influence in only two of the twelve cases examined.

The Wilsonian liberal model also did not do well in predicting the process of the public's influence. Public opinion only rarely served as a source of policy innovation, information, or direction, with the exception of Dulles's reaction in the New Look and Clinton's reaction to Bosnia. More often, when public opinion did affect policy, it did so as a policy restraint by limiting the range of policy actions that decision makers saw as viable. Those policymakers who considered public opinion mostly used it either to avoid public opposition or to generate public support for a policy rather than to implement what the public wanted. In cases in which decision makers did follow public opinion (*Sputnik*, Bosnia), they reacted more from fear of public retribution than an attempt to incorporate the public's preferences. In general, decision makers were constrained by public opinion when they felt they could not lead it and acted to lead the public when they sensed they could. A policymaker's analysis of which of the conditions prevailed at a particular time depended greatly on that person's sensitivity to public opinion, perception of the opinion context, and anticipation of the public's view.

These cases partially support the realist and Wilsonian liberal models, but decision maker's beliefs about the role of public opinion in foreign policy formulation primarily determined its degree of influence. The beliefs model suggests that an individual's normative beliefs about the desirability of the public's influencing foreign policy decisions and practical beliefs about the necessity of public support for a policy to succeed largely define the range of influence that public opinion will have on that person's choices. As indicated in table 10.1, these beliefs affected the public's influence in all twelve cases. In the one mixed case (the *Sputnik* case), even though Eisenhower tried to act consistently with his beliefs in not responding to public opinion, he did reluctantly react to public opinion when his continued strong stance against increased spending threatened to undermine support for his administration. Otherwise, across several decision contexts and presidents, the beliefs model more accurately accounted for both when and how public opinion entered the policy formulation process than did either the realist or the Wilsonian liberal perspectives.

The beliefs model suggested several orientations toward public opinion. The example of a delegate, who favors the public's input and thinks its support is necessary for a policy to succeed, was provided by Bill Clinton. In both the Somalia and Bosnia cases, he reacted to public opinion and swiftly adjusted his policies in light of public preferences. These reactions were directed at how he anticipated the public would eventually respond to his policies; thus public opinion was an important policy determinant.

The example of an executor, who favors public input but thinks its support is unnecessary, was provided by Jimmy Carter. Executors are expected to consider public opinion early in policy formulation and may be influenced by it if the public's view is a convincing one. However, because executors do not think that public support is necessary, they may ignore it if they strongly disagree with the public's view. In both the Afghanistan and Panama Canal cases, Carter considered the public's view but did not respond to it in his final policy, since he had firm positions on both issues.

Guardians reject both public input and the necessity of public support and are expected to base their decisions on their conceptions of the national interest rather than public opinion. Ronald Reagan provided the example of this type of orientation in both the Beirut and SDI cases. In both instances, he rejected public opinion as a reason to choose a particular policy and largely relied on his own conception of the national interest.

Finally, pragmatists, who see public input as undesirable but believe the public's support is necessary, are expected to base their decisions on national security and then lead the public to support their policies. If they do not think they can win the public's support, they will be swayed by the public. Because this study includes three pragmatists who varied in their assessment of a leader's ability to change public opinion, it illustrates how this variation affected their behavior. These three pragmatists believed they needed the public's support and were at times reined in by "unmalleable" public opinion. Their views of which opinions were malleable and which were not depended on their beliefs about the effectiveness of leadership efforts.

Of the pragmatists examined, Eisenhower had the least confidence in a leader's ability to sway the public. In several cases, when faced with public opposition, his mind was swiftly changed by public opinion. Dulles, who thought that elites could lead the public if given enough time, was influenced by the public only when he was surprised by the issue and had a short time to make a decision, as in the offshore islands case. Bush, who assumed that the public would largely support the policy he chose, based his decisions on national security in the Gulf War and German reunification cases. Because of his beliefs, he acted to lead the public only as an afterthought. In the one instance in which he assumed he could not lead the public (if the Gulf War became a protracted conflict, he thought the public would irretrievably oppose the policy), public opinion limited his decision. In all these cases, the president's orientation toward public opinion explains his reaction to public opinion.

The influence of beliefs also affected how the presidents attempted to generate support for the policies they selected. All tried to win support for their policies, but how they did so and how they thought about it were affected by their beliefs. Clinton, a delegate, thought about educating the public about his policies, an action that he conceived of as showing the public how his policies aligned with the public's preferences. Carter, an executor, considered public opinion when formulating policy but viewed it instrumentally when trying to implement it. He tried to generate public support only when it became necessary to influence other actors, such as Congress. Eisenhower and Bush, both pragmatists, focused their leadership efforts on saying the things they thought would persuade the public to support their policies. For example, Eisenhower made sure to frame his New Look policy as increasing security rather than as reducing costs because he thought the public would respond better to the former. Bush pondered several ways of persuading the public to support the Gulf War before deciding on nuclear weapons proliferation as a justification. Finally, Reagan, a guardian, attempted to lead the public only by referring to the national interests at stake in an issue. In essence, even though they all may have taken actions that could be broadly characterized as leading the public, the substance of their approach and their conception of their efforts varied according to their beliefs.

The realist and Wilsonian liberal views suggest that conditions in the international (in the case of the realists) or domestic (in the case of the Wilsonian liberals) environments create pressures on decision makers that cause them to behave uniformly in reaction to public opinion under the same circumstances. The findings in this book dispute these assessments. Instead, people are likely to react to the same information differently depending on their beliefs. Although the realist and Wilsonian liberal approaches maintain that knowing the decision context is sufficient to ascertain the influence of public opinion on policy formulation, the findings here demonstrate that though this may be a necessary condition to understand the public's influence, it is not enough. These models are correct in pointing to the decision context as an important factor in determining the public's influence, but they incorrectly diagnose the process and influence of public opinion, since they leave out a central component in determining the public's influence. The combined beliefs and decision context view does, however, accurately explain the influence of public opinion on policy. In sum, the beliefs model largely accounts for the influence of public opinion in situations marked by a high threat to important values in which national security considerations predominate.

Information, Decision Context, and Linkage Processes

The conventional wisdom is that policymakers have relatively little information about public opinion in crisis contexts. Except for Reagan's Lebanon case, when polling data were available from a survey in the field at the time of the Beirut bombing, polling did not affect the policies selected. Even in the Reagan case and even though his advisers placed great importance on the polling information, Reagan ignored it. The paucity of polling data as they selected a policy affected presidents in different ways. Some presidents turned to other indicators of public opinion. In the Somalia case, Clinton relied on members of Congress and their reactions to phone calls from constituents as evidence of the rising tide of public opposition. In the offshore islands case, Eisenhower used earlier information he had gathered about public opinion in deciding on American policy for the East Asian region. But Carter after the Soviet invasion of Afghanistan and Bush in the Gulf War made their decisions without any particular information about the public's views and relied on how they expected the public to respond. The polls did, however, affect how some presidents led and explained policy to the public once they reached a decision. This effect was clearest in Bush's Gulf War case.

In the longer decision-time cases, more information about public opinion was available to policymakers. Although they reacted differently to it, both Carter on the Panama Canal treaty and Clinton on Bosnia paid a great deal of attention to the polls when forming their policies. In implementing the New Look, Eisenhower commissioned an informal survey of newspaper editors to assess the extent of public support for his new emphasis on air and nuclear strike power. Bush clearly was aware of public sentiment on the issue of German reunification and his administration's approach to the Soviets. Interestingly, he regarded public opinion as sending a mixed message, depending on the source. On the one hand, he felt that elite and editorial opinion was pressing him to take dramatic action. But on the other hand, based on his private polling results, he thought that the public favored his slow and determined approach to the changes in Soviet policy. Unlike other presidents, Reagan had no specific information about public opinion on SDI, although the growing nuclear freeze movement probably confirmed in his mind that the public might view a change in policy favorably.

The information about public opinion on which these policymakers relied came from several sources (e.g., letters, congressional opinion, polls). The polls were only one source of information, and the decision makers (e.g., Eisenhower, Carter, Clinton) who wanted information about public opinion turned to other places as well. As discussed later in reference to anticipated opinion, a lack of information did not prevent decision makers from integrating public preferences into the decision process. In fact, available information about public opinion is not a strong determining factor in the influence of public opinion on foreign policy. For example, in one case in which decision makers had a great deal of information about public opinion when reaching a decision (Reagan on Lebanon), the president largely ignored it. This behavior contrasts with decisions by Eisenhower, Carter, and Clinton, who had relatively less information about the public's reaction but still incorporated it into their deliberations. In essence, if the president believed that public opinion should be an integral part of his choice, anticipated public preferences became a part of the calculation, regardless of the amount of information he had about public opinion.

For the most part, when public opinion affected policy choices, it was because the president feared losing the public's support of either the policy or the administration, and this fear was contingent on the decision maker's beliefs orientation. In only a few instances did a policymaker decide to pursue a policy because he felt that the public wanted it (Eisenhower after *Sputnik*, Clinton on Bosnia). Instead, presidents mostly reacted to public opinion because they feared a public backlash if they either did not eliminate certain policies or decided to choose a policy the public did not favor. Executors and guardians are likely not to respond at all to their fears regarding public opinion, as was the case with Carter and Reagan, even though the possibility of losing public support was specifically raised during discussions. Pragmatists are more responsive to this fear, but its effect may be mitigated somewhat, depending on their confidence in their ability to lead the public. Since Eisenhower saw a more limited capacity to change public opinion, his fear of public opposition limited his decision regarding the offshore islands. Bush, however, had more confidence in his ability to build public support, and he generally ignored his fears about public opposition. Delegates are the most likely to respond to these fears, since they tap in to both their normative views and their practical concerns. Clinton's hasty retreat in Somalia provides evidence of this tendency. In the end, although fear may push most decision makers to consider public opinion, how far and to what extent it influences them depend on their beliefs orientations.

Surprisingly, even those presidents who had a vast array of resources and the most sophisticated polling operations responded more to how they thought the public would eventually view the issue than to the current shape of public opinion.[3] For all the presidents examined in this book, most reacted only to anticipated public opinion. To be sure, the immediate indicators of public opinion, such as polls, letters, and editorial sentiment, sometimes formed the basis for this evaluation. But the presidents turned to these representations of opinion only as one harbinger of future opinion. At times, this anticipation was nothing more than a guess, rather than hard evidence of the public's sentiment. For example, in formulating the New Look, Eisenhower looked somewhat far into the future to determine how the public would react to the strategic policy that the administration was considering. Both Carter's reaction to the Soviet invasion of Afghanistan and Bush's Gulf War policy incorporated public opinion, under conditions in which there was little information about public sentiment. In other instances, such as Eisenhower on the offshore islands and Dien Bien Phu, decision makers paid more attention to the anticipated reactions of public opinion than to other available indicators of opinion.

Presidents responded to anticipated opinion for a number of reasons. Some were held back by it because of fears that their policy would fail to attract future support. In his reaction to the offshore islands case, Eisenhower based his decision to avoid war largely on anticipated public opposition and used the information about public sentiments that he had gathered in other contexts as a partial basis for this projection. The same dynamic occurred during the Dien Bien Phu decision process. After the Soviet invasion of Afghanistan, Carter had little information about public opinion, but his deliberations still took into account how the public would respond to potential policy options, with officials making fairly straightforward projections about public sentiment (e.g., farmers would oppose a grain embargo, the public would oppose the resumption of the previously unpopular draft, public sentiment would oppose boycotting the Olympics). Bush expected that public opinion would quickly turn against his Gulf policy if the United States suffered significant losses early in the deployment process or if the conflict dragged on. Given America's experience with Vietnam and Bush's reading of history, these projections did not diverge dramatically from reasonable expectations based on previous experience. As these examples show, it is not that these projections occurred in an information vacuum about public sentiment but, rather, that the presidents employed what they knew to formulate an anticipation of what they felt they needed to know—how the public would eventually respond to their policies.

Some presidents anticipated how the public's reaction to an issue at hand would affect larger questions. For example, several presidents considered how they thought public opinion might affect their success on other issues or their presidency's success in general. In the Somalia case, Clinton reacted to how he thought his handling of the issue would affect the success of an intervention in Bosnia, for which public support was particularly tenuous, and also his presidency's broader prospects for success. Eisenhower's New Look strategy was spurred in part because Eisenhower thought the public would eventually react unfavorably to the current American strategic policy.

Elections played an important part in forming these expectations. The context for Clinton's 1995 Bosnia policy was shaped in large part by how he thought the public would view his policies during the next election year. Fearing that inaction would leave him in a worse situation, he chose to act. Bush, too, decided to launch the Gulf War military attack in January 1991 in part because he feared that waiting another year would test public patience with his policy, and he wished to avoid starting a potentially disastrous attack during an election year. In addition, Eisenhower shifted his policy on the offshore islands crisis partly to keep the issue out of the forthcoming congressional elections. In all these cases, the presidents either removed or reduced the chances for an issue to color an election. Interestingly, in neither of the two cases in which a presidential election was held within one year of a decision did the presidents react to public opinion. Even though their views about the legitimacy of public opinion in the decision process differed, both Carter (about Afghanistan) and Reagan (about Lebanon) knew the electoral implications of their policies, but neither reacted to them. In making the Afghanistan decision, Carter gave extensive attention to public opinion and eventually decided he had to implement policies the public opposed. Reagan, however, in the Lebanon decision, rejected responding to public opinion entirely (although his advisers did not). Whereas the structural condition of future elections played a part in several decisions, the president's reaction to this prospect was based more on his beliefs about the public's influence than on the fact of a forthcoming election.

Decision Stages

The influence of public opinion across decision stages was mixed. Only Clinton seriously considered public opinion while setting his agenda, whereas all the presidents thought about public opinion while implementing their policies, mostly in relation to leading it. Some decision makers considered public opinion while selecting their policies, such as in Eisenhower's offshore islands, Dien Bien Phu, and *Sputnik* cases, Carter's Afghanistan and Panama cases, Bush's Gulf War case, and Clinton's Somalia and Bosnia cases. But public opinion affected only the policies selected in the Eisenhower and Clinton cases. Public opinion constrained policymakers during the definition of the situation in several Eisenhower cases (Dien Bien Phu, *Sputnik*, and the New Look) and in both Clinton cases. Public opinion was rarely considered during option generation, with the exception of Dulles in the offshore islands case, Eisenhower in the *Sputnik* case, and the two Clinton cases.

Even though the influence of public opinion varied widely among the decision makers, three general conclusions are warranted. First, policymakers tended to ignore public opinion in agenda setting. Second, when public opinion did affect policy, its strongest influence occurred during policy selection by constraining decisions, although it caused some policymakers to follow the public's preferences. Finally, decision makers almost uniformly acted to lead public opinion when implementing their policies. These results indicate that public opinion affected policy more often in the later, rather than the earlier, stages of decisions.

The influence of public opinion later, rather than early, during policy formulation contradicts some earlier studies. Earlier research on the stage at which public opinion affects policy stressed that its influence occurred mostly during agenda setting or a treaty ratification process. Thomas Graham's analysis of nuclear arms control cases across a range of administrations found that the public influenced policy choices during agenda setting and treaty ratification, but not during the negotiation or implementation of the agreements.[4] Since he defined decision stages according to the process of an arms control negotiation rather than the decision process, some of his stages (concerning a treaty's negotiation, ratification, and implementation) have no clear comparison with this book's research. In the one treaty case in this study, the Panama Canal treaty, public opinion was considered during agenda setting and as the administration pursued ratification, which is consistent with Graham's finding.

The conclusions of Graham's research concerning the influence of public opinion at the agenda setting stage may be limited, however, since across a range of security issues, I found a consistent lack of influence of public opinion at this decision stage. The cases analyzed in this book suggest that the agenda-setting function for security issues might be limited to high-profile, long-term issues about which the public is highly motivated to get involved (e.g., high-profile treaties). In most of the instances in this study, policymakers turned to an issue because they saw it as important to national security rather than because of public opinion.

National security interests were an important part of policymakers' calculations for all the decisions considered here. The realists may be correct when they say public opinion is not relevant to many national security issues during agenda setting, but they go too far when they insist that this prevents public opinion from influencing other policy aspects. For the Wilsonian liberals, public opinion is usually not a force for policy innovation or pressure to consider an issue, but it does limit the policy options that decision makers saw as available. But as I argued, any of these influences is highly contingent on the beliefs of the person making the decision.

Caveats

In this study, several factors were controlled that may affect public opinion's influence on foreign policy, such as issue type (national security rather than foreign economic), approval rating, and proximity to the next election. As these controls are relaxed, there may be less variation among decision makers and a trend toward a more uniform response to public opinion. Beliefs may act as a baseline variable that sets the extent to which a decision maker excludes public opinion from decision making. As issues become more economically focused, approval ratings drop, and elections approach, all decision makers may become more responsive to public opinion. Future research will have to determine whether as the control variables are relaxed, (1) the influence of beliefs continues, as found in this study; (2) responsiveness to public opinion in general increases; (3) leaders from different orientations tend to respond in the same way to public opinion because environmental factors overwhelm individual differences; (4) individuals with different beliefs become more responsive to the public by an equal amount, but differences between them continue because they begin from a different baseline; and (5) the changing conditions affect individuals in some orientations more than others.

First, as the presence of economic factors in a decision increases or the definition of security issues expands to include factors with more domestic components, such as trade, the environment, and nationalist and ethnic conflicts, the influence of public opinion may grow. Unlike more traditional national security issues that may not be relevant to domestic societal segments, interest groups and the public are more likely to be attracted to and become actively involved in issues that affect their pocketbooks, that relate to concerns in which they have a stake, or that contain a strong emotional element that can be communicated through television.[5] As the issue becomes less dominated by national security interests, the conditions (e.g., ambiguity, decisions at the top of the hierarchical ladder, wide range of action) that make likely the influence of beliefs are also likely to decrease. Given the post–Cold War environment, more issues like these will probably enter the policy agenda, but more traditional security issues will remain as well.

Second, this study considered cases in times when the president's approval rating was relatively high. As approval ratings drop or reach low levels, public opinion may act as a stronger restraint on foreign policy choices.[6] Decision makers may fear that difficulties in the international sphere may make a bad domestic situation even worse, or they may hope to improve the domestic situation with international success. As a result, policymakers may be more responsive to public preferences when they are unpopular than when they are popular. Consistent with this thinking, as argued in the *Sputnik* and New Look cases, Eisenhower's attention to public opinion at certain decision stages may have derived from his anticipation of future public disapproval. If foreign policy cases occur during periods when a president's approval rating is low, the constraining influence may be greater.

Finally, presidents may also become more attentive to public opinion as presidential elections draw closer. Presidential elections can act as a policy restraint on presidents by limiting the risks they may take. Earlier research implies that especially during peacetime, presidents are less inclined to use force in election years than at other times. Conversely, during wars or in the year after an election, presidents are more likely to approve uses of force.[7] Other research has found that presidents may be more inclined to use force during election years.[8] In short, public opinion seems more prone to influence decision makers when they face an upcoming election, but it remains unclear whether it causes presidents to act more forcefully or more timidly.

The evidence from the case studies is equally mixed on this issue. Two cases, the Reagan Lebanon case and the Carter Afghanistan case, barely missed the one-year qualification level for consideration but were included because they were the most "crisislike" cases in those administrations. In both cases, advisers to the president were very concerned with the cases' implications for upcoming elections. But given their beliefs, both presidents chose not to respond to these pressures. In addition, in two other cases (Clinton on Bosnia and Bush on the Gulf War), the possible use of force during an election year provided a reason for these policymakers to resolve the issue before the election. The implications of these results are twofold. First, the Carter and Reagan cases suggest a role for election-year politics in decision making, but not necessarily in policy outcomes. Since Bush and Clinton, both of whom thought public support was necessary, did respond to anticipated electoral effects, and Carter and Reagan, who did not believe in the necessity of public support, did not respond, it is not clear whether differences based on beliefs orientations disappear as elections approach. Second, as the Bush and Clinton cases suggest, the influence of elections may not be limited to the election year, given anticipation about the influence of policies on electoral outcomes. Because this study tried to limit the influence of elections, it cannot offer definite answers to these questions.

Aside from these factors, the coding of public opinion's influence on *presidential* decisions may understate the public's impact on the larger decision process, especially in regard to the influence of public opinion on the formation of presidential advisers' views. By distinguishing between presidential policy calculations and choices and an administration's other activities (such as the factors that lead advisers to offer certain policy recommendations to the president), this research may not reveal the full influence of public opinion in the policy process.

For example, in the Lebanon case, public opinion did not directly affect Reagan's decision to withdraw the marines. The data show that his advisers were highly responsive to public opinion and that it did affect their thinking on policy options. But when they advised Reagan, they framed their arguments as pertaining to national security factors. Consonant with this study's analysis of Reagan's preferences in regard to public opinion, the Reagan administration proved to be a sophisticated user of polls, which it employed primarily to build support for its policies.[9] Although the coding accurately accounts for the *president's* decision, it may understate the influence of public opinion on the entire *administration* and the place of public opinion in an *administration's* deliberations.

This understatement is likely only in a few cases, probably only when a guardian is involved. In their discussions with the president, advisers of presidents in the executor (Carter), pragmatist (Eisenhower, Bush), and delegate (Clinton) orientations were quite open about their concerns regarding public opinion. In the case of the guardian, since advisers probably are aware of the president's desire to ignore public opinion, they may have an incentive to disguise the amount of influence that public opinion has on their preferences. For this reason, public opinion may have a larger influence on the administration's deliberations than a guardian would wish. Since my research focused on presidential decision making, this broader assessment is left to other scholars.

Implications

Democratic Theory

According to democratic theory, there are two ways in which the public is best served in a democratic environment. The *delegate* perspective argues that policymakers should consider public opinion in their deliberations and try to align their policies to the broad framework of public support. The *trustee* view contends that the public dispenses with its role in policy formulation once it selects a qualified individual to represent it. Based on the assumption that public matters are complicated, proponents of the trustee perspective believe that especially concerning foreign policy, the public should allow elected officials to determine the best policy to serve the public interest without regard for the public's view on the issue. Although the Wilsonian liberal and realist perspectives derive partly from the delegate and trustee views, respectively, these democratic theories encompass normative views of both foreign and domestic policy formulation. As with the Wilsonian liberal and realist views, each of these democratic theory perspectives receives mixed support.

Elite theory, as exemplified in the writings of C. Wright Mills, provides a different picture of policymaking. Supporters of this view contend that decision makers construct policy with little regard to the public's preferences or the public interest and instead design policies to serve the elite's own economic and power interests. These proponents point out that the elite can manufacture public support to serve their interests, thereby freeing them from constraints by the public when deciding on foreign policy. Whereas the delegate perspective says that the public's opinion is considered, elite theory contends that decision makers take into account public opinion only to manipulate it (rather easily even if the public initially opposes a policy) to support the government's policy. Unlike the trustee concept, according to which decision makers act in response to the public's interests (although not necessarily in response to its opinion), elite theory suggests that the public interest is largely left out of the equation.[10] Because my research found that decision makers reacted either to public opinion or to their perception of the national interest, the power-driven motivation posited by elite theory did not receive any support.

An extreme reading of the delegate view that would make the policymaker into a mere tabulation machine of public opinion receives no support; rather, the more relaxed perspective that public opinion should be one of the primary determinants of policy receives more support, both in the beliefs of the post–World War II presidents and in the cases examined. Given the dangerous nature of international politics, probably no presidents see their role as merely registering public opinion, nor would most proponents of the delegate view believe they should. Seven of the ten presidents subscribed to the importance of public opinion to foreign policy, for either normative or practical reasons. But only two agreed with the normative view that public opinion should affect foreign policy decisions. Clinton's beliefs perhaps come closest to the delegate view of representation, since he believed he should consider how the public would have wanted him to act once all the information has come out. In this sense, Clinton was comfortable acting against the prevailing public opinion of the moment if he thought the people would come to view an issue differently. For this reason, Clinton's view is a modified delegate perspective that takes into account the informational constraints and complicated nature of foreign policy. Clinton's attention to the public's long-term sentiments, as opposed to their short-term views, comes the closest to the delegate's view of ideal behavior that this study found.

In regard to beliefs about public opinion, Clinton is the exception, however, rather than the rule, since most decision makers granted some importance to public opinion but did not allow nearly the amount of influence implied even by a more relaxed delegate perspective. Carter's views remain mainly in the delegate perspective because he valued public input into his foreign policy decisions. His openness to public opinion when reaching decisions on foreign policy and engaging it as a legitimate decision factor, rather than merely as the focus of potential manipulation, would certainly be looked upon favorably by delegate theory proponents. But in combination with his practical beliefs and as seen in the case studies, his actual foreign policy choices might not conform to the outcomes that these theorists would prefer.

Providing somewhat less support for the delegate theory are the five presidents who opposed public input into decisions but viewed public support as necessary. Here, the split among types of pragmatists based on their assessment of how readily they could lead public opinion becomes pertinent. One set, composed of Eisenhower and Kennedy, thought they had a fairly limited ability to shift public opinion. In turn, public opinion prevented them from enacting policies that they thought the public might not support, a result supported by the delegate theory. If these presidents based their policies on what the public could support, the correlation between opinion and policy that the delegate theory favors would occur in much the same way as the theory predicts.

Another set of presidents—Nixon, Ford, and Bush—assumed that nearly any policy they chose would be supported by public opinion because of the public's almost automatic support of the president's foreign policy or because they thought they could create support for a policy where none existed previously. Although they could be influenced by public opinion, these presidents' likely interaction with public opinion would probably not have matched that supported by the delegate theory because they would have been less likely to respond to public opinion.

The delegate theory is not supported by the beliefs of the three guardian presidents—Truman, Johnson, and Reagan. By rejecting public opinion as a factor on which to base their decisions, these policymakers' views directly contradicted the delegate theory's perspective.

The delegate perspective receives equally mixed support on policy behavior. Although the influence of public opinion never reached the dominating influence suggested by the extreme delegate position, it often was an important consideration in policy deliberations and broadly constrained the decisions of several presidents, as expected from the more relaxed delegate position. Public opinion was considered extensively in Eisenhower's, Carter's, and Clinton's approaches to foreign policy. A limiting influence on the use of force was found in the offshore islands and Dien Bien Phu cases in the Eisenhower administration, and the Somalia and Bosnia cases in the Clinton administration. A more minor following influence was found only for parts of Eisenhower's *Sputnik* decision and for both of Clinton's decisions. Although Carter considered public opinion in his decisions, he did not use it as a basis for his choice, thereby providing mixed support for the delegate position. Furthermore, the almost total lack of attention to public opinion by Reagan and Bush provides contradictory evidence for the delegate view.

The results for the trustee perspective are somewhat stronger than for the delegate view, since several of the presidents who wanted to incorporate public opinion into their decisions also considered their approach to policy formulation to be in line with the trustee view. Most of the decision makers thought they should act in the public's interest by focusing on national security concerns rather than responding to its opinion. Truman, Johnson, and Reagan most explicitly held this viewpoint. To a lesser extent, Nixon, Ford, and Bush agreed with this perspective but also added the necessity of public support, which they thought they could easily achieve for any policy in the national interest. Eisenhower and Kennedy provide more of a mixed view. Each held views that agreed with the trustee perspective of decision making, in that they thought they should first decide on the best policy from a national security perspective. However, they also strongly believed that they needed to compare that policy with public opinion and should carry out a policy only if they thought public support would be forthcoming, because the public either favored the view already or would after their leadership efforts. If they thought they could not change public opinion, this realization would probably limit their policy choices. This view contradicts the trustee perspective that policymakers should select the best policy to serve the public's interests. Finally, both Carter and Clinton favored including public opinion in their determination of foreign policy, a perspective countering the trustee view. In total, six of the presidents maintained beliefs that broadly agreed with the trustee view; two had beliefs that did so to a lesser extent; and two did not follow the trustee view at all.

The presidents' behavior provides mixed support for the trustee view. Eisenhower in the *Sputnik* and New Look cases, the Reagan and Bush cases, and the results of the Carter cases largely support the trustee model of decision making. But the Eisenhower offshore islands and Dien Bien Phu cases, the process of Carter's decisions, and both of Clinton's decisions do not offer much support for the trustee view, since public opinion affected their policy choices.

Even so, in those cases in which public opinion did affect the policy outcomes, decision makers were highly concerned with the national interests at stake in the decision. When the presidents did react to public opinion, it was often because they thought that the broader national interest required it. For example, Eisenhower thought that any military action that did not have public support would end in disaster, a view that restricted him in the two short decision-time cases. In the two long decision-time cases, he feared that public opposition to his policies would eventually undermine the foundation of American foreign policy and thus damage national security. In this sense, even though the influence of public opinion in these instances seems to contradict the trustee view, Eisenhower acted in a framework that emphasized the national interest, but with the realization that the public's reaction to policies could significantly affect their success. The same cannot be said of Carter's or Clinton's approaches to the decision process, since they both considered public opinion to be an important part of a decision on its own merits.

Although the delegate and trustee views individually find moderate support in this study, democratic theory as a whole is strongly supported, since the shortcomings of the delegate perspective are mirrored by the successes of the trustee view, and vice versa. In nearly every case, the presidents focused either on improving what they perceived to be the national interest or on attempting to implement what they perceived to be the public will. In no instance were the economic or power-driven motives of elite theory supported. Some decision makers' beliefs agreed with the delegate perspective, some with the trustee view, and some with a combination of these perspectives. Although democratic theory may be supported more broadly, the descriptive value of either perspective is contingent on the views of the person making the decision.

The Domestic Sources of International Relations

Some scholars, mainly those subscribing to the neorealist and classical realist perspectives, claim that domestic factors usually do not affect national security policy, but other analysts emphasize the influence of domestic considerations on a range of behaviors.[11] In fact, liberal international relations theory (of which Wilsonian liberalism is a distinct strand) stands in contrast to neorealism by proposing that the interaction between the state and society forms the basis for the state's behavior by determining its preferences.[12] This book takes the side of liberal international relations theory, which states that domestic factors can significantly alter national security policies. As argued in the case studies, foreign and security policy cannot be explained in reference only to prevailing international conditions or to perceptions of the national interest. Instead, across a range of cases, public opinion affected perceptions of possible policies, especially those of policymakers who were more open to information about public opinion. In fact, the public's influence was most noticeable in the short decision-time cases when choices involved the consideration of using force, which are the situations in which realists say that domestic factors should have the least amount of influence. When given a longer time to make a choice, decision makers often formulated their policy approach outside the public's view and with most of their attention to public opinion paid at the implementation stage. These findings imply that any influence of public opinion is unlikely to occur uniformly across decision makers or decisions. Because this book focused on the individual's sensitivity to public opinion and the decision context, future research should consider the extent to which the public's influence might be altered by other domestic and governmental processes.

Neorealists generally assume that a state's choice of goals and means is driven by the search for security in an anarchical system and is restricted by the international distribution of power capabilities, which largely leaves societal factors such as public opinion outside the explanatory framework. Although some realists may turn to domestic factors to explain irrational state policies, they largely ignore internal components when explaining the state's choice.[13] For example, Kenneth Waltz argues that "the pressures of competition weigh more heavily than ideological preferences or internal political pressures." Likewise, Fareed Zakaria concludes that "across time and space, states' positions in the anarchic international system prove to provide the simplest, shortest guide to international relations."[14] Some theorists now contend that structural realism can incorporate interactions at the foreign policy level, but other neorealists dispute this claim.[15]

This book's analysis of a single type of state (liberal, democratic, status quo–oriented, relatively powerful) demonstrates that public opinion can cause important and dramatic shifts in choices regarding policy goals and means that cannot be explained by capabilities or interests defined in terms of security or power. These results suggest that the interaction between public opinion and elites may be a potentially important source of state preferences that neorealist formulations largely ignore and cannot encompass.

Public opinion can influence a leader's perceptions of those interests that are worth committing resources to defend or support. In the offshore islands and Dien Bien Phu cases, because of domestic opposition, Eisenhower's and (to a lesser extent) Dulles's sensitivity to public opinion significantly altered the way in which they approached these issues, even to the point of making choices that risked damaging what they recognized as American national interests. In addition, public opinion broadly constrained the manner in which Eisenhower and Dulles approached the formulation of the New Look strategic policy, in both the goals and means of long-range American policy. Likewise, Clinton responded to domestic opinion about the attention he gave to and the value he placed on American intervention in Somalia. Public opinion also affected his perception of American interests in Bosnia and the policy means he chose to resolve the problem. Public opinion somewhat pressured Bush regarding the means with which he pursued his Gulf War policy. Although realism does not account for these decisions, a national interest–centered approach does explain rather well the policy choices in the Carter and Reagan cases.

Not only can the means that states use to achieve their goals be affected systematically and predictably by public opinion, but also the goals and objectives themselves may be partially determined by domestic variables rather than just by state power and security incentives. Whereas the neorealists argue that pressures from the international system determine how a state acts, this book implies that how a leader interprets the international environment may be greatly affected by his or her perceptions of domestic pressures. The president's reaction or nonreaction to public opinion can shape state policy in a manner unanticipated by neorealist models. Although international imperatives may provide a useful guide to the constraints that a state faces, it is an accurate and useful guide to a state's international behavior only if the leader's views of the domestic environment agree with neorealist assumptions. If the leader does not hold similar views, then he or she may act in a manner not predicted by neorealist formulations.

In contrast to realists who reject domestic-based explanations of international relations, some scholars who examine the domestic sources of international relations have incorporated in their work assumptions about how leaders react to domestic circumstances. Included in many of these approaches is the assumption that leaders are sensitive to how public opinion will react to their policies. Several of these models treat decision makers in democracies as if they were equally sensitive to the potential domestic costs of international behavior. For example, James Fearon argues that the potential loss of domestic support for democratic leaders who back down after making a commitment in an international dispute makes them less likely to do so and thus better able to signal their intentions than can leaders of authoritarian nations. This argument rests on the assumption that all democratic leaders are nearly equally sensitive to a potential loss of support and that all democratic leaders are more sensitive to this than their authoritarian counterparts are. A range of responsiveness by democratic leaders would undermine the signaling value of incurring domestic audience costs and make them a poor guide to international behavior, especially if that range overlapped with the sensitivities of authoritarian leaders.

Bruce Bueno de Mesquita and David Lalman contend that decisions regarding war are largely driven by domestic political imperatives, and they recommend that future research focus on determining the domestic processes that cause these pressures. They reject the notion that some leaders when reaching their choices are sensitive only to prevailing international conditions. This argument assumes that all leaders in a certain state respond in the same way to similar domestic pressures and processes.

Finally, Helen Milner examined the domestic determinants of international cooperation and found that internal factors rather than international conditions affect the propensity of states to cooperate with one another. She assumes that the policy preferences of leaders are driven in great part by their electoral concerns, and she contends that since people vote according to their economic conditions, a leader's preferences are partly determined by how a policy economically affects domestic social coalitions whose support is needed to win elections and by the direct electoral consequences of a policy based on its implications for the economy. Milner relies on the assumption that leaders are equally sensitive to their electoral fortunes in reaching foreign policy decisions.[16]

Each of these approaches assumes that leaders in the same state face the same domestic structural constraints and processes and that they react to them in the same way. But because this book found that this sensitivity varies among individuals, these models must be contingent on these processes. Unlike these models' assumptions, my findings suggest that decision makers differ in (1) how they react to the potential domestic consequences of failure in the international realm, (2) how they respond to domestic pressures, and (3) how they react to electoral consequences in their decisions. For example, because of his beliefs, Reagan did not react to domestic pressure to back out of Lebanon. Nor did he hesitate in adopting the SDI policy, which was premised on the eventual abrogation of the antiballistic missile treaty, which had significant domestic support. Likewise, Bush largely ignored the domestic consequences of his policies. After the Soviet invasion of Afghanistan, Carter took several actions that he knew would harm his chances for reelection, and he also risked public opposition to his Panama Canal treaty policy. Clinton, however, swiftly reacted to the potential electoral ramifications of his policies in Somalia and Bosnia. In addition, across a range of cases, Eisenhower was limited by potentially negative public reaction. In each of these cases, the influence of public opinion, elections, and domestic costs was determined by the policymaker's sensitivity to public opinion rather than by the prevailing domestic circumstances.

Some of the work on the domestic sources of international relations relies on assumptions that are actually contingent on individual level variables. Furthermore, the contingent nature of these assumptions could significantly contextualize or alter these findings. For Fearon's model, the domestic audience costs created by making commitments during crises may not imply the same thing for all persons, since some may be willing to accept the large domestic costs of backing down in a crisis and some may not. The fact that a democratic leader is making the decision implies nothing about his or her reaction to domestic audience costs. In addition, the beliefs model suggests that there is no reason to assume that democratic leaders are more sensitive to audience costs than are authoritarian leaders, because guardians may be just as insensitive to public opinion in their foreign policy decisions as authoritarian leaders are. In addition, public opinion might act as a restraint in following through on a commitment and could push democratic leaders to reach an accommodation rather than stand firm. Indeed, public opinion might cause them to renege on their commitments. For example, this dynamic was present in the Eisenhower offshore islands case, the Reagan Lebanon case, the Bush Gulf War case, and the Clinton Somalia case. Because the effect of domestic audience costs probably varies, the central finding of Fearon's work, that domestic audience costs make democratic leaders better able to signal their intentions, is questionable.

In contrast to Bueno de Mesquita and Lalman's war model, my research found that some leaders pay more attention to the international context rather than the domestic environment. In addition, even those leaders who are attentive to the domestic arena do not necessarily react to it in the same way. For this reason, their conclusions are actually contingent on a leader's varying sensitivity to domestic factors.

Finally, Milner's assumption that all leaders consider electoral implications when making foreign policy decisions overstates the case. Some decision makers certainly do have their electoral fortunes in mind, but others just as certainly are less sensitive to their electoral prospects and the domestic consequences of their international behavior. These varying sensitivities suggest that the domestic processes that Milner identifies may sometimes, but not always, become engaged. This book's findings do not mean that any of these models are wrong but that their accuracy depends on assumptions that are highly contingent rather than universal.

A surprising result of my research is the lack of support for the diversionary use of force. The literature on the linkage between elections and the use of force argues that politicians initiate the use of force either early in the election cycle when they see a better chance of creating public support for a policy or immediately before an election in order to inflate popular support for electoral purposes.[17] My findings, however, do not support these causal linkages. Relatively early in the election cycle, presidents (such as Eisenhower at Dien Bien Phu and in the offshore islands, Bush in the Persian Gulf, Clinton in Somalia) did not perceive a broader band in which to lead public opinion. In fact, in each of these instances, these presidents either regarded public opinion as a limiting factor or felt that the issue could damage their chances at the next election, even though it was at least two years away in each instance. In addition, in those cases that occurred closer to an election (such as Reagan on Lebanon, Carter on Afghanistan, and Clinton on Bosnia), none of these decision makers was tempted to resort to force to bolster their electoral prospects. In fact, in the Reagan Lebanon and Clinton Bosnia cases, public opinion and the next election provided arguments against using force because the administration feared casualties could jeopardize their electoral prospects (although this reasoning did not color Reagan's decision). Although in the Afghanistan case, Carter did take public opinion into consideration, policymakers did not see it as a reason to react strongly, and to the extent that public opinion was considered, it was seen as a factor discouraging a bellicose response. The explanatory value of the diversionary use of force model is undermined because every case contradicts this theory's causal logic.

The diversionary use of force theory also rests on the assumption that decision makers expect that the use of force will enhance the perception of the administration in the public's mind.[18] The findings from this book, however, point to just the opposite. Across a series of cases from different administrations, including ones for which extensive archival material was available, in no instance did any high-level official (including those in the Eisenhower administration whose views were not considered in this book) believe either that the public wanted force to be used or would react positively to the use of force. The public may have favored policy goals that entailed the use of force, but in every instance, the public was seen as opposed to the use of force to achieve these goals. Although leaders' perceptions of public opinion on the use of force did not vary, their reactions to it did. In accordance with their beliefs, some officials ignored this sentiment; some thought they could change it; and others were limited by it. However, the unanimity of perception of public preferences concerning the use of force across a range of individuals and cases belies the foundational assumptions of the diversionary use of force theory.

This argument should not be interpreted as suggesting that these decision makers did not recognize that they might lose some public support if they did not react forcefully in a particular instance. For example, Eisenhower feared he might lose public support if his action or inaction led to the "loss" of Indochina. Acting to prevent the loss of public support and acting to increase public support, however, entail different calculations. In the first instance, the policymaker sees little or no opportunity to increase public approval, only to lose it. In the second instance, he or she feels no such pressure but instead senses an opportunity to inflate the public's assessments.

Public Opinion and Foreign Policy

The scholarly literature discussed in chapter 1 on the influence of public opinion on foreign policy provides several possible explanations of the correlation between opinion and policy: (1) Elites create public support, or the public tends to support elites' decisions; (2) public opinion sets broad policy constraints; (3) elites largely follow public opinion; and (4) each of these relationships is conditional. This book supports the fourth combined perspective and argues that public opinion can be led, can constrain policymakers, or can cause them to follow the public, but how public opinion is considered largely depends on the circumstances in which a decision is made and the person making it. In essence, each of the first three perspectives can be correct, but only conditionally.

My findings lean toward supporting the conditional perspective on public opinion's influence, but they also have implications for the other perspectives. First, one strand of the literature, most closely identified with the realist perspective, contends that public opinion is fairly permissive on foreign policy and generally supports the decision makers' approach. Policymakers who were guardians, such as Reagan, or whose behavior was similar to that of a guardian, such as Bush, usually reacted in accordance with the predictions of this viewpoint. Even so, this view often did not accurately account for the decision-making dynamics. Policymakers perceived constraints by public opinion even when objective assessments of it, such as those contained in polls, were either vague or supportive of the administration's policy. For example, during the formulation of the New Look, public opinion did not dictate that the policy needed to change, but it also was not seen as open to just any policy option. This view's descriptive accuracy of the relationship between opinion and policy depends greatly on how a decision maker approaches a choice.

The public constraint view received more support. When public opinion affected policy, it mostly did so through a mechanism of policy constraint. In addition, it was largely the anticipation of potential public opposition or electoral retribution that motivated policymakers to respond to public opinion. Decision makers rarely were aware that the public desired or required a specific policy for policymakers to implement. Instead, they concluded that the public would accept a range of policy alternatives but was not wedded to just one. However, this finding was still largely conditional. In both cases, Carter perceived a band of public policy acceptance, but he still ignored these restrictions in his decisions. In the Afghanistan case, he chose to implement policies that he thought were outside the realm of public acceptance. On the Panama Canal treaty, he assumed a narrow range of public constraint but instead decided to move forward on his preferred policy. In this sense, even when decision makers recognize public constraint, its influence still is tightly conditioned by their beliefs and not just their perception of public opinion. For this reason, even though the constraint view was largely accurate when public opinion influenced policy, it did not always account for the reactions of decision makers.

The third view, buttressed by a growing set of quantitative correlational data, is that public opinion is often correlated with foreign policies and that it often changes before the policy shifts, thus implying that public opinion influences policymakers by causing them to follow it. This book does not provide much support for this model of public opinion's influence, since decision makers only rarely made policy decisions that tried to follow public opinion. The beliefs model posited that only delegates would react to public opinion in this manner. According to the case studies, it appears that the lone delegate, Clinton, did sometimes follow public opinion on foreign policy but that his broader reaction to public opinion revealed more of the interaction between opinion and policy that was posited by the constraint thesis.

In a larger sense, the case study findings contain a note of caution for correlational studies of the relationship between public opinion and foreign policy. A strict focus on coding policy outcomes and the prevailing public opinion, as reflected in the polls, might not only miss important decision-making dynamics but could also incorrectly code the relationship between opinion and policy. Because this book reveals that much of the connection between opinion and policy occurred because of policymakers' anticipations of public opinion—which might or might not be reflected in or derived from polling results—researchers must be careful in reaching conclusions about decision dynamics based solely on quantitative research.

Several examples illustrate this point. Reagan's decision making on Lebanon would appear from a correlational standpoint to be a case in which public opinion led to a shift in policy. From an aggregated perspective, public opinion shifted first, which was then followed by a policy adjustment. However, as the case analysis found, Reagan largely ignored public opinion in reaching his decision.

On the other side, Eisenhower's New Look policy would appear to be a case in which opinion did follow policy. There was no demand for a policy shift, and the aggregate readings of opinion quickly aligned with the policy once it was announced. However, this perspective overlooks the important constraining influence of Eisenhower's anticipation of long-term public support.

Finally, Clinton's Bosnia policy is a case in which an aggregate approach would point to a disjoint between opinion and policy. Aggregate readings of opinion saw the public as generally opposed to sending American troops into Bosnia under most conditions. However, as an examination of this case reveals, Clinton did consider public preferences when debating his decision. But because his reference point for public opinion was his anticipation of the public's long-term opinion of his Bosnia policy, a consideration of polling alone might miss this.

These examples do not imply that correlational analyses are incorrect in the trends they reveal but, rather, that they do not tell the whole story. If the influence of public opinion is to be understood, scholars must also look behind the numbers to confirm quantitative results. In this sense, these examples show that several research methods must be used to fully probe the complicated influence of public opinion.[19]

The case studies' findings add one other caution about the determination of public opinion's influence. As the length of decision time increased, decision makers had more information about public opinion. However, as revealed across several case studies, the greater amount of information about the public's preferences could be used in one of two ways: to respond to them or to attempt to change them.[20] In the long decision-time cases, some decision makers, Clinton in particular, saw the increased amount of information as an opportunity to construct a policy that not only could address the issue but respond to the public's preferences as well. Other decision makers, such as Eisenhower and Carter, used the added information to fashion leadership programs to enhance public support of their policies. Reagan's administration, in particular, was well known for using information about the public's views in this way. These instances serve to highlight a central finding of this study: that public opinion does not directly and objectively translate into policy outcomes. Instead, the public's influence is conditional on policymakers' perceptions and their sensitivity to public opinion. Both factors make the influence of public opinion highly conditional. However, when an individual's beliefs and the decision context are known, a fairly accurate gauge of how a policymaker will respond to public opinion and the influence the public will have on the development of a foreign policy is possible.

Security Policy After the Cold War

These findings regarding the general relationship between public opinion and foreign policy have implications for the development of

American foreign policy in the post–Cold War era. As the United States has confronted and will continue to cope with the uncertainties of the changing international environment, a debate over the goals and purposes of American foreign policy has begun. At the core of many of these discussions is the prospect of winning public support for a policy. Much of this concern focuses on the fear that the public will favor isolationism and the prospects for a continued internationalist orientation in American foreign policy.[21] Although any speculation about the future direction of public opinion is beyond the scope of this book, the reaction of presidents to any shifts and changes in American opinion does lie in its purview. This book suggests that in future crises or international affairs generally, regardless of public opinion about the use of force and the level of engagement the public favors in international affairs, it is unlikely to provide an absolute restraint on policymakers. Instead, the reaction of presidents to public opinion will largely be determined by variations in their beliefs.

Although the types of foreign policy issues that may arise after the Cold War have increased and expanded, there is no reason to believe that the dynamics that drive public opinion's influence, or the lack thereof, have changed much. A president's orientation toward public opinion is likely to have an important influence on how he or she reacts to public opinion when formulating a foreign policy in the post–Cold War era. Delegates will probably try to stay within the limits of public acceptance, on both specific policy issues and broad approaches to foreign policy. They will likely move more slowly in response to changing international events and attempt to bring their policies into line with public opinion. As demonstrated in both Clinton cases, the only president so far who came into office after the Cold War (who happens to be a delegate) behaved as anticipated by this discussion. Even in the development of broad foreign policy, the Clinton administration has been closely attuned to shifts in public opinion and has worked to ensure that its policy aligned with public preferences.[22]

Guardians, however, may be driven more by their perceptions of the national interests and be less likely to respond to the limitations of public opinion. Pragmatists, who are driven by their anticipation of public support, may try to create public support for whatever vision that they deem necessary for national security. Unlike guardians, they will be more inclined to engage the public to support whatever policy they determine to be the most appropriate. Finally, executors will be more or less responsive to the public, depending on the strength of their views. If they form a strong preference about the shape of American involvement, they will likely act more like guardians in implementing their strategy. If their views are weakly held, public opinion may restrict their actions in much the same way as that expected of delegates. The direction of public opinion in the future cannot be known, but the beliefs of the policymakers who will be reacting to it will probably have a significant impact on the role of public opinion in shaping the direction of American foreign policy.

These different approaches to public opinion may portend more for the process of policy formulation and selection than the policy's eventual success. As illustrated in the cases in this study, public opinion probably will have little influence on the placement of national security issues on the agenda and the development of policy options, but it may have an important influence when policymakers reach decisions and try to implement their policy. Still, differing approaches to public opinion can achieve successful policy results regarding the United States' involvement in the world. For example, in laying the foundations for America's post–World War II policy, President Franklin D. Roosevelt moved the United States toward an internationalist foreign policy and the establishment of the United Nations with active American participation. Nonetheless, throughout this process, he closely watched public opinion and worked to ensure that his policy aligned with what the public would support.[23] Harry Truman, however, adopted the Truman Doctrine while giving little consideration to public opinion. In fact, he attempted to lead public opinion on the policy only after being warned by the respected Republican Senate Foreign Relations Committee chairman, Arthur Vandenburg, that Congress would support his program only if he could "scare hell out of the country."[24] Even though the role of public opinion differed, both Roosevelt and Truman moved toward forming the basis of America's post–World War II policy. These instances suggest that the factors under consideration in this study have more to do with the way that policy is made than whether it serves the nation's long-term interests. Paradoxically, policies that both incorporate and overlook public opinion can succeed in fulfilling American interests.

The connection between public opinion and foreign policy is complicated and multifaceted. Because the public's influence varies in accordance with the president's normative and practical beliefs, there is no single "mode" of response to public opinion; rather it is a highly individualized response that depends on how the person making the decision sees the public's role in the decisions of a democratically elected leader of a modern republic. There is no reason to believe that the dynamic of the public's influence has shifted with the end of the Cold War. As policymakers confront the ambiguous questions of American national interests and the policies to serve them in the post–Cold War era, public opinion may play an important part in determining the direction of foreign policy. The public's support of internationalism during the Cold War and the results of earlier research indicating that public opinion is both rational and structured suggest that it can be the foundation for both long-term international engagement and a realistic policy to pursue American national interests. Public support will no doubt depend on leaders who are willing to use the "bully pulpit" to educate and inform the public about the pressing issues of the day. The burden to develop this supportive public opinion rests on policymakers who are willing to count the public in when formulating foreign policy.

Collecting Data on Beliefs

Because beliefs cannot be measured directly and must be inferred from available data, analyses must rely on statements made by the individual.[1] This method, however, raises the potential problem of the representative and instrumental use of language and communication. Although a particular communication could reflect the content of an individual's beliefs (representative use), people often use communication to persuade or convince others (instrumental use). To differentiate between these two uses, the analyst should rely on a number of sources that span time, situation, and audience to identify any possible inconsistencies.[2] The analysis in this book used both public and private statements to infer beliefs. Although private communications are more likely to reflect a person's representative beliefs, public statements can also be used to determine beliefs. A person's public utterances might influence his or her own views based on cognitive dissonance theory or his or her own self-perception.[3] Public officials also have an incentive to maintain their credibility by acting consistently with their professed intentions. Other actors may also act according to a decision maker's word, thus making certain that a decision maker's behavior complies with public statements.[4] In order to ensure separate data sources for measuring beliefs and behavior, I excluded statements regarding public opinion from the beliefs analysis if they occurred in the context of discussions pertaining to any of the decisions examined.[5]

Information regarding Eisenhower's beliefs came primarily from his private papers, located at the Eisenhower Presidential Library in Abilene, Kansas. I used "finding aids" (a list of files and their contents arranged by key words and subjects) of the papers to identify files with information about Eisenhower's beliefs concerning public opinion. All the finding aids of the Ann Whitman file (the primary collection of Eisenhower's private papers from December 1952 until January 1961) were searched for words that might indicate a reference to public opinion. Examples of words used in the finding aids to determine which documents to examine are *public relations, public opinion, politics, mail, polls*, and *political philosophy*. This source was supplemented by three others: (1) a search for prepresidential statements, as categorized in the *Reader's Guide to Periodicals* under Eisenhower's name; (2) a document-by-document search of the *FRUS* volumes dealing with basic national security policy through 1957 (the most recent available volume when his beliefs were analyzed in 1994); and (3) the Public Papers of the Presidents series.

Information on Dulles's beliefs came primarily from his private papers, at Princeton University. I also used finding aids here, as I did in the Eisenhower Library, with key words in the papers including *bipartisan policy, Cold War, foreign policy, isolationism*, and the names of significant persons (Eisenhower, Vice President Richard Nixon, etc.). In addition, since Dulles wrote all his speeches himself, I examined all of them, particularly those he gave before becoming secretary of state. I looked at all the files indicated by the finding aids for the period between the early 1940s through Dulles's death in 1959. As with Eisenhower, this source was supplemented by an examination of the *Reader's Guide* and the *FRUS* series. Dulles's *War or Peace* and Andrew Berding's *Dulles on Diplomacy*, which provides a record of Dulles's private statements, were also included.

Material for the other presidents relied on public source material, mainly memoirs and statements in the Public Papers of the Presidents series. Since the indexing of these materials varied from source to source, I searched the index for phrases that might indicate a reference to public opinion and foreign policy (e.g., views of the presidency, foreign policy). In certain instances, these materials were supplemented by other public source material, as cited in chapter 7. Unlike the data for

Eisenhower and Dulles, since many of the sources used for these presidents are public rather than private, the potential for inaccuracy is greater. But given the high accuracy of the predictions based on the analysis of the beliefs of these other presidents, this did not appear to be a problem.

Examining the Data

Any beliefs analysis of this kind is limited by the variety and quality of the available historical documentation. For the Eisenhower and Dulles beliefs data, this analysis relied on sources dated before the beginning of the Eisenhower administration. But because of a reliance on public source material for the other presidents, the data are from periods both during and after their administrations. Some of the important information on beliefs was from notes of the discussion recorded by a note taker. Since the exact phrasing of discussions was not available, and because of the relatively small number of statements available (from a statistical perspective), a quantitative content analysis of this material was not a viable alternative, and so I performed a qualitative analysis of the data instead. If the data were available in sufficient quantity, the beliefs dimensions would be amenable to a quantitative analysis. Some readers may be concerned that a qualitative content analysis (more than a quantitative content analysis) might be affected by the analyst's own opinions. Although a qualitative content analysis of the type in this study does not allow a traditional intercoder reliability assessment, I completed the beliefs analysis before examining the cases. This sequencing ensured that the beliefs analysis was not influenced by my examination of behavior. In addition, the use of oral history recollections in the Eisenhower and Dulles instances allows a rough test of the validity of the qualitative content analysis.

When I had collected the data from all the sources, I read each document and took notes on its content. These notes were organized under headings relevant to this study's analysis (e.g., is public support necessary, character of public opinion). Once I had examined all the data, I compared my findings in the groupings to discern similarities, caveats, and possible contradictions on a particular subject. I then reported these outcomes in the qualitative content analysis in the text. The content of these beliefs determined both the placement of the individual in a particular beliefs quadrant and the predictions of his behavior.

Selecting the Cases to Study and the Analysis Process

To select case studies for each administration, I first consulted significant secondary sources that provided an overview of the administration. Using these sources, I identified possible cases that might match each decision context and the control variables. Next I looked at significant secondary sources regarding the possible cases to determine further their applicability to the control variables and decision context. Finally, I selected the case studies examined in this book.[6]

Two methods were used to investigate the predictions of the various theories. First, I used a congruence procedure to determine whether a causal relationship for beliefs might exist. The congruence procedure requires first specifying the predicted theoretical relationship between the independent and dependent variables. Then, the values of the observed independent and dependent variables are determined and evaluated according to the theory's predictions. If the findings agree with the theory, a causal relationship may exist.[7] This process determines whether the behavior in regard to public opinion is consistent with the predicted behavior based on beliefs.

Second, process tracing, used by historians to make causal inferences, provides an additional way to examine possible causal relationships. The method "is intended to investigate and explain the decision process by which various initial conditions are translated into outcomes."[8] This method determines how inputs become outputs by examining the decision-making processes. In sum,

> the process tracing approach attempts to uncover what stimuli the actors attend to; the decision process that makes use of these stimuli to arrive at decision; the actual behavior that then occurs; the effect of various institutional arrangements on attention, processing, and behavior; and the effect of other variables of interest on attention, processing, and behavior.[9]

In the case studies, I examined the behavior for evidence that public opinion was on the decision makers' minds and whether it was used at important junctures in the decision making. From the manner and context in which public opinion was used, I made inferences as to its influence in a particular instance.[10]

Several questions guided my data analysis of each decision stage.[11] For agenda setting and the definition of the situation, I asked, How did the decision makers see the problem? What were the relevant considerations? For option generation, What policy options were seriously considered by the policymakers? Why did they view options favorably or unfavorably? At the policy selection stage, What was the policy choice? What factors affected their selection of the eventual alternative over the other possibilities? Finally, during policy implementation, What choices were necessary to pursue the decision reached at the previous stage? How did the decision makers respond to events that might question the previous decision? What adjustments, if any, were made to the previous decision?

Using this method, I followed each issue through the decision process and identified key factors in the decisions. I then wrote each case according to the answers I found for each of the questions. Even though the questions do not formally structure the chapters, the answers to them are implicitly integrated into the case discussions. This case presentation method is a modification of that employed by Burke and Greenstein (a largely historical analysis of the cases followed by a variable analysis and coding section).[12]

1. Linking Public Opinion and Foreign Policy

1. Robert Dahl, *Polyarchy: Participation and Opposition* (New Haven, Conn.: Yale University Press, 1971); Robert Dahl, *Democracy and Its Critics* (New Haven, Conn.: Yale University Press, 1989); Anthony Downs, *An Economic Theory of Democracy* (New York: Harper & Row, 1950); Giovanni Sartori, *The Theory of Democracy Revisited* (Chatham, N.J.: Chatham House, 1987). Related pluralist theories also suggest that public preferences are transmitted to the government via membership in interest groups and parties that compete over policy. See Charles Kegley and Eugene Wittkopf, *American Foreign Policy: Pattern and Process*, 3d ed. (New York: St. Martin's Press, 1987).

2. John G. Nicolay and John Hay, eds., *Complete Works of Abraham Lincoln*, 2 vols. (New York: Francis D. Tandy, 1905), vol. 1, p. 15; vol. 2, p. 71.

3. Roy P. Fairfield, ed., *The Federalist Papers* (New York: Anchor Books, 1961), pp. 206–7; Ross J. S. Hofman and Paul Levack, eds., *Burke's Politics* (New York: Knopf, 1949), p. 115.

4. John G. Geer, *From Tea Leaves to Opinion Polls: A Theory of Democratic Leadership* (New York: Columbia University Press, 1996), p. 7. In addition to this discussion of democracy and democratic leadership, see also Fenichel Pitkin, *The Concept of Representation* (Berkeley and Los Angeles: University of California Press, 1967).

5. Hans J. Morgenthau, *Politics Among Nations*, 5th, rev. ed. (New York: Knopf, 1978), pp. 147, 558.

6. Walter Lippmann, *Essays in the Public Philosophy* (Boston: Little, Brown, 1955), p. 20.

7. Gabriel Almond, *The American People and Foreign Policy* (New York: Praeger, 1950); Thomas A. Bailey, *The Man in the Street: The Impact of American Public Opinion on Foreign Policy* (New York: Macmillan, 1948); Ole R. Holsti, "Public Opinion and Foreign Policy: Challenges to the Almond-Lippmann Consensus," *International Studies Quarterly* 36 (1992):439–66; Lawrence R. Jacobs and Robert Y. Shapiro, "Lyndon Johnson, Vietnam, and Public Opinion: Rethinking Realists' Theory of Leadership," paper presented at the annual meeting of the Midwest Political Science Association, Chicago, April 14–16, 1994; George Kennan, *American Diplomacy, 1900–1950* (Chicago: University of Chicago Press, 1951).

8. Kenneth N. Waltz, *Theory of International Politics* (Reading, Mass: Addison-Wesley, 1979); John J. Mearsheimer, "Back to the Future: Instability in Europe After the Cold War," *International Security* 15 (1990):41. For a discussion of the unit-level application of neorealist theory, see Colin Elman, "Horses for Courses: Why Not Neorealist Theories of Foreign Policy?" *Security Studies* 6 (1996):7–53; and Waltz's response, Kenneth N. Waltz, "International Politics Is Not Foreign Policy," *Security Studies* 6 (1996):54–57.

9. Miroslav Nincic, *Democracy and Foreign Policy: The Fallacy of Political Realism* (New York: Columbia University Press, 1992); Daniel Yankelovich and I. M. Destler, *Beyond the Beltway* (New York: Norton, 1994).

10. Arthur Link, *Wilson: The New Freedom* (Princeton, N.J.: Princeton University Press, 1956); Herbert G. Nicholas, "Building on the Wilsonian Heritage," in Arthur Link, ed., *Woodrow Wilson* (New York: Hill & Wang, 1968), p. 184; Woodrow Wilson, *Leaders of Men* (Princeton, N.J.: Princeton University Press, 1952).

11. Alan D. Monroe, "Consistency Between Public Preferences and National Policy Decision," *American Politics Quarterly* 7 (1979):3–19.

12. Bernard C. Cohen, *The Public's Impact on Foreign Policy* (Boston: Little, Brown, 1973), p. 62. See also Morton Berkowitz, P. G. Bock, and Vincent J. Fuccillo, *The Politics of American Foreign Policy* (Englewood Cliffs, N.J.: Prentice-Hall, 1977); Warren E. Miller and Donald E. Stokes, "Constituency Influence in Congress," *American Political Science Review* 57 (1963):45–56.

13. Bruce E. Altschuler, *LBJ and the Polls* (Gainesville: University of Florida Press, 1990); Noam Chomsky and Edward Herman, *Manufacturing Consent* (New York: Pantheon, 1988); Michael Margolis and Gary Mauser, eds., *Manipulating Public Opinion: Essays on Public Opinion as a Dependent Variable* (Belmont, Calif.: Wadsworth, 1989); Thomas J. Christensen, *Useful Adversaries: Grand Strategy, Domestic Mobilization, and Sino-American Conflict, 1947–1958* (Princeton, N.J.: Princeton University Press, 1996); Richard C. Eichenberg, *Public Opinion and National Security in Western Europe* (Ithaca, N.Y.: Cornell University Press, 1989); Robert C. Hilderbrand, *Power and the People: Executive Management of Public Opinion in Foreign Affairs, 1897–1921* (Chapel Hill: University of North Carolina

Press, 1981); Barry Hughes, *The Domestic Context of American Foreign Policy* (San Francisco: Freeman, 1978); Lawrence R. Jacobs and Robert Y. Shapiro, "Presidential Manipulation of Polls and Public Opinion: The Nixon Administration and the Pollsters," *Political Science Quarterly* 110 (Winter 1995–96):519–38; John E. Mueller, *Policy and Opinion in the Gulf War* (Chicago: University of Chicago Press, 1994); Richard W. Steele, "News of the 'Good War': World War II News Management," *Journalism Quarterly* 62 (1985):707–16.

14. Holsti, "Public Opinion and Foreign Policy"; Ole R. Holsti, *Public Opinion and American Foreign Policy* (Ann Arbor: University of Michigan Press, 1996).

15. Bruce Russett, *Controlling the Sword: The Democratic Governance of National Security* (Cambridge, Mass.: Harvard University Press, 1990), p. 110.

16. Leonard A. Kusnitz, *Public Opinion and Foreign Policy: America's China Policy* (Westport, Conn.: Greenwood Press, 1984).

17. Philip J. Powlick, "The Attitudinal Bases for Responsiveness to Public Opinion Among American Foreign Policy Officials," *Journal of Conflict Resolution* 35 (1991):611–41; Philip J. Powlick and Andrew Z. Katz, "Defining the American Public Opinion/Foreign Policy Nexus," *Mershon International Studies Review* 42 (1998):29–61.

18. Ronald H. Hinckley, *People, Polls, and Policymakers: American Public Opinion and National Security* (New York: Lexington Books, 1992); Jacobs and Shapiro, "Lyndon Johnson, Vietnam, and Public Opinion"; Thomas Risse-Kappen, "Public Opinion, Domestic Structure, and Foreign Policy in Liberal Democracies," *World Politics* 43 (1991):479–512; Rodger A. Payne, "Public Opinion and Foreign Threats: Eisenhower's Response to *Sputnik*," *Armed Forces and Society* 21 (1994):89–111; Richard Sobel, ed. *Public Opinion in U.S. Foreign Policy: The Controversy Over Contra Aid* (Lanham, Md.: Rowman & Littlefield, 1993).

19. Benjamin I. Page and Robert Y. Shapiro, "Effects of Public Opinion on Policy," *American Political Science Review* 77 (1983):175–90; Benjamin I. Page and Robert Y. Shapiro, *The Rational Public: Fifty Years of Trends in American Policy Preferences* (Chicago: University of Chicago Press, 1992).

20. Larry M. Bartels, "Constituency Opinion and Congressional Policy Making: The Reagan Defense Buildup," *American Political Science Review* 85 (1991):457–74; Thomas Hartley and Bruce Russett, "Public Opinion and the Common Defense: Who Governs Military Spending in the United States?" *American Political Science Review* 86 (1992):361–87; Melvin Small, *Johnson, Nixon, and the Doves* (New Brunswick, N.J.: Rutgers University Press, 1988).

21. Patrick James and John R. Oneal, "The Influence of Domestic and International Politics on the President's Use of Force," *Journal of Conflict Resolution* 35 (1991):307–32; Charles W. Ostrom and Brian L. Job, "The President and the Political Use of Force," *American Political Science Review* 80 (1986):541–66. See also Ariel E. Levite, Bruce W. Jentleson, and Larry Berman, eds., *Foreign Military Intervention: The Dynamics of Protracted Conflict* (New York: Columbia University Press, 1992).

22. Lawrence R. Jacobs, "Public Opinion and Policymaking in the U.S. and Britain," *Comparative Politics*, 24 (1992):199–217; Lawrence R. Jacobs and Robert Y. Shapiro, "Disorganized Democracy: The Institutionalization of Polling and Public Opinion Analysis During the Kennedy, Johnson, and Nixon Presidencies," paper presented at the annual meeting of the American Political Science Association, New York 1994; Lawrence R. Jacobs and Robert Y. Shapiro, "Public Opinion in President Clinton's First Year: Leadership and Responsiveness," in Stanley A. Renshon, ed., *The Clinton Presidency: Campaigning, Governing, and the Psychology of Leadership*, pp. 195–211 (Boulder, Colo.: Westview Press, 1995); Lawrence R. Jacobs and Robert Y. Shapiro, "The Rise of Presidential Polling: The Nixon White House in Historical Perspective," *Public Opinion Quarterly* 59 (1995):163–95.

23. Thomas W. Graham, "The Politics of Failure: Strategic Nuclear Arms Control, Public Opinion, and Domestic Politics in the United States, 1945–1980" (Ph.D. diss., Massachusetts Institute of Technology, 1989).

24. Thomas W. Graham, "Public Opinion and U.S. Foreign Policy Decision Making," in David A. Deese, ed., *The New Politics of American Foreign Policy*, pp. 190–215 (New York: St. Martin's Press, 1994).

25. Thomas Risse-Kappen, "Masses and Leaders: Public Opinion, Domestic Structures, and Foreign Policy," in David A. Deese, ed., *The New Politics of American Foreign Policy*, pp. 238–61 (New York: St. Martin's Press, 1994).

26. Kurt Taylor Gaubatz, "Election Cycles and War," *Journal of Conflict Resolution* 35 (1991):212–44; Lawrence R. Jacobs and Robert Y. Shapiro, "The Public Presidency, Private Polls, and Policymaking: Lyndon Johnson," paper presented at the annual meeting of the American Political Science Association, Washington, D.C., September 2–5, 1993; Ben D. Mor, "Peace Initiatives and Public Opinion: The Domestic Context of Conflict Resolution," *Journal of Peace Research* 34 (1997):197–215; Miroslav Nincic, "U.S. Soviet Policy and the Electoral Connection," *World Politics* 42 (1990):370–96; Kevin H. Wang, "Presidential Responses to Foreign Policy Crises: Rational Choice and Domestic Politics," *Journal of Conflict Resolution* 40 (1996):68–97.

27. Holsti, *Public Opinion and American Foreign Policy*; Russett, *Controlling the Sword*.

28. Holsti, *Public Opinion and American Foreign Policy*; Philip J. Powlick, "Foreign Policy Decisions and Public Opinion: The Case of the Lebanon Intervention, 1982–1984," paper presented at the annual meeting of the American Political Science Association, Washington, D.C., September 1, 1988.

29. Hughes, *Domestic Context*; Russett, *Controlling the Sword*.

30. Holsti, *Public Opinion and American Foreign Policy*; Lawrence R. Jacobs and Robert Y. Shapiro, "Public Opinion and the New Social History: Some Lessons for the Study of Public Opinion and Democratic Policy-Making," *Social Science History* 13 (1989):1–24; Lawrence R. Jacobs and Robert Y. Shapiro, "Studying Substantive Democracy," *PS* 27 (1994):9–16; Benjamin I. Page, "Democratic Responsiveness? Untangling the Links Between Public Opinion and Policy," *PS* 27 (1994):25–28.

31. Margaret G. Hermann, "Ingredients of Leadership," in Margaret G. Hermann, ed., *Political Psychology: Contemporary Problems and Issues*, pp. 167–92 (San Francisco: Jossey-Bass, 1986); Robert Jervis, *Perception and Misperception in International Relations* (Princeton, N.J.: Princeton University Press, 1976); Deborah Welch Larson, *Origins of Containment: A Psychological Explanation* (Princeton, N.J.: Princeton University Press, 1985); Jerel A. Rosati, "The Impact of Beliefs on Behavior: The Foreign Policy of the Carter Administration," in Donald Sylvan and Steve Chan, eds., *Foreign Policy Decision Making* (New York: Praeger, 1984), pp. 158–91; James F. Voss and Ellen Dorsey, "Perception and International Relations: An Overview," in Eric Singer and Valerie Hudson, eds., *Political Psychology and Foreign Policy*, pp. 3–29 (Boulder, Colo.: Westview Press, 1992).

32. Richard E. Petty and John T. Cacioppo, *Attitudes and Persuasion: Classic and Contemporary Approaches* (Dubuque, Iowa: Brown, 1987), p. 7.

33. Ole R. Holsti, "The Belief System and National Images: A Case Study," *Journal of Conflict Resolution* 6 (1962):244.

34. Yaacov Y. I. Vertzberger, *The World In Their Minds. Information Processing, Cognition, and Perception in Foreign Policy Decisionmaking* (Stanford, Calif.: Stanford University Press, 1990), p. 114.

35. Alexander L. George, "The Causal Nexus Between Cognitive Beliefs and Decision-Making Behavior: The 'Operational Code' Belief System," in Lawrence S. Falkawski, ed., *Psychological Models in International Politics*, pp. 95–124 (Boulder, Colo.: Westview Press, 1979); Alexander L. George, *Presidential Decision-Making in Foreign Policy: The Effective Use of Information and Advice* (Boulder, Colo.: Westview Press, 1980); Ole R. Holsti, "Foreign Policy Formation Viewed Cognitively," in Robert Axelrod, ed., *Structure of Decision*, pp. 18–55 (Princeton, N.J.: Princeton University Press, 1976); Powlick, "Attitudinal Bases."

36. Margaret G. Hermann, "Effects of Personal Characteristics on Political Leaders on Foreign Policy," in Maurice A. East, Stephen A. Salmore, and Charles F. Hermann, eds., *Why Nations Act*, pp. 49–68 (Beverly Hills, Calif.: Sage, 1978); Margaret G. Hermann, "Personality and Foreign Policy Decision Making: A Study of 53 Heads of Government," in Donald Sylvan and Steve Chan, eds., *Foreign Policy Decision Making*, pp. 33–80 (New York: Praeger, 1984); Holsti, "Foreign Policy Formation."

37. Cohen, *Public's Impact*; Graham, "Public Opinion and U.S. Foreign Policy"; Powlick, "Attitudinal Bases."

38. Philip J. Powlick, "Attitudinal Bases," pp. 616, 637.

39. Pitkin, *Concept of Representation*, pp. 145–47.

40. James F. Byrnes, *Speaking Frankly* (New York: Harpers, 1947), pp. 233, 248; Philip J. Powlick, "The American Foreign Policy Process and the Public" (Ph.D. diss., University of Pittsburgh, 1990), p. 181.

41. Dean Rusk, *As I Saw It*, ed. Daniel S. Papp (New York: Norton, 1990), p. 551.

42. Powlick, "Attitudinal Bases," p. 623.

43. Hans J. Morgenthau, *Dilemmas of Politics* (Chicago: University of Chicago Press, 1958), p. 326.

44. Morgenthau, *Politics Among Nations*, p. 548.

45. David S. Broder, "A Clear View from Foggy Bottom," *Washington Post National Weekly Edition*, March 3, 1997, p. 4; Cohen, *Public's Impact*, p. 63.

46. Pitkin, *Concept of Representation*, p. 147.

47. Lippmann, *Essays in the Public Philosophy*, p. 15.

48. Kennan, *American Diplomacy*, pp. 73, 93.

49. George P. Shultz, *Turmoil and Triumph: My Years as Secretary of State* (New York: Scribner, 1993), p. 650; Powlick, "Attitudinal Bases," p. 627.

50. Charles F. Hermann, "International Crisis as a Situational Variable." in James N. Rosenau, ed., *International Politics and Foreign Policy*, pp. 409–21 (New York: Free Press, 1969).

51. Charles F. Hermann, *Crises in Foreign Policy: A Simulation Analysis* (Indianapolis: Bobbs-Merrill, 1969), pp. 29–30.

52. Situations with low threats to important values are less likely to involve the president and instead should be handled in the foreign policy bureaucracy. See Hermann, "International Crises as a Situational Variable." For a discussion of how public opinion is considered below the presidential level, see Powlick, "American Foreign Policy Process."

53. Hermann, "International Crisis as a Situational Variable." While accepting finite time and high threat as important variables, some of the crisis literature disputes the use of awareness in the definition of a foreign policy crisis. In the place of the awareness variable, these researchers insert the need for a high probability of involvement in hostilities. See Michael Brecher and Patrick James, *Crisis and Change in World Politics* (Boulder, Colo.: Westview Press, 1986). If this definition were used and applied to the short decision-time and high-threat cases in this study, all would still be considered crises under this new definition.

54. Hermann, "International Crises as a Situational Variable."

55. Jacobs and Shapiro, "Studying Substantive Democracy"; Holsti, *Public Opinion*, pp. 54–62; Page, "Democratic Responsiveness?"

56. V. O. Key, *Public Opinion and American Democracy* (New York: Knopf, 1961), pp. 428–31; Gladys Engel Lang and Kurt Lang, "The Future Study of Public Opinion: Symposium," *Public Opinion Quarterly* 51 (1987):S181–S182; James A. Stimson, Michael B. MacKuen, and Robert S. Erikson, "Dynamic Representation," *American Political Science Review*, 89 (1995):543–65; John R. Zaller, *The Nature and Origins of Mass Opinion* (Cambridge: Cambridge University Press, 1992); John Zaller, "Elite Leadership of Mass Opinion," in W. Lance Bennett and David L. Paletz, eds., *Taken By Storm*, pp. 186–209 (Chicago: University of Chicago Press, 1994).

57. Cohen, *Public's Impact*, pp. 197–98; Carl J. Friedrich, *Man and His Government: An Empirical Theory of Politics* (New York: McGraw-Hill, 1963).

58. Kusnitz, *Public Opinion and Foreign Policy*, pp. 8, 10.

59. Powlick and Katz, "A Two-Way Model of Public Opinion's Influence on Foreign Policy"; Powlick, "American Foreign Policy"; Russett, *Controlling the Sword*, p. 110; Stimson, MacKuen, and Erikson, "Dynamic Representation."

60. Walter Lippmann, *Public Opinion* (New York: Macmillan, 1922), p. 18.

61. Key, *Public Opinion*, p. 423.

62. Bernard Cohen, *The Political Process and Foreign Policy* (Princeton, N.J.: Princeton University Press, 1957), p. 29.

63. James N. Rosenau, *Public Opinion and Foreign Policy: An Operational Formulation* (New York: Random House, 1961).

64. Key, *Public Opinion*, p. 14.

65. Philip J. Powlick, "The Sources of Public Opinion for American Foreign Policy Officials," *International Studies Quarterly* 39 (1995):427–52.

66. Some realists incorporate domestic factors into their analyses. See Benjamin Frankel, ed., *Realism: Restatements and Renewal* (London: Frank Cass, 1997).

67. Fen Osler Hampson, "The Divided Decision-Maker: American Domestic Politics and the Cuban Crises," *International Security* 9 (Winter 1984/85):130–65; Ole R. Holsti, "Crisis Decision Making," in Philip E. Tetlock et al., eds., *Behavior, Society, and Nuclear War*, vol. 1, pp. 9–84 (New York: Oxford University Press, 1989); Christopher Layne, "Kant or Cant: The Myth of the Democratic Peace," *International Security* 19 (1994):5–49; James Meernik, "Presidential Decision Making and the Political Use of Military Force," *International Studies Quarterly* 38 (1994):121–38; James Meernik and Peter Waterman, "The Myth of the Diversionary Use of Force by American Presidents," *Political Research Quarterly* 49 (1996):573–90. The crisis literature is sizable. For other recent discussions and literature reviews on this subject, see Brecher and James, *Crisis and Change*; Michael Brecher and Jonathan Wilkenfeld, *A Study of Crisis* (Ann Arbor: University of Michigan Press, 1997); Patrick J. Haney, *Organizing for Foreign Policy Crises* (Ann Arbor: University of Michigan Press, 1997); Robert B. McCalla, *Uncertain Perceptions: U.S. Cold War Crisis Decision Making* (Ann Arbor: University of Michigan Press, 1992); Ben D. Mor, *Decision and Interaction in Crisis: A Model of International Crisis Behavior* (Westport, Conn: Praeger, 1993); John R. Oneal, *Foreign Policy Making in Times of Crisis* (Columbus: Ohio State University Press, 1982); James L. Richardson, *Crisis Diplomacy: The Great Powers Since the Mid-Nineteenth Century* (Cambridge: Cambridge University Press, 1994).

68. Richard A. Brody, "International Crises: A Rallying Point for the President?" *Public Opinion* 6 (1984):41–43, 60; Richard A. Brody and Catherine R. Shapiro, "A Reconsideration of the Rally Phenomenon in Public Opinion," in Samuel Long, ed., *Political Behavior Annual*, vol. 2, pp. 77–102 (Boulder, Colo.: Westview Press, 1989); John E. Mueller, *War, Presidents, and Public Opinion* (New York: Wiley, 1973). For a view that suggests little or no rally effect after most uses of force, see Bradley Lian and John R. Oneal, "Presidents, the Use of Military Force, and Public Opinion," *Journal of Conflict Resolution* 37 (1993):277–300.

69. John J. Mearsheimer, "The False Promise of International Institutions," *International Security* 19 (Winter 1994/95):5–49; Fareed Zakaria, "Realism and Domestic Politics: A Review Essay," *International Security* 17 (1992):177–198.

70. Andrew Moravcsik, "Taking Preferences Seriously: A Liberal Theory of International Politics," *International Organization* 51 (Fall 1997):513–54.

71. Barbara Reardon Farnham, *Roosevelt and the Munich Crisis: A Study of Political Decision Making* (Princeton, N.J.: Princeton University Press, 1997); Hampson, "The Divided Decision-Maker"; Russett, *Controlling the Sword.*

72. Bruce Bueno de Mesquita and David Lalman, *War and Reason* (New Haven, Conn.: Yale University Press, 1992); Christensen, *Useful Adversaries*; James D. Fearon, "Domestic Political Audiences and the Escalation of International Disputes," *American Political Science Review* 88 (1994):577–92; Paul K. Huth, *Standing Your Ground: Territorial Disputes and International Conflict* (Ann Arbor: University of Michigan Press, 1996); James and Oneal, "Influence of Domestic"; Patrick James and Athanasios Hristoulas, "Domestic Politics and Foreign Policy: Evaluating a Model of Crisis Activity for the United States," *Journal of Politics* 56 (1994):327–48; T. Clifton Morgan and Kenneth N. Bickers, "Domestic Discontent and the External Use of Force," *Journal of Conflict Resolution* 36 (1992):25–52; Ostrom and Job, "President and the Political Use of Force"; Susan Peterson, *Crisis Bargaining and the State: The Domestic Politics of International Conflict* (Ann Arbor: University of Michigan Press, 1996); Robert D. Putnam, "Diplomacy and Domestic Politics: The Logic of Two-Level Games," *International Organization* 42 (1988):427–60; Richard Rosecrance and Arthur A. Stein, eds., *The Domestic Bases of Grand Strategy* (Ithaca, N.Y.: Cornell University Press, 1993); Jack Snyder, *The Myths of Empire* (Ithaca, N.Y.: Cornell University Press, 1991); Wang, "Presidential Responses."

73. John G. Ikenberry, David Lumsdaine, and Lisa Anderson, "Polity Forum: The Intertwining of Domestic Politics and International Relations," *Polity* 29 (1996):293–310; Thomas Risse-Kappen, *Cooperation Among Democracies*, (Princeton, N.J.: Princeton University Press, 1995); David Skidmore and Valerie M. Hudson, eds., *The Limits of State Autonomy: Societal Groups and Foreign Policy Formulation* (Boulder, Colo.: Westview Press, 1993).

74. Gary King, Robert O. Keohane, and Sidney Verba, *Designing Social Inquiry: Scientific Inference in Qualitative Research* (Princeton, N.J.: Princeton University Press, 1994), esp. ch. 6. For a discussion of the importance of case studies in a larger literature, see Gary King, Robert O. Keohane, and Sydney Verba, "The Importance of Research Design in Political Science," *American Political Science Review* 89 (1995):475–81. This approach is not without controversy. See David D. Laitin et al., "Review Symposium: The Qualitative-Quantitative Disputation: Gary King, Robert O. Keohane, and Sidney Verba's Designing Social Inquiry: Scientific Inference in Qualitative Research," *American Political Science Review* 89 (1995):454–81.

75. This concept is a form of construct validity that refers to the idea that two measures of the same construct should reveal the same results. See Earl Babbie, *The Practice of Social Research*, 7th ed. (Belmont, Calif.: Wadsworth, 1995), pp. 127–28; Chava Frankfort-Nachmias and David Nachmias, *Research Methods in the Social Sciences*, 5th ed. (New York: St. Martin's Press, 1996), pp. 168–69.

76. Margaret Hermann and John Thomas Preston, "Presidents, Advisers, and Foreign Policy: The Effects of Leadership Style on Executive Arrangements," *Political Psychology* 15 (1994):75–96.

77. Hughes, *Domestic Context*; Meernik and Waterman, "Myth of Diversionary Force"; Bert A. Rockman, "Presidents, Opinion, and Institutional Leadership," in David A. Deese, ed., *The New Politics of American Foreign Policy*, pp. 59–75 (New York: St. Martin's Press, 1994).

78. For a discussion of this case selection technique, see Graham T. Allison, *Essence of Decision* (Boston: Little, Brown, 1971).

79. Richard A. Brody, *Assessing the President* (Stanford, Calif.: Stanford University Press, 1991); George Edwards, *The Public Presidency* (New York: St. Martin's Press, 1983); Paul Brace and Barbara Hinckley, *Follow the Leader: Opinion Polls and the Modern Presidents* (New York: Basic Books, 1992); Samuel Kernell, *Going Public* (Washington, D.C.: Congressional Quarterly Press, 1986); Richard E. Neustadt, *Presidential Power. The Politics of Leadership* (New York: Wiley, 1980); Ostrom and Job, "President and the Political Use of Force"; Douglas Rivers and Nancy L. Rose, "Passing the President's Program: Public Opinion and Presidential Influence in Congress," *American Journal of Political Science* 29 (1985):183–96.

80. Kernell, *Going Public*.

81. Morgan and Bickers, "Domestic Discontent."

82. It could be argued that decision makers may not verbalize their concern with public opinion. This situation would then (incorrectly) appear to support the no-impact view. This prospect can be accounted for in part by examining behavior before and after information about public opinion is considered. For example, an individual's policy positions can be compared both before and after an official was exposed to public opinion information to determine whether policy preferences changed. A policy change in the direction of the public's opinion would then show that the policymaker did react to public opinion.

83. In this analysis, the focus is on what decision makers try to do with their actions (e.g., attempting to lead public opinion). Whether they affected public opinion is not determined.

2. Preserving Public Support: Eisenhower and Dulles as Pragmatists

1. Memorandum of Conversation, March 20, 1956, March 1956 (2), Box 8, DDE Diary Series, DDE Papers.

2. Eisenhower to Phillips, June 5, 1953, DDE Diary December 1952–July 1953 (2), Box 3, DDE Diary Series, DDE Papers. Italics in original.

3. Eisenhower to Chynoweth, July 13, 1954, DDE Diary July 1954 (2), Box 7, DDE Diaries Series, DDE Papers.

4. Memorandum of Discussion, 157th NSC Meeting, July 30, 1953, *FRUS: 1952–1954*, vol. 2, pp. 184–85.

5. Dwight D. Eisenhower, "Give the Public the Facts," *Vital Speeches of the Day*, June 1, 1950, pp. 584–86.

6. Eisenhower to Humphrey, Summerfield, Lodge, Adams, Hall, and Stephens, November 23, 1953, DDE Diary November 1953 (1), Box 3, DDE Diary Series, DDE Papers.

7. Eisenhower to Dillon, January 8, 1953, Clarence Dillon, Box 7, Name Series, DDE Papers.

8. Ibid.

9. Memorandum of Discussion, 146th NSC Meeting, May 27, 1953, *FRUS: 1952–1954*, vol. 2, p. 1173.

10. Eisenhower, "Give the Public the Facts."

11. Diary entry, June 19, 1954, June 1954, Box 1, James C. Hagerty Papers, Eisenhower Library.

12. Memorandum of Conversation, September 2, 1955, Sigurd Larmon (2), Box 20, Administration Series, DDE Papers.

13. Eisenhower to Hughes, December 10, 1953, DDE Diary December 1953 (2), Box 4, DDE Diary Series, DDE Papers.

14. Notes by Minnich, May 22, 1953, Miscellaneous-O January 1953–January 1956, Box 1, L. Arthur Minnich Series, OSS.

15. Eisenhower, "Give the Public the Facts."

16. Memorandum of Discussion, 285th NSC Meeting, May 17, 1956, *FRUS: 1955–1957*, vol. 19, pp. 305–11; Memorandum of Discussion, 146th NSC Meeting, pp. 1169–74.

17. Memorandum of Discussion, 210th NSC Meeting, August 12, 1954, Box 5, NSC Series, DDE Papers.

18. Eisenhower to Robinson, March 12, 1954, DDE Diary March 1954 (3), Box 6, DDE Diary Series, DDE Papers.

19. Notes, October 24, 1953, ACW Diary, August–September–October 1953 (1), Box 1, Ann Whitman Diary Series, DDE Papers.

20. Eisenhower to Phillips, June 5, 1953, DDE Diary December 1952–July 1953 (2), Box 3, DDE Diary Series, DDE Papers.

21. Notes, September 28, 1953, Whitman Diary, August–September–October 1953 (3), Box 1, Ann Whitman Diary Series, DDE Papers; Eisenhower to Robinson, August 4, 1954, William Robinson, 1952–1955 (3), Box 29, Name Series, DDE Papers.

22. Memorandum of Discussion, 285th NSC Meeting, 305–11; Notes by Minnich, May 22, 1953; Eisenhower to Larmon, February 1, 1954, DDE Diary February 1954 (2), Box 5, DDE Diary Series, DDE Papers; Memorandum of Conversation, September 2, 1955.

23. Memorandum of Conversation, September 2, 1955.

24. Eisenhower to Hughes, December 10, 1953.

25. Eisenhower to Gruenther, February 1, 1955, *FRUS: 1955–1957*, vol. 2, p. 192. Italics in the original.

26. Memorandum by Dulles, May 23, 1947, John Foster Dulles Papers, Box 31, Princeton University.

27. Extemporaneous Remarks by Dulles at Conference on U.S. Foreign Policy, June 4 and 5, 1953, John Foster Dulles Papers, Box 75, Princeton University.

28. Speech "On Unity," February 27, 1952, John Foster Dulles Papers, Box 306, Princeton University; Statement, May 22, 1952, John Foster Dulles Papers, Box 286, Princeton University.

29. Speech "A New Year Resolve," January 17, 1947, John Foster Dulles Papers, Box 294, Princeton University.

30. John Foster Dulles, "Developing Bipartisan Foreign Policy," *Department of State Bulletin*, May 8 1950, p. 721.

31. Speech "The State of the World," March 5, 1946, John Foster Dulles Papers, Box 293, Princeton University.

32. Andrew H. Berding, *Dulles on Diplomacy* (Princeton, N.J.: Van Nostrand, 1965), p. 139.

33. Memorandum of Discussion, 312th NSC Meeting, February 7, 1957, *FRUS: 1955–1957*, vol. 19, pp. 413–19; see also Memorandum of Discussion, 195th NSC Meeting, May 6, 1954, *FRUS: 1952–1954*, vol. 2, p. 1425.

34. John Foster Dulles, *War or Peace* (New York: Macmillan, 1950), p. 5.

35. Extemporaneous Remarks, March 2, 1953, John Foster Dulles Papers, Box 311, Princeton University; Meeting transcript, April 14, 1958, John Foster Dulles Papers, Box 125, Princeton University.

36. Extemporaneous Remarks to American Association for the United Nations, March 2, 1953. See also Speech "Europe and the Atlantic Pact," March 23, 1949, John Foster Dulles Papers, Box 297, Princeton University.

37. Berding, *Dulles*, p. 142. See also Dulles to Acheson, March 19, 1950, John Foster Dulles Papers, Box 47, Princeton University; Dulles, *War or Peace*, pp. 121–22; Speech "National Unity in Foreign Policy," September 16, 1952, John Foster Dulles Papers, Box 308, Princeton University; Speech by Dulles, June 6, 1955, John Foster Dulles Papers, Box 40, Princeton University.

38. Extemporaneous Remarks by Dulles, June 4 and 5, 1953.

39. Speech "The Balance of Power," March 10, 1950, John Foster Dulles Papers, Box 301, Princeton University; Speech, "Foreign Policy-Ideals not Deals."

40. Speech, "Foundations of Peace," August 18, 1958, John Foster Dulles Papers, Box 366, Princeton University.

41. Dulles, *War or Peace*, p. 115; Berding, *Dulles*, p. 142; Impromptu remarks by Dulles, April 7, 1954, John Foster Dulles Papers, Box 79, Princeton University.

42. Dulles to Fuchs, December 5, 1949, John Foster Dulles Papers, Box 40, Princeton University.

43. James Hagerty Oral History, April 16, 1968, OH 91, Eisenhower Library, p. 493.

44. Kenneth W. Thompson, ed., *The Eisenhower Presidency: Eleven Intimate Perspectives of Dwight D. Eisenhower* (Lanham, Md.: University Press of America, 1984), pp. 8–9.

45. Ibid., pp. 42, 44.

46. General Andrew Goodpaster Oral History, OH 378, Eisenhower Library, pp. 107–8.

47. Thompson, *Eisenhower Presidency*, pp. 82, 83.

48. Ibid., p. 240.

49. Richard M. Nixon, John Foster Dulles Oral History Collection, Princeton University (JFDOHC), p. 12.

50. Andrew Berding, JFDOHC, p. 4; Berding, *Dulles*, pp. 139–41.

51. William Butts Macomber Jr., JFDOHC, p. 38.

52. Robert Bowie, JFDOHC, p. 8.

53. Macomber, JFDOHC, p. 37.

54. Carl McCardle Oral History, August 29, 1967, OH 116, Eisenhower Library, p. 7.

55. Roderic O'Connor, JFDOHC, p. 18.

3. The Crisis Context: Anticipating Domestic Opposition over the Offshore Islands

1. In this chapter, the Communist Chinese are also referred to as the Communists, and the Nationalist Chinese are also referred to as the Nationalists. The lowercased word *communist* refers to the broader worldwide threat that American decision makers saw emanating from the Soviet Union. Quotations from documents, of course, preserve the capitalization from the source reference. References to Chinese names and places are consistent with the American source material from that period, which used the Wade-Giles system of romanization.

2. For other discussions of the offshore islands crisis, see Robert Accinelli, "Eisenhower, Congress, and the 1954–55 Offshore Island Crisis," *Presidential Studies Quarterly* 20 (1990):329–48; Robert Accinelli, *Crisis and Commitment: United States Policy Toward Taiwan, 1950–1955* (Chapel Hill: University of North Carolina Press, 1996), esp. pp. 147–83; H. W. Brands, "Testing Massive Retaliation: Credibility and Crisis Management in the Taiwan Strait," *International Security* 12 (1988):124–51; Gordon H. Chang, "To the Nuclear Brink: Eisenhower, Dulles, and the Quemoy-Matsu Crisis," *International Security* 12 (1988):103–4; Leonard H. D. Gordon, "United States Opposition to Use of Force in the Taiwan Strait, 1954–1962," *Journal of American History* 72 (1985):637–60; Shu Guang Zhang, *Deterrence and Strategic Culture* (Ithaca, N.Y.: Cornell University Press, 1992), pp. 205–11.

3. Dwight D. Eisenhower, *Mandate for Change* (Garden City, N.Y.: Doubleday, 1963), p. 462; Memorandum of Discussion, August 6, 1954, *FRUS: 1952–1954*, vol. 14, pp. 518–19; Memorandum by Robertson, August 25, 1954, *FRUS: 1952–1954*, vol. 14, pp. 548–50; "U.S. Expected to Stay Out," *New York Times*, August 27, 1954, p. 5; "Red Attack on Quemoy Expected as Test of Nationalist Strength," *New York Times*, September 9, 1954, pp. 1, 2; "Pentagon Doubts Formosa Invasion," *New York Times*, August 19, 1954, p. 2; Secretary of State to U.S. Ambassador in Japan, August 20, 1954, JFD Chronological August 1954 (3), Box 9, JFD Chronological Series, JFD Papers; Offshore Islands Chronology of Events, June 3, 1955, Karl Rankin Papers, Box 7, Princeton University.

4. Robert Anderson to Eisenhower, September 3, 1954, *FRUS: 1952–1954*, vol. 14, p. 556; Acting Secretary of State Bedell Smith to Embassy in the Philippines, September 3, 1954, *FRUS: 1952–1954*, vol. 14, pp. 557–58; Robert J. Watson, *The Joint Chiefs of Staff and National Policy, 1953–1954*, vol. 5 of *History of the Joint Chiefs of Staff* (Washington, D.C.: Historical Division, Joint Chiefs of Staff, 1986), p. 262.

5. Secretary of State to U.S. Ambassador in Japan, August 20, 1954.

6. Harry Schwartz to Robert Bowie, August 20, 1954, *FRUS: 1952–1954*, vol. 14, pp. 543–44; William S. White, "Eisenhower Says Fleet Would Bar Formosa Invasion," *New York Times*, August 18, 1954, pp. 1, 2; Memorandum of Discussion, 211th NSC Meeting, August 18, 1954, NSC Series, Box 5, DDE Papers; "Transcript of New Conference Held by Secretary of State Dulles," *New York Times*, August 25, 1954, p. 8; Memorandum of Discussion, August 6, 1954, *FRUS: 1952–1954*, vol. 14, pp. 518–19; "Red Attack," *New York Times*.

7. Memorandum of Discussion, August 18, 1954.

8. Dwight D. Eisenhower Oral History, John Foster Dulles Oral History Collection Princeton University; Memorandum of Discussion, 214th NSC Meeting, September 12, 1954, *FRUS: 1952 1954*, vol. 14: pp. 613–24.

9. Eisenhower to Bedell Smith, September 8, 1954, *FRUS: 1952–1954*, vol. 14, pp. 577–79.

10. Memorandum of Discussion, August 18, 1954.

11. Eisenhower Telephone Conversation with Bedell Smith, September 4, 1954, Phone Calls June–December 1954 (2), Box 7, DDE Diaries Series, DDE Papers.

12. Memorandum of Discussion, August 18, 1954. A letter dated August 17 from Dulles to Wilson is referenced in Memorandum from Joint Chiefs of Staff to Wilson, September 2, 1954, 381 Far East (11 18–50), Geographic File 1954–1956, Record Group 218, National Archives; Memorandum for the Record, August 31, 1954, Reel 21, LM-152, Record Group 59, National Archives.

13. Dulles to Department of State, September 4, 1954, *FRUS: 1952–1954*, vol. 14, p. 560; Bedell Smith to Philippine Embassy, September 4, 1954, *FRUS: 1952–1954*, vol. 14, pp. 560–61.

14. Eisenhower to Bedell Smith, September 8, 1954, *FRUS: 1952–1954*, vol. 14, pp. 577–79. Eisenhower's reference to public opinion is taken from an unsent letter he proposed to send to British Prime Minister Winston Churchill. Special Report on American Opinion, November 30, 1954, China 1954–1960, Box 33, OPPS.

15. Eisenhower Telephone Conversation with Bedell Smith, September 6, 1954, Phone Calls June-December 1954 (2), Box 7, DDE Diaries Series, DDE Papers.

16. Bedell Smith to Dulles, September 6, 1954, *FRUS: 1952–1954*, vol. 14, p. 574; Eisenhower to Bedell Smith, September 8, 1954, *FRUS: 1952–1954*, vol. 14, pp. 577–79.

17. Dulles to Department of State, September 4, 1954, *FRUS: 1952–1954*, vol. 14, p. 560; Radford to Wilson, September 11, 1954, *FRUS: 1952–1954*, vol. 14, pp. 598–610; Dulles to Bedell Smith, September 5, 1954, *FRUS: 1952–1954*, vol. 14, p. 572; Memorandum of Discussion, 213th NSC Meeting, September 9, 1954, *FRUS: 1952–1954*, vol. 14, pp. 583–95.

18. Memorandum by Dulles, September 12, 1954, General Foreign Policy Matter (4), Box 8, White House Memoranda Series, JFD Papers, italics in original; Memorandum of Discussion, 214th NSC Meeting, September 12, 1954, *FRUS: 1952–1954*, vol. 14, p. 620.

19. Dulles to Rankin, September 7, 1954, *FRUS: 1952–1954*, vol. 14, p. 575; Rankin to McConaughy, September 13, 1954, *FRUS: 1952–1954*, vol. 14, pp. 624–25; Radford to Wilson, September 11, 1954, *FRUS: 1952–1954*, vol. 14, pp. 598–610.

20. Andrew Berding, John Foster Dulles Oral History Collection, Princeton University; China Telegram, September 2–8, 1954, Box 29, OPPS; China Telegram, September 9–15, 1954, Box 29, OPPS. I thank Professor Robert Accinelli for making available to me his notes regarding the China Telegram. Daily Opinion Summary, September 7, 1954, Daily Summary of Opinion Developments, Box 7, OPPS.

21. Radford to Wilson, September 11, 1954, *FRUS: 1952–1954*, vol. 14, pp. 598–610.

22. Memorandum of Discussion, 213th NSC Meeting, September 9, 1954, pp. 583–88; Radford to Wilson, September 11, 1954.

23. Memorandum of Discussion, 214th NSC Meeting, September 12, 1954, pp. 613–24. Eisenhower saw the NSC meetings as an important deliberative body from which he could gather information and then render an educated decision. Fred I. Greenstein, *The Hidden-Hand Presidency* (New York: Basic Books, 1982), pp. 246–47; Anna Kasten Nelson, "The 'Top of Policy Hill': President Eisenhower and the National Security Council," *Diplomatic History* 7 (1983):307–26.

24. NSC 146/2, November 6, 1953, *FRUS: 1952–1954*, vol. 14, p. 308; Special National Intelligence Estimate, SNIE-100–4/1–54, September 10, 1954, *FRUS: 1952–1954*, vol. 14, pp. 595–97.

25. Memorandum entitled "Congressional Attitude to Formosa Defense," September 12, 1954, President's Papers 1954 (7), Box 2, Special Assistant Series, Presidential Subseries, OSANSA.

26. Memorandum of Discussions, 214th NSC Meeting, pp. 617–19.

27. Ibid., pp. 619–20.

28. Ibid., pp. 620–21.

29. Ibid., pp. 621–22.

30. Special Report on American Opinion, November 30, 1954.

31. George Gallup, *The Gallup Poll: 1949–1958* (New York: Random House, 1972), vol. 2, p. 1273.

32. "Eisenhower Says Council Affirmed Security Policies," *New York Times*, September 14, 1954, pp. 1, 4.

33. During this period, State Department analyses of public opinion based on newspapers continued to reveal that the public would be divided over an American commitment to defend the islands. See Daily Opinion Summary, September 13, 1954, Daily Summary of Opinion Developments, Box 7, OPPS; Daily Opinion Summary, September 14, 1954, Daily Summary of Opinion Developments, Box 7, OPPS; Daily Opinion Summary, September 16, 1954, Daily Summary of Opinion Developments, Box 7, OPPS; Merchant to O'Conner, September 19, 1954, *FRUS: 1952–1954*, vol. 14, pp. 649–51. For an example of the lack of press reporting about the administration's approach, see Drew Middleton, "Full German Role in NATO Approved by U.S. and Britain," *New York Times*, September 18, 1954, p. 1.

34. Smith to Dulles, September 30, 1954, *FRUS: 1952–1954*, vol. 14, p. 669; Dulles to Smith, October 1, 1954, *FRUS: 1952–1954*, vol. 14, p. 670.

35. Dulles to Eisenhower, October 4, 1954, White House Memoranda 1954—Formosa Straits (2), Box 2, White House Memoranda Series, JFD Papers; Memorandum of Discussion, 216th Meeting of NSC, October 6, 1954, *FRUS: 1952–1954*, vol. 14, pp. 689–701.

36. Dulles Telephone Conversation with Nixon, October 5, 1954, Telephone Memos, September 1, 1954–October 30, 1954, Box 3, Telephone Calls Series, JFD Papers.

37. Memorandum of Conversation, October 5, 1954, White House Memoranda 1954—Formosa Straits (2), Box 2, White House Memoranda Series, JFD Papers; Dulles Telephone Conversation with Eisenhower, October 5, 1954, JFD Chronological, October 1954 (1), Box 9, JFD Chronological Series, JFD Papers; DDE Dictation, October 5, 1954, DDE Diary, October 1954 (2), Box 8, DDE Diaries Series, DDE Papers; Eisenhower Telephone Conversation with Dulles, October 5, 1954, Phone Calls June–December 1954 (2), Box 7, DDE Diaries Series, DDE Papers.

38. Dulles Telephone Conversation with Lodge, October 5, 1954, Telephone Memos September 1, 1954–October 30, 1954 (2), Box 3, Telephone Calls Series, JFD Papers.

39. Rankin to Department of State, October 5, 1954, *FRUS: 1952–1954*, vol. 14, p. 682.

40. Robertson to Dulles, October 7, 1954, *FRUS: 1952–1954*, vol. 14, pp. 706–7; Memorandum of Conversation, October 7, 1954, *FRUS: 1952–1954*, vol. 14, p. 708; Dulles to Walter Robertson, Douglas MacArthur, Livingston Merchant, October 7, 1954, White House Memoranda 1954—Formosa Straits (2), Box 2, White House Memoranda Series, JFD Papers; Memorandum of Conversation, October 7, 1954, *FRUS: 1952–1954*, vol. 14, p. 708.

41. Memorandum of Conversation, October 13, 1954, *FRUS: 1952–1954*, vol. 14, pp. 728–53; MacArthur to Dulles, October 14, 1954, *FRUS: 1952–1954*, vol. 14, pp. 755–56; Dulles to Rankin, October 18, 1954, *FRUS: 1952–1954*, vol. 14, p. 775; Memorandum of Conversation, October 18, 1954, Meetings with the President 1954 (1), Box 1, White House Memoranda Series, JFD Papers; Dulles Telephone Conversation with Lodge, October 19, 1954, Telephone Memo September 1, 1954–October 30, 1954 (1), Box 3, Telephone Calls Series, JFD Papers.

42. Hoover to Dulles, October 23, 1954, *FRUS: 1952–1954*, vol. 14, pp. 790–92; Memorandum of Conversation, October 27, 1954, *FRUS: 1952–1954*, vol. 14, pp. 797–801; Dulles to Eisenhower, October 28, 1954, White House Memoranda 1954—Formosa Straits (1), Box 2, White House Memoranda Series, JFD Papers; Memorandum of Conversation, October 27, 1954, *FRUS: 1952–1954*, vol. 14, pp. 797–801; Memorandum by Dulles, October 28, 1954, *FRUS: 1952–1954*, vol. 14, pp. 809–12.

43. "U.S. Is Arranging Pact with Chiang," *New York Times*, November 6, 1954, p. 1.

44. American opinion remained fairly supportive of the administration's policy toward Formosa. An October poll asked: "Do you approve or disapprove of our

government's policy toward the Chinese Nationalist government on Formosa headed by Chiang Kai-shek?" Forty-eight percent approved of the U.S. policy; 17 percent disapproved; and 35 percent gave no opinion. Special Report on American Opinion, November 30, 1954; Accinelli, "Eisenhower," p. 333; Memorandum of Conversation by Bond, November 30, 1954, *FRUS: 1952–1954*, vol. 14, pp. 961–66; Dulles to Department of State, December 17, 1954, *FRUS: 1952–1954*, vol. 14, p. 1035.

45. Kenneth W. Condit, *The Joint Chiefs of Staff and National Policy 1955–1956*, vol. 6 of *History of the Joint Chiefs of Staff* (Washington, D.C.: U.S. Government Printing Office, 1992), pp. 199–200.

4. The Reflexive Context: Boxed in by Public Opinion at Dien Bien Phu

1. Dwight D. Eisenhower Oral History, John Foster Dulles Oral Histories, Princeton University, p. 25.

2. Dwight D. Eisenhower Oral History, July 20, 1967, OH 11, Eisenhower Library, pp. 64–65.

3. Although most analysts agree that Dulles always supported multilateral intervention, there is a significant debate in the secondary literature over Eisenhower's exact position regarding intervention. I agree with the several accounts that say he honestly supported multilateral intervention. See John Burke and Fred I. Greenstein, *How Presidents Test Reality* (New York: Russell Sage Foundation, 1989); William J. Duiker, *U.S. Containment Policy and the Conflict in Indochina* (Stanford, Calif.: Stanford University Press, 1994); William Conrad Gibbons, *The U.S. Government and the Vietnam War: Executive and Legislative Roles and Relationships, Part 1, 1954–1961* (Washington, D.C.: Committee on Foreign Relations, U.S. Senate, U.S. Government Printing Office, 1984); Richard A. Immerman, "Between the Unattainable and the Unacceptable: Eisenhower and Dienbienphu," in Richard A. Melanson and David Mayers, eds., *Reevaluating Eisenhower: American Foreign Policy in the 1950s*, pp. 120–54 (Champaign-Urbana: University of Illinois Press, 1987); John Prados, *The Sky Would Fall: Operation Vulture: The U.S. Bombing Mission in Indochina, 1954* (New York: Dial Press, 1983). Others have emphasized that multilateral intervention was more a bluff and a negotiating tactic to force communist concessions at the forthcoming Geneva Convention. See George C. Herring, " 'A Good Stout Effort': John Foster Dulles and the Indochina Crisis, 1954–1955," in Richard Immerman, ed., *John Foster Dulles and the Diplomacy of the Cold War*, pp. 213–33 (Princeton, N.J.: Princeton University Press, 1990); George C. Herring and Richard H. Immerman, "Eisenhower, Dulles, and Dienbienphu: 'The Day We Didn't Go to War' Revisited," *Journal of American History* 71 (1984):343–63. Stephen Ambrose argued that Eisenhower opposed intervention for a number of reasons but mainly feared the domestic consequences of losing Indochina and set impossible standards for intervention so as to avoid domestic criticism of inaction. See Stephen E. Ambrose, *Eisenhower: The President* (New York: Simon & Schuster, 1984), vol. 2, pp. 173–85. Similarly, another finding stated that Eisenhower allowed others to erect barriers to intervention to achieve the same result. See Melanie

Billings-Yun, *Decision Against War: Eisenhower and Dien Bien Phu, 1954* (New York: Columbia University Press, 1988).

4. Memorandum of Conversation, March 24, 1953, *FRUS: 1952–1954*, vol. 13, p. 419.

5. Memorandum of Discussion, 179th NSC Meeting, January 8, 1954, *FRUS: 1952–1954*, vol. 13, p. 949.

6. Ibid., p. 952.

7. Herring, "Good Stout Effort," p. 213; Billings-Yun, *Decision Against War*, p. 16; Ambrose, *Eisenhower*, p. 173. Analogies can have a profound influence on the way decision makers interpret incoming information. See Yuen Foong Khong, *Analogies at War: Korea, Munich, Dien Bien Phu, and the Vietnam Decisions of 1965* (Princeton, N.J.: Princeton University Press, 1992).

8. Sherman Adams, *Firsthand Report* (New York: Harpers, 1961), p. 118.

9. Herring, "Good Stout Effort," p. 213.

10. Ambrose, *Eisenhower*, p. 173.

11. NSC 5405, January 16, 1954, *FRUS: 1952–1954*, vol. 13, pp. 971–76.

12. Historical Division of the Joint Secretariat, *The Joint Chiefs of Staff and the War in Vietnam: History of the Indochina Incident: 1940–1954* (Wilmington, Del.: Michael Glazier, 1982), vol. 1, p. 353. On January 19, the French had requested four hundred maintenance technicians and twenty-five B-26 aircraft. Achilles to Department of State, January 19, 1954, *FRUS: 1952–1954*, vol. 13, pp. 983–85.

13. Senator John Stennis to Radford, February 1, 1954, 091 Indochina (February 1, 1954), Record Group 218 Records of the Chairman—Arthur Radford, National Archives; Senator John Stennis to Wilson, January 29, 1954, *United States–Vietnam Relations, 1945–1967*, vol. 9, 1971, p. 239; Dwight D. Eisenhower, *Public Papers of the Presidents of the United States: Dwight D. Eisenhower, 1954* (Washington, D.C.: U.S. Government Printing Office, 1960), p. 226; Immerman, "Between the Unattainable," pp. 126–27; Telephone Calls, February 3, 1954, Phone Calls January–May 1954 (3), Box 5, DDE Diary Series, DDE Papers.

14. *Public Papers, 1954*, pp. 247, 250.

15. Telephone Calls, February 8, 1954, Phone Calls January–May 1954 (3), Box 5, DDE Diary Series, DDE Papers; Notes, February 8, 1954, Miscellaneous-I, Box 1, L. Arthur Minnich Series, OSS; Smith to Dulles, February 10, 1954, *FRUS: 1952–1954*, vol. 13, pp. 1031–32; *Public Papers, 1954*, p. 306; Billings-Yun, *Decision Against War*, p. 26.

16. Burke and Greenstein, *How Presidents Test Reality*, pp. 105–6. Burke and Greenstein speculate that this passage and the continuation of it (quoted later) were excised from the final draft because Eisenhower wanted to avoid the perception of criticizing the Kennedy administration's policies.

17. Jackson to Eisenhower, July 11, 1953, C. D. Jackson 1953 (1), Box 21, Administration Series, DDE Papers.

18. George Gallup, *The Gallup Poll 1949–1958* (New York: Random House, 1972), vol. 2, p. 1146; Special Report on American Opinion, November 16, 1953, Foreign Policy 1953, Box 1, OPPS.

19. Prados, *Sky Would Fall*, p. 10; Immerman, "Between the Unattainable," p. 123.

20. Burke and Greenstein, *How Presidents Test Reality*, pp. 106–7.

21. Minutes of Meeting Between President Eisenhower and Prime Minister of France Mayer, March 26, 1953, *FRUS: 1952–1954*, vol. 13, pp. 429–32.

22. Handwritten Notes of Legislative Meeting, January 5, 1954, Box 1, Legislative Meetings Series, OSS; Minutes of Bipartisan Legislative Meeting, January 5, 1954, Staff Notes January–December 1954, Box 4, DDE Diary Series, DDE Papers.

23. Gibbons, *U.S. Government*, p. 154.

24. Memorandum of Conversation, February 24, 1954, *FRUS, Secretary of State's Memoranda of Conversation, Microfiche Supplement, November 1952–1954* (Washington, D.C.: U.S. Government Printing Office, 1992).

25. Memorandum of Discussion, 186th NSC Meeting, February 26, 1954, *FRUS: 1952–1954*, vol. 13, pp. 1079–81.

26. Robert Griffith, ed., *Ike's Letters to a Friend* (Lawrence: University Press of Kansas, 1984), p. 122.

27. Memorandum of Discussion, 189th NSC Meeting, March 18, 1954, *FRUS: 1952–1954*, vol. 13, pp. 1132–33.

28. Gibbons, *U.S. Government*, pp. 137, 173.

29. Billings-Yun, *Decision Against War*, pp. 35–36; Gibbons, *U.S. Government*, p. 171; Stephen Jurika Jr., ed., *The Memoirs of Admiral Arthur W. Radford* (Stanford, Calif.: Hoover Institution Press, 1980), p. 393; Memorandum for the President, March 23, 1954, microfiche supplement, p. 379; Memorandum of Conversation, March 23, 1954, microfiche supplement, p. 380.

30. Billings-Yun suggests that Radford was making an implicit threat of his possible testimony in order to persuade Dulles to support more immediate intervention. Billings-Yun, *Decision Against War*, pp. 41–42.

31. Telephone Conversation Between Radford and Dulles, March 24, 1954, Telephone Memos March 1954–April 1954 (2), Box 2, Telephone Calls Series, JFD Papers.

32. *History of the Indochina Incident*, pp. 371–73; Radford to Eisenhower, March 24, 1954, *FRUS: 1952–1954*, vol. 13, pp. 1158–59.

33. Editorial Note, *FRUS: 1952–1954*, vol. 13, p. 1134; Gibbons, *U.S. Government*, pp. 176–77.

34. Robert H. Ferrell, ed., *The Diary of James C. Hagerty* (Bloomington: Indiana University Press, 1983), p. 32; Gibbons, *U.S. Government*, pp. 177–78.

35. Memorandum of Conversation, March 24, 1954, microfiche supplement, p. 382.

36. Memorandum for the Secretary of Defense, March 12, 1954, 092 Asia (6–25–48) S. 58, Record Group 218 Geographic File, National Archives; Memorandum for the Special Committee, March 17, 1953, *United States–Vietnam Relations, 1945–1967*, vol. 9, 1971, pp. 271–75; Smith to Eisenhower, March 11, 1954, *FRUS: 1952–1954*, vol. 13, pp. 1108–16.

37. Memorandum of Discussion, March 25, 1954, *FRUS: 1952–1954*, vol. 13, p. 1165.

38. Ibid., pp. 1167–68.

39. Ferrell, *Diary*, p. 35.

40. Handwritten Notes of Cabinet Discussion, March 26, 1954, Box 2, Cabinet Series, OSS; Minutes of Cabinet Meeting, March 26, 1954, Box 3, Cabinet Series, DDE Papers.

41. Immerman, "Between the Unattainable," p. 132; Memorandum of Conversation, March 30, 1954, *FRUS: 1952–1954*, vol. 13, p. 1187; Memorandum of Conversation, March 24, 1954, microfiche supplement, p. 382; Telephone Conversation Between Judd and Dulles, March 29, 1954, Telephone Memos March 1954–April 1954 (2), Box 2, Telephone Calls Series, JFD Papers; Telephone Conversation Between Hagerty and Dulles, March 31, 1954, Telephone Memos January–June 1954 (2), Box 10, Telephone Calls Series, JFD Papers; Telephone Conversation Between McCardle and Dulles, March 27, 1954, Telephone Memos March 1954–April 1954 (2), Box 2, Telephone Calls Series, JFD Papers; Robert J. Donovan, *Eisenhower: The Inside Story* (New York: Harpers, 1956), p. 259.

42. Telephone Conversation Between McCardle and Dulles, March 27, 1954, Telephone Calls Series, JFD Papers.

43. This interpretation is consistent with Billings-Yun, *Decision Against War*, pp. 63–64, 77.

44. Burke and Greenstein, *How Presidents Test Reality*, p. 47; Speech by Dulles: "The Threat of a Red Asia," March 29, 1954, John Foster Dulles Papers, Box 82, Princeton University. The reference to responding to aggression at "places and by means of free world choosing" was to his January 12, 1954, speech, entitled "The Evolution of Foreign Policy," discussed in reference to the New Look in chapter 6. See Gibbons, *U.S. Government*, p. 181; *Public Papers, 1954*, p. 366.

45. Richard Nixon, *RN: The Memoirs of Richard Nixon* (New York: Grosset & Dunlap, 1978), p. 151.

46. For a discussion of the JCS meetings, see Gibbons, *U.S. Government*, pp. 182–87; Robert J. Watson, *The Joint Chiefs of Staff and National Policy, 1953–1954*, vol. 5 of *History of the Joint Chiefs of Staff* (Washington, D.C.: Historical Division, Joint Chiefs of Staff, 1986), pp. 253–54.

47. Gibbons, *U.S. Government*, p. 182; Memorandum of Discussion, 191st NSC Meeting, April 1, 1954, *FRUS: 1952–1954*, vol. 13, pp. 1200–2.

48. Footnote, *FRUS: 1952–1954*, vol. 13, p. 1202; Gibbons, *U.S. Government*, pp. 183–84. Gibbons presents a similar analysis of these events.

49. Footnote, *FRUS: 1952–1954*, vol. 13, p. 1202.

50. Memorandum of Phone Conversations, April 1, 1954, Phone Calls January–May 1954 (2), Box 5, DDE Diary Series, DDE Papers.

51. Telephone Conversation Between Radford and Dulles, April 1, 1954, Telephone Memos March 1954–April 1954 (2), Box 2, Telephone Calls Series, JFD Papers.

52. Ferrell, *Diary*, p. 39.

53. Memorandum of Conversation with the President, April 2, 1954, *FRUS: 1952–1954*, vol. 13, pp. 1210–11; Draft Resolution Prepared by Department of State,

April 2, 1954, *FRUS: 1952–1954*, vol. 13, pp. 1211–12. The substantive part of the Joint Resolution held "that the President of the United States be and he hereby is authorized, in the event he determines that such action is required to protect and defend the safety and security of the United States, to employ the Naval and Air Forces of the United States to assist the forces which are resisting aggression in Southeast Asia, to prevent the extension and expansion of that aggression, and to protect and defend the safety and security of the United States."

54. Although it is not clear why Radford now opposed intervention, Gibbons concluded that Radford changed his mind after seeing Eisenhower's and Dulles's opposition to overt intervention and the continued opposition of the JCS. Gibbons, *U.S. Government*, pp. 185–86.

55. Memorandum for the File of the Secretary of State, April 5, 1954, *FRUS: 1952–1954*, vol. 13, pp. 1224–25.

56. Telephone Conversation Between Eisenhower and Dulles, April 3, 1954, Telephone Memos January–June 1954 (2), Box 10, Telephone Calls Series, JFD Papers; Telephone Conversation Between Senator Knowland and Dulles, April 3, 1954, Telephone Memos March 1954–April 1954 (1), Box 2, Telephone Calls Series, JFD Papers.

57. The effect of congressional sentiment on the administration's decisions continues to generate much discussion. Scholars argue that (1) Eisenhower's insistence on congressional approval was part of an intentional and determined effort to construct roadblocks to intervention (see Ambrose, *Eisenhower*, pp. 177–78); (2) congressional sentiment was sufficiently ambivalent to dictate no specific course of action (see Burke and Greenstein, *How Presidents Test Reality*, p. 66); (3) the congressional meeting was an attempt to co-opt the leadership in order to isolate proponents of unilateral intervention and to build support for multilateral action (see Leslie H. Gelb, *The Irony of Vietnam: The System Worked* [Washington, D.C.: Brookings Institution, 1979]; Gibbons, *U.S. Government*, pp. 195–203); (4) it was an attempt to gain a "blank check" from Congress, which instead served to tie the administration's hands by preventing unilateral action and thereby requiring any action to be multilateral (see Herring and Immerman, "Eisenhower, Dulles, and Dienbienphu," pp. 343–63); and (5) Eisenhower purposely required congressional authorization (which he knew he would not get) to prevent intervention and insulate the administration from criticism for the "loss" of another nation to communism (see Billings-Yun, *Decision Against War*, pp. 75–79). This use of the "hidden hand" by Eisenhower has been criticized as an "imperfectly documented conclusion." See Fred I. Greenstein, "The Hidden-Hand Presidency: Eisenhower as Leader: A 1994 Perspective," *Presidential Studies Quarterly* 24 (1994):233–41.

58. Editorial Note, *FRUS: 1952–1954*, vol. 13, p. 1236; Adams, *Firsthand Report*, p. 122.

59. Burke and Greenstein, *How Presidents Test Reality*, pp. 66–68.

60. Memorandum of Discussion, 192nd NSC Meeting, April 6, 1954, *FRUS: 1952–1954*, vol. 13, pp. 1250–65; NSC Action 1074-a, Possible U.S. Intervention in

Indo-China, April 5, 1954, *United States–Vietnam Relations, 1945–1967*, vol. 9, 1971, esp. pp. 310, 320, 325.

61. Memorandum of Discussion, 192nd NSC Meeting, pp. 1253–55.

62. Ibid.

63. Ibid., pp. 1257, 1259.

64. Ibid., p. 1259.

65. Ibid., pp. 1261–62.

66. Nixon, *Memoirs*, p. 151.

67. Dillon to Department of State, April 5, 1954, *FRUS: 1952–1954*, vol. 13, pp. 1236–38; Telephone Conversation Between Eisenhower and Dulles, April 5, 1954, Telephone Memos January–June 1954 (2), Box 10, Telephone Calls Series, JFD Papers.

68. Memorandum of Telephone Calls, April 5, 1954, Phone Calls January–May 1954 (2), Box 5, DDE Diary Series, DDE Papers.

69. Dulles to Embassy in France, April 5, 1954, *FRUS: 1952–1954*, vol. 13, p. 1242.

70. Dulles to Embassy of France, April 6, 1954, *FRUS: 1952–1954*, vol. 13, pp. 1268–69.

71. Impromptu Remarks by Dulles, April 7, 1954, John Foster Dulles Papers, Box 79, Princeton University; *Public Papers, 1954*, pp. 382–84, 389.

72. Richard H. Rovere, *Affairs of State: The Eisenhower Years* (New York: Farrar, Straus, & Cudahy, 1956), p. 193.

73. Handwritten Notes of Cabinet Meeting, April 9, 1954, Box 2, Cabinet Series, OSS.

74. Statement by Dulles, April 15, 1954, John Foster Dulles Papers, Box 82, Princeton University; Joint Statement by Dulles and Eden, April 13, 1954, John Foster Dulles Papers, Box 326, Princeton University. For details of these events, see Billings-Yun, *Decision Against War*, pp. 123–46; Herring and Immerman, "Eisenhower, Dulles, and Dienbienphu," pp. 355–61.

75. Press Conference by Dulles, April 13, 1954, John Foster Dulles Papers, Box 79, Princeton University; Dulles to Department of State, April 13, 1954, *FRUS: 1952–1954*, vol. 13, pp. 1319–20.

76. Godley to Department of State, April 21, 1954, *FRUS: 1952–1954*, vol. 13, pp. 1328–34.

77. Nixon, *Memoirs*, pp. 152–53.

78. Billings-Yun, *Decision Against War*, pp. 130–35.

79. Memorandum of Conversations, April 18, 1954, *FRUS: 1952–1954*, vol. 13, pp. 1349–50; Herring and Immerman, "Eisenhower, Dulles, and Dienbienphu," p. 357.

80. Telephone Conversation Between Nixon and Dulles, April 19, 1954, Telephone Memos March 1954–April 1954 (1), Box 2, Telephone Calls Series, JFD Papers; Burke and Greenstein, *How Presidents Test Reality*, pp. 105–6.

81. Special Report on American Opinion, April 19, 1954, South East Asia 1953–1961, Box 42, OPPS.

82. Dulles to Department of State, April 22, 1954, *FRUS: 1952–1954*, vol. 13, pp. 1361–62.

83. Telegram from Dulles, April 23, 1954, April 1954 (1), Box 2, Dulles-Herter Series, DDE Papers.

84. Dulles to State Department, April 24, 1954, DDE Diary April 1954 (1), Box 6, DDE Diary Series, DDE Papers.

85. Telephone Calls, April 24, 1954, Phone Calls January–May 1954 (1), Box 5, DDE Diary Series, DDE Papers.

86. Dulles to State Department, April 24, 1954, Indochina, Box 80, Lot 65 D101, Record Group 59 Records of the Policy Planning Staff 1954, National Archives.

87. Dulles to Smith, April 25, 1954, *FRUS: 1952–1954*, vol. 13, pp. 1404–5.

88. Notes, February 8, 1954 (of meeting on April 26, 1954), Miscellaneous-I, Box 1, L. Arthur Minnich Series, OSS.

89. Burke and Greenstein, *How Presidents Test Reality*, p. 82.

90. Hagerty Diary Entry, April 26, 1954, *FRUS: 1952–1954*, vol. 13, pp. 1410–12; *Public Papers, 1954*, pp. 427–28, 433, 436; Eisenhower to Gruenther, April 26, 1954, DDE Personal Diary January–November 1954 (2), Box 4, DDE Diary Series, DDE Papers; Robert H. Ferrell, ed., *The Eisenhower Diaries* (New York: Norton, 1981), pp. 279–80.

91. Memorandum of Discussion, 194th NSC Meeting, April 29, 1954, *FRUS: 1952–1954*, vol. 13, pp. 1431–45; Dwight D. Eisenhower, *Mandate for Change* (Garden City, N.Y.: Doubleday, 1963), pp. 354–55; Nixon, *Memoirs*, pp. 153–54.

92. Memorandum of Discussion, 194th NSC Meeting, pp. 1431–32, 1435, 1438–42.

93. Ibid., pp. 1442–45.

94. Nixon, *Memoirs*, p. 154.

95. Smith to Dulles, April 29, 1954, *FRUS: 1952–1954*, vol. 16, pp. 616.

96. Conference with Eisenhower, Dulles, MacArthur, and Cutler, May 5, 1954, Foreign Policy—Miscellaneous, Box 2, Miscellaneous Series, DDE Papers.

97. Record of Dulles's Briefing of Members of Congress, May 5, 1954, *FRUS: 1952–1954*, vol. 13, pp. 1471–77.

98. Burke and Greenstein, *How Presidents Test Reality*, p. 89–97; Herring, "Good Stout Effort," p. 227; Immerman, "Between the Unattainable," p. 45.

5. The Innovative Context: Standing Firm, Pushing Forward, and Giving Way After Sputnik

1. General historical treatments of the *Sputnik* issue include Stephen E. Ambrose, *Eisenhower: The President* (New York: Simon & Schuster, 1984), vol. 2; Robert A. Divine, *The Sputnik Challenge* (New York: Oxford University Press, 1993); John Lewis Gaddis, *Strategies of Containment* (New York: Oxford University Press, 1982); Walter A. McDougall, . . . *The Heavens and the Earth: A Political History of the Space Age* (New York: Basic Books, 1985); Rodger A. Payne, "Public Opinion and Foreign Threats: Eisenhower's Response to *Sputnik*," *Armed Forces and*

Society 21 (1994):89–111. Discussions of specific issues include Giles Alston, "Eisenhower: Leadership in Space Policy," in Shirley Anne Warshaw, ed., *Reexamining the Eisenhower Presidency*, pp. 103–20 (Westport, Conn.: Greenwood Press, 1993); Barbara Barksdale Clowse, *Brainpower for the Cold War: The Sputnik Crisis and National Defense Education Act of 1958* (Westport, Conn.: Greenwood Press, 1981); Brian R. Duchin, " 'The Most Spectacular Legislative Battle of that Year:' President Eisenhower and the 1958 Reorganization of the Department of Defense," *Presidential Studies Quarterly* 24 (1994):243–62; Iwan W. Morgan, *Eisenhower Versus 'The Spenders': The Eisenhower Administration, the Democrats, and the Budget, 1953–60* (New York: St. Martin's Press, 1990); Iwan W. Morgan, "Eisenhower and the Balanced Budget," in Shirley Anne Warshaw, ed., *Reexamining the Eisenhower Presidency*, pp. 121–32 (Westport, Conn.: Greenwood Press, 1993); Peter J. Roman, *Eisenhower and the Missile Gap* (Ithaca, N.Y.: Cornell University Press, 1995); Paul B. Stares, *The Militarization of Space: U.S. Policy, 1945–1984* (Ithaca, N.Y.: Cornell University Press, 1985)

2. Divine, *Sputnik Challenge*, pp. 8, 32–33; Roman, *Eisenhower and the Missile Gap*, pp. 1, 31–35.

3. Memorandum of Discussion, 339th NSC Meeting, *FRUS: 1955–1957*, vol. 11, p. 759.

4. Dwight D. Eisenhower, *Waging Peace* (Garden City, N.Y.: Doubleday, 1965), p. 205.

5. The approval rating control was not met for one month during the case study when the March/April 1958 Gallup poll had Eisenhower at 48 percent approval and 36 percent disapproval. Gallup Opinion Index October–November, no. 182, 1980. The March/April approval rating (the low point of the Eisenhower administration) is most likely attributable to the ongoing economic recession. See Ambrose, *Eisenhower*, p. 460. In any event, most of the critical decisions in reference to this case were made between October 1957 and March 1958. Memorandum of Discussion, 339th NSC Meeting, October 10, 1957, Box 9, NSC Series, DDE Papers; Eisenhower, *Waging Peace*, p. 206; Chester J. Pach Jr. and Elmo Richardson, *The Presidency of Dwight D. Eisenhower*, rev. ed. (Lawrence: University Press of Kansas, 1991), p. 170.

6. NSC 5520: Draft Statement of Policy on U.S. Scientific Satellite Program, May 20, 1955, *FRUS: 1955–1957*, vol. 11, pp. 723–32; Memorandum of Discussion, 250th NSC Meeting, May 26, 1955, *FRUS: 1955–1957*, vol. 11, pp. 732–33. For discussions of the early American space and missile programs, see Divine, *Sputnik Challenge*, pp. 18–42; McDougall, *Heavens*, pp. 74–140.

7. Memorandum of Discussion, December 1, 1955, 268th NSC Meeting, *FRUS: 1955–1957*, vol. 19, pp. 166–70.

8. Daily Opinion Summary, October 7, 1957, Daily Opinion Summary, Box 42, OPPS; Daily Opinion Summary, October 8, 1957, Daily Opinion Summary, Box 42, OPPS; Daily Opinion Summary, October 9, 1957, Daily Opinion Summary, Box 42, OPPS; Divine, *Sputnik Challenge*, p. xv.

9. Divine, *Sputnik Challenge*, pp. xiv–xv, 3.

10. Sherman Adams, *Firsthand Report* (New York: Harpers, 1961), p. 415.

11. Eisenhower, *Waging Peace*, p. 205.

12. Ibid., p. 211.

13. Memorandum of Discussion, 339th NSC Meeting, October 10, 1957, *FRUS: 1955–1957*, vol. 11, pp. 761, 763.

14. Minutes of Cabinet Meeting, October 11, 1957, October 1957 Staff Notes (2), Box 27, DDE Diary Series, DDE Papers.

15. Memorandum for the President from Secretary of Defense, October 7, 1954, Earth Satellites (1), Box 7, NSC Series, Briefing Notes Subseries, OSANSA.

16. Memorandum of Conference with the President, October 9, 1957 (of meeting on October 8, 1957), October 1957 Staff Notes (2), Box 27, DDE Diary Series, DDE Papers.

17. Telephone Call from Hagerty to Dulles, October 8, 1957, Telephone Memos September–December 1957 (3), Box 12, Telephone Calls Series, JFD Papers.

18. Memorandum for Quarles and Cutler from Goodpaster, October 8, 1957, Earth Satellites (1), Box 7, NSC Series, Briefing Notes Subseries, OSANSA; Telephone Call to Allen Dulles from John Foster Dulles, October 8, 1957, Telephone Memos September–October 1957 (2), Box 7, Telephone Calls Series, JFD Papers; Memorandum of Conversation with Nixon, October 9, 1957, Vice President Nixon (2), Box 6, Subject Series, JFD Papers; Divine, *Sputnik Challenge*, p. 63.

19. Memorandum of Conversation with the President, October 9, 1957 (of meeting on October 8, 1957), October 1957 Staff Notes (2), Box 27, DDE Diary Series, DDE Papers.

20. Memorandum of Conference with the President, October 8, 1957, October 1957 Staff Notes (2), Box 27, DDE Diary Series, DDE Papers.

21. Dulles to Hagerty, October 8, 1957, Satellite Announcement, Box 9, James Hagerty Papers, Eisenhower Library.

22. Memorandum of Conference with President, October 9, 1957, October 1957 Staff Notes (2), Box 27, DDE Diary Series, DDE Papers.

23. Pre-Press Conference, October 9, 1957, Box 6, Press Conference Series, DDE Papers.

24. Ambrose, *Eisenhower*, p. 429.

25. Dwight D. Eisenhower, *Public Papers of the Presidents of the United States: Dwight D. Eisenhower, 1957* (Washington, D.C.: U.S. Government Printing Office, 1958), pp. 719–35.

26. Divine, *Sputnik Challenge*, p. 8.

27. George Gallup, *The Gallup Poll: 1949–1958* (New York: Random House, 1972), vol. 2, pp. 1514–15, 1523.

28. Samuel Lubell, "*Sputnik* and American Public Opinion," *Columbia University Forum* 1 (1957):15–21.

29. *Gallup Poll*, pp. 1519–21.

30. McDougall, *Heavens*, p. 145.

31. Memorandum of Discussion, 339th NSC Meeting, October 10, 1957, *FRUS: 1955–1957*, vol. 11, pp. 761–62.

32. Memorandum of Discussion, 339th NSC Meeting, October 10, 1957, *FRUS: 1955–1957*, vol. 19, pp. 602–3. The notes do not mention whether Eisenhower was thinking of the domestic or international consequences.

33. Minutes of Cabinet Meeting, October 11, 1957, October 1957 Staff Notes (2), Box 27, DDE Diary Series, DDE Papers; Handwritten Notes of Cabinet Meeting, October 11, 1957, Box 4, Cabinet Series, OSS.

34. Memorandum of Conference with the President, October 14, 1957, October 1957 Staff Notes (2), Box 27, DDE Diary Series, DDE Papers.

35. Divine, *Sputnik Challenge*, p. 12.

36. Citations to this meeting come from Handwritten Notes of the Office of Defense Mobilization Science Advisory Committee, October 15, 1957, Science Advisory Committee (3), Box 7, Special Assistant Series, Subject Subseries, OSANSA; Memorandum of Conference with the President, October 16, 1957 (of meeting on October 15, 1957), October 1957 Staff Notes (2), Box 27, DDE Diary Series, DDE Papers.

37. Divine, *Sputnik Challenge*, p. 15.

38. Dulles Press Conference, October 16, 1957, John Foster Dulles Papers, Box 113, Princeton University.

39. Dulles to Eisenhower, no date, White House Correspondence—General 1957 (3), Box 5, White House Memoranda Series, JFD Papers.

40. Statements By Eisenhower on Unification, no date, Reorganization of Defense Department, Reorganization of, Bryce Harlow Records, Eisenhower Library; Divine, *Sputnik Challenge*, p. 85; Duchin, "Most Spectacular," pp. 244–45; Robert Griffith, ed., *Ike's Letters to a Friend* (Lawrence: University Press of Kansas, 1984), pp. 27–31.

41. Arthur Kimball Oral History, OH 66, Eisenhower Library, p. 58.

42. Eisenhower to McChesney, October 24, 1957, October 1957 DDE Dictation, Box 28, DDE Diary Series, DDE Papers.

43. Memorandum of Conference with the President, October 26, 1957 (of meeting on October 23, 1957), Budget-Military-Chronology 1957–59, Box 2, Subject Series, DOD Subseries, OSS.

44. Memorandum of Conference with the President, October 16, 1957 (of meeting on October 15, 1957), October 1957 Staff Notes (2), Box 27, DDE Diary Series, DDE Papers; Clowse, *Brainpower*, pp. 11, 25.

45. Clowse, *Brainpower*, pp. 49–50, 55.

46. Ibid., p. 55.

47. Eisenhower to Neel, November 1, 1957, November 1957 DDE Dictation, Box 28, DDE Diary Series, DDE Papers.

48. *Public Papers, 1957*, pp. 776–77.

49. Handwritten Notes of the Office of Defense Mobilization Science Advisory Committee, October 15, 1957, Science Advisory Committee (3), Box 7, Special

Assistant Series, Subject Subseries, OSANSA; Cutler to McElroy, October 17, 1957, *FRUS: 1955–1957*, vol. 11, pp. 764–65.

50. Memorandum of Conference with the President, October 8, 1957, October 1957 Staff Notes (2), Box 27, DDE Diary Series, DDE Papers; Eisenhower to McElroy, October 17, 1957, October 1957 DDE Dictation, Box 28, DDE Diary Series, DDE Papers.

51. Divine, *Sputnik Challenge*, p. 35.

52. Telephone Call Between Dulles and Quarles, November 4, 1957, Telephone Memos November–December 1957 (4), Box 7, Telephone Calls Series, JFD Papers.

53. Cutler to McElroy, October 17, 1957, *FRUS: 1955–1957*, vol. 11, pp. 764–65.

54. Memorandum of Conference with the President, October 31, 1957 (of meeting on October 30, 1957), October 1957 Staff Notes (1), Box 27, DDE Diary Series, DDE Papers.

55. Eisenhower to Altschul, October 25, 1957, DDE Diary October 1957, Box 27, DDE Diary Series, DDE Papers.

56. *Public Papers, 1957*, p. 784.

57. Dulles to Eisenhower, October 31, 1957, November 1957 (2), Box 9, Dulles-Herter Series, DDE Papers.

58. Memorandum, October 23, 1957, Guided Missiles, Box 16, Name Series, DDE Papers.

59. James R. Killian Jr., *Sputnik, Scientists, and Eisenhower* (Cambridge, Mass.: MIT Press, 1977), pp. 20–30.

60. Daily Opinion Summary, November 4, 1957, Box 42, OPPS.

61. Divine, *Sputnik Challenge*, pp. 43–45.

62. Ibid., p. 45.

63. Clowse, *Brainpower*, p. 11.

64. Memorandum of Conference with the President, November 6, 1957 (of meeting on November 4, 1957), November 1957 Staff Notes, Box 28, DDE Diary Series, DDE Papers.

65. Eisenhower to Larson, November 5, 1957, November 1957 Diary, Box 28, DDE Diary Series, DDE Papers, italics in original.

66. Divine, *Sputnik Challenge*, pp. 41–42.

67. Memorandum of Conversation with the President, November 7, 1957, Meetings with the President 1957 (2), Box 5, White House Memoranda Series, JFD Papers.

68. Griffith, *Letters*, p. 90.

69. *Public Papers, 1957*, pp. 789–99.

70. Divine, *Sputnik Challenge*, p. 46.

71. *Public Papers, 1957*, pp. 807–17.

72. Divine, *Sputnik Challenge*, p. 55.

73. Eisenhower to Hotchkis November 15, 1957, DDE Dictation November 1957, Box 28, DDE Diary Series, DDE Papers.

74. Ambrose, *Eisenhower*, pp. 436–41.

75. Gallup, *Gallup Poll*, p. 1526.

76. Divine, *Sputnik Challenge*, pp. 61–68.

77. Ibid., pp. 71–72.

78. Telephone Conversation Between Nixon and Dulles, December 6, 1957, Telephone Memos 1957 (1), Box 7, Telephone Calls Series, JFD Papers.

79. Notes of Legislative Leaders' Meeting, January 7, 1958, Legislative Minutes 1958 (1), Box 3, Legislative Meetings Series, DDE Papers.

80. Memorandum of Conference with the President, January 22, 1958 (of meeting on January 21, 1958), Staff Notes January 1958, Box 30, DDE Diaries Series, DDE Papers.

81. NSC 5724 Report to the President by the Security Resources Panel of the ODM Science Advisory Committee on Deterrence and Survival in the Nuclear Age, November 7, 1958, *FRUS: 1955–1957*, vol. 19, pp. 638–61.

82. Handwritten Notes, November 7, 1957, Military Planning 1958–61 (3), Box 6, Subject Series, DOD Subseries, OSS; Memorandum of Conference with the President, November 7, 1957, November 1957 Staff Notes, Box 28, DDE Diary Series, DDE Papers; Memorandum of Conversation with the President, November 7, 1957, Meetings with the President 1957 (2), Box 5, White House Memoranda Series, JFD Papers.

83. Memorandum of Conference with the President, November 6, 1957 (of meeting on November 4, 1957), November 1957 Staff Notes, Box 28, DDE Diary Series, DDE Papers.

84. Memorandum of Discussion, 343d NSC Meeting, November 7, 1957, *FRUS: 1955–1957*, vol. 19, pp. 630–37.

85. Memorandum of Conversation with the President, December 26, 1957, Meetings with the President 1957 (1), Box 5, White House Memoranda Series, JFD Papers; Telephone Conversation Between Dulles and Anderson, December 27, 1957, Telephone Memos November–December 1957 (1), Box 7, Telephone Calls Series, JFD Papers.

86. Gaddis, *Strategies*, pp. 184–88.

87. Memorandum of Conference with the President, November 16, 1957 (of meeting on November 11, 1957), November 1957 Staff Notes, Box 28, DDE Diary Series, DDE Papers.

88. Memorandum of Discussion, 345th NSC Meeting, November 14, 1957, *FRUS: 1955–1957*, vol. 19, pp. 677–86; National Intelligence Estimate 11–4–57 Main Trends in Soviet Capabilities and Policies, 1957–1962, November 12, 1957, *FRUS: 1955–1957*, vol. 19, pp. 665–73; Divine, *Sputnik Challenge*, p. 33.

89. Memorandum of Conference with the President, November 23, 1957 (of meeting on November 22, 1957), November 1957 Staff Notes, Box 28, DDE Diary Series, DDE Papers.

90. Memorandum of Conference with the President, November 16, 1957 (of meeting on November 11, 1957), November 1957 Staff Notes, Box 28, DDE Diary

Series, DDE Papers; Memorandum of Discussion, 346th NSC Meeting, November 22, 1957, *FRUS: 1955–1957*, vol. 19, pp. 689–95.

91. Memorandum of Discussion, 346th NSC Meeting, November 22, 1957, *FRUS: 1955–1957*, vol. 19, pp. 689–95.

92. Dulles to Eisenhower, November 25, 1957, Leadership Meeting (1), Box 12, Bryce Harlow Records, Eisenhower Library.

93. Memorandum for the Record, December 2, 1957 (of meeting on November 26, 1957), Missiles and Satellites V.1 (3), Box 6, Subject Series, DOD Subseries, OSS.

94. Congress, Senate, Senate Armed Services Committee, Preparedness Investigating Subcommittee, *Inquiry into Satellite and Missile Programs*, 85th Cong., 1st and 2d sess., November 27, 1958, p. 194.

95. Divine, *Sputnik Challenge*, pp. 73–74.

96. Memorandum of Conference with the President, December 5, 1957, Staff Notes December 1957, Box 29, DDE Diary Series, DDE Papers.

97. Divine, *Sputnik Challenge*, p. 127.

98. Ibid., pp. 70–71.

99. Memorandum of Conference with the President, November 4, 1957, November 1957 Staff Notes, Box 28, DDE Diary Series, DDE Papers.

100. Memorandum for the Record, November 6, 1957 (of meeting on November 4, 1957), November 1957 Staff Notes, Box 28, DDE Diary Series, DDE Papers.

101. Memorandum for the Record, January 15, 1958 (of meeting on January 2, 1958), Staff Notes January 1958, Box 30, DDE Diaries Series, DDE Papers.

102. Handwritten Notes of Legislative Leadership Meeting, January 7, 1958, Box 4, Legislative Meeting Series, OSS.

103. Memorandum of Conference with the President, November 6, 1957, November 1957 Staff Notes, Box 28, DDE Diary Series, DDE Papers.

104. Minutes of Cabinet Meeting, November 15, 1957, November 1957 Staff Notes, Box 28, DDE Diary Series, DDE Papers.

105. Clowse, *Brainpower*, pp. 57, 64–65, 78.

106. Alston, *Eisenhower*; Pach and Richardson, *President Eisenhower*, p. 180.

107. Stares, *Militarization*, p. 41.

108. Legislative Leadership Meeting Notes, February 4, 1958, Legislative Minutes 1958 (1), Box 3, Legislative Meetings Series, DDE Papers.

109. Memorandum of Conference with the President, March 5, 1958, Staff Notes March 1958 (2), Box 31, DDE Diaries Series, DDE Papers.

110. Memorandum for the President, March 5, 1958, NASA (3), Box 4, U.S. President's Science Advisory Committee, Eisenhower Library.

111. Memorandum for the Record, February 6, 1958, Missiles and Satellites vol. 2 (1), Box 6, Subject Series, DOD Subseries, OSS; Memorandum of Discussion, 357th NSC Meeting, March 6, 1958, Box 9, NSC Series, DDE Papers; Divine, *Sputnik Challenge*, pp. 97–112.

112. Gaither Report as Reported by Chalmers Roberts, no date, Gaither Report (1), Box 13, Subject Series, Alphabetical Subseries, OSS.

113. Divine, *Sputnik Challenge*, pp. 74–78.

114. Gallup, *Gallup Poll*, pp. 1539, 1545–46.

115. Paul O'Neil, "U.S. Change of Mind," *Life*, March 3, 1958, pp. 91–100.

116. Minutes of Cabinet Meeting, January 3, 1958, Staff Notes January 1958, Box 30, DDE Diary Series, DDE Papers.

117. Notes of Legislative Leaders Meeting, January 7, 1958, Legislative Minutes 1958 (1), Box 3, Legislative Meetings Series, DDE Papers.

118. Eisenhower, *Waging Peace*, p. 240.

119. *Public Papers, 1958*, pp. 2–15.

120. Divine, *Sputnik*, pp. 79–80.

121. Address by Dulles to the National Press Club, January 16, 1958, John Foster Dulles Papers, Box 125, Princeton University.

122. Memorandum for the Record, January 30, 1958 (of meeting on January 27, 1958), Staff Notes January 1958, Box 30, DDE Diaries Series, DDE Papers.

123. Divine, *Sputnik Challenge*, pp. 121–24.

124. Ibid., p. 120.

125. Ibid., p. 124.

126. Eisenhower to Dulles, March 26, 1958, White House General Correspondence 1958 (5), Box 6, White House Memoranda Series, JFD Papers.

127. Memorandum of Conference with the President, March 21, 1958 (of meeting on March 20, 1958), Staff Notes March 1958 (1), Box 31, DDE Diary Series, DDE Papers.

128. Divine, *Sputnik Challenge*, pp. 124–26.

129. Memorandum of Discussion, 363d NSC Meeting, April 24, 1958, Box 10, NSC Series, DDE Papers.

130. Divine, *Sputnik*, p. 127.

131. Memorandum of Conference with the President, June 23, 1958, June 1958 Staff Notes (2), Box 33, DDE Diaries Series, DDE Papers; Legislative Leadership Meeting Notes, June 24, 1958, Legislative Minutes 1958 (3), Box 3, Legislative Meeting Series, DDE Papers.

132. Legislative Leadership Meeting Notes, July 22, 1958, Staff Memos July 1958 (1), Box 35, DDE Diaries Series, DDE Papers.

133. Divine, *Sputnik Challenge*, p. 171; *Public Papers, 1958*, p. 635.

134. Legislative Leadership Meeting, January 14, 1958, Legislative Minutes 1958 (1), Box 3, Legislative Meetings Series, DDE Papers; Legislative Leadership Meeting Notes, January 28, 1958, Staff Notes January 1958, Box 30, DDE Diaries Series, DDE Papers.

135. Memorandum for the President, January 16, 1958, Defense Reorganization (2), Box 1, Miscellaneous Series, DDE Papers; Goodpaster to Brundage, January 16, 1958, Department of Defense (1957) (2), Box 6, White House Office, Office of the Special Assistant for Science and Technology: Records 1957–61, Eisenhower Library; Handwritten Notes of Cabinet Meeting, January 17, 1958, Box 5, Cabinet Series, OSS.

136. Telephone Calls, January 20, 1958, Staff Notes January 1958, Box 30, DDE Diaries Series, DDE Papers.

137. Arthur Kimball Oral History, OH 66, Eisenhower Library, p. 59.

138. Duchin, "Most Spectacular," p. 247; Arthur Kimball Oral History, OH 66, Eisenhower Library, pp. 60–61.

139. Memorandum for the Record, January 30, 1958 (of meeting on January 25, 1958), Staff Notes January 1958, Box 30, DDE Diaries Series, DDE Papers.

140. Memorandum of Discussion, 360th NSC Meeting, March 27, 1958, Box 10, NSC Series, DDE Papers.

141. Eisenhower to Larmon, January 27, 1958, Larmon, Sigurd (1), Box 20, Administration Series, DDE Papers.

142. *Public Papers, 1958*, pp. 325–34, 363–66, 378–80.

143. Memorandum of Conference with the President, April 24, 1958 (of meeting on April 21, 1958), Staff Notes April 1958 (1), Box 32, DDE Diaries Series, DDE Papers.

144. Memorandum of Conference with the President, May 12, 1958, Staff Notes May 1958 (2), Box 32, DDE Diaries Series, DDE Papers; Eisenhower *Waging Peace*, p. 251; Divine, *Sputnik Challenge*, p. 135. For a discussion of the details of this bargaining, see Duchin, "Most Spectacular"; and Divine, *Sputnik Challenge*, pp. 123–48.

145. Handwritten Notes of Cabinet Meeting, January 17, 1958, Box 5, Cabinet Series, OSS. For a discussion of the administration's dealings with Congress and congressional handling of this bill, see Clowse, *Brainpower*, pp. 78–151.

146. Divine, *Sputnik Challenge*, pp. 111–12, 144–56; McDougall, *Heavens*, pp. 157–76.

147. Legislative Leadership Meeting, March 18, 1958, Staff Notes March 1958 (1), Box 31, DDE Diary Series, DDE Papers; Handwritten Notes of Legislative Leadership Meeting, March 18, 1958, Box 5, Legislative Meeting Series, OSS.

148. Divine, *Sputnik Challenge*, pp. 109–10.

149. Killian, *Sputnik*, pp. 123–25, 288–99.

150. Divine, *Sputnik Challenge*, p. 107.

151. *Public Papers, 1958*, p. 573; Divine, *Sputnik Challenge*, pp. 147–48.

152. Gaddis, *Strategies*, p. 183.

6. The Deliberative Context: Leadership and Limitations in the Formulation of the New Look

1. National strategy or grand strategy refers to a state's policy to bring to bear all its domestic and international resources—economic, military, political, and psychological—to provide security during peace and war. See Richard Rosecrance and Arthur A. Stein, "Beyond Realism: The Study of Grand Strategy," in Rosecrance and Stein, eds., *The Domestic Bases of Grand Strategy* (Ithaca, N.Y.: Cornell University Press, 1993), p. 4.

2. Secondary sources on the New Look include Stephen E. Ambrose, *Eisenhower: The President*, vol. 2 (New York: Simon & Schuster, 1984); H. W. Brands,

"The Age of Vulnerability: Eisenhower and the National Insecurity State," *American Historical Review* 94 (1989):963–89; Saki Dockrill, *Eisenhower's New-Look National Security Policy, 1953–1961* (New York: St. Martin's Press, 1996); John Lewis Gaddis, *Strategies of Containment* (New York: Oxford University Press, 1982); Samuel P. Huntington, *The Common Defense* (New York: Columbia University Press, 1966); Douglas Kinnard, *President Eisenhower and Strategy Management* (Lexington: University Press of Kentucky, 1977); Iwan W. Morgan, *Eisenhower Versus "The Spenders": The Eisenhower Administration, the Democrats, and the Budget, 1953–60* (New York: St. Martin's Press, 1990); Glenn H. Snyder, "The 'New Look' of 1953," in Warner R. Schilling, Paul Y. Hammond, and Glenn H. Snyder, eds., *Strategy, Politics, and Defense Budgets,* pp. 379–524 (New York: Columbia University Press, 1962); Robert J. Watson, *The Joint Chiefs of Staff and National Policy, 1953–1954,* vol. 5 of *History of the Joint Chiefs of Staff* (Washington, D.C.: Historical Division, JCS, 1986); Samuel F Wells Jr., "The Origins of Massive Retaliation," *Political Science Quarterly* 96 (1981):31–52.

3. Wells, "Origins," pp. 40–41.

4. Robert H. Ferrell, ed., *The Eisenhower Diaries* (New York: Norton, 1981), pp. 209–14.

5. Iwan W. Morgan, *Eisenhower Versus "The Spenders,"* p. 50; Snyder, "New Look," pp. 389–90.

6. Watson, *Joint Chiefs,* pp. 3–4. Even though Eisenhower stressed the issue, defense spending remained a minor aspect of the public's 1952 choice in a campaign dominated by Korea and Eisenhower's personal appeal. Charges of corruption, the internal threat of communism, the policy of liberation, high prices, and high taxes played a somewhat lesser role. See Herbert Asher, *Presidential Elections and American Politics: Voters, Candidates, and Campaigns Since 1952* (Homewood, Ill.: Dorsey Press, 1976), p. 137; Barton J. Bernstein, "Election of 1952," in Arthur M. Schlesinger Jr., ed., *History of American Presidential Elections 1789–1968* (New York: Chelsea House, 1971), vol. 4, pp. 3260–61; John Robert Greene, *The Crusade: The Presidential Election of 1952* (Lanham, Md.: University Press of America, 1985), p. 226; Eugene H. Roseboom, *A History of Presidential Elections* (London: Macmillan, 1970), pp. 519–23.

7. Ambrose, *Eisenhower,* pp. 32–33; Robert J. Donovan, *Eisenhower: The Inside Story* (New York: Harpers, 1956), pp. 17–18; Snyder, "New Look," pp. 17–18.

8. Notes by Dulles, December 11, 1952, SS *Helena* Notes, Box 8, Subject Series, JFD Papers; Donovan, *Eisenhower,* pp. 17–18.

9. Memorandum for Discussion, December 29, 1952, Legislative Leaders 12/29/52, Box 1, Legislative Meetings Series, DDE Papers.

10. Dwight D. Eisenhower, *Public Papers of the Presidents of the United States: Dwight D. Eisenhower, 1953* (Washington, D.C.: U.S. Government Printing Office, 1960), p. 17.

11. Memorandum of Discussion, 133d NSC Meeting, February 24, 1953, Box 4, NSC Series, DDE Papers.

12. Memorandum of Discussion, 134th NSC Meeting, February 25, 1953, Box 4, NSC Series, DDE Papers.

13. Memorandum by Lay, February 24, 1953, President's Meeting with Civilian Consultants (2), Box 8, NSC Series, Subject Subseries, OSANSA; Memorandum of Discussion, 135th NSC Meeting, March 5, 1953, Box 4, NSC Series, DDE Papers; Memorandum by Lay, March 5, 1953, President's Meeting with Civilian Consultants, March 31, 1953 (2), Box 8, NSC Series, Subject Subseries, OSANSA.

14. Diary Entry, March 6, 1953, Emmet Hughes Papers, Box 1, Princeton University.

15. Joint Chiefs to Wilson, March 19, 1953, President's Meeting with Civilian Consultants, March 31, 1953 (8), Box 8, NSC Series, Subject Subseries, OSANSA.

16. Memorandum of Discussion, 138th NSC Meeting, March 25, 1953, *FRUS: 1952–1954*, vol. 2, pp. 258–64.

17. Statement, March 31, 1953, Documents Pertaining to Special NSC Meeting, Box 4, NSC Series, DDE Papers.

18. Memorandum of Discussion, Special Meeting of the National Security Council, March 31, 1953, *FRUS: 1952–1954*, vol. 2, pp. 269, 279; Draft Memorandum re Consensus at March 31, 1953 Meeting, no date, *FRUS: 1952–1954*, vol. 2, pp. 281–87.

19. Report to the National Security Council, April 29, 1953, *FRUS: 1952–1954*, vol. 2, pp. 305–16. New obligational authority represents the funds appropriated by Congress in a fiscal year. Expenditures represent all spending in a fiscal year from funds previously appropriated in past years and newly appropriated funds.

20. Minutes of Legislative Leadership Meeting, April 30, 1953, Staff Notes January–December 1953, Box 4, DDE Diaries Series, DDE Papers.

21. Ferrell, *Diaries*, pp. 235–36.

22. Handwritten Minutes of Legislative Leadership Meeting, April 30, 1953, Box 1, Legislative Leadership Meetings Series, OSS.

23. Diary Entry, May 1, 1953, Emmet Hughes Papers, Box 1, Princeton University.

24. Diary Entry, May 16, 1953, Emmet Hughes Papers, Box 1, Eisenhower Library; Minutes of Legislative Leadership Meeting, May 12, 1953, Staff Notes January–December 1953, Box 4, DDE Diaries Series, DDE Papers; Handwritten Notes of Legislative Leadership Meeting, May 12, 1953, Box 1, Legislative Meetings Series, OSS; Diary Entry, May 15, 1953, Emmet Hughes Papers, Box 1, Princeton University.

25. The date of this Saturday meeting comes from Diary Entry, May 2, 1953, Log 1953 (1), Box 56, C. D. Jackson Papers, Eisenhower Library. Reports of discussions at this meeting come from Robert Cutler, *No Time for Rest* (Boston: Little, Brown, 1965), pp. 307–9. These accounts verify that the specific instigation for a broad survey of basic national security policy came from Dulles. But historian Richard Immerman rejects Cutler's account and claims that Eisenhower originated the idea. See Richard H. Immerman, "Confessions of An Eisenhower Revisionist," *Diplomatic History* 14 (1990):319–42. However, Jackson's diary entry of the subsequent May 8 meeting (at which the decision to begin the strategic review was

made) between Eisenhower and the participants of the May 2 meeting indicates that the May 8 meeting was to present Dulles's May 2 idea to Eisenhower. Log Entry, May 8, 1953, Log 1953 (1), Box 56, C.D. Jackson Papers, Eisenhower Library.

26. The third alternative represented the policy of liberation or rollback that Dulles had earlier advocated and Eisenhower tacitly endorsed during the presidential campaign. See John Foster Dulles, "A Policy of Boldness," *Life*, May 19, 1952, pp. 146–60.

27. Memorandum, May 8, 1953, Project Solarium (3), Box 15, Executive Secretary's Subject File Series, White House Office: National Security Council Staff: Papers, 1948–61, Eisenhower Library.

28. Handwritten Minutes of Legislative Leadership Meeting, May 25, 1953, Box 1, Legislative Meetings Series, OSS.

29. Eisenhower to Gruenther, May 4, 1953, DDE Diary, December 1952–July 1953 (3), Box 3, DDE Diaries Series, DDE Papers.

30. Minutes of Cabinet Meeting, May 22, 1953, Box 2, Cabinet Series, DDE Papers.

31. Ibid.

32. Handwritten Minutes of Legislative Leadership Meeting, May 25, 1953.

33. Ferrell, *Diaries*, pp. 240–42.

34. George Gallup, *The Gallup Poll: 1949–1958* (New York: Random House, 1972), vol. 2, pp. 1131, 1170.

35. Memorandum, May 8, 1953, Project Solarium (3), Box 15, Executive Secretary's Subject File Series, White House Office: National Security Council Staff: Papers, 1948–61, Eisenhower Library. The labels for the three alternatives comes from Gaddis, *Strategies*, p. 146.

36. NSC 153/1, June 10, 1953, *FRUS: 1952–1954*, vol. 2, pp. 378–86.

37. Memorandum by Lay, July 22, 1953, Project Solarium, Report to the NSC by Task Force "A" (1), Box 9, NSC Series, Subject Subseries, OSANSA.

38. Memorandum by Cutler, July 16, 1953, *FRUS: 1952–1954*, vol. 2, pp. 397–98.

39. Memorandum of Discussion, 157th NSC Meeting, July 30, 1953, *FRUS: 1952–1954*, vol. 2, pp. 435–40.

40. Memorandum by Cutler, July 31, 1953, *FRUS: 1952–1954*, vol. 2, pp. 440–41.

41. Watson, *Joint Chiefs*, p. 15.

42. Telephone Call, May 11, 1953, Phone Calls February–June 1953 (1), Box 4, DDE Diaries Series, DDE Papers; Handwritten Notes of Legislative Leadership Meeting, May 12, 1953, Box 1, Legislative Meetings Series, OSS; Eisenhower, *Public Papers, 1953*, pp. 293–94; W. Barton Leach, *The New Look* (Maxwell AFB, Ala.: Air Command and Staff College, 1954), p. 25.

43. Joint Chiefs to Wilson, August 8, 1953, NSC 162/2, Box 12, Disaster File Series, White House Office: National Security Council Staff: Papers, 1948–61, Eisenhower Library.

44. Memorandum of Discussion, 160th NSC Meeting, August 27, 1953, *FRUS: 1952–1954*, vol. 2, pp. 443–55.

45. Memorandum from Cutler to Dulles, September 3, 1953, *FRUS: 1952–1954*, vol. 2, pp. 455–57; Memorandum by Cutler on August 27/53 NSC Meeting, September 1, 1953, NSC 162/2, Box 12, Disaster File Series, White House Office: National Security Council Staff: Papers, 1948–61, Eisenhower Library.

46. Eisenhower to Caffey, July 27, 1953, DDE Diaries December 1952–July 1953 (1), Box 3, DDE Diaries Series, DDE Papers.

47. Memorandum by Dulles, September 6, 1953, *FRUS: 1952–1954*, vol. 2, pp. 457–60.

48. Eisenhower to Dulles, September 8, 1953, DDE Diary August–September 1953 (2), Box 3, DDE Diaries Series, DDE Papers, italics in original.

49. Eisenhower to Dulles, April 15, 1952, John Foster Dulles Papers, Box 60, Princeton University.

50. Eisenhower to Dulles, June 20, 1954, John Foster Dulles Papers, Box 60, Princeton University.

51. Diary Entry, March 6, 1953, Emmet Hughes Papers, Box 1, Princeton University.

52. Minutes of Legislative Leadership Meeting, April 30, 1953, Staff Notes January–December 1953, Box 4, DDE Diaries Series, DDE Papers.

53. Eisenhower, *Public Papers, 1953*, p. 293.

54. Memorandum of Discussion, 163d NSC Meeting, September 24, 1953, *FRUS: 1952–1954*, vol. 2, pp. 464–75.

55. Memorandum of Discussion, 164th NSC Meeting, October 1, 1953, Box 4, NSC Series, DDE Papers.

56. Jackson to Eisenhower, October 2, 1953, *FRUS: 1952–1954*, vol. 2, pp. 1224–26.

57. Memorandum of Discussion at the NSC Planning Board, October 19, 1953, *FRUS: 1952–1954*, vol. 2, pp. 1227–32.

58. John Lewis Gaddis, "The Unexpected John Foster Dulles: Nuclear Weapons, Communism, and the Russians," in Richard H. Immerman, ed., *John Foster Dulles and the Diplomacy of the Cold War*, pp. 47–77 (Princeton, N.J.: Princeton University Press, 1990).

59. Memorandum of Discussion, 165th NSC Meeting, October 7, 1954, *FRUS: 1952–1954*, vol. 2, pp. 514–34. Comparisons in wording derive from the initial draft (Draft Statement of Policy, September 30, 1953, *FRUS: 1952–1954*, vol. 2, pp. 491–514) and the final version of the paper (Report to the National Security Council, NSC 162/2, October 30, 1953, *FRUS: 1952–1954*, vol. 2, pp. 577–97).

60. Radford to Wilson, October 2, 1953, CD 111 (1955), Box 19, Defense-Executive Office Central Decimal Files, 1953, Record Group 330, National Archives.

61. Memorandum of Discussion, 166th NSC Meeting, October 13, 1953, *FRUS: 1952–1954*, vol. 2, pp. 534–49.

62. Memorandum of Discussion, 168th NSC Meeting, October 29, 1953, *FRUS: 1952–1954*, vol. 2, pp. 567–76.

63. Report to the National Security Council, NSC 162/2, October 30, 1953, pp. 577–97.

64. JCS to Wilson, October 27, 1953, *FRUS: 1952–1954*, vol. 2, pp. 562–64.

65. Memorandum of Conversation, October 21, 1953, ACW Diary August–September–October 1953 (1), Box 1, Ann Whitman Diary Series, DDE Papers.

66. Dwight Eisenhower to Milton Eisenhower, November 6, 1953, DDE Diary November 1953 (2), Box 3, DDE Diary Series, DDE Papers.

67. Memorandum for the Record by Eisenhower, November 11, 1953, *FRUS: 1952–1954*, vol. 2, pp. 597–98.

68. Eisenhower Telephone Conversation with Wilson, December 2, 1953, Phone Calls July–December 1953 (1), Box 5, DDE Diaries Series, DDE Papers.

69. Memorandum of Discussion, 176th NSC Meeting, December 16, 1953, Box 5, NSC Series, DDE Papers; Watson, *Joint Chiefs*, p. 82.

70. Radford to Wilson, December 9, 1953, Charles E. Wilson 1953 (2), Box 39, Administration Series, DDE Papers.

71. Dwight D. Eisenhower, *Public Papers of the Presidents of the United States: Dwight D. Eisenhower, 1954* (Washington, D.C.: U.S. Government Printing Office, 1960), p. 82.

72. Eisenhower, *Public Papers, 1953*, p. 720.

73. "Wilson Hints End of Arms Balance," *New York Times*, November 11, 1953, p. A17.

74. "Wilson Cites Gains in Defense Program," *New York Times*, November 21, 1953, p. A9.

75. Leach, *New Look*, pp. 90–99; Speech by Radford, December 14, 1953, John Foster Dulles Papers, Box 74, Princeton University.

76. Leach, *New Look*, p. 143.

77. Handwritten Minutes of Bipartisan Leadership Meeting, January 5, 1954, Box 1, Legislative Meetings Series, OSS; Minutes of Bipartisan Leadership Meeting, January 5, 1954, Staff Notes January–December 1954, Box 4, DDE Diaries Series, DDE Papers.

78. Eisenhower, *Public Papers, 1954*, p. 11.

79. Ibid., p. 12.

80. Eisenhower to Howard, February 2, 1954, Roy W. Howard (3), Box 20, Administration Series, DDE Papers. Eisenhower also asked that his connection with the questions be avoided.

81. Howard to Editors, February 5, 1954, Roy W. Howard (3), Box 20, Administration Series, DDE Papers.

82. Memorandum, n.d., Roy W. Howard (3), Box 20, Administration Series, DDE Papers.

83. Diary Entry, March 17, 1954, Box 1, James C. Hagerty Papers, Eisenhower Library.

84. Eisenhower, *Public Papers, 1954*, pp. 330–31.

85. Anthony Leviero, "Eisenhower Speaks, Asks Unity—Declares Soviet Courts Ruin If It Ventures War," *New York Times*, April 6, 1954, pp. A1, A17.

86. Speech by Dulles, January 12, 1954, John Foster Dulles Papers, Box 322, Princeton University.

87. Eisenhower, *Public Papers, 1954*, p. 58.

88. John Foster Dulles to Allen Dulles, no date, John Foster Dulles Papers, Box 78, Princeton University; Memorandum of Conversation, February 24, 1954, *FRUS: Secretary of State's Memoranda of Conversation,* Microfiche Supplement, *November, 1952–1954* (Washington, D.C.: U.S. Government Printing Office, 1992).

89. Nixon Speech, February 11, 1954, Vice President Nixon (5), Box 6, Subject Series, JFD Papers.

90. Leach, *New Look,* pp. 283–90.

91. Kinnard, *President Eisenhower,* p. 35. E. Bruce Geelhoed, *Charles E. Wilson and Controversy at the Pentagon, 1953 to 1957* (Detroit: Wayne State University Press, 1979), pp. 106–7; Leach, *New Look,* pp. 313, 405. For a summary of the content of both the Senate and House hearings, see Snyder, "New Look," pp. 457–91.

92. *Congressional Quarterly Almanac,* vol. 10 (Washington, D.C.: Congressional Quarterly News Features, 1954), pp. 153–56.

93. FY55 Eisenhower budget requests are from *Congressional Quarterly Almanac,* pp. 153–56. Congress's new obligational authority and the FY55 actual expenditures are from Watson, *Joint Chiefs,* p. 86.

94. James D. Savage, *Balanced Budgets and American Politics* (Ithaca, N.Y.: Cornell University Press, 1988), p. 290.

7. Presidential Beliefs Orientations Since World War II

1. Harry S. Truman, *Public Papers of the Presidents of the United States: Harry S. Truman, 1949* (Washington, D.C.: U.S. Government Printing Office, 1964), p. 119.

2. Harry S. Truman, *Memoirs: Years of Trial and Hope* (Garden City, N.Y.: Doubleday, 1956), vol. 2, p. 196.

3. Ken Hechler, *Working with Truman: A Personal Memoir of the White House Years* (New York: Putnam, 1982), pp. 219–20. See also Harry S. Truman, *Public Papers of the Presidents of the United States: Harry S. Truman, 1951* (Washington, D.C.: U.S. Government Printing Office, 1965), p. 192.

4. Truman, *Memoirs,* p. 196.

5. Louis Harris, *The Anguish of Change* (New York: Norton, 1973), p. 18.

6. Theodore C. Sorensen, ed., *"Let the Word Go Forth": The Speeches, Statements, and Writings of John F. Kennedy* (New York: Delacorte Press, 1988), p. 22.

7. Ibid., p. 27.

8. John F. Kennedy, *Public Papers of the Presidents of the United States: John F. Kennedy, 1961* (Washington, D.C.: U.S. Government Printing Office, 1962), p. 377.

9. Harris, *Anguish of Change,* pp. 18–19. Italics in original.

10. Lyndon Baines Johnson, *Public Papers of the Presidents of the United State: Lyndon Baines Johnson, 1967,* vol. 2 (Washington, D.C.: U.S. Government Printing Office, 1968), pp. 674, 1046.

11. Lyndon Baines Johnson, *Public Papers of the Presidents of the United States: Lyndon Baines Johnson, 1966,* vol. 2 (Washington, D.C.: U.S. Government Printing Office, 1967), p. 708.

12. Lyndon Baines Johnson, *Public Papers of the Presidents of the United States: Lyndon Baines Johnson, 1966*, vol. 1 (Washington, D.C.: U.S. Government Printing Office, 1967), p. 632; Lyndon Baines Johnson, *The Vantage Point: Perspectives of the Presidency 1963–1969* (New York: Holt, Rinehart and Winston, 1971), p. 531; Harris, *Anguish of Change*, p. 24.

13. Johnson, *Vantage Point*, p. 28.

14. Other analyses also suggest that Johnson was a guardian. See Bruce E. Altschuler, *LBJ and the Polls* (Gainesville: University of Florida Press, 1990); Lawrence R. Jacobs and Robert Y. Shapiro, "Lyndon Johnson, Vietnam, and Public Opinion: Rethinking Realists' Theory of Leadership," paper presented at the annual meeting of the Midwest Political Science Association, Chicago, April 14–16, 1994.

15. Richard Nixon, *Public Papers of the President of the United States: Richard Nixon, 1972* (Washington, D.C.: U.S. Government Printing Office, 1974), p. 999; Richard Nixon, *RN: The Memoirs of Richard Nixon* (New York: Grosset & Dunlap, 1978), p. 753.

16. Richard Nixon, *Leaders* (New York: Warner Books, 1982), p. 234. See also Richard Nixon, *In the Arena* (New York: Simon & Schuster, 1990), p. 265.

17. Nixon, *Public Papers, 1972*, p. 999; Nixon, *Public Papers, 1972*, p. 1000. See also Nixon, *In the Arena*, p. 331.

18. Richard Nixon, *The Nixon Presidential Press Conferences* (New York: Earl M. Coleman Enterprises, 1978), p. 28. See also Nixon, *In the Arena*, p. 284; Nixon, *Leaders*, p. 333.

19. Richard Nixon, *No More Vietnams* (New York: Arbor House, 1985), pp. 79, 224.

20. Nixon, *Leaders*, p. 324.

21. Gerald Ford, *Public Papers of the Presidents of the United States: Gerald Ford, 1976–77*, vol. 1 (Washington, D.C.: U.S. Government Printing Office, 1979), pp. 11, 780; Robert T. Hartmann, *Palace Politics: An Inside Account of the Ford Years* (New York: McGraw-Hill, 1980), pp. 420–21.

22. Ford, *Public Papers, 1976–77*, vol. 1, p. 7.

23. Jimmy Carter, *Public Papers of the Presidents of the United States: Jimmy Carter, 1977*, vol. 2 (Washington, D.C.: U.S. Government Printing Office, 1978), p. 1174.

24. Ibid., pp. 1394–95; see also pp. 2134–35; Jimmy Carter, *Public Papers of the Presidents of the United States: Jimmy Carter, 1978*, vol. 2 (Washington, D.C.: U.S. Government Printing Office, 1979), p. 1229; Jimmy Carter, *Public Papers of the Presidents of the United States: Jimmy Carter, 1979*, vol. 2 (Washington, D.C.: U.S. Government Printing Office, 1980), pp. 1256, 1714; Jimmy Carter, *Public Papers of the Presidents of the United States: Jimmy Carter, 1980–81*, vol. 3 (Washington, D.C.: U.S. Government Printing Office, 1982), p. 2042; Jimmy Carter, *Keeping Faith: Memoirs of a President* (New York: Bantam Books, 1982), p. 80.

25. Jimmy Carter, *Public Papers of the Presidents of the United States: Jimmy Carter, 1980–81*, vol. 1 (Washington, D.C.: U.S. Government Printing Office, 1981), p. 740.

26. Carter, *Public Papers, 1979*, vol. 2, pp. 1712, 1918–19. See also Carter, *Public Papers, 1978*, vol. 2, p. 1474.

27. Carter, *Public Papers, 1978* vol. 2, pp. 1655–56. See also Carter, *Keeping the Faith*, p. 66.

28. Ronald Reagan, *An American Life* (New York: Simon & Schuster, 1990), p. 162. For a similar comment, see also "Talking with David Frost—Five Presidents," *Journal Graphics*, Transcript 59, 1996, p. 13; Ronald Reagan, *Public Papers of the Presidents of the United States: Ronald Reagan, 1984*, vol. 1 (Washington, D.C.: U.S. Government Printing Office, 1986), pp. 111, 114.

29. Leslie H. Gelb, "The Mind of the President," *New York Times Magazine*, October 6, 1985, p. 32. The former U.S. ambassador to the UN Jeanne Kirkpatrick stated that Reagan never based his decisions on public opinion or "short-range political popularity." See Ben Wattenberg, "The Consequences of Ideas: The Reagan Revolution and Beyond," *Public Opinion* 9 (Summer 1986):60.

30. Reagan, *Public Papers, 1984*, vol. 1, p. 433; "An Interview with President Reagan: Reflections on Summitry and the Soviet Challenge," *Time*, June 7, 1982, p. 11.

31. Ronald Reagan, *Public Papers of the Presidents of the United States: Ronald Reagan, 1988–89*, vol. 2 (Washington, D.C.: U.S. Government Printing Office, 1991), p. 1019. See also George P. Shultz, *Turmoil and Triumph: My Years as Secretary of State* (New York: Scribner, 1993), p. 1135.

32. Reagan, *American Life*, pp. 451, 466. Biographer Lou Cannon found that based on the experience in Vietnam, Reagan "knew that it was realistically impossible for any president to commit U.S. troops to a protracted war that lacked the support of the American people." Lou Cannon, *President Reagan: The Role of a Lifetime* (New York: Simon & Schuster, 1991), p. 336.

33. George Bush, *Public Papers of the Presidents of the United States: George Bush, 1990*, vol. 1 (Washington, D.C.: U.S. Government Printing Office, 1991), p. 354.

34. George Bush, *Public Papers of the Presidents of the United States: George Bush, 1991*, vol. 2 (Washington, D.C.: U.S. Government Printing Office, 1992), p. 941. See also Bush, *Public Papers, 1990*, vol. 1, p. 355; George Bush, *Public Papers of the Presidents of the United States: George Bush, 1992–93*, vol. 2 (Washington, D.C.: U.S. Government Printing Office, 1993), pp. 1328–29.

35. George Bush, *Public Papers of the Presidents of the United States: George Bush, 1989*, vol. 2 (Washington, D.C.: U.S. Government Printing Office, 1990), p. 1733.

36. George Bush, *Public Papers of the Presidents of the United States: George Bush, 1990*, vol. 2 (Washington,, D.C.: U.S. Government Printing Office, 1991), p. 1382.

37. David Mervin, *George Bush and the Guardianship Presidency* (New York: St. Martin's Press, 1996), pp. 212, 213.

38. George C. Edwards III, "Frustration and Folly: Bill Clinton and the Public Presidency," in Colin Campbell and Bert A. Rockman, eds., *The Clinton Presidency: First Appraisals*, p. 255 (Chatham, N.J.: Chatham House, 1996).

39. Jack Nelson and Robert J. Donovan, "The Education of a President," *Los Angeles Times Magazine*, August 1, 1993, p. 16.

40. William Clinton, *Public Papers of the Presidents: William J. Clinton, 1993* (Washington, D.C.: U.S. Government Printing Office, 1994), p. 1765.

41. Stanley A. Renshon, *High Hopes: The Clinton Presidency and the Politics of Ambition* (New York: New York University Press, 1996), p. 81.

42. William Clinton, *Public Papers of the Presidents: William J. Clinton, 1995* (Washington, D.C.: U.S. Government Printing Office, 1996), p. 1428.

43. Richard Burke, "Gore's Bandwagon Gets Big Push as Clinton Shows Enthusiasm," *New York Times*, July 14, 1997, p. A1; Jim Hoaglund, "Cabinet Politics," *Washington Post National Weekly Edition*, July 13, 1998, p. 5.

44. Press Conference by the President, December 16, 1997, U.S. Department of State, Washington, D.C., http://library.whitehouse.gov (cited May 24, 1998).

45. Richard Reeves, "Government by the Polls," *Greensboro News & Record*, December 21, 1994, p. A15. See also Dick Morris, *Behind the Oval Office* (New York: Random House, 1997), p. 11; Dick Morris, "Report on Launch of Morris Book," interviewed by Mara Liasson, January 16 1997, *Morning Edition*, National Public Radio, available from http://www.npr.org/programs/morning/archives/nb7j16.html.

46. Jack Nelson and Doyle McManus, "Clinton Rejects Foreign Policy Team Shake-Up," *Los Angeles Times*, May 28, 1994, p. A20.

47. William Clinton, *Public Papers of the Presidents: William J. Clinton, 1994* (Washington, D.C.: U.S. Government Printing Office, 1995), p. 1576.

48. Morris, *Behind the Oval Office*, p. 257.

49. "Blending Force with Diplomacy," *Time*, October 31, 1994, p. 35.

50. Burke, "Gore's Bandwagon"; Hoaglund, "Cabinet Politics."

51. Ole R. Holsti, "Public Opinion and Foreign Policy: Challenges to the Almond-Lippmann Consensus," *International Studies Quarterly* 36 (1992):439–66.

8. Crises and Recent Presidents

1. Because the invasion of Afghanistan best exemplified the crisis context of Carter's presidency, the requirement that the case occur at least one year before the next presidential election was relaxed.

2. Jimmy Carter, *Keeping Faith: Memoirs of a President* (New York: Bantam Books, 1982), pp. 471–73. Although these perceptions influenced Carter's view, the Soviets had not used troops in 1948 to overthrow the Czechoslovak government, and the Soviets saw the Afghanistan invasion as necessary to preserve a client state rather than to expand their influence. See Raymond L. Garthoff, *Détente and Confrontation: American-Soviet Relations from Nixon to Reagan*, rev. ed. (Washington, D.C.: Brookings Institution, 1994), pp. 1042–46, 1057–58.

3. Carter, *Keeping Faith*, p. 472.

4. Garthoff, *Détente and Confrontation*, pp. 1058–60; Richard Ned Lebow and Janice Gross Stein, "Afghanistan, Carter, and Foreign Policy Change: The Limits of Cognitive Models," in Dan Caldwell and Timothy J. McKeown, eds., *Diplomacy, Force, and Leadership* (Boulder, Colo.: Westview Press, 1993), pp. 110–12 .

5. Gabriella Grasselli, *British and American Responses to the Soviet Invasion of Afghanistan* (Brookfield, Vt.: Dartmouth, 1996), pp. 130, 148–49, 174–75; Garthoff, *Détente and Confrontation*, pp. 1067–68; David Skidmore, *Reversing Course: Carter's Foreign Policy, Domestic Politics, and the Failure of Reform* (Nashville: Vanderbilt University Press, 1996), pp. 98, 101. Lebow and Stein, "Afghanistan," p. 106, dispute that domestic factors in any way influenced Carter's decision.

6. Garthoff, *Détente and Confrontation*, p. 1060, Carter, *Keeping Faith*, p. 473.

7. Carter, *Keeping Faith*, pp. 476, 544.

8. Zbigniew Brzezinski, *Power and Principle: Memoirs of the National Security Advisor, 1977–1981* (New York: Farrar, Straus & Giroux, 1983), p. 431.

9. Hamilton Jordan, *Crisis* (New York: Putnam, 1982), p. 100.

10. Carter, *Keeping Faith*, p. 474; Brzezinski, *Power and Principle*, p. 431.

11. Jordan, *Crisis*, p. 100.

12. Brzezinski, *Power and Principle*, p. 437.

13. Carter, *Keeping Faith*, p. 474; Jordan, *Crisis*, pp. 112–13; Brzezinski, *Power and Principle*, p. 433.

14. Brzezinski, *Power and Principle*, p. 434; Grasselli, *British and American Responses*, p. 161.

15. Brzezinski, *Power and Principle*, pp. 431–32; Carter, *Keeping Faith*, p. 475.

16. Carter, *Keeping Faith*, pp. 482–83.

17. Ibid., p. 483; Brzezinski, *Power and Principle*, pp. 443–44; Grasselli, *British and American Responses*, p. 163.

18. Because this case best exemplified the crisis context of Reagan's presidency, the requirement that the case occur at least one year before the next election was relaxed.

19. George P. Shultz, *Turmoil and Triumph: My Years as Secretary of State* (New York: Scribner, 1993), pp. 104–9, 220–27; Ronald Reagan, *An American Life* (New York: Simon & Schuster, 1990), p. 447; Philip J. Powlick, "Foreign Policy Decisions and Public Opinion: The Case of the Lebanon Intervention, 1982–1984," paper presented at the annual meeting of the American Political Science Association, Washington, D.C., September 1, 1988, p. 19.

20. Lou Cannon, *President Reagan: The Role of a Lifetime* (New York: Simon & Schuster, 1991), p. 438; Shultz, *Turmoil and Triumph*, p. 227.

21. Cannon, *Role of a Lifetime*, p. 442; Shultz, *Turmoil and Triumph*, p. 227.

22. David Hoffman, "Administration Credibility Under Strain: Plans, Pronouncements, on Mideast Contradictory," *Washington Post*, February 12, 1984, p. A17.

23. Cannon, *Role of a Lifetime*, pp. 445, 449.

24. Reagan, *An American Life*, p. 461.

25. Cannon, *Role of a Lifetime*, pp. 449–50.

26. Powlick, "Foreign Policy Decisions," p. 21.

27. Cannon, *Role of a Lifetime*, pp. 449–51.

28. Powlick, "Foreign Policy Decisions," p. 39.

29. Reagan, *An American Life*, pp. 461–62.

30. Powlick, "Foreign Policy Decisions," pp. 40–41.

31. Ronald Reagan, "News Conference of December 20 (Excerpts)," *Department of State Bulletin* 84 (1984):7–8.

32. Cannon, *Role of a Lifetime*, p. 453.

33. Shultz, *Turmoil and Triumph*, pp. 229–30.

34. Cannon, *Role of a Lifetime*, pp. 454–56.

35. Ibid.

36. Lou Cannon and David Hoffman, "Troop Move Was Decided a Week Ago," *Washington Post*, February 9, 1984, pp. A1, A25.

37. Reagan, *An American Life*, p. 465.

38. Steven Weisman, "Aides Say President Started Pullback Process Weeks Ago," *New York Times*, February 9, 1984, pp. A1, A12.

39. David Broder, "Redeployment of Marines 'Takes the Heat Off' President," *Washington Post*, February 9, 1984, p. A21; Powlick, "Foreign Policy Decisions," pp. 40–42; Caspar W. Weinberger, *Fighting for Peace: Seven Critical Years in the Pentagon* (New York: Warner Books, 1990), p. 167.

40. Michael R. Gordon and Bernard E. Trainor, *The Generals' War* (Boston: Little, Brown, 1995), p. 49.

41. Dan Goodgame, "What If We Do Nothing?" *Time*, January 7, 1991, p. 23; John Zaller, "Elite Leadership of Mass Opinion," in W. Lance Bennett and David L. Paletz, eds., *Taken by Storm*, p. 254 (Chicago: University of Chicago Press, 1994).

42. U.S. News & World Report, *Triumph Without Victory* (New York: Times Books, 1992), p. 48; George Bush, "A Gulf War Exclusive: President Bush Talking with David Frost," Journal Graphics, Transcript 51, 1996, p. 3.

43. U.S. News & World Report, *Triumph*, p. 48.

44. Gordon and Trainor, *Generals' War*, p. 49; Bob Woodward, *The Commanders* (New York: Simon & Schuster, 1991), p. 225.

45. Thomas L. Friedman and Patrick E. Tyler, "From the First, U.S. Resolve to Fight," *New York Times*, March 3, 1991, p. I18.

46. Colin L. Powell, *My American Journey* (New York: Random House, 1995), p. 463; Woodward, *Commanders*, pp. 226–29; U.S. News & World Report, *Triumph*, pp. 50–51.

47. Powell, *American Journey*, p. 464.

48. Gordon and Trainor, *Generals' War*, p. 37; U.S. News & World Report, *Triumph*, p. 66; Woodward, *Commanders*, pp. 236–38.

49. U.S. News & World Report, *Triumph*, p. 72.

50. James A. Baker III, *The Politics of Diplomacy: Revolution, War, and Peace, 1989–1992* (New York: Putnam, 1995), p. 277; U.S. News & World Report, *Triumph*, pp. 93–94.

51. Zaller, "Strategic Politicians," p. 252.

52. Baker, *Politics*, p. 277.

53. Lawrence Freedman and Efraim Karsh, *The Gulf Conflict, 1990–1991* (Princeton, N.J.: Princeton University Press, 1993), p. 94; U.S. News & World Report, *Triumph*, pp. 48, 141.

54. U.S. News & World Report, *Triumph*, p. 80.

55. Gordon and Trainer, *Generals' War*, p. 49.

56. Goodgame, "What If," p. 26; Freedman and Karsh, *Gulf Conflict*, pp. 203–4; Mueller, *Policy and Opinion*, p. 116; Woodward, *Commanders*, p. 301.

57. Powell, *American Journey*, pp. 476, 478, 480.

58. Tom Mathews, "The Road to War," *Newsweek*, January 28, 1991, p. 63; Powell, *American Journey*, p. 489; Woodward, *Commanders*, pp. 318, 320; Zaller, "Strategic Politicians," p. 258.

59. Freedman and Karsh, *Gulf Conflict*, pp. 222, 224; U.S. News & World Report, *Triumph*, pp. 174–75, 179; Woodward, *Commanders*, pp. 316–17.

60. Mathews, "Road to War," p. 64.

61. Freedman and Karsh, *Gulf Conflict*, p. 211; Goodgame, "What If," p. 24; Mathews, "Road to War," pp. 63–64; David Mervin, *George Bush and the Guardianship Presidency* (New York: St. Martin's Press, 1996), p. 190.

62. Mathews, "Road to War," p. 64–65; U.S. News & World Report, *Triumph*, p. 184; Woodward, *Commanders*, p. 337.

63. Woodward, *Commanders*, p. 325.

64. Powell, *American Journey*, p. 499.

65. Bush, "Gulf War Exclusive," p. 5.

66. U.S. News & World Report, *Triumph*, p. 197.

67. John E. Mueller, *Policy and Opinion in the Gulf War* (Chicago: University of Chicago Press, 1994), p. 121.

68. Woodward, *Commanders*, p. 339.

69. Mathews, "Road to War," p. 65.

70. Mueller, *Policy and Opinion*, pp. 180–81, 217–21.

71. Ann Devroy and R. Jeffrey Smith, "Clinton Reexamines a Foreign Policy Under Siege," *Washington Post*, October 17, 1993, pp. A1, A28; Carolyn J. Logan, "U.S. Public Opinion and the Intervention in Somalia," *Fletcher Forum of World Affairs*, 20 (1996):170, 172.

72. Sidney Blumenthal, "Why Are We in Somalia?" *New Yorker*, October 25, 1993, pp. 48, 60; Elizabeth Drew, *On the Edge: The Clinton Presidency* (New York: Simon & Schuster, 1994), p. 323; Elaine Sciolino, "Pentagon Changes Its Somalia Goals as Effort Falters," *New York Times*, September 28, 1993, pp. A1, A17; Thomas W. Lippman and Barton Gellman, "A Humanitarian Gesture Turns Deadly," *Washington Post*, October 10, 1993, pp. A1, A44; Clifford Krauss, "White House Tries to Calm Congress," *New York Times*, October 6, 1993, p. A16.

73. Andrew Kohut and Robert C. Toth, "Arms and the People," *Foreign Affairs* 73 (1994):52; Logan, "U.S. Public Opinion," pp. 160–61.

74. Carroll J. Doherty, "Clinton Calms Rebellion on Hill by Retooling Somalia Mission," *Congressional Quarterly Weekly Report*, October 9, 1993, p. 2750; Drew, *Edge*, p. 318.

75. Drew, *Edge*, pp. 317, 326.

76. Ann Devroy, "New Deployment Raises Confusion on U.S. Goals," *Washington Post*, October 6, 1993, pp. A1, A16; Ann Devroy and John Lancaster, "Clinton to Add 1,500 Troops in Somalia," *Washington Post*, October 7, 1993, pp. A1, A38.

77. Drew, *Edge*, pp. 326–27.

78. Ibid.; Thomas L. Friedman, "Bid to Clarify Aims," *New York Times*, October 6, 1993, pp. A1, A16.

79. Blumenthal, "Somalia," p. 51; Doherty, "Clinton Calms," p. 2751; Drew, *Edge*, p. 328.

80. Krauss, "White House"; Logan, "U.S. Public Opinion," p. 159.

81. Helen Dewar, "Senate Vote on Pullout Delayed," *Washington Post*, October 7, 1993, p. 39.

82. Drew, *Edge*, pp. 3328–29; Ruth Marcus and Ann Devroy, "Clinton to Double Force in Somalia," *Washington Post*, October 8, 1993, pp. A1, A20.

83. Marcus and Devroy, "Clinton to Double Force," pp. A1, A20.

84. Drew, *Edge*, pp. 328–29; John L. Hirsch and Robert B. Oakley, *Somalia and Operation Restore Hope* (Washington, D.C.: U.S. Institute of Peace Press, 1995), p. 128; Marcus and Devroy, "Clinton to Double Force," pp. A1, A20.

85. Devroy and Lancaster, "Clinton to Add;" Thomas L. Friedman, "Clinton Sending More Troops to Somalia," *New York Times*, October 7, 1993, pp. A1, A10.

86. Marcus and Devroy, "Clinton to Double Force."

87. Drew, *Edge*, p. 329.

88. Helen Dewar, "Congress's Reaction to TV Coverage Shows Ambivalence on Foreign Policy," *Washington Post*, October 9, 1993, p. A14; Doherty, "Clinton Calms," p. 2750; Douglas Jehl, "Clinton Doubling U.S. Force in Somalia," *New York Times*, October 8, 1993, pp. A1, A14; Clifford Krauss, "Clinton Gathers Congress Support," *New York Times*, October 8, 1993, p. A14.

89. B. Drummond Ayres Jr., "A Common Cry Across the U.S.: It's Time to Exit," *New York Times*, October 9, 1993, pp. 1, 6.

90. Patrick J. Sloyan, "Clinton's Tough Encounter with the Wounded," *Newsday*, December 8, 1993, p. 17; Michael R. Gordon and John H. Cushman Jr., "After Supporting Hunt for Aidid, U.S. Is Blaming U.N. for Losses," *New York Times*, October 18, 1993, pp. A1, A8.

91. Clifford Krauss, "Senators Seek Early Pullout of U.S. Troops from Somalia," *New York Times*, October 12, 1993, pp. A1, A10.

92. Hirsch and Oakley, *Somalia*, pp. 132, 144; Clifford Krauss, "Clinton Resists Earlier Somalia Pullout," *New York Times*, October 14, 1993, p. A12.

9. Deliberative Cases and Recent Presidents

1. Gaddis Smith, *Morality, Reason, and Power: American Diplomacy in the Carter Years* (New York: Hill & Wang, 1986), p. 111.

2. George D. Moffett III, *The Limits of Victory: The Ratification of the Panama Canal Treaties* (Ithaca, N.Y.: Cornell University Press, 1985), pp. 19–47. See also John Major, *Prize Possession: The United States and the Panama Canal, 1903–1979* (Cambridge: Cambridge University Press, 1993); William L. Furlong and Margaret E. Scranton, *The Dynamics of Foreign Policymaking: The President, the Congress, and the Panama Canal Treaties* (Boulder, Colo.: Westview Press, 1984).

3. Moffett points to these instances to bolster this view. See Moffett, *Limits of Victory*, pp. 51–52.

4. Jimmy Carter, *Keeping Faith: Memoirs of a President* (New York: Bantam Books, 1982), p. 155.

5. Ibid., pp. 155–56.

6. Furlong and Scanton, *Dynamics*, pp. 86–87; Zbigniew Brzezinski, *Power and Principle: Memoirs of the National Security Advisor, 1977–1981* (New York: Farrar, Straus & Giroux, 1983), p. 134.

7. Cyrus Vance, *Hard Choices: Critical Years in America's Foreign Policy* (New York: Simon & Schuster, 1983), p. 140.

8. Furlong and Scranton, *Dynamics*, pp. 83–85; Moffett, *Limits of Victory*, pp. 48–70; Skidmore, *Reversing Course*, pp. 111–13.

9. Carter, *Keeping Faith*, p. 156.

10. Ibid., p. 158.

11. Vance, *Hard Choices*, p. 146.

12. Carter, *Keeping Faith*, p. 155; Vance, *Hard Choices*, p. 147.

13. J. Michael Hogan, *The Panama Canal in American Politics: Domestic Advocacy and the Evolution of Policy* (Carbondale: Southern Illinois University Press, 1986), p. 89.

14. Carter, *Keeping Faith*, p. 162; Vance, *Hard Choices*, pp. 150–51.

15. Skidmore, *Reversing Course*, pp. 114, 117, 121; Moffett, *Limits of Victory*, pp. 76, 80–81; Furlong and Scranton, *Dynamics*, p. 96; Carter, *Keeping Faith*, p. 162.

16. Carter, *Keeping Faith*, pp. 178, 184; Moffett, *Limits of Victory*, pp. 76–77.

17. Moffett, *Limits of Victory*, p. 116.

18. For a more extensive discussion, see Furlong and Scranton, *Dynamics*, pp. 128–66; Hogan, *Panama Canal*, pp. 83–208; and Moffett, *Limits of Victory*, pp. 71–202.

19. Reagan's approval rating was in the low 40 percent range in late 1982 and after February 1983, and in the mid-30 percent range in January 1983 (the lowest of his presidency). See *The Gallup Report*, no. 277, October 1988, p. 10.

20. Lou Cannon, *President Reagan: The Role of a Lifetime* (New York: Simon & Schuster, 1991), p. 320; Edward Reiss, *The Strategic Defense Initiative* (Cambridge: Cambridge University Press, 1992), p. 45; George P. Shultz, *Turmoil and Triumph:*

My Years as Secretary of State (New York: Scribner, 1993), p. 261; Casper W. Weinberger, *Fighting for Peace: Seven Critical Years in the Pentagon* (New York: Warner Books, 1990), p. 309.

21. Martin Anderson, *Revolution* (New York: Harcourt Brace Jovanovich, 1988), p. 83.

22. Cannon, *Role of a Lifetime*, p. 320; Ronald Reagan, *An American Life* (New York: Simon & Schuster, 1990), pp. 547–48; Anderson, *Revolution*, pp. 71–73; Don Oberdorfer, *The Turn* (New York: Poseidon Press, 1991), pp. 25–26; Shultz, *Turmoil and Triumph*, pp. 246, 253.

23. Anderson, *Revolution*, pp. 89–96.

24. Cannon, *Role of a Lifetime*, pp. 323–25.

25. Ibid., pp. 223–28; Anderson, *Revolution*, p. 97; Reiss, *Strategic Defense*, p. 44.

26. Cannon, *Role of a Lifetime*, pp. 228–29.

27. David Hoffman, "Reagan Seized Idea Shelved in '80 Race," *Washington Post*, March 3, 1985, pp. A1.

28. Hedrick Smith, *The Power Game* (New York: Random House, 1988), p. 605.

29. Weinberger, *Fighting for Peace*, p. 304.

30. Reiss, *Strategic Defense*, pp. 44–45; Cannon, *Role of a Lifetime*, p. 330.

31. Smith, *Power Game*, pp. 607–9.

32. Cannon, *Role of a Lifetime*, p. 331; Smith, *Power Game*, pp. 603–4.

33. Cannon, *Role of a Lifetime*, p. 331.

34. Oberdorfer, *The Turn*, p. 28.

35. Cannon, *Role of a Lifetime*, pp. 330–31.

36. Reagan, *An American Life*, p. 571.

37. Smith, *Power Game*, p. 609.

38. Ronald H. Hinckley, *People, Polls, and Policymakers: American Public Opinion and National Security* (New York: Lexington Books, 1992), p. 72.

39. Philip L. Geyelin, "The Strategic Defense Initiative: The President's Story," in Simon Serfaty, ed., *The Media and Foreign Policy*, p. 30 (New York: St. Martin's Press, 1990); Reiss, *Strategic Defense*, pp. 41, 51, 83, 167.

40. Robert L. Hutchings, *American Diplomacy and the End of the Cold War* (Baltimore: Johns Hopkins University Press, 1997), p. 97; Philip Zelikow and Condoleezza Rice, *Germany Unified and Europe Transformed* (Cambridge, Mass.: Harvard University Press, 1995), p. 24.

41. Michael R. Beschloss and Strobe Talbott, *At the Highest Levels* (Boston: Little, Brown, 1993), pp. 11–12, 24, 45, 74.

42. Zelikow and Rice, *Germany*, pp. 26–28.

43. Beschloss and Talbott, *Highest Levels*, p. 74.

44. Zelikow and Rice, *Germany*, pp. 24–25.

45. James A. Baker III, *The Politics of Diplomacy: Revolution, War, and Peace 1989–1992* (New York: Putnam, 1995), p. 159.

46. Zelikow and Rice, *Germany*, pp. 28–29.

47. Ibid., p. 81.

48. Thomas Friedman, "U.S. Officials Look to Policy on East Germany as Next Big Challenge," *New York Times*, October 20, 1989, p. A13.

49. R. W. Apple, "Possibility of a Reunited Germany Is No Cause for Alarm, Bush Says," *New York Times*, October 25, 1989, pp. A1, A12.

50. Baker, *Politics*, p. 164.

51. Zelikow and Rice, *Germany*, p. 105.

52. Hutchings, *Diplomacy*, p. 98; Mervin, *George Bush*, pp. 172–73; Stephen F. Szabo, *The Diplomacy of German Unification* (New York: St. Martin's Press, 1992), pp. 41–42; Zelikow and Rice, *Germany*, pp. 25, 105, 112.

53. Baker, *Politics*, pp. 167–68; Hutchings, *Diplomacy*, p. 100; Szabo, *Unification*, pp. 38–44; Zelikow and Rice, *Germany*, p. 117.

54. George Skelton, "Americans Optimistic but Cautious on East Bloc Reform," *Los Angeles Times*, November 21, 1989, pp. A1, A12; George Skelton, "One Germany: U.S. Unfazed, Europeans Fret," *Los Angeles Times*, January 26, 1990, pp. A1, A10.

55. Jack Nelson and David Lauter, "Bush Aides Hope Malta Has Sparkle," *Los Angeles Times*, December 1, 1989, pp. A18.

56. Beschloss and Talbott, *Highest Levels*, p. 184.

57. Ibid., p. 188; Szabo, *Unification*, p. 58;

58. Baker, *Politics*, pp. 196–99; Oberdorfer, *The Turn*, p. 393; Zelikow and Rice, *Germany*, pp. 167–68, 172, 193–95.

59. Beschloss and Talbott, *Highest Levels*, pp. 219–20, 227, 238.

60. Szabo, *Unification*, pp. 23, 118–20; Zelikow and Rice, *Germany*, pp. 367–68.

61. Susan L. Woodward, *Balkan Tragedy: Chaos and Dissolution After the Cold War* (Washington, D.C.: Brookings Institution, 1995); William J. Durch and James A. Schear, "Faultlines: U.N. Operations in the Former Yugoslavia," in William J. Durch, ed., *U.N. Peacekeeping, American Politics, and the Uncivil Wars of the 1990s*, pp. 193–274 (New York: St. Martin's Press, 1996).

62. According to the Gallup poll, during May through November 1995, Clinton's approval rating was in the mid- to high 40 percent and low 50 percent range, with more approval than disapproval except for the September 14–17 poll in which an equal number (44%) approved and disapproved of his job performance. *The Gallup Poll Monthly*, no. 365 (1996):6.

63. Richard Sobel, "U.S. and European Attitudes Toward Intervention in the Former Yugoslavia; *Mourir pour la Bosnie?*" in Richard H. Ullman, ed., *The World and Yugoslavia's Wars*, pp. 148–51 (New York: Council on Foreign Relations, 1996).

64. Stephen Engelberg, "How Events Drew U.S. into Balkans," *New York Times*, August 19, 1995, pp. A1, A4.

65. Bob Woodward, *The Choice* (New York: Simon & Schuster, 1996), p. 255.

66. Ibid., pp. 256–57.

67. Thomas W. Lippman and Ann Devroy, "Clinton's Policy Evolution," *Washington Post*, September 11, 1995, pp. A1, A16.

68. Ibid.

69. Stephen Engelberg and Alison Mitchell, "A Seesaw Week for U.S. Policy in the Balkans," *New York Times*, June 5, 1995, pp. A1, A8.

70. Woodward, *The Choice*, pp. 258–59.

71. Michael Dobbs, "Bosnia Crystallizes U.S. Post-Cold War Role," *Washington Post*, December 3, 1995, pp. A1, A34.

72. Lippmann and Devroy, "Clinton's Policy."

73. Engelberg, "How Events."

74. Woodward, *The Choice*, p. 260.

75. Dobbs, "Bosnia Crystallizes."

76. Durch, "Faultlines," p. 246; Alison Mitchell, "Clinton Lays out His Case for U.S. Troops in Balkans," *New York Times*, November 28, 1995, pp. A1, A15.

77. Woodward, *The Choice*, pp. 261–63.

78. Ibid., p. 265.

79. Dick Morris, *Behind the Oval Office* (New York: Random House, 1997), pp. 248–49.

80. Ibid., pp. 244–65; Lippman and Devroy, "Clinton's Policy."

81. Dobbs, "Bosnia Crystallizes"; Lippman and Devroy, "Clinton's Policy."

82. Woodward, *The Choice*, pp. 265–66.

83. Ann Devroy, "Europeans Respond Favorably to Ideas for Bosnia Settlement, Clinton Is Told," *Washington Post*, August 16, 1995, p. A16; Engelberg, "How Events."

84. Durch, "Faultlines," pp. 246–47.

85. Morris, *Behind the Oval Office*, pp. 255–56, 339.

86. Dana Priest and Ann Devroy, "White House to Ask $1 Billion for Bosnia Troop Deployment," *Washington Post*, September 28, 1995, p. A24.

87. Ann Devroy and Dana Priest, "Clinton Aides Debate Size of U.S. Peacekeeping Force for Bosnia," *Washington Post*, September 21, 1995, pp. A24.

88. Alison Mitchell, "Clinton's Next Task Will Be to Sell Plan to the U.S. Public," *New York Times*, November 22, 1995, pp. A1, A11.

89. Ann Devroy and Helen Dewar, "U.S. Troops Vital to Bosnia Peace, Clinton Says," *Washington Post*, November 28, 1995, pp. A1, A9; Helen Dewar and Guy Gugliott, "Senate Backs Troops to Bosnia," *Washington Post*, December 14, 1995, pp. A1, A39.

90. Woodward, *The Choice*, p. 368.

10. Conclusions and Implications for Theory and Practice

1. Fen Osler Hampson, "The Divided Decision-Maker: American Domestic Politics and the Cuban Crises," *International Security* 9 (1984/85):130–65; Ole R. Holsti, "Crisis Decision Making," in Philip E. Tetlock et al., eds., *Behavior, Society, and Nuclear War*, vol. 1, pp. 9–84 (New York: Oxford University Press, 1989); Christopher Layne, "Kant or Cant: The Myth of the Democratic Peace," *International Security* 19 (1994):5–49; James Meernik, "Presidential Decision Making and the Political Use of Military Force," *International Studies Quarterly* 38 (1994):121–38;

James Meernik and Peter Waterman, "The Myth of the Diversionary Use of Force by American Presidents," *Political Research Quarterly* 49 (1996):573–90.

2. See also Bruce W. Jentleson, "The Pretty Prudent Public: Post Post-Vietnam American Opinion on the Use of Military Force," *International Studies Quarterly* 36 (1992):49–74; Benjamin I. Page and Robert Y. Shapiro, *The Rational Public: Fifty Years of Trends in American Policy Preferences* (Chicago: University of Chicago Press, 1992).

3. This finding is consistent with other research that focused more closely on the use of polls in the Carter and Reagan administrations. See Robert Britt Mattes, "The Politics of Public Opinion: Polls, Pollsters, and the President" (Ph.D. diss., University of Illinois at Urbana-Champaign, 1992).

4. Thomas W. Graham, "The Politics of Failure: Strategic Nuclear Arms Control, Public Opinion, and Domestic Politics in the United States: 1945–1980" (Ph.D. diss., Massachusetts Institute of Technology, 1989). In a study of the content of presidential State of the Union speeches and mostly on domestic issues, Jeffrey Cohen found that the public could force an issue onto the agenda if it became interested in it but that presidents were not responsive to public opinion during policy formulation. See Jeffrey E. Cohen, *Presidential Responsiveness and Public Policy-Making* (Ann Arbor: University of Michigan Press, 1997).

5. Ole R. Holsti, *Public Opinion and American Foreign Policy* (Ann Arbor: University of Michigan Press, 1996), pp. 192–95.

6. Patrick James and John R. Oneal, "The Influence of Domestic and International Politics on the President's Use of Force," *Journal of Conflict Resolution* 35 (1991):307–32; Charles W. Ostrom and Brian L. Job, "The President and the Political Use of Force," *American Political Science Review* 80 (1986):541–66.

7. Kurt Taylor Gaubatz, "Election Cycles and War," *Journal of Conflict Resolution* 35 (1991):212–44; Richard J. Stoll, "The Guns of November: Presidential Reelections and the Use of Force, 1947–1982," *Journal of Conflict Resolution* 28 (1984):231–46.

8. James and Oneal, "Influence of Domestic"; Bruce M. Russett, "Economic Decline, Electoral Pressure, and the Initiation of Interstate Conflict," in Charles S. Gochman and Alan Ned Sabrosky, eds., *Prisoners of War?* pp. 123–40 (Lexington, Mass.: Lexington Books, 1990); Kevin H. Wang, "Presidential Responses to Foreign Policy Crises," *Journal of Conflict Resolution* 40 (1996):68–97.

9. Holsti, *Public Opinion and American Foreign Policy*, p. 199.

10. C. Wright Mills, *The Power Elite* (New York: Oxford University Press, 1956); Richard J. Barnet, *Roots of War* (New York: Penguin Books, 1972); Richard J. Barnet, *The Rocket's Red Glare* (New York: Simon & Schuster, 1990); G. William Domhoff, *Who Rules America Now?* (New York: Simon & Schuster, 1986); Gabriel Kolko and Joyce Kolko, *The Limits of Power: The World and United States Foreign Policy, 1945–1954* (New York: Harper & Row, 1972).

11. On the lack of domestic influences, see, for example, John J. Mearsheimer, "The False Promise of International Institutions," *International Security* 19

(1994/95):5–49; and Fareed Zakaria, "Realism and Domestic Politics: A Review Essay," *International Security* 17 (1992):177–98. On the influence of domestic politics, see, for example, John G. Ikenberry, David Lumsdaine, and Lisa Anderson, "Polity Forum: The Intertwining of Domestic Politics and International Relations," *Polity* 29 (1996):293–310; Robert D. Putnam, "Diplomacy and Domestic Politics: The Logic of Two-Level Games," *International Organization* 42 (1988):427–60; Randolph M. Siverson, ed., *Strategic Politicians, Institutions, and Foreign Policy* (Ann Arbor: University of Michigan Press, 1998); and David Skidmore and Valerie M. Hudson, eds., *The Limits of State Autonomy: Societal Groups and Foreign Policy Formulation* (Boulder, Colo.: Westview Press, 1993).

12. Andrew Moravcsik, "Taking Preferences Seriously: A Liberal Theory of International Politics," *International Organization* 51 (1997):513–54.

13. Randall L. Schweller and David Priess, "A Tale of Two Realisms: Expanding the Institutions Debate," *Mershon International Studies Review* 41 (1997):7, 14, 24. For an example of a realist using domestic-level explanations to explain irrational policy outcomes, see Jack Snyder, *Myths of Empire* (Ithaca, N.Y.: Cornell University Press, 1991).

14. Kenneth N. Waltz, "A Response to My Critics," in Robert O. Keohane, ed., *Neorealism and Its Critics*, p. 323 (New York: Columbia University Press, 1986); Zakaria, "Realism and Domestic Politics," p. 198.

15. Jennifer Sterling-Folker, "Realist Environment, Liberal Process, and Domestic Level Variables," *International Studies Quarterly* 41 (1997):1–25; Colin Elman, "Horses for Courses: Why Not Neorealist Theories of Foreign Policy?" *Security Studies* 6 (1996):7–53; Kenneth N. Waltz, "International Politics Is Not Foreign Policy," *Security Studies* 6 (1996):54–57.

16. James Fearon, "Domestic Political Audiences and the Escalation of International Disputes," *American Political Science Review* 88 (1994):577–92; Bruce Bueno de Mesquita and David Lalman, *War and Reason* (New Haven, Conn.: Yale University Press, 1992), pp. 41, 46, 265–71; Helen V. Milner, *Interests, Institutions, and Information* (Princeton, N.J.: Princeton University Press, 1997), p. 16.

17. Steve Chan, "In Search of Democratic Peace: Problems and Promise," *Mershon International Studies Review* 41 (1997):59–91; Gaubatz, "Election Cycles"; Ross Miller, "Domestic Structures and the Diversionary Use of Force," *American Journal of Political Science* 39 (1995):760–85; Alastair Smith, "Diversionary Foreign Policy in Democratic Systems," *International Studies Quarterly* 40 (1996):133–53.

18. Jack S. Levy, "The Diversionary Theory of War: A Critique," in Manus I. Midlarsky, ed., *The Handbook of War Studies*, pp. 259–88 (Boston: Unwin Hyman, 1989); Meernik and Waterman, "Myth of Diversionary Force"; Miller, "Domestic Structures"; Diana Richards et al., "Good Times, Bad Times, and the Diversionary Use of Force," *Journal of Conflict Resolution* 37 (1993):504–35; Russett, "Economic Decline"; Stoll, "Guns of November."

19. Ole R. Holsti, "Public Opinion and Foreign Policy: Challenges to the Almond-Lippmann Consensus," *International Studies Quarterly* 36 (1992):439–66;

Lawrence R. Jacobs and Robert Y. Shapiro, "Studying Substantive Democracy," *PS* 27 (1994):9–16; Benjamin I. Page, "Democratic Responsiveness? Untangling the Links Between Public Opinion and Policy," *PS* 27 (1994):25–28; Philip J. Powlick and Andrew Z. Katz, "Defining the American Public Opinion / Foreign Policy Nexus," *Mershon International Studies Review* 42 (1998):29–61.

20. Lawrence R. Jacobs and Robert Y. Shapiro, "The Rise of Presidential Polling: The Nixon White House in Historical Perspective," *Public Opinion Quarterly* 59 (1995):163–95.

21. Miroslav Nincic, "Domestic Costs, the U.S. Public, and the Isolationist Calculus," *International Studies Quarterly* 41 (1997):593–610; Arthur Schlesinger Jr., "Back to the Womb: Isolationism's Renewed Threat," *Foreign Affairs* 74 (1995):2–8; John Gerard Ruggie, "The Past as Prologue? Interests, Identity, and American Foreign Policy," *International Security* 21 (1997):89–125. Recent research has suggested that although the public is not as internationalist as elites are, it still supports an active American role in the world. See Ole R. Holsti, "Public Opinion and U.S. Foreign Policy," in James M. Scott, ed., *After the End: Making U.S. Foreign Policy in the Post-Cold War Environment* (Durham, N.C.: Duke University Press, 1998), pp. 18–69. For a discussion of several possible American policies, see Barry R. Posen and Andrew L. Ross, "Competing Visions for U.S. Grand Strategy," *International Security* 21 (1996/97):5–53.

22. Posen and Ross, "Competing Visions," pp. 44–50.

23. Ruggie, "Past as Prologue," pp. 98–102.

24. *Encyclopedia of U.S. Foreign Relations*, s.v. "Truman Doctrine"; David McCullough, *Truman* (New York: Simon & Schuster, 1992), pp. 541–61.

Methods Appendix

1. Deborah Welch Larson, "The Role of Belief Systems and Schemas in Foreign Policy Decision-Making," *Political Psychology* 15 (1994):17–33.

2. Ole R. Holsti, "Foreign Policy Formation Viewed Cognitively," in Robert Axelrod, ed., *Structure of Decision*, pp. 18–55 (Princeton, N.J.: Princeton University Press, 1976); Jerel A. Rosati, "The Impact of Beliefs on Behavior: The Foreign Policy of the Carter Administration," in Donald Sylvan and Steve Chan, eds., *Foreign Policy Decision Making*, p. 163 (New York: Praeger, 1984).

3. Deborah Welch Larson, *Origins of Containment: A Psychological Explanation* (Princeton, N.J.: Princeton University Press, 1985).

4. Rosati, "The Impact of Beliefs," p. 163.

5. Fred I. Greenstein, *Personality and Politics: Problems of Evidence, Inference, and Conceptualization* (New York: Norton, 1975); Ole R. Holsti, "Foreign Policy Decision-Makers Viewed Psychologically: Cognitive Processes Approaches," in G. M. Bonham and M. J. Shapiro, eds., *Thought and Action in Foreign Policy*, pp. 10–74 (Basel: Birkhauser Verlag, 1977).

6. Gary King, Robert O. Keohane, and Sydney Verba, *Designing Social Inquiry* (Princeton, N.J.: Princeton University Press, 1994).

7. Alexander L. George and Timothy J. McKeown, "Case Studies and Theories of Organizational Decision Making," *Advances in Information Processing in Organizations* 2 (1985):21–58.

8. Ibid., p. 35.

9. Ibid.

10. Yuen Foong Khong, *Analogies at War: Korea, Munich, Dien Bien Phu, and the Vietnam Decisions of 1965* (Princeton, N.J.: Princeton University Press, 1992).

11. Alexander L. George, "Case Studies and Theory Development: The Method of Structured, Focused Comparison," in Paul Gordon Lauren, ed., *Diplomacy: New Approaches in History, Theory, and Policy*, pp. 43–68 (New York: Free Press, 1979).

12. John Burke and Fred I. Greenstein, *How Presidents Test Reality* (New York: Russell Sage Foundation, 1989).

Manuscript Collections

Dwight D. Eisenhower Presidential Library, Abilene, Kansas
  • John Foster Dulles Papers (JFD Papers)
    JFD Chronological Series
    Subject Series
    Telephone Calls Series
    White House Memoranda Series
  • Dwight D. Eisenhower: Papers as President of the United States, 1953–1961
    (Ann Whitman File) (DDE Papers)
    Administration Series
    Ann Whitman Diary Series
    DDE Diaries Series
    Dulles-Herter Series
    Legislative Meetings Series
    Miscellaneous Series
    Name Series
    NSC Series
    Press Conference Series
  • James C. Hagerty Papers
  • Bryce Harlow Records
  • C. D. Jackson Papers

- National Security Council Staff, Papers, 1948–1961
    - Executive Secretary's Subject File Series
    - Disaster File Series
- Office of the Special Assistant for National Security Affairs (OSANSA), Records, 1952–1961
    - NSC Series, Administration Subseries
    - NSC Series, Briefing Notes Subseries
    - NSC Series, Subject Subseries
    - Special Assistant Series, Presidential Subseries
    - Special Assistant Series, Subject Subseries
- Office of the Special Assistant for Science and Technology: Records, 1957–1961
- Office of the Staff Secretary (OSS): Records, 1952–1961
    - Cabinet Series
    - Legislative Meetings Series
    - L. Arthur Minnich Series
    - Subject Series, Alphabetical Subseries
    - Subject Series, DOD Subseries
- U.S. President's Science Advisory Committee
- Oral Histories
    - Dwight D. Eisenhower, OH 11
    - Andrew J. Goodpaster OH 378
    - James C. Hagerty OH 91
    - Arthur A. Kimball OH 66
    - Carl McCardle OH 116

National Archives, Washington, D.C.
- Diplomatic Branch
    - General Records of the Department of State, Record Group 59
    - Office of Public Opinion Studies (OPPS), 1943–1965, Record Group 59
- Modern Military Records Branch
    - Joint Chiefs of Staff Records, Record Group 218
        - Geographic File, 1954–1956
        - Records of the Chairman Arthur Radford
- Records of the Secretary of Defense, Record Group 330
    - Defense-Executive Office, Central Decimal Files, 1953

Seeley G. Mudd Manuscript Library, Princeton University, Princeton, New Jersey (used by permission of the Princeton University Libraries)
- John Foster Dulles Oral History Collection
    - Andrew H. Berding
    - Robert R. Bowie

Dwight D. Eisenhower
William Butts Macomber
Richard M. Nixon
Roderic L. O'Connor
• John Foster Dulles Papers
• Emmet Hughes Papers
• Karl Lott Rankin Papers

Selected Books and Articles

Accinelli, Robert. *Crisis and Commitment: United States Policy Toward Taiwan, 1950–1955*. Chapel Hill: University of North Carolina Press, 1996.

Accinelli, Robert. "Eisenhower, Congress, and the 1954–55 Offshore Island Crisis." *Presidential Studies Quarterly* 20 (1990):329–48.

Adams, Sherman. *Firsthand Report*. New York: Harpers, 1961.

Allison, Graham T. *Essence of Decision*. Boston: Little, Brown, 1971.

Almond, Gabriel. *The American People and Foreign Policy*. New York: Praeger, 1950.

Alston, Giles. "Eisenhower: Leadership in Space Policy." In Shirley Anne War- shaw, ed., *Reexamining the Eisenhower Presidency*. Westport, Conn.: Green- wood Press, 1993, pp. 103–20.

Altschuler, Bruce E. *LBJ and the Polls*. Gainesville: University of Florida Press, 1990.

Ambrose, Stephen E. *Eisenhower: The President*. Vol. 2. New York: Simon & Schus- ter, 1984.

Anderson, Martin. *Revolution*. New York: Harcourt Brace Jovanovich, 1988.

Asher, Herbert. *Presidential Elections and American Politics: Voters Candidates, and Campaigns Since 1952*. Homewood, Ill.: Dorsey Press, 1976.

Babbie, Earl. *The Practice of Social Research*. 7th ed. Belmont, Calif.: Wadsworth, 1995.

Bailey, Thomas A. *The Man in the Street: The Impact of American Public Opinion on Foreign Policy*. New York: Macmillan, 1948.

Baker, James A. III. *The Politics of Diplomacy: Revolution, War and Peace 1989–1992*. New York: Putnam, 1995.

Barnet, Richard J. *Roots of War*. New York: Penguin Books, 1972.

Bartels, Larry M. "Constituency Opinion and Congressional Policy Making: The Reagan Defense Buildup." *American Political Science Review* 85 (1991):457–74.

Berding, Andrew H. *Dulles on Diplomacy*. Princeton, N.J.: Van Nostrand, 1965.

Berkowitz, Morton, P. G. Bock, and Vincent J. Fuccillo. *The Politics of American Foreign Policy*. Englewood Cliffs, N.J.: Prentice-Hall, 1977.

Bernstein, Barton J. "Election of 1952." In Arthur M. Schlesinger Jr., ed., *History of American Presidential Elections 1789–1968*. Vol. 4, pp. 3215–66. New York: Chelsea House, 1971.

Beschloss, Michael R., and Strobe Talbott. *At the Highest Levels*. Boston: Little, Brown, 1993.

Billings-Yun, Melanie. *Decision Against War: Eisenhower and Dien Bien Phu, 1954*. New York: Columbia University Press, 1988.

Brace, Paul, and Barbara Hinckley. *Follow the Leader: Opinion Polls and the Modern Presidents*. New York: Basic Books, 1992.

Brands, H. W. "The Age of Vulnerability: Eisenhower and the National Insecurity State." *American Historical Review* 94 (1989):963–89.

Brands, H. W. "Testing Massive Retaliation: Credibility and Crisis Management in the Taiwan Strait." *International Security* 12 (Spring 1988):124–51.

Brecher, Michael, and Patrick James. *Crisis and Change in World Politics*. Boulder, Colo.: Westview Press, 1986.

Brody, Richard A. *Assessing the President*. Stanford, Calif.: Stanford University Press, 1991.

Brody, Richard A. "International Crises: A Rallying Point for the President?" *Public Opinion* 6 (1984):41–43, 60.

Brody, Richard A., and Catherine R. Shapiro. "A Reconsideration of the Rally Phenomenon in Public Opinion." In Samuel Long, ed., *Political Behavior Annual*. Vol. 2, pp. 77–102. Boulder, Colo.: Westview Press, 1989.

Brzezinski, Zbigniew. *Power and Principle: Memoirs of the National Security Advisor, 1977–1981*. New York: Farrar, Straus & Giroux, 1983.

Bueno de Mesquita, Bruce, and David Lalman. *War and Reason*. New Haven, Conn.: Yale University Press, 1992.

Burke, John, and Fred I. Greenstein. *How Presidents Test Reality*. New York: Russell Sage Foundation, 1989.

Bush, George. *Public Papers of the Presidents of the United States: George Bush, 1989*. Vol. 2. Washington, D.C.: U.S. Government Printing Office, 1990.

Bush, George. *Public Papers of the Presidents of the United States: George Bush, 1990*. Vol. 1. Washington, D.C.: U.S. Government Printing Office, 1991.

Bush, George. *Public Papers of the Presidents of the United States: George Bush, 1990*. Vol. 2. Washington, D.C.: U.S. Government Printing Office, 1991.

Bush, George. *Public Papers of the Presidents of the United States: George Bush, 1991*. Vol. 2. Washington, D.C.: U.S. Government Printing Office, 1992.

Bush, George. *Public Papers of the Presidents of the United States: George Bush, 1992–93*. Vol. 2. Washington, D.C.: U.S. Government Printing Office, 1993.

Byrnes, James F. *Speaking Frankly*. New York: Harpers, 1947.

Cannon, Lou. *President Reagan: The Role of a Lifetime*. New York: Simon & Schuster, 1991.

Carter, Jimmy. *Keeping Faith: Memoirs of a President*. New York: Bantam Books, 1982.

Carter, Jimmy. *Public Papers of the Presidents of the United States, Jimmy Carter, 1977*. Vol. 2. Washington, D.C.: U.S. Government Printing Office, 1978.

Carter, Jimmy. *Public Papers of the Presidents of the United States, Jimmy Carter, 1978*. Vol. 2. Washington, D.C.: U.S. Government Printing Office, 1979.

Carter, Jimmy. *Public Papers of the Presidents of the United States, Jimmy Carter, 1979*. Vol. 2. Washington, D.C.: U.S. Government Printing Office, 1980.

Carter, Jimmy. *Public Papers of the Presidents of the United States, Jimmy Carter, 1980–81*. Vol. 1. Washington, D.C.: U.S. Government Printing Office, 1981.

Carter, Jimmy. *Public Papers of the Presidents of the United States, Jimmy Carter, 1980–81*. Vol. 3. Washington, D.C.: U.S. Government Printing Office, 1982.

Chan, Steve. "In Search of Democratic Peace: Problems and Promise." *Mershon International Studies Review* 41 (1997):59–92.

Chang, Gordon H. "To the Nuclear Brink: Eisenhower, Dulles, and the Quemoy-Matsu Crisis." *International Security* 12 (1988):96–123.

Chomsky, Noam, and Edward Herman. *Manufacturing Consent*. New York: Pantheon, 1988.

Christensen, Thomas J. *Useful Adversaries: Grand Strategy, Domestic Mobilization, and Sino-American Conflict, 1947–1958*. Princeton, N.J.: Princeton University Press, 1996.

Clinton, William J. *Public Papers of the President of the United States: William J. Clinton, 1993*. Washington, D.C.: U.S. Government Printing Office, 1994.

Clinton, William J. *Public Papers of the President of the United States: William J. Clinton, 1994*. Washington, D.C.: U.S. Government Printing Office, 1995.

Clinton, William J. *Public Papers of the President of the United States: William J. Clinton, 1995*. Washington, D.C.: U.S. Government Printing Office, 1996.

Clowse, Barbara Barksdale. *Brainpower for the Cold War: The Sputnik Crisis and National Defense Education Act of 1958*. Westport, Conn.: Greenwood Press, 1981.

Cohen, Bernard. *The Political Process and Foreign Policy*. Princeton, N.J.: Princeton University Press, 1957.

Cohen, Bernard. *The Public's Impact on Foreign Policy*. Boston: Little, Brown, 1973.

Cohen, Jeffrey E. *Presidential Responsiveness and Public Policy-Making*. Ann Arbor: University of Michigan Press, 1997.

Condit, Kenneth W. *The Joint Chiefs of Staff and National Policy 1955–1956*. Vol. 6 of *History of the Joint Chiefs of Staff*. Washington, D.C.: U.S. Government Printing Office, 1992.

Congressional Quarterly Almanac. Vol. 10. Washington, D.C.: Congressional Quarterly News Features, 1954.

Cutler, Robert. *No Time for Rest*. Boston: Little, Brown, 1965.

Dahl, Robert. *Democracy and Its Critics*. New Haven, Conn.: Yale University Press, 1989.

Dahl, Robert. *Polyarchy: Participation and Opposition*. New Haven, Conn.: Yale University Press, 1971.

Divine, Robert A. *The Sputnik Challenge*. New York: Oxford University Press, 1993.

Dockrill, Saki. *Eisenhower's New-Look National Security Policy, 1953–1961*. New York: St. Martin's Press, 1996.

Donovan, Robert J. *Eisenhower: The Inside Story*. New York: Harpers, 1956.

Downs, Anthony. *An Economic Theory of Democracy*. New York: Harper & Row, 1950.

Drew, Elizabeth. *On the Edge: The Clinton Presidency*. New York: Simon & Schuster, 1994.

Duchin, Brian R. " 'The Most Spectacular Legislative Battle of that Year:' President Eisenhower and the 1958 Reorganization of the Department of Defense." *Presidential Studies Quarterly* 24 (1994):243–62.

Duiker, William J. *U.S. Containment Policy and the Conflict in Indochina*. Stanford, Calif.: Stanford University Press, 1994.

Dulles, John Foster. "Developing Bipartisan Foreign Policy." *Department of State Bulletin*, May 8, 1950, p. 721.

Dulles, John Foster. "A Policy of Boldness." *Life*, May 19, 1952, pp. 146–60.

Dulles, John Foster. *War or Peace*. New York: Macmillan, 1950.

Dulles, John Foster. "A Policy of Boldness." *Life*, May 19, 1952, pp. 146–60.

Durch, William J., and James A. Schear. "Faultlines: U.N. Operations in the Former Yugoslavia." In William A. Durch, ed., *U.N. Peacekeeping, American Politics, and the Uncivil Wars of the 1990s*, pp. 193–274. New York: St. Martin's Press, 1996.

Edwards, George. "Frustration and Folly: Bill Clinton and the Public Presidency." In Colin Campbell and Bert A. Rockman, eds., *The Clinton Presidency: First Appraisals*, pp. 234–61. Chatham, N.J.: Chatham House, 1996.

Edwards, George. *The Public Presidency*. New York: St. Martin's Press, 1983.

Eichenberg, Richard C. *Public Opinion and National Security in Western Europe*. Ithaca, N.Y.: Cornell University Press, 1989.

Eisenhower, Dwight D. *Mandate for Change*. Garden City, N.Y.: Doubleday, 1963.

Eisenhower, Dwight D. *Public Papers of the Presidents of the United States: Dwight D. Eisenhower, 1953*. Washington, D.C.: U.S. Government Printing Office, 1960.

Eisenhower, Dwight D. *Public Papers of the Presidents of the United States: Dwight D. Eisenhower, 1954*. Washington, D.C.: U.S. Government Printing Office, 1960.

Eisenhower, Dwight D. *Public Papers of the Presidents of the United States: Dwight D. Eisenhower, 1957*. Washington, D.C.: U.S. Government Printing Office, 1958.

Eisenhower, Dwight D. *Waging Peace*. Garden City, N.Y.: Doubleday, 1965.

Elman, Colin. "Horses for Courses: Why Not Neorealist Theories of Foreign Policy?" *Security Studies* 6 (1996):7–53.

Fairfield, Roy P., ed. *The Federalist Papers*. New York: Anchor Books, 1961.

Farnham, Barbara Reardon. *Roosevelt and the Munich Crisis: A Study of Political Decision Making*. Princeton, N.J.: Princeton University Press, 1997.

Fearon, James D. "Domestic Political Audiences and the Escalation of International Disputes." *American Political Science Review* 88 (1994):577–92.

Ferrell, Robert H., ed. *The Diary of James C. Hagerty*. Bloomington: Indiana University Press, 1983.

Ferrell, Robert H., ed. *The Eisenhower Diaries*. New York: Norton, 1981.

Ford, Gerald. *Public Papers of the Presidents of the United States: Gerald Ford, 1976–77*. Vol. 1. Washington, D.C.: U.S. Government Printing Office, 1979.

Frankel, Benjamin, ed. *Realism: Restatements and Renewal*. London: Frank Cass, 1997.

Frankfort-Nachias, Chava, and David Nachmias. *Research Methods in the Social Sciences*. New York: St. Martin's Press, 1996.

Freedman, Lawrence, and Efraim Karsh. *The Gulf Conflict, 1990 1991*. Princeton, N.J.: Princeton University Press, 1993.

Friedrich, Carl J. *Man and His Government: An Empirical Theory of Politics*. New York: McGraw-Hill, 1963.

Furlong, William L., and Margaret E. Scranton. *The Dynamics of Foreign Policymaking: The President, the Congress, and the Panama Canal Treaties*. Boulder, Colo.: Westview Press, 1984.

Gaddis, John Lewis. *Strategies of Containment*. New York: Oxford University Press, 1982.

Gaddis, John Lewis. "The Unexpected John Foster Dulles: Nuclear Weapons, Communism, and the Russians." In Richard H. Immerman, ed., *John Foster Dulles and the Diplomacy of the Cold War*. Princeton, N.J.: Princeton University Press, 1990.

Gallup, George. *The Gallup Poll: 1949 -1958*. Vol. 2. New York: Random House, 1972.

Gallup Opinion Index 182. October–November 1980.

Garthoff, Raymond L. *Détente and Confrontation: American-Soviet Relations from Nixon to Reagan*. Rev. ed. Washington, D.C.: Brookings Institution, 1994.

Gaubatz, Kurt Taylor. "Election Cycles and War." *Journal of Conflict Resolution* 35 (1991):212–44.

Geelhoed, E. Bruce. *Charles E. Wilson and Controversy at the Pentagon, 1953 to 1957*. Detroit: Wayne State University Press, 1979.

Geer, John G. *From Tea Leaves to Opinion Polls: A Theory of Democratic Leadership*. New York: Columbia University Press, 1996.

Gelb, Leslie H. *The Irony of Vietnam: The System Worked*. Washington, D.C.: Brookings Institution, 1979.

Gelb, Leslie H. "The Mind of the President." *New York Times Magazine*, October 6, 1985, pp. 21 ff.

George, Alexander L. "Case Studies and Theory Development: The Method of Structured, Focused Comparison." In Paul Gordon Lauren, ed., *Diplomacy: New Approaches in History, Theory, and Policy*, pp. 43–68. New York: Free Press, 1979.

George, Alexander L. "The Causal Nexus Between Cognitive Beliefs and Decision-Making Behavior: The 'Operational Code' Belief System." In Lawrence S. Falkawski, ed., *Psychological Models in International Politics*, pp. 95–124. Boulder, Colo.: Westview Press, 1979.

George, Alexander L. *Presidential Decision-Making in Foreign Policy: The Effective Use of Information and Advice*. Boulder, Colo.: Westview Press, 1980.

George, Alexander L., and Timothy J. McKeown. "Case Studies and Theories of Organizational Decision Making." *Advances in Information Processing in Organizations* 2 (1985):21–58.

Geyelin, Philip L. "The Strategic Defense Initiative: The President's Story." In Simon Serfaty, ed., *The Media and Foreign Policy*, pp. 19–32. New York: St. Martin's Press, 1990.

Gibbons, William Conrad. *The U.S. Government and the Vietnam War: Executive and Legislative Roles and Relationships*. Part 1: *1954–1961*. Washington, D.C.: U.S. Senate Committee on Foreign Relations, U.S. Government Printing Office, 1984.

Gordon, Leonard H. D. "United States Opposition to Use of Force in the Taiwan Strait, 1954–1962." *Journal of American History* 72 (1985): 637–60.

Gordon, Michael R., and Bernard E. Trainor. *The Generals' War*. Boston: Little, Brown, 1995.

Graham, Thomas W. "The Politics of Failure: Strategic Nuclear Arms Control, Public Opinion, and Domestic Politics in the United States, 1945–1980." Ph.D. diss., Massachusetts Institute of Technology, 1989.

Graham, Thomas W. "Public Opinion and U.S. Foreign Policy Decision Making." In David A. Deese, ed., *The New Politics of American Foreign Policy*, pp. 190–215. New York: St. Martin's Press, 1994.

Grasselli, Gabriella. *British and American Responses to the Soviet Invasion of Afghanistan*. Brookfield, Vt.: Dartmouth College Press, 1996.

Greene, John Robert. *The Crusade: The Presidential Election of 1952*. Lanham, Md.: University Press of America, 1985.

Greenstein, Fred I. *The Hidden-Hand Presidency*. New York: Basic Books, 1982.

Greenstein, Fred I. "The Hidden-Hand Presidency: Eisenhower as Leader. A 1994 Perspective." *Presidential Studies Quarterly* 24 (1994):233–41.

Greenstein, Fred I. *Personality and Politics: Problems of Evidence, Inference, and Conceptualization*. New York: Norton, 1975.

Griffith, Robert, ed. *Ike's Letters to a Friend*. Lawrence: University Press of Kansas, 1984.

Hampson, Fen Osler. "The Divided Decision-Maker: American Domestic Politics and the Cuban Crises." *International Security* 9 (Winter 1984/85): 130–65.

Haney, Patrick J. *Organizing for Foreign Policy Crises*. Ann Arbor: University of Michigan Press, 1997.

Harris, Louis. *The Anguish of Change*. New York: Norton, 1973.

Hartley, Thomas, and Bruce Russett. "Public Opinion and the Common Defense: Who Governs Military Spending in the United States?" *American Political Science Review* 86 (1992):361–87.

Hartmann, Robert T. *Palace Politics: An Inside Account of the Ford Years*. New York: McGraw-Hill, 1980.

Hechler, Ken. *Working with Truman: A Personal Memoir of the White House Years*. New York: Putnam, 1982.

Hermann, Charles F. *Crises in Foreign Policy: A Simulation Analysis*. Indianapolis: Bobbs-Merrill, 1969.

Hermann, Charles F. "International Crisis as a Situational Variable." In James N. Rosenau, ed., *International Politics and Foreign Policy*, pp. 409–21. New York: Free Press, 1969.

Hermann, Margaret G. "Effects of Personal Characteristics on Political Leaders on Foreign Policy." In Maurice A. East, Stephen A. Salmore, and Charles F. Hermann, eds., *Why Nations Act*, pp. 49–68. Beverly Hills: Sage, 1978.

Hermann, Margaret G. "Ingredients of Leadership." In Margaret G. Hermann, ed., *Political Psychology: Contemporary Problems and Issues*, pp. 167–92. San Francisco: Jossey-Bass, 1986.

Hermann, Margaret G. "Personality and Foreign Policy Decision Making: A Study of 53 Heads of Government." In Donald Sylvan and Steve Chan, eds., *Foreign Policy Decision Making*, pp. 33–80. New York: Praeger, 1984.

Hermann, Margaret, and John Thomas Preston. "Presidents, Advisers, and Foreign Policy: The Effects of Leadership Style on Executive Arrangements." *Political Psychology* 15 (1994):75–96.

Herring, George C. " 'A Good Stout Effort': John Foster Dulles and the Indochina Crisis, 1954–1955." In Richard Immerman, ed., *John Foster Dulles and the Diplomacy of the Cold War*, pp. 213–33. Princeton, N.J.: Princeton University Press, 1990.

Herring, George C., and Richard H. Immerman. "Eisenhower, Dulles, and Dienbienphu: 'The Day We Didn't Go to War' Revisited." *Journal of American History* 71 (1984):343–63.

Hilderbrand, Robert C. *Power and the People: Executive Management of Public Opinion in Foreign Affairs, 1897–1921*. Chapel Hill: University of North Carolina Press, 1981.

Hinckley, Ronald H. *People, Polls, and Policymakers: American Public Opinion and National Security*. New York: Lexington Books, 1992.

Hirsch, John L., and Robert B. Oakley. *Somalia and Operation Restore Hope*. Washington, D.C.: United States Institute of Peace Press, 1995.

Historical Division of the Joint Secretariat. *History of the Indochina Incident: 1940–1954*. Vol. 1 of *The Joint Chiefs of Staff and the War in Vietnam*. Wilmington, Del.: Michael Glazier, 1982.

Hofman, Ross J. S., and Paul Levack, eds. *Burke's Politics*. New York: Knopf, 1949.

Hogan, J. Michael. *The Panama Canal in American Politics: Domestic Advocacy and the Evolution of Policy*. Carbondale: Southern Illinois University Press, 1986.

Holsti, Ole R. "The Belief System and National Images: A Case Study." *Journal of Conflict Resolution* 6 (1962):244–52.

Holsti, Ole R. "Crisis Decision Making." In Philip E. Tetlock et al., eds. *Behavior, Society, and Nuclear War*. Vol. 1, pp. 9–84. New York: Oxford University Press, 1989.

Holsti, Ole R. "Foreign Policy Decision-Makers Viewed Psychologically: Cognitive Processes Approaches." In G. M. Bonham, and M. J. Shapiro, eds., *Thought and Action in Foreign Policy*, pp. 10–74. Basel: Birkhauser Verlag, 1977.

Holsti, Ole R. "Foreign Policy Formation Viewed Cognitively." In Robert Axelrod, ed., *Structure of Decision*, pp. 18–55. Princeton, N.J.: Princeton University Press, 1976.

Holsti, Ole R. *Public Opinion and American Foreign Policy*. Ann Arbor: University of Michigan Press, 1996.

Holsti, Ole R. "Public Opinion and Foreign Policy: Challenges to the Almond-Lippmann Consensus." *International Studies Quarterly* 36 (1992):439–66.

Holsti, Ole R. "Public Opinion and U.S. Foreign Policy." In James M. Scott, ed., *After the End: Making U.S. Foreign Policy in the Post-Cold War*, pp. 18–69. Durham, N.C.: Duke University Press, 1998.

Huntington, Samuel P. *The Common Defense*. New York: Columbia University Press, 1966.

Hutchings, Robert L. *American Diplomacy and the End of the Cold War*. Baltimore: Johns Hopkins University Press, 1997.

Huth, Paul K. *Standing Your Ground: Territorial Disputes and International Conflict*. Ann Arbor: University of Michigan Press, 1996.

Ikenberry, John G., David Lumsdaine, and Lisa Anderson. "Polity Forum: The Intertwining of Domestic Politics and International Relations." *Polity* 29 (1996):293–310.

Immerman, Richard H. "Between the Unattainable and the Unacceptable: Eisenhower and Dienbienphu." In Richard A. Melanson and David Mayers, eds., *Reevaluating Eisenhower: American Foreign Policy in the 1950s*, pp. 120–54. Champaign-Urbana: University of Illinois Press, 1987.

Immerman, Richard H. "Confessions of An Eisenhower Revisionist." *Diplomatic History* 14 (1990):319–42.

Jacobs, Lawrence R. "Public Opinion and Policymaking in the U.S. and Britain." *Comparative Politics* 24 (1992):99–217.

Jacobs, Lawrence R., and Robert Y. Shapiro. "Disorganized Democracy: The Institutionalization of Polling and Public Opinion Analysis During the

Kennedy, Johnson, and Nixon Presidencies." Paper presented at the annual meeting of the American Political Science Association, New York, 1994.

Jacobs, Lawrence R., and Robert Y. Shapiro. "Lyndon Johnson, Vietnam, and Public Opinion: Rethinking Realists' Theory of Leadership." Paper presented at the annual meeting of the Midwest Political Science Association, Chicago, April 14–16, 1994.

Jacobs, Lawrence R., and Robert Y. Shapiro. "Presidential Manipulation of Polls and Public Opinion: The Nixon Administration and the Pollsters." *Political Science Quarterly* 110 (Winter 1995/96):519–38.

Jacobs, Lawrence R., and Robert Y. Shapiro. "Public Opinion and the New Social History: Some Lessons for the Study of Public Opinion and Democratic Policy-making." *Social Science History* 13 (1989):1–24.

Jacobs, Lawrence R., and Robert Y. Shapiro. "Public Opinion in President Clinton's First Year: Leadership and Responsiveness." In Stanley A. Renshon, ed., *The Clinton Presidency: Campaigning, Governing, and the Psychology of Leadership*, pp. 195–211. Boulder, Colo.: Westview Press, 1995.

Jacobs, Lawrence R., and Robert Y. Shapiro. "The Public Presidency, Private Polls, and Policymaking: Lyndon Johnson." Paper presented at the annual meeting of the American Political Science Association, Washington, D.C., September 2–5, 1993.

Jacobs, Lawrence R., and Robert Y. Shapiro. "The Rise of Presidential Polling: The Nixon White House in Historical Perspective." *Public Opinion Quarterly* 59 (1995):163–95.

Jacobs, Lawrence R., and Robert Y. Shapiro. "Studying Substantive Democracy." *PS* 27 (1994):9–16.

James, Patrick, and Athanasios Hristoulas. "Domestic Politics and Foreign Policy: Evaluating a Model of Crisis Activity for the United States." *Journal of Politics* 56 (1994):327–48.

James, Patrick, and John R. Oneal. "The Influence of Domestic and International Politics on the President's Use of Force." *Journal of Conflict Resolution* 35 (1991):307–32.

Jentleson, Bruce W. "The Pretty Prudent Public: Post Post-Vietnam American Opinion on the Use of Military Force." *International Studies Quarterly* 36 (1992):49–74.

Jervis, Robert. *Perception and Misperception in International Relations*. Princeton, N.J.: Princeton University Press, 1976.

Johnson, Lyndon Baines. *Public Papers of the Presidents, Lyndon Baines Johnson, 1966*. Vol. 1. Washington, D.C.: U.S. Government Printing Office, 1967.

Johnson, Lyndon Baines. *Public Papers of the Presidents, Lyndon Baines Johnson, 1966*. Vol. 2. Washington, D.C.: U.S. Government Printing Office, 1967.

Johnson, Lyndon Baines. *Public Papers of the Presidents, Lyndon Baines Johnson, 1967*. Vol. 2. Washington, D.C.: U.S. Government Printing Office, 1968.

Johnson, Lyndon Baines. *The Vantage Point: Perspectives of the Presidency, 1963–1969*. New York: Holt, Rinehart and Winston, 1971.

Jordan, Hamilton. *Crisis*. New York: Putnam, 1982.

Jurika, Stephan Jr., ed. *The Memoirs of Admiral Arthur W. Radford*. Stanford, Calif.: Hoover Institution Press, 1980.

Kegley, Charles, and Eugene Wittkopf. *American Foreign Policy: Pattern and Process*. 3d ed. New York: St. Martin's Press, 1987.

Kennan, George. *American Diplomacy, 1900–1950*. Chicago: University of Chicago Press, 1951.

Kennedy, John F. *Public Papers of the Presidents of the United States: John F. Kennedy, 1961*. Washington, D.C.: U.S. Government Printing Office, 1962.

Kernell, Samuel. *Going Public: New Strategies of Presidential Leadership*. Washington, D.C.: Congressional Quarterly Press, 1986.

Key, V. O. *Public Opinion and American Democracy*. New York: Knopf, 1961.

Khong, Yuen Foong. *Analogies at War: Korea, Munich, Dien Bien Phu, and the Vietnam Decisions of 1965*. Princeton, N.J.: Princeton University Press, 1992.

Killian, James R., Jr. *Sputnik, Scientists, and Eisenhower*. Cambridge, Mass.: MIT Press, 1977.

King, Gary, Robert O. Keohane, and Sydney Verba. *Designing Social Inquiry: Scientific Inference in Qualitative Research*. Princeton, N.J.: Princeton University Press, 1994.

King, Gary, Robert O. Keohane, and Sydney Verba. "The Importance of Research Design in Political Science." *American Political Science Review* 89 (1995):475–81.

Kinnard, Douglas. *President Eisenhower and Strategy Management*. Lexington: University Press of Kentucky, 1977.

Kohut, Andrew, and Robert C. Toth. "Arms and the People." *Foreign Affairs* 73 (1994):47–61.

Kusnitz, Leonard A. *Public Opinion and Foreign Policy: America's China Policy*. Westport, Conn.: Greenwood Press, 1984.

Laitin, David D., et al. "Review Symposium: The Qualitative-Quantitative Disputation: Gary King, Robert O. Keohane, and Sidney Verba's Designing Social Inquiry: Scientific Inference in Qualitative Research." *American Political Science Review* 89 (1995):454–81.

Lang, Gladys Engel, and Kurt Lang. "The Future Study of Public Opinion: Symposium." *Public Opinion Quarterly* 51 (1987):S181–S182.

Larson, Deborah Welch. *Origins of Containment: A Psychological Explanation*. Princeton, N.J.: Princeton University Press, 1985.

Larson, Deborah Welch. "The Role of Belief Systems and Schemas in Foreign Policy Decision-Making." *Political Psychology* 15 (1994):17–33.

Layne, Christopher. "Kant or Cant: The Myth of the Democratic Peace." *International Security* 19 (1994):5–49.

Leach, W. Barton. *The New Look*. Maxwell Air Force Base, Ala.: Air Command and Staff College, 1954.

Lebow, Richard Ned, and Janice Gross Stein. "Afghanistan, Carter, and Foreign Policy Change: The Limits of Cognitive Models." In Dan Caldwell and Timothy J. McKeown, eds., *Diplomacy, Force, and Leadership*, pp. 95–128. Boulder, Colo.: Westview Press, 1993.

Levite, Ariel E., Bruce W. Jentleson, and Larry Berman, eds. *Foreign Military Intervention: The Dynamics of Protracted Conflict*. New York: Columbia University Press, 1992.

Levy, Jack S. "The Diversionary Theory of War: A Critique." In Manus I. Midlarsky, ed., *The Handbook of War Studies*, pp. 259–88. Boston: Unwin Hyman, 1989.

Lian, Bradley, and John R. Oneal. "Presidents, the Use of Military Force, and Public Opinion." *Journal of Conflict Resolution* 37 (1993):277–300.

Link, Arthur. *Wilson: The New Freedom*. Princeton, N.J.: Princeton University Press, 1956.

Lippmann, Walter. *Essays in the Public Philosophy*. Boston: Little, Brown, 1955.

Lippmann, Walter. *Public Opinion*. New York: Macmillan, 1922.

Logan, Carolyn J. "U.S. Public Opinion and the Intervention in Somalia." *Fletcher Forum of World Affairs* 20 (1996): 155–80.

Lubell, Samuel. "*Sputnik* and American Public Opinion." *Columbia University Forum* 1 (1957):15–21.

Major, John. *Prize Possession: The United States and the Panama Canal, 1903–1979*. Cambridge: Cambridge University Press, 1993.

Margolis, Michael, and Gary Mauser, eds. *Manipulating Public Opinion: Essays on Public Opinion as a Dependent Variable*. Belmont, Calif.: Wadsworth, 1989.

Mattes, Robert Britt. "The Politics of Public Opinion: Polls, Pollsters, and the President." Ph.D. diss., University of Illinois, Champaign-Urbana, 1992.

McCalla, Robert B. *Uncertain Perceptions: U.S. Cold War Crisis Decision Making*. Ann Arbor: University of Michigan Press, 1992.

McCullough, David. *Truman*. New York: Simon & Schuster, 1992.

McDougall, Walter A. . . . *The Heavens and the Earth: A Political History of the Space Age*. New York: Basic Books, 1985.

Mearsheimer, John J. "Back to the Future: Instability in Europe After the Cold War." *International Security* 15 (1990):5–56.

Mearsheimer, John J. "The False Promise of International Institutions." *International Security* 19 (Winter 1994/95):5–49.

Meernik, James. "Presidential Decision Making and the Political Use of Military Force." *International Studies Quarterly* 38 (1994):121–38.

Meernik, James, and Peter Waterman. "The Myth of the Diversionary Use of Force by American Presidents." *Political Research Quarterly* 49 (1996):573–90.

Mervin, David. *George BUSBL and the Guardianship Presidency*. New York: St. Martin's Press, 1996.

Miller, Ross. "Domestic Structures and the Diversionary Use of Force." *American Journal of Political Science* 39 (1995):760–85.

Miller, Warren E., and Donald E. Stokes. "Constituency Influence in Congress." *American Political Science Review* 57 (1963):45–56.

Mills, C. Wright. *The Power Elite*. New York: Oxford University Press, 1956.

Milner, Helen V. *Interests, Institutions, and Information*. Princeton, N.J.: Princeton University Press, 1997.

Moffett, George D., III. *The Limits of Victory: The Ratification of the Panama Canal Treaties*. Ithaca, N.Y.: Cornell University Press, 1985.

Monroe, Alan D. "Consistency Between Public Preferences and National Policy Decision." *American Politics Quarterly* 7 (1979):3–19.

Mor, Ben D. *Decision and Interaction in Crisis: A Model of International Crisis Behavior*. Westport, Conn.: Praeger, 1993.

Mor, Ben D. "Peace Initiatives and Public Opinion: The Domestic Context of Conflict Resolution." *Journal of Peace Research* 34 (1997):197–215.

Moravcsik, Andrew. "Taking Preferences Seriously: A Liberal Theory of International Politics." *International Organization* 51 (1997):513–54.

Morgan, Iwan W. "Eisenhower and the Balanced Budget." In Shirley Anne Warshaw, ed., *Reexamining the Eisenhower Presidency*, pp. 121–32. Westport, Conn.: Greenwood Press, 1993.

Morgan, Iwan W. *Eisenhower Versus 'The Spenders': The Eisenhower Administration, the Democrats, and the Budget, 1953–60*. New York: St. Martin's Press, 1990.

Morgan, T. Clifton, and Kenneth N. Bickers. "Domestic Discontent and the External Use of Force." *Journal of Conflict Resolution* 36 (1992):25–52.

Morgenthau, Hans J. *Dilemmas of Politics*. Chicago: University of Chicago Press, 1958.

Morgenthau, Hans J. *Politics Among Nations*. 5th rev. ed. New York: Knopf, 1978.

Morris, Dick. *Behind the Oval Office*. New York: Random House, 1997.

Mueller, John E. *War, Presidents, and Public Opinion*. New York: Wiley, 1973.

Mueller, John E. *Policy and Opinion in the Gulf War*. Chicago: University of Chicago Press, 1994.

Nelson, Anna Kasten. "The 'Top of Policy Hill': President Eisenhower and the National Security Council." *Diplomatic History* 7 (1983):307–26.

Nelson, Jack, and Robert J. Donovan. "The Education of a President." *Los Angeles Times*, August 1, 1993, pp. 12 ff.

Neustadt, Richard E. *Presidential Power: The Politics of Leadership*. New York: Wiley, 1980.

Nicholas, Herbert G. "Building on the Wilsonian Heritage." In Arthur Link, ed., *Woodrow Wilson*, pp. 178–92. New York: Hill & Wang, 1968.

Nicolay, John G., and John Hay, eds. *Complete Works of Abraham Lincoln*. Vols. 1–2. New York: Francis D. Tandy, 1905.

Nincic, Miroslav. *Democracy and Foreign Policy: The Fallacy of Political Realism*. New York: Columbia University Press, 1992.

Nincic, Miroslav. "U.S. Soviet Policy and the Electoral Connection." *World Politics* 42 (1990):370–96.

Nixon, Richard. *In the Arena*. New York: Simon & Schuster, 1990.

Nixon, Richard. *Leaders*. New York: Warner Books, 1982.

Nixon, Richard. *The Nixon Presidential Press Conferences.* New York: Coleman, 1978.

Nixon, Richard. *No More Vietnams.* New York: Arbor House, 1985.

Nixon, Richard. *Public Papers of the President of the United States: Richard Nixon, 1972.* Washington, D.C.: U.S. Government Printing Office, 1974.

Nixon, Richard. *RN: The Memoirs of Richard Nixon.* New York: Grosset & Dunlap, 1978.

Oberdorfer, Don. *The Turn.* New York: Poseidon Press, 1991.

Oncal, John R. *Foreign Policy Making in Times of Crisis.* Columbus: Ohio State University Press, 1982.

Ostrom, Charles W., and Brian L. Job. "The President and the Political Use of Force." *American Political Science Review* 80 (1986):541–66.

Pach, Chester J. Jr., and Elmo Richardson. *The Presidency of Dwight D. Eisenhower.* Rev. ed. Lawrence: University Press of Kansas, 1991.

Page, Benjamin I. "Democratic Responsiveness? Untangling the Links Between Public Opinion and Policy." *PS* 27 (1994):125–28

Page, Benjamin I., and Robert Y. Shapiro. "Effects of Public Opinion on Policy." *American Political Science Review* 77 (1983):175–90.

Page, Benjamin I., and Robert Y. Shapiro. *The Rational Public: Fifty Years of Trends in American Policy Preferences.* Chicago: University of Chicago Press, 1992.

Payne, Rodger A. "Public Opinion and Foreign Threats: Eisenhower's Response to Sputnik." *Armed Forces and Society* 21 (1994):89–111.

Peterson, Susan. *Crisis Bargaining and the State: The Domestic Politics of International Conflict.* Ann Arbor: University of Michigan Press, 1996.

Petty, Richard E., and John T. Cacioppo. *Attitude and Persuasion: Classic and Contemporary Approaches.* Dubuque, Iowa.: Brown, 1987.

Pitkin, Fenichel. *The Concept of Representation.* Berkeley and Los Angeles: University of California Press, 1967.

Posen, Barry R., and Andrew L. Ross. "Competing Visions for U.S. Grand Strategy." *International Security* 21 (Winter 1996/97):5–53.

Powell, Colin L. *My American Journey.* New York: Random House, 1995.

Powlick, Philip J. "The American Foreign Policy Process and the Public." Ph.D. diss., University of Pittsburgh, 1990.

Powlick, Philip J. "The Attitudinal Bases for Responsiveness to Public Opinion Among American Foreign Policy Officials." *Journal of Conflict Resolution* 35 (1991):611–41.

Powlick, Philip J. "Foreign Policy Decisions and Public Opinion: The Case of the Lebanon Intervention, 1982–1984." Paper presented at the annual meeting of the American Political Science Association, Washington, D.C., September 1, 1988.

Powlick, Philip J. "The Sources of Public Opinion for American Foreign Policy Officials." *International Studies Quarterly* 39 (1995):427–52.

Powlick, Philip J., and Andrew Z. Katz. "Defining the American Public Opinion / Foreign Policy Nexus." *Mershon International Studies Review* 42 (1998):29–61.

Powlick, Philip J., and Andrew Z. Katz. "A Two-Way Model of Public Opinion's Influence on Foreign Policy." Paper presented at the annual meeting of the American Political Science Association, San Francisco, August 29–September 1, 1996.

Prados, John. *The Sky Would Fall: Operation Vulture: The U.S. Bombing Mission in Indochina, 1954.* New York: Dial Press, 1983.

Putnam, Robert D. "Diplomacy and Domestic Politics: The Logic of Two-Level Games." *International Organization* 42 (1988):427–60.

Reagan, Ronald. *An American Life.* New York: Simon & Schuster, 1990.

Reagan, Ronald. *Public Papers of the Presidents of the United States, Ronald Reagan, 1984.* Vol. 1. Washington, D.C.: U.S. Government Printing Office, 1986.

Reagan, Ronald. *Public Papers of the Presidents of the United States, Ronald Reagan, 1988–89.* Vol. 2. Washington, D.C.: U.S. Government Printing Office, 1991.

Reiss, Edward. *The Strategic Defense Initiative.* Cambridge: Cambridge University Press, 1992.

Renshon, Stanley A. *High Hopes: The Clinton Presidency and the Politics of Ambition.* New York: New York University Press, 1996.

Richards, Diana, T., et al. "Good Times, Bad Times and the Diversionary Use of Force." *Journal of Conflict Resolution* 37 (1993):504–35.

Richardson, James L. *Crisis Diplomacy: The Great Powers Since the Mid-Nineteenth Century.* Cambridge: Cambridge University Press, 1994.

Risse-Kappen, Thomas. *Cooperation Among Democracies: The European Influence on U.S. Foreign Policy.* Princeton, N.J.: Princeton University Press, 1995.

Risse-Kappen, Thomas. "Masses and Leaders: Public Opinion, Domestic Structures, and Foreign Policy." In David A. Deese, ed., *The New Politics of American Foreign Policy*, pp. 238–61. New York: St. Martin's Press, 1994.

Risse-Kappen, Thomas. "Public Opinion, Domestic Structure, and Foreign Policy in Liberal Democracies." *World Politics* 43 (1991):479–512.

Rivers, Douglas, and Nancy L. Rose. "Passing the President's Program: Public Opinion and Presidential Influence in Congress." *American Journal of Political Science* 29 (1985):183–96.

Rockman, Bert A. "Presidents, Opinion, and Institutional Leadership." In David A. Deese, ed., *The New Politics of American Foreign Policy*, pp. 59–75. New York: St. Martin's Press, 1994.

Roman, Peter J. *Eisenhower and the Missile Gap.* Ithaca, N.Y.: Cornell University Press, 1995.

Rosati, Jerel A. "The Impact of Beliefs on Behavior: The Foreign Policy of the Carter Administration." In Donald Sylvan and Steve Chan, eds., *Foreign Policy Decision Making*, pp. 158–91. New York: Praeger, 1984.

Roseboom, Eugene H. *A History of Presidential Elections.* London: Macmillan, 1970.

Rosecrance, Richard, and Arthur A. Stein, eds. *The Domestic Bases of Grand Strategy*. Ithaca, N.Y.: Cornell University Press, 1991.

Rosecrance, Richard, and Arthur A. Stein. "Beyond Realism: The Study of Grand Strategy." In Richard Rosecrance and Arthur A. Stein, eds., *The Domestic Bases of Grand Strategy*, pp. 3–21. Ithaca, N.Y.: Cornell University Press, 1993.

Rosenau, James N. *Public Opinion and Foreign Policy: An Operational Formulation*. New York: Random House, 1961.

Rovere, Richard H. *Affairs of State: The Eisenhower Years*. New York: Farrar, Straus & Cudahy, 1956.

Ruggie, John Gerard. "The Past as Prologue? Interests, Identity, and American Foreign Policy." *International Security* 21 (1997):89–125.

Rusk, Dean. *As I Saw It*. Ed. Daniel S. Papp. New York: Norton, 1990.

Russett, Bruce. *Controlling the Sword: The Democratic Governance of National Security*. Cambridge, Mass.: Harvard University Press, 1990.

Russett, Bruce. "Economic Decline, Electoral Pressure, and the Initiation of Interstate Conflict." In Charles S. Gochman and Alan Ned Sabrosky, eds., *Prisoners of War?* pp. 123–40. Lexington, Mass.: Lexington Books, 1990.

Sartori, Giovanni. *The Theory of Democracy Revisited*. Chatham, N.J.: Chatham House, 1987.

Savage, James D. *Balanced Budgets and American Politics*. Ithaca, N.Y.: Cornell University Press, 1988.

Schlesinger, Arthur Jr. "Back to the Womb: Isolationism's Renewed Threat." *Foreign Affairs* 74 (1995):2–8.

Schweller, Randall L., and David Priess. "A Tale of Two Realisms: Expanding the Institutions Debate." *Mershon International Studies Review* 41 (1997):1–32.

Shultz, George P. *Turmoil and Triumph: My Years as Secretary of State*. New York: Scribner, 1993.

Siverson, Randolph M., ed. *Strategic Politicians, Institutions, and Foreign Policy*. Ann Arbor: University of Michigan Press, 1998.

Skidmore, David. *Reversing Course: Carter's Foreign Policy, Domestic Politics, and the Failure of Reform*. Nashville: Vanderbilt University Press, 1996.

Skidmore, David, and Valerie M. Hudson, eds. *The Limits of State Autonomy: Societal Groups and Foreign Policy Formulation*. Boulder, Colo.: Westview Press, 1993.

Small, Melvin. *Johnson, Nixon, and the Doves*. New Brunswick, N.J.: Rutgers University Press, 1988.

Smith, Alastair. "Diversionary Foreign Policy in Democratic Systems." *International Studies Quarterly* 40 (1996):133–54.

Smith, Gaddis. *Morality, Reason, and Power: American Diplomacy in the Carter Years*. New York: Hill & Wang, 1986.

Smith, Hedrick. *The Power Game*. New York: Random House, 1988.

Snyder, Glenn H. "The 'New Look' of 1953." In Warner R. Schilling, Paul Y. Hammond, and Glenn H. Snyder, eds., *Strategy, Politics, and Defense Budgets*, pp. 379–524. New York: Columbia University Press, 1962.

Snyder, Jack. *Myths of Empire*. Ithaca, N.Y.: Cornell University Press, 1991.

Sobel, Richard. "U.S. and European Attitudes Toward Intervention in the Former Yugoslavia; *Mourir pour la Bosnie?*" In Richard H. Ullman, ed., *The World and Yugoslavia's Wars*, pp. 145–81. New York: Council on Foreign Relations, 1996.

Sobel, Richard, ed. *Public Opinion in U.S. Foreign Policy: The Controversy over Contra Aid*. Lanham, Md.: Rowman & Littlefield, 1993.

Sorensen, Theodore C., ed. *"Let the Word Go Forth": The Speeches, Statements, and Writings of John F. Kennedy*. New York: Delacorte Press, 1988.

Stares, Paul B. *The Militarization of Space: U.S. Policy, 1945–1984*. Ithaca, N.Y.: Cornell University Press, 1985.

Steele, Richard W. "News of the 'Good War': World War II News Management." *Journalism Quarterly* 62 (1985):707–16.

Sterling-Folker, Jennifer. "Realist Environment, Liberal Process, and Domestic-Level Variables." *International Studies Quarterly* 41 (1997):1–26.

Stimson, James A., Michael B. MacKuen, and Robert S. Erikson. "Dynamic Representation." *American Political Science Review* 89 (1995):543–65.

Stoll, Richard J. "The Guns of November: Presidential Reelections and the Use of Force, 1947–1982." *Journal of Conflict Resolution* 28 (1984):231–46.

Thompson, Kenneth W., ed. *The Eisenhower Presidency: Eleven Intimate Perspectives of Dwight D. Eisenhower*. Lanham, Md.: University Press of America, 1984.

Truman, Harry S. *Memoirs: Years of Trial and Hope*. Vol. 2. Garden City, N.Y.: Doubleday, 1956.

Truman, Harry S. *Public Papers of the Presidents: Harry S. Truman, 1949*. Washington, D.C.: U.S. Government Printing Office, 1964.

Truman, Harry S. *Public Papers of the Presidents: Harry S. Truman, 1951*. Washington, D.C.: U.S. Government Printing Office, 1965.

U.S. Congress, Senate. Senate Armed Services Committee. Preparedness Investigating Subcommittee. *Inquiry into Satellite and Missile Programs*. 85th Cong., 1st and 2d sess., November 27, 1958.

U.S. Department of Defense. *United States–Vietnam Relations: 1945–1967*. Vol. 9. Washington, D.C.: U.S. Government Printing Office, 1971.

U.S. Department of State. *Foreign Relations of the United States*. Secretary of State's Memoranda of Conversation, Microfiche Supplement, November 1952–1954. Washington, D.C.: U.S. Government Printing Office, 1992.

U.S. Department of State. *Foreign Relations of the United States, 1952–1954*. Vol. 2. Washington, D.C.: U.S. Government Printing Office, 1984.

U.S. Department of State. *Foreign Relations of the United States, 1952–1954*. Vol. 13. Washington, D.C.: U.S. Government Printing Office, 1982.

U.S. Department of State. *Foreign Relations of the United States, 1952–1954*. Vol. 14. Washington, D.C.: U.S. Government Printing Office, 1987.

U.S. Department of State. *Foreign Relations of the United States, 1952–1954*. Vol. 16. Washington, D.C.: U.S. Government Printing Office, 1984.

U.S. Department of State. *Foreign Relations of the United States, 1955–1957*. Vol. 2. Washington, D.C.: U.S. Government Printing Office, 1986.

U.S. Department of State. *Foreign Relations of the United States, 1955–1957*. Vol. 11. Washington, D.C.: U.S. Government Printing Office, 1988.

U.S. Department of State. *Foreign Relations of the United States, 1955–1957*. Vol. 19. Washington, D.C.: U.S. Government Printing Office, 1990.

U.S. News & World Report. *Triumph Without Victory*. New York: Times Books, 1992.

Vance, Cyrus. *Hard Choices: Critical Years in America's Foreign Policy*. New York: Simon & Schuster, 1983.

Vertzberger, Yaacov Y. I. *The World in Their Minds: Information Processing, Cognition, and Perception in Foreign Policy Decisionmaking*. Stanford, Calif.: Stanford University Press, 1990.

Voss, James F., and Ellen Dorsey. "Perception and International Relations: An Overview." In Eric Singer and Valerie Hudson, eds., *Political Psychology and Foreign Policy*, pp. 3–29. Boulder, Colo.: Westview Press, 1992.

Waltz, Kenneth N. "International Politics Is Not Foreign Policy." *Security Studies* 6 (1996):54–57.

Waltz, Kenneth N. "A Response to My Critics." In Robert O. Keohane, ed., *Neorealism and Its Critics*, pp. 322–46. New York: Columbia University Press, 1986.

Waltz, Kenneth N. *Theory of International Politics*. Reading, Mass.: Addison-Wesley, 1979.

Wang, Kevin H. "Presidential Responses to Foreign Policy Crises: Rational Choice and Domestic Politics." *Journal of Conflict Resolution* 40 (1996):68–97.

Watson, Robert J. *The Joint Chiefs of Staff and National Policy, 1953–1954*. Vol. 5 of *History of the Joint Chiefs of Staff*. Washington, D.C.: Historical Division, Joint Chiefs of Staff, 1986.

Wattenberg, Ben. "The Consequences of Ideas: The Reagan Revolution and Beyond." *Public Opinion* 9 (1986):17–26, 57–60.

Weinberger, Caspar W. *Fighting for Peace: Seven Critical Years in the Pentagon*. New York: Warner Books, 1990.

Wells, Samuel F. Jr. "The Origins of Massive Retaliation." *Political Science Quarterly* 96 (1981):31–52.

Wilson, Woodrow. *Leaders of Men*. Princeton, N.J.: Princeton University Press, 1952.

Woodward, Bob. *The Choice*. New York: Simon & Schuster, 1996.

Woodward, Bob. *The Commanders*. New York: Simon & Schuster, 1991.

Woodward, Susan L. *Balkan Tragedy: Chaos and Dissolution After the Cold War*. Washington, D.C.: Brookings Institution, 1995.

Yankelovich, Daniel, and I. M. Destler, eds. *Beyond the Beltway*. New York: Norton, 1994.

Zakaria, Fareed. "Realism and Domestic Politics: A Review Essay." *International Security* 17 (1992):177–98.

Zaller, John R. "Elite Leadership of Mass Opinion." In W. Lance Bennett and David L. Paletz, eds., *Taken by Storm*, pp. 186–209. Chicago: University of Chicago Press, 1994.

Zaller, John R. *The Nature and Origins of Mass Opinion*. Cambridge: Cambridge University Press, 1992.

Zelikow, Philip, and Condoleezza Rice. *Germany Unified and Europe Transformed*. Cambridge, Mass.: Harvard University Press, 1995.

Zhang, Shu Guang. *Deterrence and Strategic Culture*. Ithaca, N.Y.: Cornell University Press, 1992.